T0330108

Growing an
Entrepreneurial Business

Growing an Entrepreneurial Business

Concepts and Cases

Edward D. Hess

STANFORD BUSINESS BOOKS
An Imprint of Stanford University Press
Stanford, California

Stanford University Press
Stanford, California

Special discounts for bulk quantities of Stanford Business Books are available to corporations, professional associations, and other organizations. For details and discount information, contact the special sales department of Stanford University Press. Tel: (650) 736-1782, Fax: (650) 736-1784

Printed in the United States of America on acid-free, archival-quality paper

Library of Congress Cataloging-in-Publication Data
Hess, Edward D. author.
  Growing an entrepreneurial business : concepts and cases / Edward D. Hess.
     pages cm.
  Includes bibliographical references and index.
  ISBN 978-0-8047-7141-2 (cloth : alk. paper)
  1. Small business—Growth—Textbooks. 2. Small business—Management—Textbooks.
3. Entrepreneurship—Textbooks. I. Title.
  HD62.7.H484 2010
  658.4'063—dc22   2010043504

Typeset by Classic Typography in 10.5/14 Bembo

This book is dedicated to the memory of Frank Batten Sr., whose vision, leadership, and generosity founded the Batten Institute at the Darden Graduate School of Business, University of Virginia.

Brief Contents

Contents

Acknowledgments

With each book, I am humbled because my work builds upon my earlier works with the unifying focus of decoding the DNA of enduring, high-performance organizations. My research has examined public companies, family businesses, start-ups, and now private growth companies. I again thank and acknowledge the continuing contribution of all those acknowledged in previous books--too many to be named here.

No one writes a book alone.

This book began with a research question: "What were the major management challenges faced by leaders of high-growth private companies?" Professor Jeanne Liedtka, who at the time of my research was Executive Director, Batten Institute, Darden Graduate School of Business, and Professor Sankaran Venkataraman, Research Director, Batten Institute, supported my curiosity and agreed that the Batten Institute and the Darden Foundation would fund this research.

Fifty-four high-growth private companies located in 23 states generously participated in my study. A special thank you goes to the CEOs who agreed to participate in developing Darden cases with us and sharing their learning experiences.

Elizabeth O'Halloran, Sean Carr, Shizuka Modica, and Gosia Glinska of the Batten Institute all played key roles in making this book happen. I'd like to give a special thank you to Research Assistant Cassy Eriksson, for her research, critique, good ideas, and perfectionist production of this book.

Margo Beth Crouppen of Stanford University Press has been a good partner in making it possible that others may learn from the entrepreneurs I studied. Jessica Walsh and David Horne did a tremendous job in preparing the book for publishing. A special thanks goes to Jim Collins, who quickly and graciously encouraged me to go ahead with this book.

Dean Robert Bruner; Associate Dean of the Faculty Jim Freeland; and Michael Lenox, Executive Director, Batten Institute of the Darden Graduate School of Business, through their leadership, encouragement, and positivity make the Darden community an energizing entrepreneurial environment. It is a privilege to be part of that environment.

Many of us teach because so many teachers made positive contributions to our life. I have been blessed by many wonderful, generous teachers who encouraged me along my journey and opened new avenues for me.

My first teachers were my parents, who were both entrepreneurs--although at the time I did not know that. My first paying job, at age six, was distributing flyers for their clothing store in Carrollton, Georgia, for which I was paid 25 cents. My parents worked hard, long hours building a business comprising four clothing stores in rural Georgia. Their hard work enabled me to embark upon my own continuing entrepreneurial journey.

To my wife, Katherine Leigh, thank you for sharing your expertise by editing the text and for the goodness of your heart. Your entrepreneurial life journey is inspirational to all who know you.

Growing an Entrepreneurial Business

Introduction

A Bird's-Eye View

This book is designed for courses that explore entrepreneurship beyond the start-up phase, as well as for classes in managing small businesses. Its focus is on the common issues faced by businesses as they attempt to scale.

I have spent much of my non-academic career representing growth companies like those discussed in the cases, as a lawyer, an investment banker, or a strategy consultant. And now, my interest in growth companies has carried over into my academic research and teaching at the Darden Graduate School of Business. As a result, this book draws on both practical experience and academic research. All of the theories and many of the cases have been used in my own course, Managing Smaller Enterprises.

The book is divided into two parts—text and cases—to provide professors maximum flexibility in customizing course content. The thirty-three cases can be used in conjunction with the text or independent of it. Eleven cases were written as narratives with many teaching points but without a focused decision or conundrum. The remaining twenty-two cases were written to require students to make and defend business decisions. The case portion of the book contains discussion questions for each case and a matrix (table) that indicates which cases cover key issues that users (professors and students alike) may wish to explore.

The text portion of the book discusses key issues derived from research and consulting, and is meant to accompany the case method of teaching, raising issues for conversation and an exchange of views. It does not provide a comprehensive review of the literature or a discussion of *all* issues facing growing businesses. Rather, the text is focused on enabling classroom conversations about key issues for small firms that are aiming to grow. Questions are provided to stimulate reflective thought and discussion. Most have been battle-tested in the classroom, and have generated lively and challenging responses. A finely honed recommended readings list is provided to guide readers in broadening their knowledge beyond the foundation of this book. As I hope is evident, a hallmark throughout this presentation is *focus*—on presenting issues that matter most to growing businesses, on providing tangible examples of those issues for readers, and on building a foundational understanding of the promise and challenges that come with growth.

A First Word About Growth

Growing a business is a major inflection point for both the small business and the entrepreneur. Growth challenges people and processes and necessitates changes. Growth is particularly challenging for small businesses because they generally have limited resources: capital, people, time, and managerial experience. As the text discusses, if not properly managed, growth can pose significant risks to a business's viability and survivability.

As you read through this book, you will find several recurring themes that have an impact on people, processes, and culture. By *people* I mean everyone in the organization: the entrepreneur, managers, and line employees. *Processes* include how things are done and which checklists, information, and controls are needed to effectively manage the business. *Culture* is the environment created by the entrepreneur in which all of this happens. Following are the key themes throughout the text and cases:

1. *Growth is change.* Growth changes what many employees do; growth changes what the entrepreneur must do; growth necessitates different people and processes; and growth changes the organizational environment and the personal dynamics within the business.

2. *Growth is evolutionary.* Growth results in the evolution of the entrepreneur, the management team, and the processes and controls. Many times the business model and customer value proposition evolve too, as the company grows. This evolution is continuous.

3. *Growth requires learning.* The entrepreneur and employees must constantly be open to learning and adapting in an incremental, iterative, and experimental fashion. Growing businesses generally do not experience much sameness, stability or predictability until they become quite large—for example larger than $100 million in revenue.

4. *Growth requires focus.* The business generally must focus strategically on its differentiating customer value proposition and operational excellence. The entrepreneur's focus changes from every business detail to developing people as the business grows.

Chapter Overview

The text that makes up the first part of the book is divided into nine stand-alone chapters exploring common critical issues related to growing a business. The chapters contain embedded questions for discussion, and some also contain related commentaries previously written by me. Each chapter contains one case with case discussion questions. At the end of each chapter is a list of cases in this book that contain issues relevant to the chapter topic, allowing for multiple case discussions with regard to each chapter's content.

Chapter 1, "Growth Can Be Good and Growth Can Be Bad," challenges the common business assumptions that businesses must "grow or die," that growth is always good, that bigger is always better, and that growth should be the key objective of every business. In place of these assumptions, a more nuanced theory of growth is advanced, based on research demonstrating that, depending on the circumstances, growth may be either good or bad. Growth should never be assumed but rather should be a strategic decision made only after careful weighing of the pros and cons of growth at each stage of a business's life cycle. Often growth is not linear, and it rarely happens smoothly or predictably. Mistakes, detours, or bumps along the road are common. The point is that growth creates risks that must be effectively managed. If not properly managed, growth can (1) outstrip the capabilities and competencies of a business or its management team, (2) stress quality and financial controls, (3) dilute a business's culture, (4) dilute a business's customer value proposition, or (5) propel a business into a new competitive space, exposing it to bigger and better competition.

Chapter 1 introduces two tools: a Growth Risks Audit for companies to assess the wisdom of growth at a particular time and a Growth Decision Template that challenges entrepreneurs to think about why they want to grow, how much growth they can undertake without exposing the company and themselves to material risks, and other potential ramifications of growth.

Chapter 1 ends with the "Eyebobs Eyewear, Inc." case that tells the story of how Julie Allinson intentionally grew her business in a growth risk management manner.

Chapter 2, "Darden Private Growth Company Research (DPGC)," summarizes the key findings from my research: The Darden Private Growth Research Project, funded by the Batten Institute at the Darden Graduate School of Business and the Darden Foundation. This project involved semi-structured interviews with 54 CEOs of recognized high-performance private companies located in 23 different states. Twenty-one of the companies were primarily product companies with the remainder being primarily service companies. The average age of the companies was 9.6 years and the average revenue for 2008 was $60 million. Revenue ranged from $5 million to $343 million. A preview of these findings was first published in a chapter in my book *Smart Growth: Building an Enduring Business by Managing the Risks of Growth*,[1] which focused primarily on public company growth issues. Chapter 2 ends with the "Octane Fitness, Inc: The Power of Focus" case, which tells a story of how two entrepreneurs used strategic focus to build a market-leading business.

Chapter 3, "Growth Is More Than a Strategy," introduces the concept that growth is much more than a strategy—it is a system: a Growth System. To continuously produce quality growth, an internal, seamless, consistent, self-reinforcing Growth System has to be built linking strategy, structure, culture, HR policies, leadership model, execution processes, measurements, and rewards to drive desired behaviors. This Growth System requires constant tweaking as a business grows so that the critical components remain aligned to drive the desired behaviors.

Aligning all of the above requires the entrepreneur to become sensitized to the impact of people, process, and cultural changes as well as to the risks posed by a collection of small, dilutive changes that when added together produce a big, unintended consequence. A Growth System not only enables growth but helps manage and limit the risks of growth. Chapter 3 ends with the "Room & Board" case, which illustrates how one entrepreneur chose to grow at his own desired pace, building a Growth System that became his competitive advantage.

Chapter 4, "The 4Ps of Growth: Planning, Prioritization, Processes, and Pace," moves to granular findings of the DPGC research to explore how growth happens on the ground level. Much to my surprise, few of the companies researched systematically and proactively planned for their growth. Instead, in most cases, they reacted to growth. Most CEOs reported having to manage the pace of growth so it did not create material execution, quality, or financial risks to the company. Growth created the need for more processes, and this chapter discusses how CEOs prioritized what processes to create. Processes can be thought of as the step-by-step recipes for doing the critical tasks necessary to produce and consistently deliver high-quality products and services in a timely manner.

Many CEOs found it challenging to grow while simultaneously installing the necessary processes because growth and process implementation require different mindsets or perspectives. Too often, the result was a "gas pedal" approach to growth—growing until problems emerged and then letting up on the growth pedal to allow the processes to catch up. The challenge was managing the tension of slowing growth long enough to add sufficient processes and controls to mitigate risks without losing critical business opportunities. Another management tension was installing enough process while not becoming too bureaucratic and thus losing the entrepreneurial feel of the business.

---

1. Edward D. Hess, *Smart Growth: Building an Enduring Business by Managing the Risks of Growth* (New York: Columbia Business School Publishing, 2010).

Chapter 4 also discusses the necessity of strategic focus as a growth accelerator and how our sample of CEOs created heuristics to help them decide what to focus on each day. In the chaos of fast-paced growth, entrepreneurs were constantly prioritizing how they spent their time on the basis of what the most critical need was that day, while expressing the need for "firehouse time" to think strategically and not to just "fight fires." Chapter 4 ends with the "SecureWorks" case, which tells the story of how Mike Cote grew a business substantially while dealing with the challenges of planning, processes, prioritization, and pace.

Chapter 5, "The Entrepreneur Must Grow, Too!," focuses on the finding that in order for a business to grow the entrepreneur must grow, too. The entrepreneur must evolve from being primarily a doer to being a manager. He or she must learn how to delegate and how to accept the fact that no one will do the task like the entrepreneur would do it. This "letting go" continues as the business grows and the entrepreneur evolves into being both a leader and ultimately a coach and mentor for the managers in the business.

For the entrepreneur, growth requires significant change not only in what he or she does but also in how he or she does it. Many entrepreneurs must step back from being a functional specialist and learn to be a generalist (general manager) in the early phases of a business. As the business grows, however, the entrepreneur often starts moving back to being a specialist, spending more time in the functional area he or she enjoys.

Evolving toward becoming a leader and coach is challenging for many entrepreneurs because both roles require emotional intelligence, people engagement, and the ability to relate to individuals in a way they find meaningful. Coaching requires that time be spent getting to know people, listening, caring, understanding their emotional needs, and helping them grow. Coaching takes patience and a degree of personal emotional intimacy that many entrepreneurs are not able to achieve. It requires a continuation of the mind shift from "me the entrepreneur" and "my way" to "it is really all about them." Many entrepreneurs found this process very difficult, and some neither relished nor excelled in this role. As the business grows, some entrepreneurs evolve into more of a CEO or chairman, focusing on strategy, culture, and big issues while delegating the daily operational management to a chief operating officer (COO).

Chapter 5 ends with the "Defender Direct, Inc.: A Business of Growing Leaders" case, which tells the story of how Dave Lindsey, the entrepreneur, grew as his business grew, eventually evolving into the role of a servant leader.

Chapter 6, "The Challenges of Building an Effective Management Team," focuses on the finding that most CEOs had difficulties building an effective management team. Challenges varied, but included evaluating technical competencies in a functional area in which the CEO lacked sufficient experience or training, such as finance or technology; failing to follow interviewing best practices; hiring big-company people who could not adjust to a small-company environment; hiring small-company people who had no scaling experience; managing the interpersonal dynamics among new managers brought into the business; and adjusting to the challenge of upgrading managers when the business outgrew their capabilities. The result was that many management positions required multiple hires to get it right, taking extensive time, incurring costs, causing lost opportunities, and stressing the emotional dynamics of the business.

Chapter 6 contains the "Global Medical Imaging, LLC" case, which discusses how Ryan Dienst, the CEO, had to build an effective management team that was capable of scaling the business.

Chapter 7, "Culture—Creating a High-Performance Environment," looks at the importance of culture in setting standards and bounds for employee behavior and in creating an environment that results in high employee engagement and productivity. Developing a positive employment culture is important because employees who find meaning in their work and view it as more than just a paycheck are generally more engaged and productive.

This chapter discusses the inherent management tension of creating a "family" environment while requiring high accountability. It contains a discussion not only of my studies but also of the leading academic research on employee engagement done at the University of Michigan, Stanford University, Case Western Reserve University, and Harvard University. Chapter 7 shares some of the ways that successful entrepreneurs built environments that enabled high employee engagement. The "Leaders Bank: Creating a Great Place to Work" case is used at the end of this chapter to illustrate a growth business that built a high employee engagement environment.

Chapter 8, "Growth Thrusters: 'Replication' and 'Boosters,'" introduces the different ways businesses can grow beyond the start-up phase. Growth generally occurs either by scaling or through new growth initiatives. Scaling is the fastest way to grow and involves a strategy of replication. Executing a replication strategy is called "replicution." To scale quickly, entrepreneurs have to make critical decisions about what parts of their value chain they will scale and what parts they will outsource. Scaling has its limitations, and once scaling reaches its limits a business needs new "growth boosters" in order to continue growing. Different kinds of "growth boosters" are discussed with references to the various cases. This chapter attempts to put into perspective the interrelationship between scaling a business, constantly improving a business, and business innovation. It concludes with the "Enchanting Travels" case, which sets forth a scaling challenge.

Chapter 9, "The Added Complexity of Managing a Family Business," examines the added complexity when a growth business is also a family business. Having family members working in the business, owning stock in the business, or both adds a level of family dynamics complexity that has to be managed separately and in addition to the business. This chapter distills key points from my book *The Successful Family Business: A Proactive Plan for Managing Both the Family & the Business*.[2] Family business leaders need to proactively manage both the family and the business so that family issues do not have a negative impact on the business and business issues do not create family disharmony. Processes and policies need to be put in place that allow for the raising, discussing, and resolving of family issues that become apparent as family members age and their needs and wants change. In many cases an entrepreneur's business management style is not conducive to effectively managing family issues, and the entrepreneur or family leader has to adapt. Many find this difficult. This chapter ends with the "Edens & Avant" case, which tells the story of how Joe Edens institutionalized his family business while managing the succession process.

---

2. Edward D. Hess, *The Successful Family Business: A Proactive Plan for Managing Both the Family & the Business* (Westport, CT: Praeger, 2006).

PART I

1 Growth Can Be Good and Growth Can Be Bad

We live in a country that values individual spirit, entrepreneurship, and growth. Business growth generally is assumed to be good; bigger is assumed to be better. These assumptions underlie the mantra that businesses must "grow or die," which propels many business decisions, sometimes undermining the very viability of those businesses. The purpose of this chapter is to challenge those assumptions by presenting real-world examples of some of growth's pitfalls as well as empirical data to encourage business students to develop a more nuanced view of growth.

CLASS DISCUSSION QUESTIONS

1. Why must every business continuously grow?
2. When should a business grow?
3. When should a business stop growing?
4. Is growth the right objective for every business?
5. What are other alternative objectives for a business?

In *Smart Growth: Building an Enduring Business by Managing the Risks of Growth*, I challenged the "grow or die" mantra and the "Wall Street Rules," which assert that public company growth should be continuous, smooth, and linear, and should occur quarterly. Most view corporate quarterly reports of steady growth as the crucial metric of a public company's health. However, after reviewing relevant research in economics, finance, strategy, organizational design, complexity theory, and even biology, I concluded that there was no empirical basis for the "grow or die" axiom or for the Wall Street Rules. Given the lack of empirical basis to support the axiom that businesses must "grow or die," it is surprising that it continues to dominate both Wall

Street thinking and graduate business education. An examination of how businesses actually grow shows us that continuous, smooth, linear growth is the exception rather than the rule and that growth actually can bring about significant problems for the company, sometimes leading to the premature death of the company.

The Reality of Growth

Business growth is a complex process involving strategy choices, execution challenges, competitor responses, and changing customer needs. Although many business theories assume efficiency and rational decision making, this does not translate well in the real world. Growth results from the interactions of imperfect people who make mistakes. Moreover, people have cognitive limitations and biases that make certainty and predictability difficult. The reality of business is that individuals do not always behave efficiently or rationally, and neither do markets. As a result, business growth is unlikely to be smooth, linear, or continuous.

Instead, growth is a dynamic, interactive, interdependent process that generally involves false starts, learning as you go, adaptation, and failed initiatives. Growth is messy; growth is change; and growth has spurts, detours, downturns, and spikes. Growth requires constant learning and improvement. Growth requires people, processes, and culture to be aligned in order to drive desired value-creating behaviors. Businesses make people mistakes, process mistakes, and alignment mistakes. Growth, if not well-planned and managed, can stress people, processes, and controls and often can outstrip the capabilities of people and companies. In fact, growth creates another category of business risks that must be proactively managed.

I am not anti-growth. I am simply presenting my research findings, which challenge the basic business assumptions that a business must "grow or die" and that all growth is good. I want to begin a conversation about the realities of business growth based on empirical research and real-world business experience. Growth should not be accepted as a given. Rather, growth should be a strategic decision made only after the risks of growing and the risks of not growing have been assessed. As important, I have suggested a more nuanced view of growth that replaces the mantra "grow or die" with a more accurate but less catchy "all businesses must constantly improve so as to continuously meet customer needs better than the competition." Businesses do not have to grow but they do have to constantly improve.

My research on high-growth companies has led me to the following conclusions:

1. Growth can be good or bad;

2. Bigger is not always better;

3. There is nothing wrong with a business maintaining a steady state provided it continues to meet customer needs better than its competitors;

4. Growth should be an informed strategic decision made only after analysis of the pros and cons of growing and not growing;

5. Growth can stress people, processes, controls, culture, and customer value propositions;

6. Growth usually means adding employees, and having more employees requires building a larger management team, both of which are disruptive to a business and challenging to execute well;

7. Growth sometimes catapults businesses into a different competitive space where they will be forced to compete against bigger and better competition;

8. Growth materially changes the role of the entrepreneur who built the business and often requires the entrepreneur to enlarge his or her activities into areas where there is neither expertise nor enjoyment; and

9. To manage the risks of growth entrepreneurs must manage the pace of growth.

Growth is change. Growth requires the entrepreneur and the organization to evolve, which changes the personal dynamics and inner workings of the business. All of these changes in people and processes increase the risks that quality and financial controls may be violated and that culture and customer value proposition may become diluted, both of which are not good.

When Is Growth Bad?

There are several reasons why an unquestioning quest for growth can lead to bad outcomes. First, growth can be bad for a business if it requires the business to increase the magnitude of output so quickly that quality declines below customers' expectations. This produces dissatisfied customers who will then look elsewhere. Second, growth can be bad if it requires significant investment ahead of when the anticipated increased revenue will be received. The result can be that the business runs out of cash and cannot pay its bills. Third, growth can be bad if a business diversifies into a new related business that, while it might have looked good on paper, turns out to be too different from the core business and causes unexpected losses to occur. Fourth, growth can be bad if the business expands geographically without adequate management depth, causing a dilution of leadership since it is impossible for the entrepreneur to be in two places at the same time.

Growth also can be bad if an entrepreneur assumes that success in one area of business will ensure success in a different business area. For example, why does a successful residential real estate developer think he can build an office building or a shopping mall?

What may not be obvious is that growth requires more and qualitatively different controls and processes, plus a culture to drive desired behaviors to avoid negatively impacting quality, brand reputation, customer relationships, and financial stability or viability.

Why Should a Business Grow?

Common reasons given by the DPGC research entrepreneurs as to why they should grow their business were

- To make more money;
- Because more customers kept showing up;
- To give my employees a chance to grow in their jobs;
- To be more competitive;
- Because businesses are supposed to grow;
- Because I [the entrepreneur] am bored;
- Because my banker wants me to grow; and
- Businesses either "grow or die."

Are any of those reasons valid? Why? Why or under what circumstances do you think a business should grow? Why does a business have to grow revenues by more than the rate of expenses inflation?

In the next section, we will examine some growth tools that were generated by my research findings and developed for both my consulting practice and Darden Executive Education programs: the Growth Decision Template, the Growth Risks Audit, and the Managing the Risks of Growth Plan. These tools were designed to enable entrepreneurs to systematically assess the risks and benefits of growing their business.

Strategic Growth Decisions

I developed an appreciation for the necessity of strategic growth decisions and managing the risks of growth from research not of public companies but of private high-growth companies. This is somewhat surprising because, unlike publicly traded companies that are strongly affected by the public markets' push for quarterly growth, private company CEOs should, arguably, be free from such pressures. Why were these private company CEOs more aware of and concerned about the risks of growth than the public company CEOs? I do not know the answer to that question. Could it have something to do with the fact that private company CEOs in many cases have invested their own money, often a significant portion of their wealth, in their business?

In general, what I found was that entrepreneurs who had previous bad entrepreneurial experiences were more aware and respectful of the challenges and risks presented by growth. These experiences resulted in caution and sensitivity to the need to pace growth.

Growth Decision Template

In *Smart Growth*, I advised business managers to make decisions about growth only after systematically weighing the reasons and opportunities to grow against the risks of growth. For example, an entrepreneur should continually ask the following:

1. Should we grow?
2. Why should we grow?
3. How much should we grow?
4. Are we ready to grow? What preconditions for growth from a cultural, structural, management, people, capital, process, controls, and technology perspective need to be met?
5. What are our growth alternatives?
6. What are the pros and cons of each alternative?
7. Have we completed the Growth Risks Audit?
8. Have we designed a Growth Risks Management Plan to manage those risks?

Growth is change and change is risky. Growth challenges people and internal systems. When companies grow, they change beyond simply getting bigger.

Growth Risks Audit

The purpose of the Growth Risks Audit is to sensitize an entrepreneur to the proposition that managing growth includes managing risks as well as opportunities. I have used the Growth Risks Audit (Figure 1.1) in some executive education and consulting work, and it has worked well, but by no means should it be viewed as the only possible tool. Each company has its own stresses and fault lines, so any audit tool should be modified accordingly.

The next step after completing the Growth Risks Audit is to create a plan to manage the risks identified. I have found in my work with companies that it takes a different perspective to think about growth risks and their management than to think about growth. I have found very few managers who can switch back and forth quickly from a risk management mindset to a growth mindset. As a result, one has to put in place processes that give early warnings of growth risks issues, and one has to allocate specific management time to monitoring growth risks frequently. This takes discipline and focus.

Let me emphasize again that I have found no empirical basis for the commonly held beliefs that a business must "grow or die," nor for the assumption that growth should be continuous. I suggest that the corollary to "grow or die" is in some cases "grow and die." That is why growth should be a strategic decision, not just assumed as a rule of the business game. Businesses do not have to grow past a certain stage, but they do have to constantly improve.

Figure 1.1.

Growth Risks Audit

1. For each growth initiative, evaluate if, how, and to what extent that initiative will put material stress on your

   - Culture;

   - Structure;

   - Management team;

   - Employees;

   - Execution processes;

   - Quality controls;

   - Customer value proposition;

   - Customer experience;

   - Financial controls;

   - Financial safety net; and

   - Image and brand reputation.

2. What specific behaviors create material business risks for you? Will growth increase the likelihood of those behaviors?

3. Based on your answers to questions 1 and 2, prioritize those risks in order of harm to your business.

4. How do you know if those risks are occurring? What is your early warning system for each material risk? How do you monitor and detect those risk-inducing behaviors? How do you manage against creeping additive risks?

5. Does your measurement and reward system encourage or discourage those risky behaviors?

6. Managing growth requires a far different mindset or perspective than for managing the risks of growth. How do you put in place processes and time for you to do both?

7. What changes to your execution processes, quality control processes, and financial and information systems do you need to make to better manage the risks of growth?

8. Do you need to balance your internal communications about growth with communications about the specific growth risks you want to avoid?

9. Do you need to pace growth?

10. Under what conditions will you slow down or pause growth?

11. What is your risk management plan for each key material internal risk?

12. Will growth change whom you compete against?

13. If so, how will your new competitors likely respond?

14. Will that new competition impact your ability to maintain current customers? How? How will you ward off those new competitors? On what basis are you at a disadvantage with respect to the new competition? Do they have the capabilities to offer a better customer value proposition than you offer? Could the new competition put your business more at risk?

15. What changes do you need to make from strategy, structure, cultural, execution processes, quality control, financial controls, information management, measurements, and rewards perspectives to manage these risks of growth? In what priority?

16. Have you created a risk management execution plan with timelines, milestones, and responsibilities?

17. How do you collectivize growth risk management across your employee team?

Growth risk management accepts the fact that growth is change and that change can have unintended consequences on people, culture, quality, and financial controls. Some of those consequences may seem small but when they are added to other small consequences, they may result in a big negative impact.

CLASS DISCUSSION QUESTIONS

1. Why should growth be a strategic decision?

2. What can entrepreneurs do to prepare for growth and minimize the risks of growth?

3. Is it ever smart to turn away new business? Why?

4. When should a business grow?

5. When should a business not grow?

6. What factors might contribute to a business "growing and dying?"

The Elephant in the Room

Underlying our discussion is a critical question for every entrepreneur: What are the personal and financial objectives of the entrepreneur? To answer that question, one must first understand the goals of the entrepreneur. For example, is the goal to build a business and sell it or is the goal to build something that continues to be fun and that will support the entrepreneur and his or her family for years to come? How much income is enough? Why build this business? Why mess with success?

Thinking about these questions up front in the business-building process will help entrepreneurs decide if, when, and how much to grow their business. Growth should not be undertaken without rigorous assessment of the risks of growing and not growing and a systematic analysis of how to manage the risks.

Eyebobs Eyewear, Inc.

Let us move to the Eyebobs Eyewear, Inc. case. This story presents one entrepreneur's views about the risks of growth and why she turned away growth opportunities and certain large potential customers because of those risks.

CASE DISCUSSION QUESTIONS

1. Put yourself in Julie's shoes; why was she so risk averse?

2. What was consistent about Julie's attitude about financing her business and her product?

3. What were Julie's big concerns that drove many of her decisions?

4. Julie's life experiences prepared her to be a business builder—what were they and what did she learn?

5. Chart how Julie built the production and distribution parts of her business and explain her risk management thinking.

6. You are a writer for your school newspaper. Write a 250-word story that summarizes the Eyebobs case.

CASE
STUDY

EYEBOBS EYEWEAR, INC.

Eyebobs Eyewear, Inc. (Eyebobs), based in Minneapolis, Minnesota, was a private company specializing in optician-grade ready-to-wear reading glasses with an attitude, or "eyewear for the irreverent and slightly jaded," as the company's tagline proclaimed. The artsy frames in striking colors, innovative shapes, and tongue-in-cheek names such as Board Stiff, Barely Lucid, and Hostile Makeover had a cult-like following among people with a playful streak. Eyebobs were sold at optical centers, high-end department stores such as Nordstrom and Neiman Marcus, and upscale clothing boutiques from coast to coast.

Eyebobs president and CEO Julie Allinson was a 40-year-old former banker and president of a start-up for children's clothing when she quit her job to launch an eyewear business in 2000. She used her life's savings as seed capital and funded growth entirely out of cash flow. It took her six long years to earn $1 million in sales. But in 2007, her company of 10 employees pulled in $4.5 million in revenues. In 2008, in the midst of an economic downturn, Allinson proudly handed out year-end bonus checks to her staff and was looking to hire more people. Reflecting on her decision to bootstrap her company and eschew external funding sources, Allinson emphasized the long-term benefits of debt-free growth and the freedom it allowed her:

I didn't borrow money; I didn't take on investors, and that allowed me to make all the decisions on how to allocate that tiny pool of money I had myself. I didn't want anybody beating on my back, "Grow faster, grow faster," if I wasn't comfortable with it. I've had many a sleepless night at Eyebobs, going over my decisions. But they are the decisions that I've made, not somebody else pushing me, wanting a certain return. We are trying to be realistic here, and we say that as we make decisions in the office every day: Do we want to take on more private label? Do we want to take on this customer? Do we want to create another brand that's cheaper? And often, the answer is, No, we don't have to have every single dollar in the marketplace. Just be true to ourselves, deliver a beautiful product that's high-end—to stay in that niche. And that's a discipline all by itself.

The Founder—A Country Girl Goes Corporate

Julie Allinson was born in 1958 and grew up on a small farm in Iowa. "We had no idea how poor we were," Allinson said. Her upbringing provided many lessons, which she later applied to running her own business. "What's driven home in a farm situation is common sense, and common sense really isn't very common," Allinson

Case Study UVA-ENT-0139 © 2009 by the University of Virginia Darden School Foundation. This case was prepared by Senior Researcher Gosia Glinska and Edward D. Hess as a basis for class discussion rather than to illustrate effective or ineffective handling of an administrative situation.

said. "You learn how to take care of yourself on a day-to-day basis, and you learn how to take care of your little business, because every farmer is an entrepreneur."

As a child of parents who, no matter how hard they worked, lived lives of constant uncertainty, Allinson valued planning and predictability. "I hated that type of existence where you couldn't have control," she said. But, reflecting on the similarities between her and her parents' lives, she admitted that maybe she "ended up just like them." She explained:

I can remember my parents praying for rain and then praying for it to stop. I never wanted to live that way. But being an entrepreneur is very much the same: you pray for the business, and you pray that you can handle the business, that you can deliver a quality product. And a lot of that is out of your hands—by virtue of having employees, manufacturers, etc.—because it's not just you who's involved.

Following her parents' advice, Allinson held various steady jobs during her teens. After graduating from high school, she attended the University of Iowa, where she majored in business. Even though she wanted to work in the area of marketing, for which she had a natural affinity, she gave up the idea. "I didn't think it was practical," she said. "I went into the numbers business, because I'm competitive. I wanted to challenge myself and become very good at it."

After graduating in 1980, Allinson moved to Minneapolis, Minnesota, and became an operations manager for the brokerage firm Piper Jaffray & Co., followed by a short stint as a stockbroker. "I didn't like the telephone sales, which is what it really was," she said. She spent the next 10 years managing loan portfolios for FirstBank. But she felt out of place in the corporate environment. "I was the square peg in a round hole," she said.[1] She also chafed at the lack of independence she experienced in large organizations. A free spirit at heart, Allinson admitted that she "always wanted to live and die by [her] own sword."

Mack & Moore—A Crash Course in Running a Start-Up

An opportunity to work outside the United States occurred in 1995, when a friend introduced Allinson to the founders of a Minneapolis-based clothing start-up, Mack & Moore, Inc. Gerri Mack and Susan Moore persuaded Allinson to come onboard as president. Heading a $1.5 million venture, which specialized in high-end children's clothes sold at Nordstrom and Neiman Marcus, was all-consuming, but "it was an incredible learning experience," Allinson said. "I got my PhD overnight, every day at work."

---

1. Allie Shah, "Eye-Conoclast: Meet the Brains Behind Some of the Wackiest Glasses You'll Ever See," *Star Tribune*, August 24, 2006.

When Allinson reviewed the company's financial statements, she realized that the owners had run themselves into debt and needed to raise capital. "They were artists," Allinson said, "and they had a great product, but I looked at their financials and said, 'You're going to be bankrupt in three or four weeks.'"

Reflecting on the lessons learned as president of a struggling start-up, Allinson stressed the importance of keeping a close eye on the numbers:

You can call it finance, or you can call it common sense, but you have to know where the money is coming from, where it went, and how much you can spend. So that's what I learned at Mack & Moore—profitability is king. Just because you've got great ideas doesn't mean you can do it quickly, without a great plan in place and without funding. You have to keep in mind that you need to spend the money to create money, and that it can be a very long path before you turn a profit.

A Business of Her Own

Five years into her tenure as president of Mack & Moore, Allinson grew increasingly frustrated with her job. "I had no real ownership of the company," she admitted. Despite her title, "I really was the relationship manager getting investors," she said, adding that she had "all the responsibility and none of the authority." She also began to feel the entrepreneurial itch. She had wanted to run her own business but "wanting a business and starting a business are two different things," she said. "You really have to find something you have a passion for in order to quit your job and stick your life savings into it."[2]

Ironically, she found that "something" when she developed presbyopia, the farsightedness that accompanied aging and happened to most people entering their 40s and 50s. Allinson realized she needed a pair of reading glasses, so she went to see her friend Jason, who worked at an optical store. "[He] was happy to sell me hip reading glasses, but at a price that I couldn't afford," Allinson said. "So he showed me alternatives—at Walgreens." But Allinson did not like the cheap off-the-rack drug-store readers. "Isn't there anything in between?" she asked her optician friend. "Not really," he said. "That was my *aha* moment," Allinson remembered.[3]

Retail sales of nonprescription reading glasses in 1999 were about $350 million, up 6.5% from the previous year, according to optical-industry research.[4] With studies showing that 1.5 million people turned 40 each year and someone turned 50 every few seconds, there was a large potential pool of people with blurred vision.

---

2. Melissa Colgan, "People Who Do Cool Things: Julie Allinson," mspmag.com (accessed January 2008).

3. Colgan.

4. Lauren Lipton, "Going Loopy Over an Eyeglass Holder," *Wall Street Journal*, July 6, 2001.

In 2002, sensing a business opportunity, Allinson quit her job at Mack & Moore and plunged into a life of risk and uncertainty—she was going to start her own company. She reflected on the inspiration behind her decision to make affordable but hip reading glasses:

I loved going to work every day—that really turned me on. I liked having people around me. I like solving problems, all that kind of thing. But what I envied about [my optician friend] was that he had a genuine love for the product. I was in banking and at brokerage firms, where you don't have a tangible product. And so that always kind of hung with me, something you could put in your hand, something you could sell, something you could look at and improve.

The first year after leaving Mack & Moore, Allinson lived off her savings. She was "a student of [her] own business," as she put it, "trying to figure out how to get Eyebobs up and running." She went to China, Italy, and Chicago to talk to plastic manufacturers. She developed a business plan, asking herself the following questions:

Where am I going to have it manufactured? What kind of hinges should I use? How am I going to get this distributed? How am I going to get this packaged? How am I going to present it at the stores?

Bootstrapping Like Crazy

Rounding up funds for her venture did not involve looking for investors or knocking on banks' doors: Allinson used her personal savings as seed capital and was determined to fund growth from the company's own cash flow, instead of borrowing large sums. "Because my parents grew up during the Depression," Allinson said, "I pay for everything with cash. I've never had a bank loan for the business. Sometimes, I ask myself, am I being too conservative?"

Another reason behind eschewing debt was a family health scare. Soon after she started Eyebobs, Allinson's husband Paul had a heart attack. During his recovery, the couple talked about ways to minimize factors that increased his risk of heart disease. "We asked, 'Okay, what's creating stress in Paul's life?'" Allinson recalled. "And the answer was, 'Well, my starting a business.' What the hell could be more stressful?" She elaborated:

We talked about the numbers—a business could take a lot of cash if you let it—and how do you keep it from just eating you alive kind of thing. And the other thing was owning a house, so we moved into a condo, and we just bootstrapped this thing like crazy, because I couldn't have Paul stress out about the business.

Supply Chain Management

When Allinson set out on her entrepreneurial journey, she wanted to produce optical-grade reading glasses with stylish frames equipped with lenses that were scratch and chip resistant. Because she valued quality, she traveled to China to visit manufacturers in order to see their operations. "I interviewed between 24 to 30 people in one week," Allinson said. She learned the importance of staying well-connected with one's partners and suppliers and checking on them in person:

Getting to know your supply side is crucial. If you're going through a middleman, you don't know stink. You don't know what the hell's going on at the factory. You don't know who owns it, who's getting priority, and what the product looks like. Going back to my upbringing—don't be afraid to get your hands dirty. Don't just make a phone call, get out there. I was gonna end up wiring my life's savings to an optical manufacturer, and the only way I was comfortable doing this was to go there first to meet them eye to eye.

For Allinson, the sourcing trip to China provided many other insights. "I learned so much during that trip about hinges and materials and where the good stuff was coming from," she said, adding that it soon became apparent that she should go talk to the Italian plastic manufacturers in person. "I wanted a higher-end product, and to this day, Italy is the place where they make the latest and the greatest," she said. As it turned out, her Italian manufacturers also had plants in China, so that's where her Eyebobs frames were made.

Allinson believed that the reason she was able to develop successful partnerships with Italian manufacturers was because she made the effort to visit them early on. She explained, "When you're small and you say, 'I'm going to do 1,000 pieces' or some ridiculous amount like that, something I do in a day now, how do you get the attention of these people? Well, they know you're serious because you were crazy enough to go over there to find out." As a result of her efforts, Eyebobs reading glasses would be made with the same top-grade Italian plastic and hinges used by the more expensive frame companies. Having optical-quality frames also would allow Allinson's customers to have prescription lenses cut for their Eyebobs frames.

Eyewear for the Discerning

For the next step, Allinson again turned to her friend Jason; this time it was to help her design the first line of Eyebobs. "I said, 'I want to do some conservative things and some outrageous things,'" she recalled. "I came up with the frames, and Jason helped me with the bridge work—the most difficult part because everybody's nose is different." Next she contacted a team of designers at an optical manufacturer. With their help and feedback, Allinson's dream of creating reading glasses became a reality. "They said, 'Yes, we can do it, it will be more expensive if we do it this way, and less expensive if we do it that way,'" Allinson said.

Allinson aimed for a niche in the reading glasses market and she targeted customers who valued style as well as quality. The bulk of her clientele were baby boomers who needed nonprescription reading glasses but also wanted to look good. For them, glasses were a fashion accessory. An extrovert, Allinson favored eyewear that was "nonconforming, a little twisted, that [said] something about the nature of the person wearing it." She liked to say that Eyebobs readers were not for most people and that she and her staff wanted to appeal to discerning people like herself.

From the beginning, Allinson was deeply involved in the design process. "I always have a final say on a design," she said. "And you get a few of those who say, 'Well Julie, nobody's done that.' And I say, 'I think I'm going to.' Don't be afraid to do it differently." For example, one year, when the big color for the fall was grey, one of Allinson's customers pointed out that the Eyebobs' line did not have a single grey frame. "You're making a huge mistake," she told Allinson. But Allinson knew better. "I had nothing grey, because if you're wearing grey, then your eyewear should be red," she said.

Allinson looked for colors and styles that would stand out on a person's face and be memorable. "When working on a design, we think about the personality of the individual who might wear it, and what that person would want to communicate about themselves," she said.[5] Because she often drew inspiration from old Hollywood movies, many Eyebobs glasses had a retro feel, yet looked distinctly modern. She was not afraid to do frames with old-fashioned, round lenses, in purple or neon green. "The wackier I get," she said, "the more people love them."[6] She continued:

That's one of the blessings of not having been in the business previously. "We've always done it this way," wouldn't even occur to me. I don't know how they did it—I don't care. Again, that's the advantage of going to your end users to find out what they want, because if I'd gone to the retailer, I would have had a nickel-and-dime product that was a pile of crap that looked like everything else on the shelf.

Meeting satisfied customers was part of the fun of running Eyebobs. During one of her trips to Italy, where she sourced plastic, Allinson and one of her staffers went to Venice for a couple of days. "We're walking in Venice, and somebody's wearing Eyebobs," Allinson recalled. "I went and handed her my card, and she said, 'Oh my God, I love these glasses, you wouldn't believe how often I get stopped.' She was thrilled, I was thrilled . . . it seemed so silly. It's a kick, it really is."

The Right Distribution Channels

The most obvious distribution channel Allinson tried first was the eyewear stores. In 2001, she attended an optical trade show, Vision Expo in New York City, hoping that eyewear retail stores would pick up her reading glasses. "I basically sold noth-

---

5. Colgan.
6. Colgan.

ing," she recalled and lamented that she opened only one new account. "The first two years I really struggled. I kept trying to sell in the optical market because you're thinking, where do people go with their eye troubles?" Her reasoning was correct, but she did not realize that optical stores resisted selling nonprescription readers for fear these glasses would detract from their high-margin prescription business. Allinson explained:

It was shocking to me how a lot of [eyewear stores] would keep Eyebobs under the counter because they didn't want people to know they carried a reader line. I'd go to these places knowing they'd bought the product and ask, "Where is it?" And they'd be, like, "Oh, we don't show that to anybody." I sat there for two years scratching my head, going, "What am I doing wrong?" I was just dumb enough to stay at it. The first couple of years in the business world you sweat bullets. You have to believe in your vision for a long time.

Hubert White—Allinson's Lucky Break

Allinson's belief in her product kept her going forward. The feedback she was getting from her focus groups and her first customers, as well as from friends and family, confirmed that all of them wanted Eyebobs. "I had to find a different way to get them distributed," she said.

One day, Allinson visited Hubert White, an upscale men's clothing store in downtown Minneapolis, to make a pitch. Brad Sherman, the store's general manager, agreed to display a few pairs of Eyebobs readers for eight weeks, but he was not optimistic. "He said to me very honestly," recalled Allinson, "'Julie, I'll work with you because you're local, but I've done it all. I've done belts, gloves, and scarves. None of this stuff sells.'" Two weeks later, Allinson received a phone call from Sherman. "I'm sold out to the piece," he announced.

Sherman ordered more Eyebobs, and he even helped Allinson design an elegant display case for the store. "I still use it today," Allinson said, adding that "everybody in the market had knocked it off." Over time, Hubert White sold "at least one or two pairs a day every single day of the year," and Eyebobs became one of the store's "most successful items," according to Sherman.[7] "And from there—it just went like wildfire," Allinson said.

Hitting the Trade-Show Circuit

Sherman told Allinson that she should start attending fashion-industry trade shows to generate new sales leads. At the time, renting a 10-foot by 10-foot exhibit booth for each show for roughly $10,000 was an expensive proposition for Allinson. "Well, that scared the bejesus out of me," she said. "You know, money's tight in small companies."

---

7. Shah.

So, Allinson decided to dip her toes into the world of trade shows, and in 2002, she signed up for the ENK Men's Show in New York City.[8]

Forming relationships with retailers, however, took time and persistence. At the first ENK Men's Show she attended, everyone who stopped by her booth loved the stylish Eyebobs readers. "I sold to every sales rep in the place," Allinson said. "But a lot of them would buy for themselves and wouldn't buy for their store." The following year, at the same show, "it went gangbusters," Allinson said and explained:

[The sales reps] realized that everything I had told them was true: the product was not disposable—it hung together. They realized I was a woman of my word, it built up that trust, and the orders started coming in. But it's not all a bed of roses. My product was too high-priced for some of the stores that bought it. Others were pushing me to go to an even higher-priced product. But I got that swath in the middle, that 60% to 80% that understood it and wanted it.

After her first ENK success, Allinson attended the men's fashion show in New York City, followed by one in Las Vegas and another in Chicago, eventually adding the women's accessory show to her roster. "After Brad Sherman introduced me to men's shows, that's when the sales really started to happen," she said and added:

And that's how the company has grown, and I just keep adding these shows. But it's not, like, "I'm going to do all these shows," throwing stuff at the wall and hoping that it sticks. It was very methodical, very bootstrapped. If the show pays for itself, then I can do the next show.

In 2008, Allinson and 12 of her staff members attended 22 national trade shows; however, Allinson believed that her presence alone was not generating new sales leads. "Most of it comes from word of mouth," she said. "It's because somebody else bought my product, and they're a believer. Three retailers are being dragged by one of their friends who sells it already."

Building the Eyebobs Team

Like many entrepreneurs who bootstrap their start-ups, in the beginning Allinson did everything herself. "I created the designs, got the inventory stocked, took orders," she said. "I was the only salesperson, packer, shipper, and bookkeeper." An extrovert, Allinson went to lunch with the mailman twice a week, "just to have human interaction," she said.

One day, Allinson realized that her company demanded more than she could handle alone. "That's when you start to get really excited about your business," she said. "That's what you dream of—not being able to do it all yourself." In 2002 she hired her first part-time employee. "The first person you hire is a minimum-

---

8. ENK was the leading fashion-industry tradeshow organization, conducting 25 events per year. Upscale fashion retailers representing specialty and department stores from around the world attended ENK events.

wage kind of person, just to pickup the phone," Allinson said. "Really, you take all the phone calls, but they'll get the one line that rolls over." After her first employee moved out of state, Allinson hired a professional customer service rep/bookkeeper, who was excellent at the job, and who hired two of her relatives as packers and shippers.

Unfortunately, the new hire started charging personal items to Allinson's business credit card. "She thought that because she paid the credit-card bill, I would not catch on," Allinson said. But Allinson, who monitored her credit-card statement online every day, caught the embezzler in her tracks. "And so I fired all of them," she said. Losing all employees, including an entire shipping department, during one of the busiest times of the year was tough on the fledgling company. "It was one of my big surges when I was catching on right before Christmas when the retailers count on you," she said.

Getting It Right

In 2004, through personal referrals from friends, Allinson hired a part-time operations manager named Saul and a full-time customer-service rep named Kim, who had 20 years of experience in the optical business. By now, Allinson was self-aware enough to know her own strengths and weaknesses and admitted that while she "was not a great customer-service person," Kim was an excellent one. As Allinson recalled, she often asked Kim to handle the problem phone calls:

[Kim] just knew how to do that. And I thought, "Wow, that's really good!" That illustrates how you've got to pull that talent around you. Kim would say, "Yeah Julie, I can do that all day long, but I couldn't have started this business. So, I guess, we're made for each other."

Allinson understood the importance of having someone to take care of the nuts and bolts of the business, and she particularly valued Saul, who came to Eyebobs from an upscale department-store chain. "He set a really high bar for us," Allinson said. "He never gets sick of checks and balances—'What do we have in today? How do I get these people organized? How can I get them to be more effective in their jobs?'"

Having two knowledgeable and experienced employees freed Allinson up and allowed her to focus more on growing the business. "I was able to go on the road more to talk to customers," she said, and added that she was "completely blessed with [Saul and Kim] . . . it was beyond my dreams." But the transition from working solo for two years to delegating was not without wrinkles. Allinson explained:

Now I can't even go out to the shipping desk and put together a package I'm so proud of, but I'm so glad they have figured out 10 different ways to automate it and do it better than I did. Frankly, my biggest adjustment was handing over my customers to somebody else. Having them take ownership of my customers and letting them talk to my customers. There's a certain tone that I like to have at Eyebobs—it's well-informed smart ass, somebody who can give them the answer but have fun talking to them and kind of pull their chain. Make it a memorable part of their day.

Building the IT Function

When Allinson started building the IT function of her fledgling company, her husband Paul proved to be an invaluable resource. Although working full time for a major bank, he came to Allinson's office after hours to set up servers and computer networks or create Web interfaces. "He saved us money from day one," Allinson said, adding that "when you have a company that's growing like Eyebobs, the technical piece can make you buckle at the knees. When your system goes down—those charges can be enormous." Describing her husband's contributions to Eyebobs, Allinson emphasized the importance of the "technical piece" he provided:

We have a direct interface from our Web site to our accounting software that eliminates rekeying, which eliminates most errors. That's huge for us. Everything we do, he creates an interface for us. We have direct interface with UPS. We never rekey any of that information, either. That's hours of manpower that we don't have to worry about.

Allinson's husband joined Eyebobs full time in 2007. In addition to being responsible for the IT function, he oversaw the accounting function of the business. Allinson's only regret about hiring her husband was not having done it sooner. "But he was my bread-and-butter-man," she said. "He was the guy who allowed me to be an entrepreneur."

A Team of Hardworking "Nut Cases"

In 2009, Eyebobs had 12 full-time employees. "The people who work at Eyebobs today are the best thing to happen to this company," Allinson said. "Each one is a hardworking nut case, and I derive so much positive energy from them." Allinson was proud of her diverse group, which included one national-sales manager, responsible for the independent-sales reps; two people responsible for bookkeeping, accounting, and data entry; one person who managed the company's Web site, blog, and all of the social networks. "Everybody else is the packer, shipper, and phone person," Allinson said, and added that all her packers and shippers also served as customer-service reps. "They are all too smart for packing jobs, and I needed to engage them in other ways. By answering the phone, they know that their mistakes are immediately felt by the customers."

Allinson's optician friend, Jason, who had been assisting with the designs since the Eyebobs' launch, joined the company full time in early 2009 as a customer-service rep and designer. In spite of a grim economic environment, Eyebobs was growing, and Allinson wanted to expand her staff. "I'm now interviewing marketing companies," she said. "I want one cohesive message going out to my end users and my wholesalers. I want to either bring somebody in-house or hire a marketing company."

Allinson liked to say that one of the most enjoyable aspects of running Eyebobs was handing out bonus checks to her employees. She was proud that she had not had to face any layoffs and that her employees were not "sitting with an axe over their neck every day." She continued:

I'm happy to know them each very well and not treat them like a number, like they are disposable. That's one of the big joys I get out of running Eyebobs. I surround myself with people I genuinely like. We have a 401(k)-type situation, and I'm just starting to look at ESOPs and things like that. It's important to me to take care of these people.

Allinson's Evolving Role—Growing Sales

As her company grew and she expanded her staff, in addition to her focus on design, Allinson's priority became growing sales. "Marketing comes very naturally to me," Allinson said, "but not the sales part; I had to figure out how to do it inexpensively and effectively. So my attention went to how to get that done."

Over the years, Allinson developed a sales strategy to help her grow Eyebobs. As she saw it, one of its main components was a well-stocked inventory, which carried a risk, but which helped her differentiate her business and engender customer loyalty:

Reading glasses are not a seasonal product. You're trying to create an annuity for the retailer and for yourself . . . So the whole sales strategy is trying to keep that inventory full so that people always have something to go back to. You're trying to educate the retailer that once a month or once a week they need to be reordering Eyebobs. If a customer loses a frame, if they like that frame, they can continue to reorder it from you. And that's really not what customers are used to. They are used to calling for a special order and being told, no we don't have it. And I want to say, Yes, we have it, we'll ship it for you today. Most companies do not carry inventory—we do. I've changed that paradigm, and that's my real risk in my business.

Managing Growth

For many entrepreneurs, the business catchphrase "grow or die" meant "grow at breakneck speed or die." Allinson did not see it that way. Unmanaged, "growth could easily swallow you up," she cautioned. She knew that unmanaged growth was a sure sign of growing too fast. Unlike the cocky upstarts who took on debt swiftly to fund expansions only to crash and burn, Allinson grew her company slowly, out of her own cash flow, and was careful not to overstretch her resources. It took her six years to hit the $1 million in revenue mark. "I spent my money sourcing the product and trying to get the very best product," she said, "and I didn't have money to blow on marketing. I had to be happy to grow a little bit at a time, to get the word out."

Once the word got out about her product, Allinson started getting offers from retailers across the country, but she was very selective about her clients. "It's important who you say no to," she said. "Why would I take on customers who can't pay me?

We are very careful about who we extend credit to." She explained how her financial background was a huge asset in dealing with clients and managing risk:

Cash flow is king, no doubt about it. Now, I'm in a situation where I'm always looking at the balance sheet, I'm looking at inventory, looking at where the money is. Because I extend terms to my customers, I don't have factors in the middle of this. I take all the risk of all these small customers I do business with. Because I understand the collections process and cash flow, we've stayed on top of that. You can't let that become the last thing—it has to be the first thing.

Allinson also tried to broaden her customer base to prevent a crisis that inevitably happened when a company's chief customers suddenly pulled orders. She was not afraid to say "no, thank you" to prospective buyers who posed too much risk to her company's financial health. She explained why she turned away a lot of business:

I didn't want them to be 80% of my business. What if they go away? I do have two or three big customers—they all have a big slice, but it's still a small part of my business. I feel I'm a boutique business. Not everybody wants an expensive reader or is comfortable wearing fashion. So, I'm better off selling to boutiques.

Allinson thought that "it's easy to get into business, but it's hard to stay in business." She understood the perils of undisciplined growth and the importance of the continuous monitoring of inventory levels:

You think, oh yeah, I want to sell to everybody, bring on the business. Bullshit. You've got to manage that, pay for that inventory. And you better know who you're going to sell it to, and how long it's going to take you to see it out. I feel I have a significant amount of inventory. When I was running Mack & Moore, one of our investors, who used to be the president of Target, would say over and over again, "Julie, inventory is not like fine wine, it does not get better with age." So even if it's $25,000 worth of inventory that's just sitting there, get rid of it.

Allinson considered 2005 a breakthrough year for the fledgling company because Eyebobs pulled in $840,000 in revenues. "When I hit that number, I can remember I thought we've made it," she said. In 2006, her start-up generated $1 million in revenue, followed by $4.5 million in 2007. In 2008, Allinson expanded her Minneapolis office and pumped money into a new phone system better equipped to handle the increasing number of calls. She said:

Because we're growing by leaps and bounds right now, we are expanding our area. One of the ideas for the new phone system is that when you're on hold, we want people telling their Eyebobs story. Some funny story and we want it to be a customer, preferably an end user, who's talking about how they found Eyebobs.

Beating the Copycats

Growing a company from zero to $4.5 million in sales in seven years, with no outside investors or credit lines, would make many entrepreneurs complacent, but Allinson did not dwell on her extraordinary achievement. "I never focus on my success," she said. "I always focus on the things I'm going to fix and do next. You just put something else on your worry plate."

In 2009, her "worry plate" was full of copycats who were knocking off her reading glasses and funky designs, using inferior materials and selling them for less. Imitation may be the sincerest form of flattery but, for an entrepreneur like Allinson, whose success was born of creativity and innovation, it was a big problem.

To beat the competition whose only game was imitation, she was forced to be more innovative and take charge of the market, which was not an easy feat in a time of economic downturn. In lieu of offering a lower-priced product, which was what many in the fashion-accessories business were doing, Allinson decided to "add some other value," and make her product "even more interesting." Instead of the usual protective case for her Eyebobs readers, she created an innovative leather case with room for car keys and credit cards. She explained:

I want to add value to the product rather than increase or decrease the price. My costs have gone up, but I'm not passing that on to the customer. Other reading-glasses companies are knocking us off—that's why I'm changing my cases; I want to do more for my customer for $65. I want to add value so the customer sees us as the leader. Eventually, instead of saying, "Where are my reading glasses?" I want people to say, "Where are my Eyebobs?"

And, when asked about keeping her Eyebobs business ahead of the copycat pack in the future, Allinson said:

I have to stay at the front; I have to be more creative. I really work hard not to look at people who are knocking me off. What am I going to do? Stand there with my head looking over my shoulder? No, I want to look straight ahead, doing all the things that they are not thinking of doing. They are busy trying to be me, but they are not me.

List of Relevant Cases

3 Fellers Bakery

Enchanting Travels

Eyebobs Eyewear, Inc.

Mellace Family Brands, Inc.: Building a Socially Responsible Enterprise

Room & Board

Sammy Snacks (A)

Sammy Snacks (B)

Students Helping Honduras

Valley-Wide Health Systems, Inc.

Author's Commentaries

This chapter aims to challenge beliefs about the goals of business growth and discuss the potential risks of growth and strategies for managing them. What follows are additional commentaries I've written on these topics.

"Rapid Growth: Be Careful What You Ask For"[9]

Every business builder feels pressure to strive for growth—as much and as fast as possible. Every entrepreneur has to be cognizant of the fact that growth can be bad if not properly managed. Entrepreneurial ventures often fail for one of three reasons:

1. The entrepreneur has a business idea, but the idea is not a good business opportunity;

2. The entrepreneur has a good business opportunity, but does not attract enough profitable customers fast enough to support the business and thus, runs out of money; and

3. The entrepreneur has a good business opportunity, is able to attract sufficient profitable customers, but is unable to scale the business successfully to accommodate growth.

Growth requires a business builder to

1. Hire more people quickly;

2. Get them productive quickly;

3. Put in place structure and controls;

4. Teach a business culture;

5. Transition from being a doer to becoming more of a manager; and

6. Not lose the entrepreneurial spirit and not lower quality standards.

Growth requires the business builder to change and the business to change. Many business builders are good doers but are not able to transition successfully to managing people. Some are overwhelmed by the process issues.

Growth can be good or bad. Managing growth requires a disciplined process. It depends on the personality, skills, adaptability, and willingness of the entrepreneur to change and be resilient. Doing something you love and are good at is far easier than delegating and managing people. Management is hard—it is getting people to do what you want, when you want and how you want. How do you instill the pride, the quest for excellence, the love of the product into others? How do you hire, train, critique, manage, sell, and compete at the same time? How do you do all of this and still have fun? How do you make it fun for your employees?

---

9. Edward D. Hess, "Rapid Growth: Be Careful What You Ask For," *The Catalyst*, July 2003.

It is a major transition. No longer can entrepreneurs have the direct contact with employees and customers they once had. However, only through others can you leverage your business and grow. It is through others that you will or will not survive the growth stage.

Every business as it grows will face the following conflicting tensions:

1. Flexibility vs. rules;
2. Employee autonomy vs. controls;
3. Informality vs. formality;
4. No bureaucracy vs. creating bureaucracy—administrators;
5. Decentralization vs. centralization;
6. One leader vs. managers;
7. Vertical structure vs. horizontal hierarchy;
8. Open communication vs. need-to-know;
9. Hands-on informal reporting vs. functional or product reporting;
10. Informal HR policies and reviews vs. formal HR policies and reviews; and
11. Entrepreneur involvement in everything vs. delegation.

The time to think about these issues is *before* you face them. Business builders should think about the "what ifs?" of growth. Think about what your business will look like if you double in size or even quadruple in size. Disciplined, managed growth is good; undisciplined, unmanaged growth will kill your business.

You need to answer the following questions before you face them:

1. What type of skills and personalities will you be looking for in the people you hire?
2. How will you teach the new people? How many can you teach at one time?
3. How will you make sure the new people will not destroy the good employee chemistry you currently enjoy?
4. How will you organize people? Everyone cannot report directly to you.
5. Who will you make managers? How will you teach them to manage?
6. What results or objectives will you measure? How often? How will you manage by objectives?
7. How will you manage by exceptions?
8. How will you make sure you get the problems resolved quickly? How will you make sure you know what the problems are?
9. What will you reward? How? When?
10. What business information will be communicated and to whom? When? How often?
11. What are the values or meaning that you want to preserve?

Every business builder needs to keep in mind these three questions as he or she considers growth:

1. What are our values and purpose? Why should someone join us, and what are we trying to build?
2. What personality traits and skills are most important for our business?
3. What is the key economic measure that all employees must focus on every day?

Growing requires you to refocus part of your time away from customers to hiring and teaching. It is a time-consuming and daily process.

Growth will change you, it will change what you do, it will change what you focus on, and growth will scare your employees. Will growth be constructive and productive or chaotic and demoralizing? Will the growth preserve the essence of what you are trying to build or will growth destroy it? What do you need to do in order not to lose control? What are the mission critical items you must not lose control of?

As you grow, keep in mind the U.S. Army Leader's Recon: The leader's job is to ask three questions every day. What is happening? What is not happening? What do I need to do to influence the outcome?

The message of this perspective is quite simply: If you wait to think through these issues when you have the problems of growth, it may be too late.

In a later perspective, we will talk about one way of thinking through these issues. Remember—growth can be good. But poorly managed growth can be your downfall!

"When Should Your Business Stop Growing?"[10]

The business world is a believer—a believer in growth. With sayings like "grow or die" and "eat or be eaten," the growth mantra implies that you must keep growing or bad things will happen to you. Growth is the goal. Expand! Acquire! Go! Go! Go!

Very few people—consultants, writers, stock analysts, academics—challenge the underlying growth assumption and few assert that maybe, yes, maybe growth is not a clear-cut issue. Just maybe growth can be bad for you.

When should you stop growing? When the risks of growth outweigh the benefits. Risks can be of two types—risks inherent or internal to the business and risks external to the business. Internal risks can be lack of management expertise or depth, increased capital needs due to increased fixed overhead, people needs, low tolerance for bureaucracy, controls, and accountability. External risks can be changing market conditions, reliance on too few customers, and increased competition from bigger and better players.

Every growth decision should be a risk/reward analysis along with an analysis of the risks to you of not growing.

---

10. Edward D. Hess, "When Should Your Business Stop Growing?" *The Catalyst*, March 2004.

Not growing is not a steady state analysis—in other words, things will not stay the same—stuff happens—what are the risks of not growing? What are the risks of growing? Which risks are more palatable for you? Let's explore.

Internal Factors

The issue of whether to grow raises the issue as to what size is optimum for the owner's risk profile or risk tolerance. How much income is enough? How reliable is your income? How replaceable is your income? When will the financial risks or quality control risks, or people risks be too much? At what point does growth require a new level of bureaucracy, technology, and maybe even new management? When does growth push the business beyond current management's capabilities? When does growth change the culture from being fun to being a job?

Most companies can tolerate incremental growth or growth to replace unprofitable customers fairly easily over time. Successive years of high growth challenge the competencies and risk tolerances of most companies. So the issue of growth is really two issues: (1) At what pace or rate should you grow and (2) what is your capacity and risk tolerance for growth?

As a small home builder said to me recently, "I make a good living building four houses a year—why should I stretch and build eight a year?"

That home builder is comfortable with himself, what he makes, and has ability to make it in good times and in bad times. He has a tolerance which he understands only for so much overhead—personal and business.

What is the costs side of growth? New people? More expensive people? New systems? New controls? Can you tolerate psychologically the economic risk of the growth? And likewise, can you tolerate the risk of not growing?

Most business people look at growth with an optimistic framework. Maybe to counterbalance that approach a different framework is needed. Maybe you should grow when the risks to you of not growing clearly are higher than the risks of growing. Maybe the decision is not what is the most upside but rather what is the best downside protection.

External Factors

By growing at high rates for several years—yes, you will capture market share but also you rise on the business food chain and come into the sights of very big, well-capitalized, highly-efficient, and well-managed competitors. As you grow, your competition changes. As you grow, you become both a threat and a target. Growth reminds me of three sayings I heard over and over growing up in rural Georgia:

1. A sports analogy—"Remember—there are always many people faster and bigger than you are";
2. "Honey attracts bees—your profits will attract competitors"; and
3. "The elephant will wake up—the big player who can exist far longer than you on selling at very low prices will attack you at some point."

Most industries have two or three giant competitors who control a huge market share. Your chances of taking them on head-to-head and winning are very small. Remember that all business is probability theory. At some point as you grow, you will pass the stage of being unnoticed by bigger competitors, or even pass the stage of being a nuisance or annoyance, and then the big competitor will want to Darwinally destroy your livelihood.

At some point, growth will change the competitive landscape for your company.

No, I am not against growth. But like everything else in life, it comes with risks and costs. What I am advocating is a risk management approach to growth—first, understand the internal and external risks, and second, do not accept the mantra that all growth is good. It is not.

The bigger you become, the more you have to manage risks—risks of disruptions, supply risks, fixed overhead costs, competitive risks, and customer risks. The bigger you become, the more working capital, key man life insurance, legal protection, and financial and quality controls you will need. The bigger you are, the more personal liability you will have with your banks.

And remember—growth will change your business and you. And growth will change the players you will be competing against. Be aware.

2 Darden Private Growth Company Research (DPGC)[1]

In 2008, I began a research project focusing on how private companies cope with the challenges of growth. I was curious about the following:

1. How managers managed simultaneously across business functions;
2. How they executed growth initiatives with limited time and resources;
3. How they prioritized what they focused on each day;
4. How they balanced growth with executing existing business;
5. Whether they invested ahead of or behind the growth curve;
6. How they learned to delegate;
7. How they met the challenges of building a management team; and
8. Whether they managed or paced growth or took whatever came through the door; and when and in what order they installed more controls and processes.

Private High-Growth Companies

I did not research entrepreneurial start-ups. Rather, I looked at companies that were part of the small group that had survived the start-up phase and had been through a high-growth phase.

I was fortunate. Fifty-four CEOs of high-growth private companies agreed to participate. Each participated in a recorded interview or series of interviews, which were analyzed by me and independently by my research students. Almost all of the

---

1. This chapter was adapted from Chapter 8 of *Smart Growth: Building an Enduring Business by Managing the Risks of Growth*, by Edward D. Hess, copyright © 2010 Columbia Business School Publishing. Reprinted with permission of the publisher; Edward D. Hess, "Darden Private Growth Research Project," 2008.

companies had been publicly acknowledged as high-growth companies by one of the big-four public accounting firms or by magazines such as *Inc.* or *Entrepreneur*. The companies were diversified across industries and located in twenty-three different states. Twenty-one companies primarily produced products and thirty-three were primarily service companies. They had an average age of 9.6 years of activity and an average estimated 2008 revenue of $60 million. Although the average revenue was $60 million, the range was $5 million to over $300 million.

This research was primarily qualitative and descriptive—not predictive. So far, I have been unsuccessful in convincing CEOs who failed the high-growth phase to discuss these failures and the causes.

The CEOs were predominately males but included five females. Of the 54 CEOs, 34 started companies in an industry in which they had substantial prior experience. Of the 54 CEOs, 28 had no prior start-up experience. Forty companies had no institutional funding at start-up.

Research Findings

I looked for best practices and decision heuristics or templates. I found that managing growth was fundamentally a change management process because growth changed the companies—their culture, their people, and how they did business. Growth changed the human dynamics of how people communicated and with whom they communicated. It challenged peoples' competencies and interpersonal skills. Furthermore, for these companies the human dynamic of growth proved to be one of the biggest challenges of managing growth. And this challenge recurred as the companies grew because many management teams were not able to manage a bigger or more complex business. As a result, CEOs had to continuously upgrade management teams and face the difficulties of hiring and integrating new players into existing management teams, which often stirred up difficult emotional and loyalty issues for remaining team members.

These human dynamics made growth difficult to manage, making smooth and continuous growth rare. Following are some other findings.

1. Most companies did not plan for growth. In some cases, it just happened. Those CEOs regretted not thinking about what a bigger company would look like and about how much growth their company could accommodate. Some companies were so overwhelmed by growth they had to put the brakes on growth to survive. Some understood the risks of growing rapidly without having put the people, quality, and financial processes in place and sometimes turned away business until they were more prepared. Many companies attempted to accommodate the growth by upgrading people, processes, and controls in parallel with the growth: a challenging proposition.

CEOs with prior entrepreneurial experience, in general, had learned from that experience that they needed to prepare for the company's growth. Consequently, they devoted time to visualizing and designing what their company should look like from people, structure, and process perspectives at different points along the growth spectrum.

Several CEOs experienced at least one business life-threatening challenge as they grew. Causes of these near-death experiences were myriad, but included growing too fast, poor financial controls, geographic expansion too distant from the home base of business, losing a major customer, and adopting inflexible customer business models.

Growth often created real financial stresses because, usually, it required the outlay of significant cash ahead of the receipt of new revenue. Many companies failed to plan for that mismatch of funds, and even when they did plan for it, they failed to estimate it reliably, creating severe cash flow pressures. These experiences humbled many of the CEOs, who made statements such as, "We were lucky to survive that phase" or "We nearly lost control of the ship then."

The CEOs I interviewed, however, had beaten the odds by successfully steering their companies through significant growth, surviving nearly 10 years and, in 53 cases, building profitable companies. That process raised their awareness of the potential risks of growth. Several told me that, given the challenges of growth, they learned to step back and question why their companies should grow. Some CEOs stated that growth in itself was not the endgame for them. Growth became secondary to building a good company that serves its customers well and is a good place to work.

Several told me they learned that generation of more revenue once a company reached a certain stage of profitability was not a valid reason for pushing growth. Stating it another way, experiencing the challenges and complexities of managing through growth changed some of the CEOs. Prior to their experiences with growing their companies, many had never thought critically about growth and automatically accepted "grow or die" as axiomatic. However, after learning that successfully managing growth was not a foregone conclusion, many fundamentally changed their view of growth. They became more respectful of the difficulty of managing growth.

2. The necessity of managing the pace of growth was one of the take-away lessons for the CEOs. Many CEOs said that their companies fared better when they learned when to say no to new opportunities. Essential to managing the pace of growth was the matching of funding and people capacity with opportunities. Managing the pace of growth required them to learn to focus on the capacity of the company to meet the demands of new business opportunities and being strategic in taking on business. For many, matching growth with resources led to a "sweet-spot" strategy.

3. Growth changes a company fundamentally. Routines, structures, staffing, and processes are shuffled, and the impact of these changes and how they are managed determines the success or failure of growing the company. In my study, growth changed the content of what the CEO did, what the employees did, and who they interacted with. Growth usually required adding people and implementing more processes. Adding new people and new managers to the company's staff created different human dynamics. The chemistry of the company changed—and not always for the good. When the management teams expanded, the interpersonal dynamics multiplied, and the people complexities impacted execution. Growth also increased the complexity of communications, raising the likelihood of miscommunications and interpersonal misunderstandings. Communication complexities often led to mistakes, inefficiency, and a lack of focus, which undermined a smooth growth process.

As these private companies grew, the roles of CEOs evolved, often dramatically. CEOs who initially *did* everything had to shift to *managing* everything, to managing managers, and then to coaching managers and leading culture and strategy. As one CEO stated, growth required the CEO "to continuously redefine his or her relationship to the business." CEOs struggled to remove themselves from the daily business of putting out fires to devoting time to think strategically about how to deal with the big issues facing the business. They needed "firehouse time." One CEO told me the only way he got time to think was to leave for an hour some days and take a drive in the country. Another CEO told me he took a day a week and went elsewhere to think about the five most important challenges the company was facing.

4. A bigger company and more staff required CEOs to learn how to delegate. As one CEO said, "Delegation is not a natural act." Delegation consistently was a difficult issue for CEOs. How do you learn to delegate? Who teaches a course in "letting go"? CEOs overcame their hesitation because they were not able to continue doing everything they had previously done and delegated grudgingly because of necessity.

5. Most companies experienced difficulties in building a management team because of multiple financially and emotionally costly hiring mistakes. There were several reasons for the hiring failures. CEOs had particular difficulty in evaluating expertise outside their functional domains. Many experienced hires from big companies could not adapt to the entrepreneurial environment of a smaller, private company. Likewise, many individuals hired from small companies lacked the experience to scale a business. Multiple hires were particularly common for the positions of senior managers in finance, human resources, and technology. Many companies went through more than two hiring mistakes for key positions, and several had to make four or five such hires.

6. Even if assembling a management team went well, many CEOs were surprised at the difficulty of getting that team to work together effectively. To overcome this hurdle, some companies hired psychologists or executive coaches to help the man-

agement team learn how to communicate and relate to each other constructively. Again, the human dynamics of growth were frequently the biggest management challenge, often undermining the ease of business growth. Surprisingly, people issues were more difficult than customer or competitor issues in most cases.

7. Most CEOs learned that growth required them to upgrade their people. This caused stress because such changes adversely affected loyal employees who had helped build the business. Many CEOs stated that they had to undertake these difficult upgrades more than once. Given the risks of making mistakes in hiring as described above, the added stress of disrupting loyal employees and changing team dynamics was wearing on the CEOs who yearned for team stability. Many CEOs said the challenges of hiring and managing a leadership team were the hardest part of the job.

8. Growth was not easy for any of these companies, and the various tensions generated usually resulted in a zig-zag growth pattern instead of a smooth, linear one. Managing company growth created tensions between high employee accountability and the more family-oriented environment of a small company; between the pace of growth and delivering quality; between being concerned about turning away business and being cautious that too much business would overwhelm a company's people and processes. As one CEO stated, "Managing a growing business is like sailing—you know where you are and you know where you want to go and you have to be able to execute a whole lot of tacking to get there."

9. Many CEOs stressed that at some point in growing their companies they had to get honest with themselves and question why they should push their companies to continue to grow and whether that growth would change them and their company so much that the business would no longer be fun. Some had concluded that companies needed to grow for the right reasons and that simply to generate more money was not a good enough reason.

10. The CEOs with outside institutional capital (private equity) at their inception had a different view of growth. They pushed growth as fast as they could and focused more on revenue growth than profits. In some cases, these private equity supported companies outgrew their capabilities but their CEOs were less concerned because of the financial safety net supplied by the company's institutional shareholder. Interestingly, my research showed that in spite of this rush to grow those companies took longer to reach certain revenue levels than non-institutionally funded companies.

11. Some of the CEOs were aware that at a certain revenue level they were likely going to engage bigger, well-capitalized competition. That competition would expose them to significant risk and perhaps require taking on an institutional partner or selling. Both alternatives meant big changes for the company, the CEO, and the employees. In some cases, the CEO's goal was to keep his or her revenue level below that inflection point.

CEO Quotes

Presented to illustrate the points made in sections 1 through 11, the following are remarks made by some of the CEOs in the study.

Growth Risks

"It's easy to get into business but hard to stay in business."

"You don't want to bring on all the business that you can—growth can easily swallow you."

"Understand that growth puts you in different competitive space."

"Paradox of getting the one big customer."

"It takes one set of skills to manage a company and an entirely different set of skills to grow a company."

"Paradox of success. Once a business recognizes that if we do this, this, and this and we get results then they will run that play over and over until it hits an inflection point."

Process and Focus

"Focus on the one thing you can do better than anyone else and then figure out how to make that thing attractive to a big market."

"If you are making mistakes you are making progress."

"I don't want a single-person point of failure."

"When scaling focus first on those processes-systems that generate cash."

"Focus. Be two inches wide and two miles deep."

"5Ps: Plan, People, Passion, Pace, Process."

"Work your business plan until it fits on one page—people-products-market-where you are going—and give that to every employee."

"Prioritize what is critical to making it to the next month; next quarter; next year."

"Build a wheel of life: a clock picture of what drives your business—in this case marketing drives sales, which drives installs, which drives admin/finance. Faster we spin the wheel the faster we grow. CEO focuses on bottlenecks in the wheel."

"Make sure each manager is involved in the development of his/her metrics and that they actually sign up for performance and results."

"Make sure that some percentage of everyone's compensation plan embraces some cross-functional objectives to drive team objectives."

"I've kind of got a philosophy that that which is not audited will always get worse, never better, and will create surprises."

"Don't get involved in all the brush fires—focus on the thing with the biggest impact."

"I collectivize problems."

"We always want to put out the fire and leave the fire extinguisher behind."

"I do not pay you to get everything done every day—I pay you to get the most important things done."

"Everyday we have cascading meetings starting with the leadership team, and by ten o'clock all employees will have had a daily focus meeting."

"Being a great place to work is like owning a house. It takes work. If you don't do anything to your house it falls apart. It actually takes proactive effort to keep it going."

"Stones sharpen stones."

People

"Want smart people who play well in the sandbox."

"I've never been able successfully to get someone to switch seats on the bus—my experience is that they have to get off the bus."

"Dump stars who are not nice."

"You can build a star system or a team system."

"Don't save time trying to save bad people."

"I built a stab-you-in-the-chest culture not a stab-you-in-the-back culture."

"If you want your people to think like owners, make them owners."

"The average person is the worst enemy of a business."

"Hire slowly—fire fast."

"Most people can't develop as fast as the business can grow."

"Profile success and hire against that profile."

"Celebrate success often . . . awards . . . pizza . . . trips . . . schooling."

"Businesses do not grow, people do."

"Upgrading the management team is hard."

Entrepreneur's Evolution

"Ultimately you have to delegate everything not in your unique skill set."

"I delegate until a problem arises—then I micromanage."

"I tell my managers, I am not your co-pilot."

"I focus on big opportunities and big crises."

"Give yourself an afternoon a week to close the door and think about five things going on in the business and make sure you are focused on big opportunities or problems."

"Delegation is the most difficult thing to learn."

"Delegation is not a natural human characteristic for a manager."

"Ego fails. Control freaks fail. Listen until it hurts."

"Entrepreneurs think we know everything. And the quicker we recognize that we don't and we open up our ears and our eyes instead of our mouths, things start going well."

What comes through from these CEOs is that growth is difficult, and it is rarely smooth and continuous. Further, growth has risks. By growing too fast, a company risks outstripping its capabilities, people, processes, and controls. To avoid these pitfalls, growth should be proactively managed as a process on a daily basis.

CLASS DISCUSSION QUESTIONS

1. What findings surprised you? Why?

2. What courses available at your school are most relevant to these findings and CEO quotes?

3. What kind of role did competitor analysis play in their growth strategies?

4. Do you think you can learn how to delegate in a course?

5. Why do you think prior start-up experience may be helpful in growing the next company?

6. Why do you think prior experience in the industry may be helpful in being successful?

7. Were you surprised that it took these companies on average nearly 10 years on average to reach $60 million in revenue?

8. Review all the CEO quotes and pick the top five in your judgment that give you the secret of building a growth business. What do those five quotes say about you? How did your training or work experience influence your choices?

Other Research Findings

The research also produced some interesting quantitative data that provides another view of the companies and growth and raises questions for further research (Table 2.1). Because of the small sample size, although the results are suggestive, they are not statistically significant. The findings suggest that prior start-up experience can lead to faster revenue generation.

Table 2.1 Time Needed to Reach Revenue Levels

Revenue Level	Years/CEO with No Prior Start-Up Experience	Years/CEO with Prior Start-Up Experience
$1 million	3.6	2.2
$5 million	5.6	3.8
$10 million	6.9	4.8
$20 million	7.3	5.9
$50 million	9.2	6.5

CLASS DISCUSSION QUESTIONS

1. Product companies reached $10 million, $20 million, and $50 million of revenue a minimum of sixteen months faster than service companies. Could it be easier to scale a product company than a service company? Why?

2. Companies with two founders reached $1 million, $5 million, and $10 million revenue levels faster than companies with one, three, or four founders. There was no real difference at $20 million and higher. Why do you think that was the case?

3. In the progression of revenue growth, it took on average 2.98 years from start to reach $1 million in revenue; 4.8 years from start to reach $5 million; 6.0 years from start to reach $10 million in revenue; 6.7 years from start for those reaching $20 milvlion; 7.86 years from start for those reaching $50 million; and 9.75 years from start for those reaching $100 million in revenue. Notice the length of time between each revenue level. Did it consistently decrease? Why?

4. CEOs with prior experience in their business's industry achieved revenue levels faster from a time of 1.0 to 2.6 years. Why do you think that result occurred?

Octane Fitness, Inc.

A good example of an entrepreneur who, with others, built a successful growth business is Dennis Lee of Octane Fitness. As you read the case focus on strategic focus, critical growth processes, and the people aspect of growth.

CASE DISCUSSION QUESTIONS

1. Why was Octane Fitness able to achieve $6 million in revenue in its first year of operations?

2. Octane Fitness has hired you to prepare a speech titled "The Keys to Success: The Octane Fitness Way" to be given at your school by the founders. Please create a PowerPoint presentation.

3. Do you think the founders made a good or bad decision in selling part of their company?

4. What was their biggest challenge in building the business?

5. Why are their current challenges harder than even their start-up challenges?

OCTANE FITNESS, INC.:
THE POWER OF FOCUS

Octane Fitness, Inc. (Octane), based in Brooklyn Park, Minnesota, was a privately held company specializing in the design and distribution of elliptical cross-training machines for the commercial and consumer markets. Cofounders Dennis Lee and Tim Porth launched their business in September 2001, after leaving their jobs at the national exercise-equipment manufacturer Life Fitness. The two men pooled their savings, mortgaged their homes, and set up shop in Lee's basement, with the goal of developing the best elliptical-exercise machine on the market.

In November 2002, Lee and Porth delivered four ellipticals to 2nd Wind Exercise Equipment, an Eden Prairie, Minnesota–based fitness specialty chain. The first unit sold less than an hour after the retailer had put it out on the floor. In the following weeks, Octane's 2002 sales climbed to $280,000, from the 38 stores in five states selling its ellipticals.[2] By the end of 2003, the company had 40 dealers and 210 stores in North America and had made $6.9 million in revenue.

In January 2005, North Castle Partners, LLC, a private equity firm based in Connecticut, bought a majority interest in Octane. With Lee at the helm as president and CEO and Porth working as executive vice president for product development and marketing, the business continued to grow. By 2008, Octane was a global operation with 50 employees and offices in the Netherlands and the United Kingdom pulling in $41 million in sales.

The entrepreneurs attributed their company's success to some key decisions they made early on. First, they decided to focus solely on elliptical cross trainers. "We had something different from the rest of the crowd," Lee said. "There wasn't anybody else that did just ellipticals. Our goal was to be the number-one market-share leader for consumer ellipticals, and one reason we attained it was because we set it as our goal, and we focused on it."

Second, the founders committed to doing what they knew best and outsourced the core competences they lacked. Lee explained:

When we started, we said, if we didn't put time into [manufacturing, warehousing, and logistics] but instead focused our energies on the two core drivers—product innovation and sales and service excellence—just think of what we could do. . . . Our business model is set up so

---

Case Study UVA-ENT-0141 © 2009 by the University of Virginia Darden School Foundation. This case was prepared by Senior Researcher Gosia Glinska and Edward D. Hess as a basis for class discussion rather than to illustrate effective or ineffective handling of an administrative situation.

2. Dick Youngblood, "Fit for Business," *Star-Tribune*, May 18, 2003.

that everything we do has to do with product innovation and sales and service, because that's what we're really good at.[3]

The Founders

Cofounder Lee was born in 1963 and grew up in North Minneapolis, Minnesota. After high school, he enrolled at Hamline University in St. Paul, where he earned a BS degree in business administration.

Between 1987 and 1998, Lee managed sales at ParaBody, Inc., a manufacturer of strength-training products for the home, based in Ramsey, Minnesota. During his tenure at ParaBody, Lee's sales team was recognized as number one in the industry for sales and service excellence by American Sports Data, Inc. In 1998, Illinois-based Life Fitness, a global manufacturer of commercial- and consumer-fitness equipment, acquired ParaBody, and Lee became director of sales and service, eventually rising to vice president of sales, service, and logistics for consumer products.

The other founder, Porth, was born in 1968, in Buffalo Grove, Illinois. He earned a BS degree in industrial design from Western Michigan University in Kalamazoo, Michigan. After working as an industrial designer for several firms that specialized in medical and consumer products, Porth landed a job with NordicTrack in Chaska, Minnesota, where he worked as an industrial design and product manager at the Franklin Park location of Life Fitness as senior business director of cardiovascular products. In that position, he managed financial performance and strategic direction for commercial and consumer treadmills, cross trainers, and Lifecycle upright and recumbent exercise bikes and stair climbers.

Launching Octane

The Octane cofounders met in 1998, the same year Life Fitness acquired ParaBody. At first, the notion of starting a fitness-equipment company together was just idle talk. "It was sort of an idea-a-month thing, after which we'd figure out why it wouldn't work," Lee said.[4] Things took a serious turn, however, after Lee tried out an elliptical cross trainer. A former linebacker for Hamline University's football team, Lee had repaired ligaments in both knees, so that every time he used high-impact exercise equipment he experienced pain. "The first time I got on a standing elliptical I thought to myself, 'Oh my goodness! I can work on this every day,'" he said.

In August 2001, Lee and Porth quit their jobs, drained their bank accounts, and remortgaged their houses. "I left my job at Life Fitness," recounted Lee, "where I was

---

3. Todd Messelt, "Sporting Chance: Octane Fitness Takes a Shot at Building a Better Machine," *Minnesota Business*, April 2007.
4. Youngblood.

doing pretty well, and walked into my unfinished basement, which now was the new 'world headquarters,' and right above in the living room, I had five kids making noise, and sometimes I'd hit the ceiling with a broomstick to get them to quiet down."[5]

The two entrepreneurs had their work cut out for them. Realizing the importance of having a well-defined, unique business plan when starting a company, Lee and his partner thought long and hard about how they were going to differentiate their start-up. Lee described their thinking:

It's a competitive world out there, and it's not enough just to be passionate and maybe good at something that 10 other people are doing. Here's what it boils down to: "Do you have a shot at being number one, two, or three?" Preferably one or two. Because if you can't be there, the odds are you're not going to make money.

From the beginning, what set Octane apart from its key competitors, the large exercise-equipment manufacturers Nautilus, Life Fitness, and Precor and their broad product lines, was its exclusive focus on ellipticals. "The idea was that if we focus on one segment of the exercise market, we could do it better than all of the big boys who are trying to be all things to all people. We eventually distilled that idea down to focusing on elliptical trainers and developed a business plan around it," Lee said.[6]

The timing could not have been better. The elliptical machines, which provided a total body workout by mimicking running and walking motions, had been gaining in popularity since the late 1990s because they burned more calories with what was perceived as less exertion. In addition, the low-impact cardio workout they delivered made them especially attractive to aging baby boomers, who could achieve a desired heart rate without having to suffer the aches and pains that accompanied high-impact workouts. Not surprisingly, elliptical sales grew 25% between 2001 and 2005, becoming the fastest-growing segment in the wholesale fitness-equipment market.[7]

Fine-Tuning the Business Model

Once Lee and Porth decided to focus on becoming innovation leaders in the elliptical category, they began fine-tuning Octane's strategy and business model. A book by Michel Robert provided them with the foundation.[8] Lee explained:

Robert puts forth this idea that depending on what type of business you're in, you have a certain strategic driver. We are a product-driven company. And in a product-driven company,

---

5. Cati Vanden Breul, "Octane Fitness Founders Thrived with Focus, Flexibility," *Minneapolis St. Paul Business Journal*, August 31, 2007.

6. Messelt.

7. Fran Howard, "Why This Start-Up Is Working Out," *Twin Cities Business*, February 2007.

8. Michel Robert, *Strategy Pure and Simple: How Winning Companies Dominate Their Competitors* (New York: McGraw-Hill, 1993).

the two "areas of excellence" required are product innovation and sales/service excellence. When we started the business we had that as a backdrop, and we got to the point where we said, "What if we just outsourced everything that didn't fall into one of those two categories?"

The entrepreneurs concentrated on the development, sales, and service of their product. "The other core competencies that we did not have, we tried to bring in through a third party," Lee said. They decided to look for a manufacturer in Asia and outsource logistics and warehousing to Superior Logistics, a St. Paul–based start-up.

Developing a Business Plan

Lee thought that a detailed business plan was an absolute necessity for entrepreneurs to have in place before they started spending their start-up capital. "This might sound rudimentary," Lee said, "but I run into so many people who really haven't thought through the whole thing. They haven't laid it all out in a document." He admitted that he and Porth had spent a considerable amount of time on their business plan. The result was a document they changed here and there as they went along but which they followed with confidence. Lee continued:

Every once in a while, I'll go grab that original plan, and you know what? It's pretty good. At that stage, you have to ask yourself, what is your idea? Why is it going to work? What are all the things that could really screw this up? And have some contingencies built into the plan. And when you're trying to sell it to investors: underpromise and overdeliver. Don't set the bogies so high that everything is going to have to go right to get there. Set the bogies where a few things are going to go wrong, and you can still exceed the plan.

Raising Capital

One of the biggest challenges facing the Octane founders was access to capital. Raising money was especially difficult in the aftermath of the terrorist attacks of September 11, and the entrepreneurs were unable to secure a bank loan. "People think that they're going to go get a small business loan, or the bank will do some financing, but in our instance that just really didn't work out well," Lee said. "And the SBA doesn't want to loan you money unless you have some collateral, like a building or equipment-type thing."

For months, Lee and Porth bootstrapped their business, working in the basement of Lee's Brooklyn Park home. "It just meant we stayed at home and worked in the basement longer, and it forced us to be diligent with money," Porth said. "When your life savings is in the company, it can be scary."[9]

It took approximately a year to bring investors on board. The entrepreneurs managed to raise $1.2 million through private placement, even before they had taken a

9. Breul.

single order for their elliptical machine. "The company cash flowed from there," said Lee, adding that he and Porth were able to pay back the investors 13 times the value of their original investment in two-and-a-half years. "To me that was one of the most important things," Lee said. "It was about our success, but I wanted to be successful because I wanted to take care of the people who had invested in us."

Keeping a Close Eye on the Numbers

As the designer in the partnership, Porth was instrumental in developing Octane's elliptical machine, while Lee oversaw the business side of the start-up, including the finance and accounting area. One of Lee's mentors had always emphasized the importance of paying close attention to the numbers. "He said that [start-ups] have problems because they don't think they need to have that finance person, and you really do." Therefore, from the beginning, Lee worked with a seasoned CFO, who stayed with Octane for almost two years. "He helped us with the preparation of the financial information in the private placement, with the monthly P&L," Lee said. "Without having him involved in the business, it would have been a lot more complex." Lee explained:

A lot of start-ups that I talk to, I ask them, have you put together a cash flow for that first two years and have you broken it down monthly? And have you really thought through what happens if you're off your revenue plan by 20%? What is that going to mean? And are you raising enough cash to cover that kind of a scenario?

Outsourcing Manufacturing

As industry veterans, Lee and Porth knew who manufactured fitness equipment in Asia. "We had an idea of who were the right people we needed to talk to," Lee said, "and that helped us." Strapped for cash, the entrepreneurs hoped the manufacturer would see the potential of their elliptical machine and form a partnership with Octane or support the start-up with liberal financing. Lee recalled:

We went to Taiwan with a PowerPoint presentation, and we were trying to sound like we knew what we were doing and sell manufacturers on the idea that they should be participating with us in this venture. Your tooling to get things going back then was about a $300,000 bill, so we were looking for somebody that would believe in us. They participated in the tooling, but they wanted the money, because we had no history.

The next hurdle was developing a satisfactory relationship with manufacturers in Taiwan. It proved more challenging than Lee had expected. "Culturally and communication-wise, there was a lot to learn," Lee said. He and Porth also discovered that their expectations regarding product quality differed from those of manufacturers. "We constantly had to work that back and forth," Lee said. "It got really frustrating, and there were a lot of phone calls at two in the morning to Taiwan."

When the first shipment of elliptical machines arrived from Asia, Lee and Porth were not exactly thrilled with what they saw. Lee complained that "something wasn't quite right when we wanted to move this or tighten that or adjust this—a handful of little things." He added:

Some of that we probably could have passed on to the customer. But that's not the way we operate. So we ended up reworking our first 30 containers of product. And that was painful. But in the long run, those are the right decisions because you're establishing who you are and how customers perceive you.

Octane's First Elliptical Cross Trainer

Lee and Porth wanted their elliptical machine to provide a total-body workout and, at the same time, be low impact. "Something you can use every day and not wake up feeling beat-up or sore," Lee said. Their sole focus on the elliptical machines gave them time to perfect their first model while paying special attention to ergonomics. "We spent a lot of time making sure the machine fit people's bodies," Lee said. They developed a unique quad-link-drive system after tinkering with the length and position of the links to ensure the most natural and comfortable motion possible.

Martin Bruder, an executive at 2nd Wind Exercise Equipment (2nd Wind), was among the many industry insiders invited to Lee and Porth's basement office to test the prototype. Bruder was particularly impressed with the entrepreneurs' openness to feedback. "They tweaked it with a lot of people's input and did an excellent job making a product the consumer wanted by listening to the advice of people in the industry," he said.[10] Bruder's company became the first retailer to offer Octane elliptical machines for sale. Octane's sole focus on product development speeded up the delivery of the elliptical cross-trainers to retailers. "No one in the industry has brought a product to market so quickly and been so successful," Bruder said.[11]

Early Sales and Distribution

Octane sold its first four machines to 2nd Wind in November 2002. "We put them on the back of a truck, dropped one in Coon Rapids at 3 P.M., one in Maple Grove at 5:30 P.M., and the others in St. Louis Park at 8 P.M. When I got in my car at 8:45 P.M. to go home, I had a voice mail from the Maple Grove sales manager, saying he had just sold our first product," Lee said.[12]

Their long tenures in the fitness-equipment industry translated into thorough knowledge of distribution channels for the founders. "We knew who we wanted to sell to, who the good retailers were, and who was going to pay their bills," Lee

---

10. Breul.
11. Breul.
12. Howard.

recalled. Also because of that knowledge, they avoided making the mistakes made by so many start-ups when it came to choosing their distributors. "They often pick the wrong guy to sell to," Lee said.

Octane sold to most retailers on terms. Knowing which retailers were in strong financial shape gave Lee and Porth the opportunity to award discounts to those who could pay up front. "When we first started," Lee said, "we offered that to a few folks and that helped us in the cash position, too."

Getting It Right—Quality Control

After a rough start with their first manufacturer, over time the founders gained a clear understanding of what was important to most of them: They wanted to work with a company that had experience with fitness equipment but did not produce its own brand. "And we wanted to be the number-one or number-two customer for that factory," Lee said. "And that's exactly where we are right now. We have two wonderful manufacturing facilities in Taiwan that understand fitness, and the relationships are great." Octane had learned the importance of "being on top of the relationship" with another manufacturer. Lee explained:

If you think, I get this thing into production and the thing goes right out of the gate; it takes a little while, and then I can just let it run. Well, that ain't how it works. You've got to be on it all the time. We have folks on the line that are inspecting. We inspect inbound over here. I don't want to imply that inspection is the right way to building quality, but we are definitely all over the products to make sure that they're being built to spec. If people are going to put down $2,000 to $4,000 for our product, it's got to be right.

To ensure the excellence of the Octane brand and show that the company took quality control seriously, a U.S. engineer conducted an inspection every month. In addition, three employees worked out of an Octane office in Taiwan to make sure that quality was never compromised. All the focus on product innovation and maintenance of high standards was rewarded with blistering sales and numerous awards that Octane's elliptical cross trainers started to receive in 2004 (Exhibit 2.1).

Enter North Castle

In 2004, North Castle Partners, LLC (North Castle), a Connecticut-based private equity firm, approached Octane with a buy-out offer. "They started chatting with us in July," Lee said. North Castle invested in consumer businesses that fit into the category of "healthy living and aging" and that appealed to Lee and Porth. "[North Castle] really figured out the idea on the equity side of the advantages of being focused and how the companies in the portfolio can play off each other to help each other grow," Lee said.

On January 7, 2005, North Castle closed the deal and purchased Octane. Lee and Porth each retained a minority interest and a seat on Octane's board of directors. At first, Lee admitted, "Our biggest fear was . . . those horror stories, and you think, 'Am I going to get myself into something like this?'" But the partnership between North Castle and Octane was a success. "They've been a wonderful partner," Lee said. In 2008, the equity firm awarded Lee the North Castle 2007 CEO of the Year award, for achieving financial results that included growing sales by 27%.[13] Lee commented:

What's interesting about private equity was the use of debt. A significant portion of what we got paid out got financed via debt versus equity. So they came in and bought us out. And it was the perfect scenario. They gave us this unique opportunity to monetize the risk that we put forward going in and to take care of our families. They also gave us the chance to continue to nurture this baby, our company, and be a part of taking it to the next level.

Building the Octane Team

In 2008, Octane had 50 employees. In addition to Lee and four others on the executive team, Octane's work force consisted of engineers and designers on the product side as well as the sales and customer-service reps.

It had taken Lee and Porth a lot of time and effort to build a team. In the process, the founders had learned the importance of hiring great people "through a school of hard knocks," as Lee put it. Having had problems with some early employees, they developed an appreciation for implementing a disciplined hiring process. "We do multiple interviews. We do background checks. We do assessments," Lee said. "We have an outside-party interview, so that we're not caught up in the emotions of it."

In Lee's opinion, businesses suffered in the long run from settling on average or good-enough new hires. "It's really tough when you need that position filled, and you've got about 20 million balls in the air," he said. He admitted that getting great people could be quite a challenge, especially for a start-up; however, he thought it was worth "sweating it further to make sure that even if it takes a little bit longer, you're going to get great people. The return is just incredible." Lee continued:

Jim Collins in *Good to Great* talks about getting the right people on the bus. The way I think about that is, the average person is the worst enemy of a business. The bad guys, you smoke them out right away. The great guys are the ones you want. The average ones stick around and don't really advance the business. So we really push on our folks not to settle. Even if you really need somebody today, let's not settle for "He's pretty good." We want great people.

---

13. "North Castle Partners Name Dennis Lee of Octane Fitness as CEO of the Year" (joint press release), May 22, 2008.

Goals and Incentives

Lee said that to encourage each Octane employee to "participate in the business as a business person and think as a business person," the company implemented a profit-sharing plan, culminating in an annual profit bonus tied to corporate and individual goals and performance. "We set up our corporate goals going into the year, and every team member sets up three to four goals that tie as much as possible into our corporate goals," Lee explained. Then the Octane management team spent considerable time reviewing these goals.

During the company's quarterly meetings, Lee gave updates on the progress of corporate goals, and the individual team members talked about their goals and achievements. "It's a wonderful thing," Lee said, "because for their successes, it gives them a chance to stand up and pound their chests a little bit." To discuss issues in the areas where they struggled, Octane team members met in smaller groups. "The engineers meet together, the sales and service group meets together, the admin people meet together," he said. "We give them feedback on different ideas for attacking the problems they're having."

During monthly lunch meetings, the executive team shared Octane's financial data with all employees in an open-book style. "We review the previous month's P&L," Lee said. "We talk about where we're at relative to our annual profit bonus, and we go through the different areas of how we're doing just to keep everybody abreast as to the things that aren't in their direct area."

Less Is More—Avoiding Organizational Complexity

Having worked for large corporations, the Octane founders understood the perils of growth, where layers of management and complex organizational structures often stifled innovation and entrepreneurial spirit in a small organization. So as their company grew, they tried to prevent bureaucracy from setting in. Lee explained:

When you have a large group of people, you have to have procedures and structure. And those things, if not done right, get in the way. And politics gets in the way. And all of that, plus more, adds to the complexity. And I kind of tie that back to my old company. They should kick our butt. I mean, they've got so many more resources than we do. But when the entity is more complex, it's hard to get those resources deployed in an efficient way to the right spot.

Sales and Distribution—2008

In 2008, Octane offered four commercial models for sale to health clubs, sports teams, personal-training facilities, universities, and corporate-fitness facilities. According to Lee, "A company like us might do 20 to 25 shows around the commercial segment annually." In addition, the company's sales reps from offices in the Netherlands and the United Kingdom "did a bunch of shows, regionally in different parts of the world," he said. Octane also sold seven consumer models to fitness specialty retailers, which Lee described as a "fairly small niche market" with one major annual trade show—a health and fitness retail show in Denver, Colorado. Lee continued:

There are probably 700 fitness specialty stores in North America, and we deal with about 350 of them. They're fragmented—it's a lot of regional players. There have been one or two consolidators, but for the most part, we deal with a number of great regional customers.

Winning Market Share

In 2008, the global market for elliptical cross trainers was $450 million. Octane had a 9% share of that market, with a lead in the premium-consumer business. One of the biggest challenges facing Octane in 2008 was increasing market share internationally and in the commercial segment of the United States. "If we're looking at a $450-million global market, I still have some runway there. If I can excel in the commercial and international channels, I have the ability to grow the business," Lee said. In striving for a foothold in the commercial U.S. market and the international market, Lee aimed for one of the top-three spots, and the relative newness of the global-market territory did not dampen his aspirations.

In Lee's opinion, his company had a real shot at becoming one of the top three global sellers in the elliptical category. In addition to being ergonomically superior and loaded with great features, Octane's machines were a "relative value on the commercial side," Lee said. He was confident that Octane's ability to deliver a high-quality, innovative product at a price lower than its competitors was a source of the company's competitive advantage:

It all comes back to our business model. The two biggest competitors we have, Precor and Life Fitness, make great products. But they are traditional, vertically integrated manufacturing companies. Think about a front office that's got a big factory behind it. Our front office doesn't have the plant attached to it. So we don't have those expenses tied to our business. We are buying from the low-cost producer in Asia. That gives us a competitive advantage. Even more importantly, our focus on what we do gives us a competitive advantage, too. Instead of competing on price, it allows us to charge a premium because we're coming up with new innovative features on a consistent basis.

Staying on Course

Octane's founders started out with a vision of becoming innovation leaders in the elliptical cross-trainer category. Their disciplined focus enabled them to perfect the elliptical concept and ensured its success. "We could have said after we got that first elliptical out, well, hey, treadmills are the biggest category out there," Lee said. "Let's go get us a treadmill now. We're selling to these guys already." But Lee and Porth stayed on course and resisted the temptation to add another category to their product portfolio. Their focus on the elliptical forced them to "dig deeper," as Lee said, and become more innovative. He explained:

If we would have gone to the treadmill, we wouldn't have figured out how to do something called Smart Stride that adjusts your stride length to the intensity level. And when you walk, jog, and run, your stride length actually changes to a walk/jog/run stride. We wouldn't have had to dig to get to that next thing because we would've been on to the other revenue producer.

Over time, the founders modified their original vision only slightly. "The more we got into it, the more we focused on the low-impact cardio market. And we've got a number of products in our pipeline that will expand the way people think of low-impact cardio," said Lee. In 2008, Octane unveiled another innovative product in the low-impact-cardio category—a seated elliptical machine. "Imagine you can sit down on a product and work through a big range of motion with your legs," Lee said. "It's activating more muscle, getting your heart rate up easier, and it's got an upper-body component so that you can cross-train and do total body from a seated position."

The real test of the founders' disciplined focus came after North Castle acquired Octane, when suddenly the prospect of expanding their focus became as tempting as low-hanging fruit. Lee vividly recalled how tough it was to stay true to their original vision. "You've got somebody that does acquisitions, and so you're getting these opportunities put in front of you all the time." He continued:

Well, we could double our revenues. We could leverage our sales force. But, boy, if it doesn't fit our focus on low-impact cardio, is it something that we really want to do? And we've passed on every acquisition that's been put in front of us so far because they didn't fit that spot.

As Octane continued to grow, Lee kept returning to what had made it a success in the beginning and what seemed to work best for it in the long run. He explained his take on the power of focus and the danger of trying to be "everything to all people":

No matter whether you're a start-up or you're Life Fitness and you're the largest premium manufacturer in the world, you have limited resources. I've been fortunate to be able to live in both worlds. I don't want to knock Life Fitness. I'm just going to use it as a comparison. They've got 10, 20 times the resources in people that we had looking at design. But it doesn't really matter because if you are fighting on seven fronts you're diluting your resources. And you can only be so good. So our focus on elliptical was a strategic move and, frankly, probably a necessity in the early days; the only way we were going to fight this guerilla war and win was if we fought on a narrow front. That's what started it, but we believed so much in the focus thing that we just said, "If we got runway to go on this low-impact cardio thing, we just need to stay focused, because we're going to continue to innovate and good things are going to happen because of it."

Exhibit 2.1.

Awards

Octane Fitness ellipticals have earned many awards and best-buy designations from leading consumer publications such as *Health, Consumer Guide, Prevention,* and *Today's Health and Wellness.*

Specialty fitness retailers named Octane Fitness the *best supplier in the industry* in 2007 and have cited its products as the *top-selling ellipticals* three times. Octane founders Dennis Lee and Tim Porth won the Ernst & Young Entrepreneur of the Year 2007 award in the consumer-products category.

2009   Voted No. 1 Elliptical Brand Annual Specialty News Fitness Retailer Survey, two years in a row.

2009   Voted No. 1 Best Supplier two years in a row in 2008 Annual Specialty News Fitness Retailer Survey, two years in a row.

2008   Octane Q47ce named best elliptical cross trainer by FitnessProfessorReview.com.

2008   Octane Q37ce named best elliptical under $3,000 by FitnessProfessorReview.com.

2007   Voted top-selling elliptical by specialty fitness retailers in Gear Trends 2007 Retailer Survey.

2007   Voted best supplier in the fitness industry in Gear Trends 2007 Retailer Survey.

2007   *Health Magazine*'s Best Fitness award for Q37e elliptical trainer.

2007   Octane Q37e and Q37ce named best buys by *Best Buy*, leading consumer publication.

2007   Q45: Premium Elliptical Choice in 2007 by *Prevention* magazine.

2007   ShapeYou 2007 Great Gear of the Year, Octane Q47 series silver award.

2007   ShapeYou 2007 Great Gear of the Year, Octane Q37 series sliver award.

2007   ShapeYou 2007 Octane Q35 seal of excellence.

2006   *Health Magazine* Best Fitness award for Q45e elliptical trainer.

2006   Named the top-selling brand of elliptical cross trainer by specialty fitness retailers in the fourth annual Specialty News Fitness Retailer Survey.

2005   Octane Q45e named a best buy by *Consumer Guide.*

2005   *Named the leading seller of elliptical trainers by* specialty fitness retailers in the third annual Specialty News Fitness Retailer Survey.

2004   Octane Q35e named a best buy by *Consumer Guide.*

———————

source: Octane Fitness Web site.

List of Relevant Cases

3 Fellers Bakery

Eyebobs Eyewear, Inc.

Global Medical Imaging, LLC

Green Copier Recycling: Entrepreneur Meets Private Equity

Jeff Bowling at the Delta Companies: From Baseball Coach to CEO

Mellace Family Brands, Inc.: Building a Socially Responsible Enterprise

Octane Fitness, Inc.: The Power of Focus

Room & Board

Sammy Snacks (B)

Students Helping Honduras

Valley-Wide Health Systems, Inc.

3 Growth Is More Than a Strategy[1]

In this chapter I will discuss a growing body of research around Growth Systems in public companies, for two reasons. First, some of those research findings are consistent with some of the findings of my Darden Private Growth Company research (DPGC) and thus offer the opportunity for further learning. Second, they introduce the concept of a Growth System and take growth out of the strategy domain and place it in the holistic general management domain, which is relevant to every growing private business.

Organic Growth—Then and Now

When I began my exploration into the area of organic growth in 2002, I was surprised to find that the academic research on organic growth was quite limited and not a focus of either business managers or academics. Organic growth was defined as non-acquisitive growth and generally measured by increases in sales, employees, or net assets. Very little additional information on organic growth was available.

Now, over seven years later, many companies have organic growth strategies and make organic growth financial disclosures. Organic growth has been the featured topic in business magazine articles. During the intervening years, I have learned that (1) there is no commonly accepted definition of organic growth; (2) there is no commonly accepted way to measure it; (3) in consistent high organic growth companies, organic growth is more than a strategy, it is a system; and (4) consistent high organic growth companies manage a diversified portfolio of growth initiatives, both to create

---

1. Portions of this chapter are adapted from Edward D. Hess, "Organic Growth—Lessons from Market Leaders," (Working paper, 2007).

new streams of income to replicate over a large customer base and to leverage their core operating competencies. This portfolio is built using an experimental learning process and is managed across a two-by-two matrix: top-line revenue growth and bottom-line operating efficiencies, from both a short-term and a long-term perspective. This portfolio consists of both improvements and innovations.

Organic growth can be defined as growth "the old-fashioned way." By that I mean adding new customers, new products, new services, selling more to existing customers in arm's-length transactions, and achieving margin-enhancing operating efficiencies. Organic growth is not growth created by accounting elections, valuations, classifications, related party transactions, investment income, financial or structured finance transactions, currency gains, hedging income, nor the serial acquisition of income.

Until recently, strategy has been the primary intellectual home for growth theories. That academic area is rich with the concepts of 5 Forces, SWOT analysis, sustainable competitive advantage, leveraging core competencies, differentiators, customer value propositions, business models, alignment of strategy and structure, and hypercompetition. Within public companies, growth generally has been the domain of corporate strategists, senior management, and management consultants. In consistent high organic growth companies, growth is more than just strategy—it is a system, involving managers and employees across functional areas. Growth strategies have to be executed by line employees. Execution requires a systems approach aligning growth strategies with culture, structure, execution processes, HR policies, accountability, and measurement and reward policies.

Organic Growth Index

I began my organic growth research studying public companies because data was more readily available and because of the timeliness of it after the Enron earnings scandal. With a team of students and research assistants, we built a model called the "Organic Growth Index" (OGI) with the purpose of illuminating public companies that created significant economic value by outcompeting their industry competitors by primarily growing organically for time frames of five years or more. The OGI (until it was modified in 2010) had six tests: (1) EVA/Capital rankings; (2) Sales and Cash Flow From Operations (CFFO) Compound Annual Growth Rate (CAGRs) versus industry average CAGRs; (3) Comparison of annual sales growth to account receivables growth; (4) (CFFO)/Net Income; (5) Net Income/Modified S&P Core Earnings; and (6) a merger and acquisitions screen. To my surprise, the data from that work showed and continues to show that less than 10% of the public companies studied are able to achieve consistent high organic growth for time periods of five years or longer. Consistent high organic growth is the exception, not the rule. OGI is discussed in much more detail in Hess and Kazanjian, *The Search for Organic Growth*;[2] Hess, *The Road to Organic Growth*;[3] and on my website: www.EDHLTD.com.

The DNA of Successful HOGs

Being surprised at the results described in the previous section, I was curious as to how the high-organic-growth (HOG) companies were able to achieve their results. This led me to study 23 such companies. My hypotheses were based upon my professional experiences as an investment banker and as a strategy consultant. They were (1) these companies produced unique products and services; (2) they had visionary, charismatic leaders; (3) they had diversified portfolios of strategies; (4) they had outsourced or offshored all non-core activities; (5) they had the best talent; and (6) they were the most innovative in their industry. My hypotheses were neither unique nor original but reflected the views espoused by many academics and management consulting firms.

What my study found was that none of those hypotheses were necessary to produce consistent high organic growth. I found that high organic growth companies had the following characteristics or attributes: (1) they had simple, easy-to-understand, focused strategies; (2) their leaders were not visionaries but were humble, passionate operators who grew up in the business and were focused on the details of the business; (3) most did not substantively offshore or outsource; (4) they did not necessarily have the best talent but they got the most out of their talent by achieving high employee engagement; (5) they were execution champions; (6) they acted with a small company "soul" in a large company body; (7) no company had unique products or services; and (8) most companies were not the most innovative, but they had a constant-improvement, "be better" DNA.

Further study revealed that high-organic-growth companies proactively and simultaneously managed a portfolio of growth initiatives. Underlying most of these initiatives was an iterative, incremental improvement mentality—not the search for or creation of big "wow" innovations. Growth Systems had two overriding objectives: (1) to create new income streams that can be replicated quickly and efficiently across a large distribution or customer base and (2) to leverage core operating competencies into new income streams or new cost efficiencies.

Interestingly, in studying these high-organic-growth companies, I found different kinds of cultures. Some were customer-centric; some were employee-centric; some were growth-centric; some were product-centric; and some were brand-centric. It did not

2. Edward D. Hess and Robert K. Kazanjian, eds., *The Search for Organic Growth* (Cambridge: Cambridge University Press, 2006).

3. Edward D. Hess, *The Road to Organic Growth* (New York: McGraw-Hill, 2007).

seem to matter as long as their systems were aligned to send consistent messages that enabled and promoted the desired growth-producing behaviors. Irrespective of the culture, every company had underlying "be better" DNA. This "be better" focus was the underpinning of every growth initiative, whether it was top-line, bottom-line, or new concepts.

Growth Systems

The goal of a Growth System is to create new, scalable streams of income or cost efficiencies. High organic growth companies manage a diversified portfolio of growth initiatives. When you chart company growth initiatives over time, you discover that most companies go through the same general type of initiatives in the same sequence. These companies generally took the following steps:

1. First growing geographically—domestically and then internationally;
2. Then adding complementary products for existing customers;
3. Next entering new customer segments; and
4. Then adding complementary services for existing customers and looking to sell those services to new customers.

Once those top-line initiatives are underway, the focus turns to bottom-line cost efficiencies and productivity. In doing so, these companies took the following steps in this sequence:

5. Focused on supply chain efficiencies;
6. Concentrated on logistics and distribution efficiencies;
7. Focused on manufacturing or operations efficiencies and productivity;
8. Improved customer management;
9. Revised measurement systems; and
10. Implemented better HR hiring, training, and promotion processes.

After focusing on bottom-line efficiencies, companies then moved to these steps:

11. Created new concepts based on core competencies; and
12. Redefined their business models so as to compete in a larger market space.

By now, you must be asking, "What is the relevance of this research?" Interestingly, many of my public company research findings are consistent with the DPGC research findings discussed in the following chapters and the CEO quotes listed in the previous chapter. Successful public and private companies both had focused strategies, high employee engagement, a small-company feel, and continuous improvement.

Many of the public companies I studied (Sysco, UPS, Best Buy, Tiffany & Co., and TSYS) and some of the private companies shared one commonality. They iterated until they had a Growth System that consistently, seamlessly, and in a self-reinforcing manner linked strategy, structure, culture, leadership philosophy, employee policies, measurements, and rewards to drive desired behaviors. Both public and private companies reached this result through iteration and learning. In Chapter 4 you will see that many private company CEOs who had prior experience growing another business started designing their Growth System on day one. Almost all private company CEOs without such prior experience figured out the need for consistency, alignment, and measuring the key value-creating behaviors as they grew. In all cases, the Growth System has to be improved as one grows. The "Defender Direct, Inc.: A Business of Growing Leaders" and "SecureWorks" cases are examples of this.

Creating a Growth System

The creation of a Growth System is both an art and a science. The science part is the engineering process of drilling down to identify the specific employee behaviors that create value and then creating consistent policies, measurements, and rewards to drive those desired behaviors. The art part is managing the inherent tensions in a Growth System between the need for centralized controls and the need for decentralized entrepreneurial activities, and the tensions between high employee accountability and high employee engagement. To be successful, these holistic Growth Systems require (1) a maniacal sensitivity to inconsistency of messages and unintended consequences and (2) a paranoiac vigilance against complacency, hypocrisy, and hubris. These Growth Systems are hard to build, need constant tweaking, and need constant vigilance to ward off inconsistencies. Many public companies I studied that, over a period of years, have iterated to such a system believe it is a competitive advantage because it is so hard to build and maintain.

These Growth Systems focused on behaviors, believing that if the right behaviors occurred, then the financial results would follow. This is different from the approach of some CEOs who put tremendous emphasis on growth and pressured their people to hit financial metrics. My research found that consistent growth can result from building a Growth System. The big difference between the public companies and private companies I studied are differences in scale and resources dedicated to the work of system building.

Communication was also critical. Communications have to be concise, clear, and capable of being understood and internalized by line employees. Employees in the public companies I studied were able to focus on the task of being better daily because they generally believed that if they worked hard and performed they would be treated fairly and have the opportunity to advance. Other interesting consistencies across the companies were the following:

1. Focus on measuring behaviors and not just financial results;
2. High employee engagement, retention, productivity, and stock ownership;
3. Promotion from within policies;

4. Relatively stable and highly transparent measurement and reward policies engendering trust in the system;

5. One set of rules for both management and employees with the devaluation of elitist perks; and

6. Positive learning environments instead of environments of fear, vicious politics, or autocratic patriarchy.

At some point in the evolution of some private companies, I did find that several began to focus more on aligning culture, measurements, and rewards. Case study examples in this book are "Room & Board"; "Defender Direct, Inc.: A Business of Growing Leaders"; "Mellace Family Brands, Inc.: Building a Socially Responsible Enterprise"; "Trilogy Health Services, LLC: Building a Great Service Company"; "Leaders Bank: Creating a Great Place to Work"; "SecureWorks"; and "Valley-Wide Health Systems, Inc.".

Room & Board

In the fall of 2007, while reading *BusinessWeek* magazine, I came across an article that caught my attention: "Room & Board Plays Impossible to Get—Private Equity Sees Growth for the Retailer but Founder John Gabbert Prefers His Own Pace."[4] The reporter, Jena McGregor, wrote, "By all conventional standards, Room & Board should be bigger than it is."[5] Given my interest in corporate growth, I was intrigued by the story, which illuminated a contrarian view. I wrote to John Gabbert and asked if I could do a case study on Room & Board because I thought business students needed to hear his views. He graciously agreed, and the Room & Board story follows.

CASE DISCUSSION QUESTIONS

1. Put yourself in John Gabbert's shoes. What were your goals in starting your own business, and how does Room & Board's business model reflect those goals?

2. Explain how John elegantly designed Room & Board's culture, structure, leadership model, and human resource policies to consistently create the right environment to attract the right people (customers and employees) to Room & Board.

3. If John wants to institutionalize his business beyond his life, why doesn't he take Room & Board public?

4. What are the biggest risks of John's business model?

5. Why did John disclose the company's financials to his employees?

6. Would you want to go to work at Room & Board? Why?

---

4. Jena McGregor, "Room & Board Plays Impossible to Get: Private Equity Sees Growth for the Retailer but Founder John Gabbert Prefers His Own Pace," *BusinessWeek*, October 1, 2007.

5. McGregor, 80.

CASE
STUDY

ROOM & BOARD

Room & Board was a privately owned home-furnishings retailer, offering products that combined classic, simple design with exceptional quality. Approximately $250 million of revenue a year was generated through Room & Board's fully integrated and multichannel sales approach, consisting of its eight national retail stores, an annual catalog, and its Web site. Based in Minneapolis, Minnesota, Room & Board had a story of contrarian success as a company that had abandoned the standard retail-industry business model, disavowed debt and equity-growth financing, and embraced a unique multiple-stakeholder model that valued quality and relationships ahead of the bottom line while producing stellar financial results. That the company had achieved consistency and harmony between its values and actions also added to its uniqueness. Its culture supported an energized, positive growth environment for its employees that fostered high employee engagement and, in turn, high customer engagement.

Room & Board was wholly owned by John Gabbert, who had created it more than 25 years earlier. Now Gabbert, having reached the age of 60, was confronting his biggest challenge: how to institutionalize the unusual business model, culture, and employee environment he had built. His primary objective was to preserve and protect his "relationship" business model, which was the heart and soul of Room & Board's success.

History

Gabbert grew up working in a family retail business that sold traditional home furnishings, and at the age of 24 succeeded his father as the CEO. Family dynamics proved challenging, so when he was 33, he left the family furniture business to pursue his own business model, initially basing his furniture company on IKEA's business model. He also diversified into other businesses, but by the late 1980s, feeling overextended and unfulfilled, he decided to focus all his energy on building a business with people he liked and on a model that represented quality. All this drew him into the design aspect of the furniture business.

To Gabbert, quality relationships were just as important as quality home furnishings. This belief had helped shape Room & Board into a business focused on creating long-lasting relationships with customers, vendors, and employees, who were all fully integrated into the model of selling quality furnishings. At Room & Board, quality was also about providing value. That value was inherent in its products, which lasted and whose style and design were timeless—furniture that customers could count on enjoying for many years. But Room & Board went further by believing that a customer's home should be a favorite place where a customer should be able to create

Case Study UVA-S-0150 © 2008 by the University of Virginia Darden School Foundation. This case was prepared by Edward D. Hess as a basis for class discussion rather than to illustrate effective or ineffective handling of an administrative situation.

a meaningful special environment. This customization was made attractive by offering customers a multitude of special-order products, ranging from fabric choices on throw pillows to customer-designed solid-wood storage pieces.

Supply Chain

The retail-furniture industry was generally controlled by large manufacturers that dictated style, product availability, and price, and that made many products overseas with cheaper labor than could be found in the United States. Room & Board decided early on that it did not want to play that game, so the company created its own supply chain of approximately 40 different vendors, nearly all privately owned family businesses, many having grown alongside Room & Board over the years. Soon, more than 85% of the company's products were made in the United States—in places like Newton, North Carolina; Martinsville, Virginia; Minneapolis, Minnesota; Grand Forks, North Dakota; Shell Lake, Wisconsin; and Albany, Oregon—by craftsmen and artisans using hardwoods, granite, and steel of high quality. Most of these products were made exclusively for Room & Board, and more than 50% of the products were manufactured by 12 of its key vendors. Room & Board met with its vendors frequently to plan growth, discuss needs, and share financials to ensure that everyone was making a fair living while creating high-quality, well-designed products.

These vendor relationships evolved over the years into true partnerships, which allowed Room & Board to set an annual goal of having 85% of its products in stock at all times, contributing to quick deliveries. Special-order products were programmed ahead of normal production with the aim of delivering the product as fast as possible to the customer.

Under this model, Room & Board was more in control of its destiny; it had control over product quality, inventory availability, and the risk of supply-chain disruptions. This unique model carried its own risk, however, as almost all of Room & Board's suppliers were private, family businesses that shared the company's challenge of growing at a rate that sustained their economic health.

Culture

Room & Board had rejected common attributes of private company culture: hierarchy, command and control from the top, information on a need-to-know basis, and, in the retail industry, high turnover resulting in customer-service challenges. Its culture was based on the principles of trust, respect, relationships, transparency, entrepreneurial ownership of one's job and career, and the importance of a balanced life. Room & Board eschewed rules, lengthy policy manuals, and elitism. Rather, it believed individuals thrived in an environment where they were empowered to make decisions, and everyone's view was heard and respected. These core beliefs were outlined in its *Guiding Principles*, partially based on the following expectation:

At Room & Board we hope you find meaning in your work. There is both tremendous productivity for the company and personal fulfillment for each staff member when someone finds their life's work. It's a wonderful circle of success.

Room & Board tried to achieve this "circle of success" by creating an environment of collaboration and engagement. This engagement was evidenced by deep relationships with customers, fellow employees, and suppliers. Respect for different views, openness to feedback, and responsibility for one's actions all drove the staff's behavior.

What worked for Room & Board as it tried to achieve balance was defined by Gandhi: Happiness exists when what you think, what you say, and what you do are in harmony. Many businesses talked a good game, but Room & Board actually tried to "walk the talk." In this company environment, there was a heightened sensitivity regarding the impact of actions across functions and an awareness of the real message being communicated.

Room & Board believed that success was rooted in shared accountability; therefore, there were no rules for personal leave or sick pay. All 670 employees were shown the company's annual strategy priorities and a complete detailed financial package every month, so everyone could understand the goals and the business. All financial and operating numbers were transparent to encourage responsibility for owning and, in turn, effecting Room & Board's success. In discussing the company's normal eight-hour day, Gabbert stated:

I learned a long time ago that most people only have so many productive hours a day—it is the number of productive hours that count, not the number of hours at work. We strive to have an environment which results in energy and productivity. That is why we have a full physical-fitness facility with classes going on during the workday, a masseuse, as well as a great kitchen for employees to prepare healthy lunches.

Room & Board also operated on the principle that people who have a balanced life, with a life outside work, were happier and dealt well with customers and with each other. Gabbert, understanding that what set his company apart was its engaged employees, who tried to make every customer experience special, said:

I never wanted to be the biggest. I never thought about size. I just wanted to be the best and to spend my time at work with good people doing something more meaningful than just making money or keeping score.

Employees

The retail industry was generally known for its high employee turnover, with many part-time employees to keep expenditures on employee benefits low and commission-based compensation to lower fixed costs. But Room & Board was proof that a very profitable, quality business could be built by not following any of those common retail practices.

Instead, Room & Board had very low employee turnover, mostly full-time employees, and full benefits for part-time employees, and paid its retail sales staff on a salary basis rather than on individual sales. The rejection of a commission-based structure, together with its integrated and multichannel purchasing options, allowed Room & Board customers to shop and purchase in the manner that made the most sense to them. "We want customers to rely on us for the best advice and to trust that we have their best interests in mind—sales commissions run against that type of trust," said Gabbert. Room & Board employed over 670 staff members, as shown in Table 3.1.

Table 3.1   Room & Board Staff Divisions

Type	Number
Store personnel	237
Delivery personnel	220
Store and delivery leadership team	62
Central office staff	100

SOURCE: Room & Board.

Room & Board stores more than five years old had average employee tenure of over five years, which was very high for the retail industry. Delivery and warehouse personnel in delivery centers open for more than four years had an average tenure of five years. Employee tenure was 5.7 years for the central office, and total employee tenure for the company averaged nearly five years.

Room & Board also took a different approach to measuring employee satisfaction: by tracking how many employees referred family and friends for jobs and how many employees participated in the company's 401(k) program. Room & Board believed that these measures truly contributed to long-term employee engagement. Following the philosophy that employees needed good physical, mental, and financial health, Room & Board offered an extensive physical-fitness facility, a healthy-lunch program, and personal financial-planning services and 401(k) investment advice from an outside financial consulting firm at no cost. In addition, all employees could buy Room & Board products at a substantial discount.

Leadership Team

Room & Board was led by a six-member advisory board made up of John Gabbert and the members shown in Table 3.2. The leadership team was incentivized by a generous bonus program if key company objectives were met.

Key Expectations for Employees and Leaders

Room & Board's *Guiding Principles* was the foundation for the company's expectations and also served as a tool to help employees understand their connection to the

Table 3.2 Leadership Team Members

Member	Title	Tenure
Bruce Champeau	Vice President of Distribution, Delivery/Technology	16 years
Kimberly Ruthenbeck	Vice President of Retail Customer Experience and Vendor Management	15 years
Mark Miller	Chief Financial Officer	11 years
Betsey Kershaw	Director of Brand Experience	5 years
Nancy McGough	Director of Human Resources	16 years

SOURCE: Room & Board.

business. The document, which spoke primarily to respect, individual accountability, and engaging the business, included the following statements:

- Respect is foundational to our work environment. Everyone is expected to build relationships based upon mutual respect and collaboration.

- Use good judgment when making decisions and apply principle, not rules, to each situation.

- The more you seek to understand how your role is related to our business objectives and tied to the broader success of the company, the more rewarding, enjoyable, and challenging the effort.

Just as all employees were expected to understand and embrace the core beliefs outlined in *Guiding Principles*, leaders were expected to adhere to their own additional roadmap. Room & Board set forth a number of leadership objectives for its central office, store, and delivery/distribution leadership team, including the following:

- You take ownership for your business—you're independent and therefore do not wait to be told what to do.

- You lead less with rules and rely more on principles.

- You value building relationships; collaboration is much more important to you than competition.

You appreciate and desire longevity within your role. You do not seek to move from location to location or from department to department to get ahead; your growth occurs from richer experiences within your current role.

Financial Results

The Skokie, Illinois, store opened in 1986; the Edina, Minnesota, store in April 1989; the Denver, Colorado, store in 1991; and the Chicago, Illinois, store in 1993. See Exhibits 3.1 and 3.2 for more information.

Delivery Centers

Another point of differentiation from other retailers was Room & Board's philosophy regarding deliveries. Many furniture chains outsourced their deliveries. Room & Board did not, operating its own delivery centers staffed by full-time Room & Board professionals. These teams delivered all the local products. For national deliveries, Room & Board had an exclusive relationship with a Minneapolis company. To ensure ongoing collaboration, a few employees from the national shipping company's office worked out of Room & Board's central location.

In addition, the company had dedicated delivery teams for just Room & Board products. It was not unusual for customers to assume that these delivery professionals were Room & Board employees, not just because of their Room & Board uniforms, but also because they adhered to the same principles that all Room & Board employees followed: namely, that the customer experience during every step of the process was hassle-free and treated as an opportunity to create long-lasting relationships. The individuals who had the last interaction with customers about purchases were viewed as brand ambassadors and acted as such.

Room & Board's goal of providing a great customer experience at every step of the buying-and-receiving process required delivery personnel to deliver and set up the product and leave the customer happy. Delivery times were scheduled to allow time for customer interaction, discussions, and the proper placement of the new purchases. If there was a problem, delivery personnel were empowered to solve it on the spot because they were trained to "leave the customer in a good place." The focus on interaction with the customer, from the beginning of the experience to the end, drove customer satisfaction, in terms of loyalty and referrals, to a rate of more than 95%.

Real Estate

To avoid the high rent typical in retail malls, Room & Board owned most of its locations, and searched out freestanding sites with ample parking and easy access for customers. The company often chose to renovate an existing location, blending its store in with a particular environment rather than building a new one. This practice served as inspiration to customers who dealt with similar challenges when designing and furnishing their own spaces. Moreover, it prevented Room & Board from adopting a "cookie cutter" image for its stores and fostered the company's philosophy of unique design. The central-office facility was furnished with Room & Board products, so even employees who were not in customer-facing roles understood what the company sold, its quality, and its lasting design.

Pricing Model

Room & Board's pricing model was simple: no sales, no volume discounts, and no discounts for interior designers. Everyone paid the same price. As John Gabbert put it:

Nothing makes me madder than to buy something and then see it go on sale. I feel taken advantage of. That is why we have no sales, and we guarantee all prices for a year after purchase for each calendar year. If we sell a product within a year of your purchase for less than you paid, we will refund the difference.

Competition

Direct comparison with other retailers was impossible to make because Room & Board's exclusive designs, corporate structure, and long-lasting heirloom-quality products were not paralleled by any other company. Ultimately, Room & Board was competing for any of the dollars that customers spent on their homes no matter what the other retailer sold. Design Within Reach and Crate and Barrel were two companies that carried similar modern home furnishings and midcentury products.

Design Within Reach is a public company. In fiscal 2006, it had $110 million in sales through its 63 stores, which ranged in size from 1,100 square feet to 11,000 square feet. Although Room & Board stores were fewer in number, they were much bigger, at 30,000 square feet to 45,000 square feet.

Crate and Barrel had grown from a small, family business based in Chicago, started in 1962, to a chain of over 160 mall-based stores owned by the private German company Otto, which also owned Spiegel and Eddie Bauer. Over 50% of Crate and Barrel products were imported from Europe.

Conclusion

Room & Board had achieved the enviable market position of managing its growth and avoiding the capital-market pressures produced by debt financing and equity partners or by being a public company. It had built a loyal and highly engaged work force dedicated to its way of doing things, and managed to be a model of productivity and engagement without sacrificing quality. The company did not strive for the lowest operational costs, but instead embraced a vertically integrated business model and earned good net margins.

The beauty of the Room & Board success story is how it had created a consistent, seamless, self-reinforcing system that cut across culture, structure, execution philosophy, employee hiring, and benefits. The result was a company with a high-performance environment that manufactured 85% of its products in the United States, paid its people well, sold quality products, and made good profits.

Room & Board had adhered to a multiple-stakeholder philosophy of capitalism, much like the European model and less like the sole-stakeholder model more common in the United States. It believed it would do well if its customers, employees, and suppliers did well. To create shareholder value had not been Room & Board's sole purpose. But now the company was looking at expanding—into Los Angeles, Seattle, Atlanta, Miami, and Washington, D.C.—but at its own pace and on its own terms.

Room & Board's task was figuring out how to institutionalize its way of doing business beyond the life of its founder and how to strengthen its culture and high employee and customer engagement, while growing at a rate that sustained its economic health.

Exhibit 3.1   Room & Board Financial Results I

Year	Sales (in millions)	New-Store Openings
1995	$33	
1996	45	
1997	53	Oakbrook, IL
1998	67	
1999	82	
2000	98	
2001	92	
2002	95	South Coast, CA
2003	10	
2004	132	New York; downtown Chicago store moves to Rush and Ohio location
2005	173	San Francisco
2006	208	
2007	229	

SOURCE: Room & Board.

Exhibit 3.2   Room & Board Financial Results II

Key Metrics	Goals
Sales growth	10% annually
Net profit	8% pretax
Customer satisfaction	>96%
Product in warehouse at time of sale	>85%
Vendor lead time	<7 weeks

Channels of Distribution	Approximate Breakdown
Store sales	70%
Phone sales	12%
Web sales	18%

Markets	($ in millions)
Colorado	$18
Minneapolis	$24
Chicago	$44
San Francisco	$33
Southern California	$23
New York City	$46
National sales	$42

Main Product Lines	
Sofas and chairs	36%
Bedroom	17%
Dining room	12%

SOURCE: Room & Board.

List of Relevant Cases

Defender Direct, Inc.: A Business of Growing Leaders

Enchanting Travels

James Abrams @ Clockwork Home Services, Inc.: Lessons from a Serial Entrepreneur

Mellace Family Brands, Inc.: Building a Socially Responsible Enterprise

SecureWorks

Trilogy Health Services, LLC: Building a Great Service Company

Valley-Wide Health Systems, Inc.

4 The 4Ps of Growth
Planning, Prioritization, Processes, and Pace

In the research on successful private companies that had met challenges of growth, four concepts came up repeatedly in my interviews: (1) the power of planning ahead for growth; (2) the introduction of processes in the right amounts, at the right times, and in the right order to manage growth; (3) adoption by the entrepreneur of prioritization heuristics to focus his or her time on critical areas, which changed frequently; and (4) proactive management of both the pace and the focus of growth.[1]

Three Tensions

This chapter introduces three fundamental growth management tensions. (1) Some entrepreneurs left bigger companies because they disliked the bureaucracy, rules, countless meetings, and inefficiencies caused by processes. Now their growing business needed processes. So, the compromise is to install just enough processes but not too much. (2) Selling to more customers and growing the business requires a different mindset and skill set than analyzing what processes are needed to better manage quality, finances, and other functions and installing them. Making it a point to think differently is hard when thinking about growth is more fun for many entrepreneurs. And many entrepreneurs have no experience in process thinking or implementation. (3) Growth is change and requires companies to evolve. The processes put in place to better manage a $5 million revenue business may not be good enough or the right kind for a $20 million revenue business. Processes have to evolve as the revenues, number of employees, and entrepreneur grow. As a business grows, more and/or different processes may be needed. Process implementation is not a one-time event.

---

1. All quotes from the Darden Private Growth Company Research project are anonymous.

Planning for growth requires planning for process. Planning for growth and planning for process requires prioritization and managing the pace of both, understanding that growth drives process needs.

Planning

Anonymous Quotes from DPGC CEOs on Planning

"Begin with the end in mind."

"We set up as if we were a larger company right from the start."

"Work your business plan until it fits on one page."

"Understand that growth puts you in a different competitive space."

"Plan from the beginning—know what it is you are setting out to do with the end in mind."

Structure

Many of the companies I have studied or worked with did not plan for growth. Growth happened and the entrepreneurs reacted. The exceptions to this were companies led by entrepreneurs who had previous start-up/growth experience and had learned from that experience that they needed to plan ahead for growth. How did they do this? They asked themselves several questions: What will our organizational structure look like at $5 million or $10 million in revenue? Will the organizational structure need to change at $25 million in revenue? At $50 million in revenue? At $100 million in revenue? When will the company need to add more processes, managers, and structure? Most entrepreneurs used the number of employees to describe inflection points that triggered change. Common inflection points were 10 employees; 25 employees; 50 employees; and 100 employees.

While no entrepreneur used the following way of describing those inflection points, they reflected the organizational structure utilized by the U.S. Army and U.S. Marine Corps for combat troops. Both the Army and Marine Corps have created organizational structures to manage and keep control in fast-paced, intense, chaotic, changing environments. The Army organizes basically into squads of 9 to 10 people; platoons made up of 3 squads (30 people); and a company made up of 3 platoons (90 people). The Marine Corps adopts a "Rule of 3". Its basic structure is a rifle team made up of 3 people plus a leader. Three rifle teams plus a leader constitute a squad of 13 people, 3 squads plus a leader constitute a platoon of 40 people, and 3 platoons plus a leader equal a company of 121 people. What can we learn from the military?

Depending on the circumstances, a business probably will need managers once it has more than 9 employees, and at around 25 to 30 employees it will need a different management structure, and another structure at around 90 to 100 employees. Several entrepreneurs stated that they had to create a completely new structure every couple of years. Because of this, one entrepreneur stated that building a company is like building a house. That is, "be sure you go ahead and pre-wire the electrical and stub-in the plumbing for rooms you will need to finish in the future." In other words, plan ahead for your infrastructure, processes, and people needs. Make flexible, adaptable investment decisions, especially on software and phone systems.

Infrastructure

There was a constant tension between closely watching the bottom line in the short run and investing for the possibility of growth. Should one invest in more infrastructure than is needed now, assuming that it will be needed in the future? Should one buy only what one needs in the short run or should one financially stretch and buy more than one needs to accommodate future growth?

Some entrepreneurs planned by drawing organizational charts of their business at different sizes and visualizing a range of variables, including what their space requirements would be; number of employees by function; management team structure; information and technology needs; and how they would process every step of the value chain. They thought about what kinds of people, skills, and processes they would need in the future and took those future needs into account when making current hires, installing technology, implementing processes, or deciding which administrative functions to outsource now. They took each functional area such as accounting, manufacturing, HR, sales, information technology, and customer service and drilled down, mapping each component of the value chain at different revenue levels, including an organization chart and number of employees doing each job.

Outsourcing

At different phases in the growth process, most entrepreneurs resorted to some form of outsourcing. Almost all outsourced payroll processing, HR benefits processing, and some accounting functions. One company outsourced interviewing; many relied on staffing companies for periodic workers; and many had learned to engage executive recruiters for hiring experienced managers. In the accounting area, most traversed through the common path of hiring a part-time accountant, moving to a full-time controller, and ultimately moving to a vice president of finance or CFO. Likewise, in HR many started out with an administrative person handling HR matters, moved to a junior HR professional at around 25 employees, and upgraded to an experienced HR professional at around 50 employees. Outsourcing was common in the finance, accounting, and HR areas. As companies grew, they then in-sourced more of those functions.

Outsourcing—Manufacturing

Many of the product companies outsourced manufacturing, primarily to China. Some entrepreneurs with prior industry experience outsourced to known reputable sources. Entrepreneurs without that experience spent considerable time on the ground in the foreign country interviewing potential outsourcing partners. Outsourcing of manufacturing required entrepreneurs to plan for manufacturing quality controls on-site because doing quality control upon receipt of the products in the United States was inefficient and most manufacturers required payment prior to shipping. To ensure quality, entrepreneurs either hired on-site quality control representatives or made frequent inspection trips to the factories during their product runs. Even with diligent planning for manufacturing quality many entrepreneurs recounted horror stories of receiving containers of bad products.

One positive outsourcing story was told by Octane Fitness. After a rough start with their first manufacturer, over time the founders gained a clear understanding of what they believed to be important in ensuring quality. They wanted to work with a company that had experience with fitness equipment but did not produce its own brand. "And we wanted to be the number-one or number-two customer for that factory," Dennis Lee, the CEO, said. "And that's exactly where we are right now. We have two wonderful manufacturing facilities in Taiwan that understand fitness, and the relationships are great." Octane Fitness had learned the importance of "being on top of the relationship" from their negative experience with another manufacturer.

To ensure the excellence of the Octane Fitness brand and to show that the company took quality control seriously, a U.S. engineer conducted an inspection every month. In addition, three employees worked out of an Octane Fitness office in Taiwan to make sure that quality was never compromised. The company's focus on product quality and maintenance of high standards was rewarded with phenomenal sales and numerous awards that Octane Fitness's elliptical cross trainers started to earn in 2004.

Planning for Growth

Planning meant different things to different entrepreneurs. One entrepreneur took planning so seriously that he had a rolling three-year plan focusing on head count, revenue plan, and expense plan. Others focused annually on creating a one-year plan that was rigorously followed with respect to what additional business the company would be willing to take on. One had his management team meet at the end of the year to create the next annual plan. They iterated until that plan fit on a single piece of paper that could be distributed to every employee so everyone understood where the business was going and not going in the next year. That entrepreneur understood the dual function of strategic planning: it not only prioritizes what you focus on but also tells you what not to do.

"Firehouse Time"

Several entrepreneurs emphasized the need to allocate time to get away from the business to think clearly about what the business needed to do. They were unable to think strategically in the daily "heat of battle" and had to get away from the business to focus on thinking strategically. One entrepreneur emphasized the need for this by saying, "Give yourself an afternoon a week to think about five critical things going on in the business and make sure you are focused on big opportunities or problems." One of my colleagues calls this time for strategic thinking "firehouse time." Thinking strategically or on a macro-level is different from thinking tactically and reactively.

Thinking strategically and focusing on tactics such as choosing processes to install are two different ways of thinking, and both require that entrepreneurs who want to successfully grow allocate specific time to each need. Managing a growing business requires mental agility to think both strategically and tactically. This dual mindset encompasses both planning for growth and managing the risks of growth. Agility is also needed to understand that most decisions are subject to review and change as the business grows and evolves.

CLASS DISCUSSION QUESTIONS

1. How have you learned to think strategically?
2. How have you learned to think tactically?
3. What is the difference for you between thinking strategically and thinking tactically?
4. What templates or tools do you use to think strategically?
5. What templates or tools do you use to think tactically?

Prioritization

Anonymous Quotes from DPGC CEOs on Prioritization

"Don't get involved in all the brush fires—focus on the thing with the biggest impact."

"I focus on big opportunities and big crises."

"I do not pay you to get everything done everyday. I pay you to get the most important things done."

"Prioritize what we needed to do that was critical to knowing about cash flow."

"We are a product company. I focus on quality, innovation, and sales."

"For me, the most difficult part is figuring out what not to do."

"If the CEO pays attention to something, he can influence it."

"First thing is to make payroll. Then I focus on sales. Once we got growth, I did not focus enough on profits."

Bottlenecks

One purpose of my research was to learn how entrepreneurs prioritized their time under high-velocity growth conditions. I was looking for templates and heuristics. What I found were common sense approaches. Some were similar to what the military teaches team leaders and junior officers: assess the situation and go where you can have the most critical impact relative to the mission. Others created a flow chart showing each critical step in the process of generating cash—the lifeblood of a business. They then thought of the flow chart as a pipeline or funnel and monitored flows to determine where there were bottlenecks or flow delays. They then focused on the bottlenecks and, not surprisingly, found that wherever they focused, things improved.

Priorities

One entrepreneur prioritized his focus simply as customers, quality, and cash flow. He stated that if an issue did not have an impact directly and materially on one of those three areas, it could wait. A condition precedent to knowing where to spend your time is having reliable current data or information about critical metrics regarding value drivers. Simply put, entrepreneurs first need to use reliable data to assess the situation in order to define their priorities. Then they need to effectively communicate the priorities to the rest of the team. Finally, systems must be put in place, such as a strong company culture and metrics that reinforce the identified priorities.

For most entrepreneurs and growing businesses, it is all about cash flow—the oxygen of a business. One entrepreneur stated her priorities this way: "You don't eat if you don't sell. You don't sell if you don't have a customer. You don't have a customer if you don't offer a good service." Another successful serial entrepreneur stated his priorities this way: "Set up three or four priorities that take precedence over everything else: (1) manage cash flow; (2) focus on customers and quality service; (3) accelerate revenue growth; and (4) all the rest—unless something is on fire—can wait." Another serial business builder stated it this way: "Focus on the areas of the business that are critical to making it to next month, next quarter, and next year."

Why is prioritization so important? Because the growing business has resource constraints: limited people, only so much time, and limited capital. So it is critical that the entrepreneur spend his or her time on the most important areas that can drive success. These priorities are not static, however, and can change often. What we seem to know is that where the entrepreneur spends time has a multiplier effect that influences the focus of other employees. As I learned from one entrepreneur in my study (Dave Lindsey of Defender Direct), this multiplier effect was compounded when the process was transparent, enabling the employees to work together with Lindsey to fix the problem.

Huddles

How did entrepreneurs communicate their priorities? Several entrepreneurs held a "start-of-the-day huddle" to set priorities for the day and an "end-of-the-day huddle" to review the day. Another entrepreneur had a meeting every morning at 8:30 A.M. with his direct reports, and then the direct reports had meetings with their direct reports, and those meetings cascaded down the line until by 10:30 A.M. every employee in the company had been in a meeting talking about the priorities of the day.

Prioritization for the entrepreneur will change as the business grows and as a successful management team is built. As the business evolves and the entrepreneur's role evolves, his or her focus will change. Prioritization also is influenced by a business culture and its information systems. Culture helps keep employees focused on what is important and can deter aberrant behaviors. Timely and reliable measurement systems illuminate deviances, helping entrepreneurs to know about and focus on key problem areas or mistakes to be corrected. Consistent deviances or mistakes highlight the need for more process.

CLASS DISCUSSION QUESTIONS

1. You are building a service company. Create a good general heuristic to help you set your priorities every day. What is mission-critical for your success?
2. You are building a product company. Create a good general heuristic to help you set your priorities every day. What is mission-critical for your success?

Processes

Anonymous Quotes from DPGC CEOs on Processes

"We always want to put out the fire and leave a fire extinguisher behind."

"I do not want a single point of failure."

"I've got a philosophy that that which is not audited will always get worse, never better, and will create surprises."

"Get process good enough then improve it constantly."

"I've been in enough small companies to know that you can't strangle them with too much process."

"Understand that accounting and HR people by nature are process oriented."

What Are Processes?

As businesses grow the entrepreneur loses the ability to be hands-on with respect to everything going on in the business. How does an entrepreneur increase the probability that others will do the task as he or she would do it? The entrepreneur implements processes. Processes are the directions, the recipes, the instructions, and the standards for how to do specific tasks. Processes include rules or controls for mitigating financial and quality risks. Most processes are designed to tell an employee how to do something or what not to do. Other processes have a different goal—to produce reliable, timely data that will reveal variances or mistakes. These types of processes are designed to get the key data in the hands of the entrepreneur faster and faster as the business grows.

Purpose of Processes

Process implementations are intended to produce consistency and reliability. Process improvement is an ongoing, never-ending job for a growing business. As a business grows it will encounter problems that it never faced before, requiring new processes. Failing to anticipate potential problems is particularly risky for small businesses without the corresponding financial cushions that a larger or more established company would have in place to absorb those risks. Processes are needed to manage those risks. In every functional area, a growth company will need processes to ensure the production and delivery of products or services on time, defect free, with caring customer service. And a growing business needs processes to ensure that cash flow stays positive, that inventory is managed, that the right people are hired and trained, and that bad hires are terminated quickly.

Two points need to be made here. First, as a company grows, an entrepreneur will face problems he or she may have never experienced before. One serial entrepreneur told me that he hit that "wall" at $100 million of revenue and, comparing his business to an airplane hitting its maximum speed tolerance, said his business "started shaking, tilting, and rolling" and he thought he was going to "lose control and crash." Second, as a business grows, an entrepreneur has to hire skilled people who have managed functional areas of a business through such growth inflection points. Michael Cote of SecureWorks is an example of such a hire, and his story is at the end of this chapter.

Process Challenges

Common challenges faced by several entrepreneurs in my study were (1) not knowing what processes were needed nor how to put them in because of their lack of experience in all functional areas; (2) difficulty of balancing the pace of growth with process implementation—that is, the difficulty of doing both at the same time; (3) not enjoying process implementation because it was not as much fun as selling and finding customers; (4) assuming that process implementation was a one-time event rather than an ongoing priority that evolved through the life of the business; (5) underestimating the time and costs to install processes; (6) purchasing software process tools that could not scale; (7) not involving employees in the development of critical processes; (8) delegating too much of the process implementation to new, unproven managers; (9) struggling with the tension of investing ahead of future growth or always playing catch-up; and (10) failing to prioritize what processes to implement first and, as a result, trying to do too much at once.

Successful Process Implementation

One of the more successful entrepreneurs I studied, Dave Lindsey of Defender Direct, relied heavily on Michael Gerber's book *The E-Myth Revisited*,[2] stating, "the entrepreneur's job is to create the process, management's job is to make sure the process is followed, and the technician's job is to use the process."[3] Several other entrepreneurs stressed that the development and writing of processes should be part of an employee's job; everyone should create a process that someone else could follow when the employee was absent because of illness or vacation. This helped the business achieve the goal of "not having a single point of failure." Embedding the development and improvement of business processes into each employee's job description "collectivizes problems" and empowers line employees to think about how to constantly improve.

Successful entrepreneurs prioritized what they needed to know and what processes were necessary to acquire and maintain happy customers. They trained employees to do multiple jobs; measured and rewarded the right behaviors; posted daily production or customer service data so all employees knew how the business was doing; and created a culture of high performance. A key challenge for an entrepreneur is deciding what processes to put in place first and putting in enough processes to get the job done but not so much that it kills the small-firm entrepreneurial feel.

Many entrepreneurs thought they could easily deal with process implementation by hiring managers from big companies. Too many times, however, they learned that such managers could not adapt to the pace and realities of a fast-growing entrepreneurial environment. They were simply too corporate and were used to having support, tools, and resources that small companies lack. Several found that managers with both big-company experience and successful entrepreneurial small growth company experience were more likely to be successful.

Complexity

By now, I hope you are developing an understanding of the complexity of these issues. There is no one right answer. Entrepreneurs are constantly managing tensions arising from too many potential opportunities; too much to do every day; cash flow

---

2. Gerber, Michael E., *The E-Myth Revisited: Why Most Small Businesses Don't Work and What to Do About It* (New York: HarperCollins, 1995).
3. Hess, Edward D. "Defender Direct, Inc.: A Business of Growing Leaders" Case Study UVA-ENT-0115. University of Virginia Darden School Foundation, Charlottesville, 2009.

needs; people and time constraints; and the daily need to manage quality, brand reputation, legal risks, and financial risks while pushing people to be better, faster, and more cost efficient. As discussed earlier, entrepreneurs also must address the tension of whether to invest in people, software, and processes that one can afford now or to stretch and invest in what will be necessary at the next levels of growth.

For most entrepreneurs process choice and implementation was a risky, iterative, learn-as-you-go process requiring constant adjustment. By the time a business reaches $5 million in revenue, it generally has some financial cushion to absorb process iteration and even process implementation mistakes. Most successful businesses made and survived multiple process and people mistakes. As one entrepreneur stated, "if you are growing, you will make mistakes."

CLASS DISCUSSION QUESTION

You opened a successful New York–style deli sandwich shop and now want to grow by opening up a second location. Create the process (step-by-step instructions) for how to make a turkey club sandwich.

Pace and Strategic Focus of Growth

Anonymous Quotes from DPGC CEOs on Pace

"You do not want to bring on all the business that you can because growth can easily swallow you."

"We did not hire unless we had cash flow in house to pay their salary and benefits for three to four months."

"Going from $8 million to $13 million in sales in one year, I had to promise everyone that we would stop selling until we caught up."

"We were growing just to grow instead of being as calculated as we should have been."

"Management challenge is when to let up on the gas pedal and let people and processes catch up to growth."

Pacing Growth

How often have you read that entrepreneurs must manage the risks of growth? How many times in business school have you discussed the challenges of growth? Almost everyone in business has heard of the axiom "grow or die," but how many of you have heard of "grow and die"? Mismanaged growth can kill a business. Too much growth too quickly can create serious quality, people, and financial problems for a business. We know that the pace of growth has to be managed so growth does not outstrip capabilities, processes, and controls. Many entrepreneurs learned this the hard way, having to put the brakes on growth in order to play process catch-up. Several in my study learned it through the failure of their first entrepreneurial venture.

Growth creates risks that need to be managed. Pushing people and systems too hard will likely create more problems or mistakes than usual. The recognition of this was a key finding in my research. One entrepreneur whose business grew too fast, losing millions of dollars, reported the following lessons: "(1) Before you grow, prove your concept—make it scalable; (2) Have the right people and processes in place; (3) Walk before you run; (4) Do not overbuy and overpay for corporate managers; (5) Have clear lines of authority and reporting—not matrix reporting; and (6) Telecommuting for senior managers does not work."

Pacing growth requires entrepreneurs to turn away business in order to allow for the time to put in processes and controls. This can be either a "catch-up" need or a planned precondition of taking on more business. The need to pace growth is directly related to the planning section in the beginning of this chapter. If you plan ahead you can pace growth so that time, resources, and money can be allocated to process implementation so that you have the infrastructure in place to take on more business. Or, as was the case with many entrepreneurs, they had to stop taking on new business until they installed the necessary processes because the risks of destroying their brand and quality reputation were too high without more controls and processes. Sometimes these "catch-up" periods lasted as long as a year.

Many entrepreneurs yearned for that next big customer or that marketing breakthrough that would bring thousands of new customers while knowing that if that happened there was no way they could properly service those customers. Some were fortunate, taking on the big opportunity and somehow performing well enough to get past the first big order and then righting the infrastructure. Others were not so lucky and had to retrench and hunker down to repair the damage.

In the cases you will see different approaches. For example, compare Julie Allinson of Eyebobs in Chapter 1 with Ryan Dienst of Global Medical Imaging in Chapter 6.

Anonymous Quotes from DPGC CEOs on Strategic Focus

"Focus—be two inches wide and two miles deep."

"In a high-growth business it is easy to get spread too thin trying to be too many things to too many people."

"Diversification kills focus."

"The more we focused and said no, the more we grew."

"As you grow it is going to be very appetizing to take on disparate products and technology that may ultimately start to pull the company apart as they compete for resources."

"Focus on one thing you can do better than anyone else and then focus on finding a way to make it appealing to a big market."

The Importance of Strategic Focus

In the spring of 2009, I had lunch in Tysons Corner, Virginia, with two very successful serial entrepreneurs. One specialized in starting companies, getting them to $5 million in revenues, and then selling them. He had never grown a company above $5 million in revenue. The second entrepreneur had built two large private companies, selling one and taking the other public. I asked him to tell me the critical thing he learned from those experiences. He stated plainly, "Have a disciplined strategic focus and keep improving your customer value proposition." From his perspective there are two reasons to turn down new business: (1) It may be too risky, and (2) it falls outside your strategic focus sweet spot.

Another key finding was that successful entrepreneurs focused on what their key differentiator was to customers and from competitors. They asked, "What can we be known for?" which led them to "Focus on the one thing you can do better than anyone else and then figure out how to make that thing attractive to a big market." To do this, you must "know your competition incredibly well."

SecureWorks

Michael Cote took over as CEO of SecureWorks, a company with a proven product but not enough sales. Cote put in place processes, people, and focus to grow the business.

CASE DISCUSSION QUESTIONS

1. In his second year as CEO, Michael Cote was able to grow sales 8X. Why was he able to achieve that result?

2. Put yourself in Michael's shoes. You are a "911" CEO. Where do you start? People? Process? Strategic focus? Please explain.

3. How did Michael align SecureWorks' culture with the processes he put in place?

4. SecureWorks' private equity investors want to use this story as a teaching story for other companies in their investment portfolio. They ask you to prepare a PowerPoint presentation of no more than five slides titled "Lessons from Michael." Please do so.

5. Why was Michael's redefinition of the business so important? By redefining the business, what was he trying to accomplish?

6. Would you want to be Michael's co-pilot? Is he a good leader? Why? Is he an inspiring leader? Why?

7. What does he mean when he says, "It's all about people"?

SECUREWORKS

SecureWorks is a privately held company in Atlanta, Georgia, specializing in information-security services. It was launched in 1999, during the first Internet gold rush, by two former CompUSA employees, Joan Wilbanks and Michael Pearson.

The startup's technology established it as an expert in preventing external Internet attacks on commercial computer networks and attracted large investors. The two co-founders raised $30 million from Mellon Ventures and GE Equity, among others. The technology focus, however, was a double-edged sword. SecureWorks' management was so busy with the company's technical development that it neglected sales and marketing efforts, and revenue suffered. At the end of 2001, SecureWorks had fewer than 100 clients and was burning roughly $900,000 a month on less than a million in sales with only $9 million of the original cash raised left in the bank.

In February 2002, Wilbanks stepped down as CEO and made room for Michael Cote. A high-tech industry veteran with a strong financial background, Cote brought in a new management team, changed the sales strategy, and, most important, developed a strong customer-focused culture. Under Cote's leadership, client retention became SecureWorks' number one goal. "[It's] pure gold—it's between 96% and 97%," Cote said.[4]

The payoff was tremendous. Sales for 2003 topped $8 million. Since then, the company had seen triple-digit growth, year after year. Unlike many fast-growth companies, SecureWorks had grown through increased sales, rather than through mergers and acquisitions. Its client base included organizations of all sizes, with more than 10% of them listed on the Fortune 500. In 2008, SecureWorks had more than 2,000 customers worldwide and pulled in $53.9 million in revenue.

In 2009, *SC Magazine* honored the 300-employee company with a Reader Trust Award for the Best Managed Security Service for the fourth year in a row. In addition, SecureWorks had earned the spot on the *Inc.* 500, *Inc.* 5,000, and Deloitte Technology Fast 500 lists of fastest-growing companies.

SecureWorks—Company History

SecureWorks co-founders Joan Wilbanks and Michael Pearson met at CompUSA, Inc., a personal-computer retailer headquartered in Dallas, Texas. Wilbanks, a sales director for CompUSA's integration team, and Pearson, a technical-account executive, became aware of a market void in Internet-security systems for small and medium-sized companies.[5]

Case Study UVA-ENT-0140 © 2009 by the University of Virginia Darden School Foundation. This case was prepared by Senior Researcher Gosia Glinska and Edward D. Hess as a basis for class discussion rather than to illustrate effective or ineffective handling of an administrative situation.

4. *The Wall Street Transcript*, April 26, 2004; http://www.twst.com/tt/issues.htm.

5. Nicole Harris, "Startup Offers Web Security to Smaller Firms, *Wall Street Journal*, February 2001.

In the late 1990s, large companies were forking over millions of dollars to fortify their computer networks against unauthorized use by increasingly sophisticated intruders. Smaller companies that did not have the resources to install firewalls and other protective systems, which required trained personnel to monitor them, were virtually defenseless against computer-network attacks, and the big Internet-security players had little interest in addressing their needs.

Sensing a business opportunity, Wilbanks and Pearson decided to start a company that would offer affordable Internet-security systems to this largely neglected customer base. In March 1999, they launched SecureWorks in Atlanta, Georgia, with Wilbanks as president and CEO and Pearson as chief technology officer.

Rounding Up Capital

Consulting gigs provided early funding. Wilbanks coached sales teams at large security-software providers, such as Internet Security Systems, on how to improve their pitches.[6] But the serious money started flowing in when SecureWorks attracted the attention of an Atlanta-based venture-capital firm at a local technology trade show. The early round of funding from Noro-Moseley Partners, Alliance Technology Ventures, and ITC Holdings generated more than $10 million for the start-up. In November 2000, SecureWorks snagged an additional $20 million in a second round of funding, which was led by Mellon Ventures of Mellon Financial Corporation and included investors such as General Electric's GE Equity and SBK Capital.[7]

Developing the Technology

Flush with capital, SecureWorks now could develop the technology to deliver cost-effective, round-the-clock Internet security monitoring and response service. The service was ideal for companies with 250 or fewer network users per location, such as medical and law practices, accounting firms, insurance agencies, and other businesses that handled sensitive information but did not have in-house IT security personnel to protect their computer networks against denial-of-service attacks, information and identity theft, Web site vandalism, and viruses.

In addition to managing the intrusion-detection systems and providing firewalls, which protected its clients' networks from unauthorized access, the start-up's security center could respond to security breaches in real time, thanks to its proprietary iSensor technology (Exhibit 4.1).

Engineers at SecureWorks made sure the technology met the needs of small companies. The security system they developed did not take too much bandwidth on

---

6. Harris.

7. "SecureWorks Receives $20 Million in Second-Round Funding," *PRNewswire*, November 16, 2000.

the small companies' networks, and the user-friendly Web interface enabled small-business owners who had little technical expertise to easily review the data.[8]

The Revolving Door at the Top

The young company had technology that worked and a market hungry for its services; it had cash and a solid investor base. But all was not well at SecureWorks. In August 2000, the board brought in a former MCI WorldCom executive as the new president and chief operating officer in charge of building distribution channels and directing sales, marketing, operations, and finance.[9] In February 2001, co-founder Wilbanks stepped down as CEO, retaining her role as chairman of the board.[10] Robert Minkhorst, former CEO of Atlanta-based Philips Consumer Electronics for North America, took over the reins of the fledgling company.[11]

At the end of 2001, SecureWorks was a weak regional player with fewer than 100 clients. It was losing $800,000 to $900,000 a month on less than $1 million in sales. There was little doubt in board members' minds that, unless they challenged the status quo, the troubled start-up was not going to survive in the long term.

Enter Michael Cote

When Michael Cote took the helm of SecureWorks on February 1, 2002, he was the company's third CEO in three years. Cote explained what attracted him to the start-up:

I came for several reasons. I believed that Internet security had good potential, and the Secure-Works technology was up and running, not just a gleam in somebody's eye. I was impressed with the company's investor group, which has turned out to be one of the best I've run across. SecureWorks had cash, which meant there wasn't a working-capital issue, and I didn't have to go out and look for money. And finally, I felt the company needed to be redirected and focused from a sales and marketing perspective.[12]

Despite having no CEO experience, Cote had a track record of growing innovative technology companies in CFO and COO roles. A graduate of Boston College with a double major in computer science and accounting, Cote started his career as a certified public accountant. He spent two years in London, England, with KPMG Peat Marwick and five years as the chief financial officer of a public company that grew from $50 to $750 million in revenue. During his tenure as partner and COO

8. Harris.

9. "Former MCI WorldCom Executive Joins SecureWorks as President/COO," *PR Newswire*, August 17, 2000.

10. In February 2003, Wilbanks resigned from the SecureWorks board to head a start-up in security-patch-management services.

11. "SecureWorks Names CEO," *PR Newswire*, February 22, 2001.

12. *The Wall Street Transcript*, April 26, 2004.

of a privately held software company, MSI Solutions, Inc., revenue growth topped 75% every year. Prior to joining SecureWorks, Cote was a CFO at Talus Solutions, a pricing and revenue-management software firm acquired by Manugistics Group, Inc., in 2000.

During a career that spanned nearly 20 years, Cote negotiated the sale of two companies in which he was a shareholder and senior officer: one for $450 million and another for $65 million. He completed 41 acquisitions worth $1.6 billion and led equity offerings that generated $261 million.[13]

First Things First

The newly minted CEO had his work cut out for him. "The most important thing I knew we had to drive was to get the right people on the bus, and in the right seats," Cote said, describing his priorities during the first 90 days of his tenure at Secure-Works.[14] "And then we had to focus on driving the revenue," he said. "Because that's what we needed in order to survive."

Getting the Right People on the Bus in the Right Seats

Among Cote's initial tasks was to interview each SecureWorks employee to find out what they did. "When I met with the guy who was running sales," Cote recalled, "he looked at me and said 'I've never run sales before. I don't want to be in this position. I hope you can move me somewhere else where I can produce.'" The unhappy sales director was transferred to the product-management area, where he ended up excelling. "That was an example of putting someone in the right seat," Cote said. Filling the top executive positions, however, was more challenging. In order to "get the right people on the bus," Cote had to tap the talent pool outside the company.

Finding the right CFO was a high priority for Cote. "I spent nine years in public accounting and then was a CFO of a public company, so I came up through the finance route," Cote said and noted the importance of financial discipline. In February 2002, he hired Michael Vandiver as SecureWorks' CFO. Vandiver, whom Cote had met a year before during his own job search, had "broad experience dealing with venture-backed, privately held, and public technology companies," Cote said.[15] In March 2002, Cote brought in Chris Coleman as CMO. Coleman was a former owner of the largest technology-marketing company in the southeast and had more than 25 years of marketing experience.

---

13. *The Wall Street Transcript.*

14. Jim Collins, *Good to Great: Why Some Companies Make the Leap . . . and Others Don't* (New York: Harper-Collins, 2001), 13.

15. *The Wall Street Transcript.*

With the help of an executive recruiter, Cote found Tyler Winkler, a vice president of sales at SafeNet, a manufacturer of hardware and software for corporate-network security located in Belcamp, Maryland. "[He] had years of experience selling Internet security space," Cote said.[16] Winkler joined SecureWorks in April 2002 as senior vice president of sales and business development.

The new management team was fully assembled by June 2002. In a cost-cutting effort, Cote reduced the SecureWorks headcount from approximately 80 employees to 40 employees. "Then, I put a new budget in front of the board starting July 1st of 2002," Cote said.

Driving Revenue

Cote was painfully aware that that the start-up would not survive without a focused effort on driving revenue and that his cost-cutting efforts could only go so far. He explained:

We are a heavy fixed-cost business. I have backup diesel generators. I'm in a fully redundant, biometric secured facility because we do 24 by 7 by 365 managed Internet security. I've got a lot invested in technology. I could not cut costs there. If we didn't drive revenue, we were done—we were out of business. And we had a nine-month life when I joined.

Cote could not drive revenue with what he had inherited, however; the sales and marketing departments were in need of big overhauls. The company was technology-focused and, as Cote said, "It had the most dysfunctional sales and marketing departments I had ever seen."[17] Rather than selling directly to businesses, the company sold through distributors and resellers, which did not make any sense to Cote. "If we can't sell our services directly, how can we expect someone else to sell them? And we are a service business; we have to touch our clients," he said.

But, at the time, no one at SecureWorks seemed to realize that. "When I joined," Cote recalled, "the company had no idea who they were. They didn't know if they were a software company or a licensing company or a service company or what they did." He continued:

The biggest thing that I struggled with then, and, quite frankly, has become a struggle with us, is focus and business model. We're not in the software business. We're not in the product business. We're a service company. Our goals have been pretty much the same for six years: daily living our team values of integrity, service excellence, reliability, open honest communication and innovation, client retention rate, and our growth and revenue because with growth comes excitement and profitability. And for six years now, those are posted in our offices.

---

16. *The Wall Street Transcript.*

17. "Seeing Double: How Four Companies Overhauled Their Sales Strategies to Spur Growth," *Sales & Marketing Management*, September 1, 2004.

Making Over the Sales Department

Cote had hired Tyler Winkler to attack the problem of low sales. To Winkler, the solution was clear: a top-to-bottom makeover of the sales department. Rather than continuing to sell exclusively to channel partners, SecureWorks adopted the direct-to-customer sales model. In addition, the start-up narrowed its focus to four markets: banks, credit unions, hospitals, and utilities, which enabled it to be "narrow and deep, rather than wide and shallow," Cote said.[18]

Winkler was appalled by the lack of accountability and sales processes in place and set specific goals for the people in sales. He greeted the sales team with "Make your numbers in three months or you're out." But he made sure they were ready for the fight by ensuring that all sales reps received intensive training from internal and external trainers. They were also given a new tool—a Webinar presentation for potential clients.[19]

Now, a sales rep who brought in $5,000 in sales in a month despite a quota of $50,000, "was gone that afternoon," Winkler said.[20] Out of a staff of six salespeople, he fired four. Yet, his militant approach produced results: Within nine months after he took over the sales department, revenues for 2002 totaled $1.9 million. Two years later, the department had grown to 30 employees, while the number of SecureWorks' clients had grown tenfold.

"Tyler has grown and developed," said Cote in 2008. "And today, he not only has all sales and business development, he recently picked up our consulting-services group and has somewhere in the neighborhood of 75 of our 300 people working for him."

And the salespeople? "They have commission checks in a month today that are bigger than what they used to make annually," said Cote.[21]

HR Issues

Revenue growth meant growing headcount. In 2007, the company hired 120 new employees, and 40 more in the first few months of 2008. To handle an influx of employees, the company had a full-time recruiter who "did nothing but recruit and focus on bringing the people onboard and making sure we pay them and all that," Cote said, adding that SecureWorks used Automatic Data Processing, Inc., (ADP) for payroll services. ADP also managed the company's benefits package and dealt with "reviews and interviews and that type of thing," Cote said.[22]

---

18. "Seeing Double."
19. "Seeing Double."
20. Betsy Cummings, "The Whip Cracker," *Fortune Small Business*, October 1, 2004.
21. Cummings.
22. Automatic Data Processing, Inc., was a provider of HR, payroll, tax, and benefits administration solutions.

Compensation

SecureWorks took compensation management seriously, using it as a way to improve performance and manage talent. Cote understood that offering the right compensation for each person was critical to attracting and retaining high-quality employees. "I have a very personal vested interest in how we compensate people and what the benefits are," Cote said.

The total compensation at SecureWorks had three components: base pay, variable compensation, and equity. "My philosophy is, look to go on the lower end of base from a market perspective—the bottom 50%. And then have variable compensation that can bring you above or at the high end of the total market," Cote said.

Compensation was tied to individual and corporate performance. "It's 60% tied to the company performance, 40% individual," Cote said. "But there are hurdles the company has to hit for you to be eligible at all. The bonuses typically get paid out in the spring after the audit has been completed." In the fall, the employees were paid the equity component of their entire compensation. "I've granted equity to the entire employee base in some shape or form every fall," Cote said.

Turnover

The turnover rate at SecureWorks ran "somewhere in the neighborhood of 15%, both voluntary and involuntary," Cote said. He admitted that because SecureWorks was a "high-energy, heavily driven" organization, it attracted a certain type of driven, high-producing individual. "And what happens is that if somebody joins the team and is not producing at the same caliber that others on the team are, they tend to push them out," Cote said. In some cases, those who did not fit in SecureWorks' fast-paced, high-charging culture left on their own. "But I don't think we lose a lot of people for other reasons, such as them being recruited away," Cote said, adding that, although he had let the marketing executive he hired in 2002 go, the CFO and the SVP of sales and development had been with the organization almost as long as he had.

Cote's Management Style

As SecureWorks grew, so did the man at the helm. The CEO's evolving leadership role was "one of the things we struggle with a lot and talk about a lot here," Cote admitted. A believer in open communication, Cote created a PowerPoint slide presentation titled "Who Am I?" intended for members of SecureWorks' board and executive team. "If I'm the one running this ship, and I'm the chairman, CEO, and president of the company, you'd better know who you're working with and what my management style is," said Cote.

One of the tag lines in Cote's presentation was, "Stop talking before I stop listening." "I don't have a lot of time to waste," Cote explained. "And if you want to come in, let's talk, but get to the point." He continued:

The second thing is, "Don't strap me in the copilot seat." Don't look for me to solve your problems. I'm paying you good money to run a department. And if you want to talk about something, then that's fine. Come in and say, "I don't have the answer, and I want to run this by you." But it is your problem, and you come up with a solution. I don't manage my folks. I look to hire high-quality people. Just like I manage the board; I look for them to manage me.

The SecureWorks executive team consisted of twelve members, including the CEO, but only six of them reported directly to Cote: the CFO, the CTO, the CMO, and the heads of operations, engineering, and sales and business development (Exhibit 4.2). As Cote told the members of his executive team, "As a CEO, I shouldn't be making routine decisions." The same principle applied to the members of his executive team: Cote wanted SecureWorks executives focused on making strategic decisions and for their direct reports to handle the easy ones. He devoted a lot of the time in meetings with his executive team to questions such as, "What am I spending my time on? What *should* I be spending my time on? And if that's the case, what should *they* be spending *their* time on? And how do I get the reports or information from them? And how do we get our relationship to work?"

Cote worked well with people who valued open communication and transparency in the same way he did. In his opinion, the ability to communicate well, which required good rapport and a certain level of "mutual respect, trust, and understanding," was an essential element of a good work relationship. To describe his philosophy of working with the executive team, Cote said:

I'm the leader of the team, but we're all in this boat together. The enemy's not in the room. And we're all executive people looking to drive this thing. And we need to be able to have a rapport and work well together and understand where we're all driving. And there's a clear handoff from one department to another of what's being done and where we're going.

Managing Time

As the company grew, one of the challenges Cote faced was deciding how to allocate one of his scarcest resources: his time. He said, "Probably the most difficult part is figuring out what not to do." He continued:

It's not that I'm not delegating. But I may be doing things or looking over someone's shoulder where, quite frankly, it doesn't matter anymore; I can't afford to put my time in that area. The one thing I perhaps do not do frequently enough is try and sit back and ask, Where am I spending my day, and is it effective? I'm trying to make sure I divide my time between . . . how I am working with the board, how I am thinking through how we're going to grow five times the size we are today, interviewing new board members, and dealing with how I pull the most out of what the next stages are.

In 2006, Cote hired an executive assistant—he did not have one for the first four years—with whom he sat down regularly and reviewed his schedule. Now he said, "No, I can't meet with this person. With 15 companies that want us to buy them and 20 companies that want us to partner with them, these people can't be on my calendar anymore."

Cote also reorganized SecureWorks every 18 months, in part to give himself time to devote to the things that mattered most for the growing company. In 2008, Cote said, "I had nine direct reports six months ago. I've reorganized down to six." He tried to limit the time he was available to direct reports seeking his advice. "My calendar's booked. Schedule it later," he told them. "And my hope is that in many of those instances they end up making the decision, because I've blocked out my calendar so I can't meet with them for two or three days," Cote said.

Information Management

For years, Cote had used Excel spreadsheets and "long hours of smart people" to help make sound financial and managerial decisions. Then, in July 2008, he implemented Microsoft's Great Plains accounting and business software to produce the data for SecureWorks' financial statements.

Cote, who had been CFO with enough companies with revenue ranging from $800,000 to $800 million to know, said that "there are different stages and different elements of where you can kind of manhandle your way through it." He added:

You sort of hit a wall with $5 million in revenue. And you sort of hit another wall in that $10 to $15 million threshold. And then my experience in buying companies is that companies are paid a higher multiple once they cross to $25 million in revenue because with $25 million in revenue it can't be manhandled anymore. You have to have systems, policies, and procedures in place. So that's sort of where we began to hit the next threshold.

One of the tools critical in the management-decision-making process at Secure-Works was the board book, which was distributed to the directors in advance of meetings. Cote said:

We have a board book that's pretty extensive. Our business is like an insurance company as far as predictability. One client is over 2% of our revenue. We've only missed one month a year from a sales perspective or a new contract perspective and have never missed an EBITDA monthly target. But it's a pretty diverse client base, pretty easy to predict. And we trend a lot—there are a lot of graphs and a lot of financial information in our board book.

Internal Controls

Cote set up adequate financial controls immediately after he took over as CEO. "From the control-of-cash perspective, the first thing I did was make sure the only two people who were allowed to sign on behalf of the company were the CFO and myself," he said. Cote added that "pretty tight controls" were put around anything that could put the company at risk. He continued:

We work heavily on the budget. Each department head has control over their expenditures. They're tied to their variable comp plan. They each have their own expenses and, if applicable, their revenue budget. And that rolls up to full corporate finances. But if it's things that relate to serving the client, running a department, there's a fair amount of latitude that has been given.

For example, the sales reps had the authority to discount the service 10% off the list price. The two vice presidents of sales had the authority to discount another five points, and the CFO could take off twenty-five points. "And anything over that, he brings it to me," Cote said. "So there are some discounting functions in place like authority to sign the company, big critical things of that nature. My operations guy may give away two, five months of free service. And I've never questioned them on any of that."

Because client retention was the company's number-one goal, Cote gave Secure-Works employees the authority to make decisions that had an impact on the client relationship. "We're human. We make mistakes," he said and recalled an exchange he had had with a staff member in charge of operations: "I asked him, in front of his staff, 'What do you think your authority is in order to fix a problem that we created relating to a client relationship?' And he looked at me and said, 'I don't know.' And I said, 'When have I ever said no to you on anything you've ever wanted to do?' It's whatever you want to do and whatever you think needs to be done."

Managing Growth

Under Cote's leadership SecureWorks experienced stellar growth. In May 2008, he said, "Today, we have almost 300 employees and about $50 million in revenue. And we'll do about $70 to $80 million in bookings or contracts this year."

In addition to a stable client base, which was a source of recurring revenue, SecureWorks was winning new clients, including international ones, every day. "As all of that grows, I have a lot of open direct conversations with my executive team. Some of this may sound exciting and sexy. But I want to make sure they truly understand what international travel means if we get to that point," Cote said.

In 2008, one of the biggest challenges facing Cote was taking the company to the next level—from $50 million to $250 million in revenue. The issues related to managing growth were the focus of many board meetings. "We spend a lot of time on whether we have the right people. And if they are the right people, what things they need to work on to make sure they've got the skill set to take them to the next level," Cote said.

One of Cote's 2008 hires was the vice president of human resources, whose mandate was to work with members of the executive team to identify their constraints and deficiencies and ensure they received the right training to succeed in their evolving roles. Cote explained:

Of the 12 people on the executive team, there's only one who's been in [his current] role in a quarter-of-a-billion-dollar company before. I've been in an $800 million publicly traded company, but as the CFO, not the CEO. And some folks on the executive team, it's sort of 50/50 that they will be the ones running their departments four or five years from now. They may be here in different roles, or they may be able to continue to evolve as we grow as a company. I was with a company, in the CFO position, that we grew from $40 million to $800 million in revenue in three-and-a-half years, all through acquisitions. So I lived through situations where we grew beyond people's capabilities. And we ended up promoting them too far, and, eventually, we had to fire them. So, when it comes to making people decisions . . . pull the trigger quicker.

In July 2009, SecureWorks acquired VeriSign's managed security-services division to increase its market share and boost its international presence. According to Cote, the acquisition also resulted in an addition of "some technical capabilities and name-brand enterprise accounts."

As of October 2009, the company had approximately 2,700 clients, $110 million in run-rate revenue, and about 525 employees in offices in Atlanta, Georgia; Chicago, Illinois; Providence, Rhode Island; Myrtle Beach, South Carolina; and London, as well as partnerships in Spain, Mexico, South America, Taiwan, and Saudi Arabia.

Staying Focused

With success came new challenges. Early on, Cote had helped the troubled start-up find its focus; six years later he strove to maintain it. Cote said:

The biggest issue for the leadership—the thing I harped on six years ago, and I'm harping on again—is focus. Does this fit who we are? Does it fit what we're doing? We've gone from one service line to seven or eight service lines. But we're not trying to be everything to everyone. We are a value-added Internet security-service provider—we are not your low-cost provider. Our gross margin runs in the mid-70% range. We've got to know who we are, know what we're doing, and stay focused on our knitting.

Cote admitted that it was hard to stay focused on what was important when confronted with all the opportunities that accompanied exponential growth. The dozens of high-tech companies interested in partnering with SecureWorks or wanting to be acquired by it presented distractions. "If we don't stay focused, we end up getting ourselves all wrapped around where we are as an executive team and find the whole organization spending time on stuff that's a waste of time," Cote stated.

To help the organization stay true to what it was and not lose sight of its core values, the executive team developed a culture book and distributed it to all Secure-Works employees. All new hires received a copy during orientation.

It's All About People

At the beginning of 2002, SecureWorks was one of a few dozen information-security start-ups. With its sales stagnant and totaling under $1 million, it was on the verge of extinction; under new leadership, however, the company found its focus and thrived.

By 2008, SecureWorks emerged as one of the three or four survivors in the industry it had helped kick-start, along with companies such as ISS and CipherTrust. "We are clearly the largest and fastest-growing company from an organic growth perspective. I often get asked, 'Why have you guys been able to do it?'" Reflecting on the driving force behind SecureWorks' success, Cote answered:

If you boil all of it down, it's people, people, and people. It's the passion we have. And we've got a focused business model. We know who we are, what we do, and what we don't do. Everybody in the company knows that if clients call, they'd better be doing cartwheels to respond to them. We may not be able to fix the problem. We may not be able to put in a new feature they want. But we're going to be open, honest, and communicate with them. And if we make a mistake, we're going to admit it and apologize. We're going to figure out how to make it right. We've got probably the best technology in the industry. But the only reason we have that technology is because we have people. We're able to focus on what clients want, and we'll continue to improve it.

Exhibit 4.1   The SecureWorks Security Services in 2009

On-demand SIM (security information management)	Aggregation, correlation, and analysis of log data from network devices, security devices, and other key assets
Log monitoring	24 X 7 real-time analysis of logs and alerts from security devices and critical IT assets by certified experts
Intrusion prevention systems (IPS)/intrusion detection systems (IDS)	Intrusion prevention/intrusion detection at the network perimeter or interior to the network
Threat intelligence	Reporting from the SecureWorks counter-threat-unit research team
Firewall	Control over network access and egress
Host IPS	Targeted intrusion prevention on key systems
Vulnerability scanning	Evaluation and inventory of network assets
Log retention	Comprehensive archiving of device logs
Encrypted email	Protection for email messages in transit
Consulting services	Consulting, assessment, and testing

SOURCE: SecureWorks Web site.

Exhibit 4.2   The SecureWorks 2009 Executive Team

Michael R. Cote, Chairman and CEO
Michael R. Vandiver, Executive Vice President and CFO
Jon Ramsey, CFO
Kathy Jaques, CMO
Tyler T. Winkler, Executive Vice President
Tony Hawk, Vice President, Human Resources
Jeff Browning, Senior Vice President, Engineering
Erik Petersen, Vice President, Consulting Services
Bill Buchanan, Vice President, Risk Management
Jim Ulam, Vice President, General Counsel and Secretary
Robert Scudiere, Vice President, Engineering
Scott Magrath, Vice President, Global Strategy

SOURCE: SecureWorks Web site.

List of Relevant Cases

Planning

3 Fellers Bakery

Defender Direct, Inc.: A Business of Growing Leaders

Enchanting Travels

Global Medical Imaging, LLC

Octane Fitness, Inc.: The Power of Focus

SecureWorks

Students Helping Honduras

Trilogy Health Services, LLC: Building a Great Service Company

Valley-Wide Health Systems, Inc.

Prioritization

3 Fellers Bakery

Defender Direct, Inc.: A Business of Growing Leaders

Global Medical Imaging, LLC

Jeff Bowling at the Delta Companies: From Baseball Coach to CEO

Octane Fitness, Inc: The Power of Focus

SecureWorks

Students Helping Honduras

Processes

C.R. Barger & Sons, Inc. (B)

Defender Direct, Inc.: A Business of Growing Leaders

Enchanting Travels

Global Medical Imaging, LLC

James Abrams @ Clockwork Home Services, Inc.: Lessons from
a Serial Entrepreneur

Leaders Bank: Creating a Great Place to Work

Octane Fitness, Inc.: The Power of Focus

Room & Board

SecureWorks

Valley-Wide Health Systems, Inc.

Pace of Growth

3 Fellers Bakery

Enchanting Travels

Eyebobs Eyewear, Inc.

Global Medical Imaging, LLC

Mellace Family Brands, Inc.: Building a Socially Responsible Enterprise

Room & Board

Sammy Snacks (A)

Sammy Snacks (B)

SecureWorks

Students Helping Honduras

Trilogy Health Services, LLC: Building a Great Service Company

Valley-Wide Health Systems, Inc.

5   The Entrepreneur Must Grow, Too!

Anonymous Quotes from DPGC CEOs

"If the business makes it three or four years, it hits a ceiling. Not a business or opportunity ceiling but an entrepreneur ceiling."

"A lot of entrepreneurs get trapped in the 'well, I will just do it myself' syndrome."

"My biggest struggle was reinventing myself to the business."

"Businesses do not grow—people do."

"Ego fails. Control freaks fail. Listen till it hurts."

"Delegation is not a natural human characteristic."

"Delegation is the most difficult management skill to learn."

"My biggest struggle has been constantly reinventing my relationship to the business. You go from a business that's in an extra bedroom to 200 employees nationwide, $150 million in sales, and that is a huge challenge in itself, both in terms of process, skill, and psychologically. Every year I say to my wife that I have to reinvent my relationship to the business."

Change, Evolution, and Learning

In the Introduction and Chapter 1, I outlined the unifying theme of this text: that growth is change, evolution, and learning. Nowhere is this more definitive than in how entrepreneurs themselves must change and evolve as the business grows. This chapter focuses on how the growth of a business changes the entrepreneur and how in order for the business to grow the entrepreneur must change. As a business grows, an entrepreneur must change not only the content of what he or she does but also how he or she interacts with employees and outside entities. In addition, these shifting roles and responsibilities are not one-time events because as the business continues to grow the entrepreneur must continue to adapt and evolve with the changing needs of the business. Growth changes both what the entrepreneur does and how he or she does it. Growth requires the entrepreneur to continuously redefine his or her relationship to the business and to its employees. Because growth changes what the entrepreneur does each day, his or her focus necessarily will change, requiring the development of new skills—often quite different from those entrepreneurial skills that made the business successful in the first place.

This redefinition of the role of the entrepreneur as the business grows can be viewed along three dimensions: (1) the movement from a hands-on doer to a manager to a leader to ultimately a coach or mentor of others; (2) from a functional specialist to a general manager back to a functional specialist and ultimately to a strategy and culture "conductor"; and (3) from having a passionate belief in the primacy of oneself to having a belief in others to having a belief in the importance of working toward something more than just the financial rewards of the business.

At any one of these change points along any of the three dimensions, the entrepreneur may need to realize that he or she may not be the right person to be the CEO of the growing business. In such cases, the entrepreneur has the choice of bringing in a CEO with the appropriate skill sets or deciding that the business has reached a comfortable size that he or she can continue to manage and additional growth is no longer the goal. Even if the entrepreneur chooses the latter, steady-state option, the business goal must change from growth to continuously improving the customer value proposition and defeating the competition.

Delegating: Learning to Manage

By definition, entrepreneurs who reach the stage of focusing on business growth have successfully traversed the start-up challenge—a victory in and of itself. They generally struggled, adapted, and iterated while being passionately consumed with the business, working long hours, and doing anything that needed to be done. In the best cases, this success at building a business builds self-confidence; in the worst cases, it builds arrogance and/or hubris. Many entrepreneurs of successful start-up companies develop a view of management that is top-down, a "my way or the highway" approach. That management style does not translate well when business growth is the target but, given its initial success, many entrepreneurs have difficulty in moving toward more of a partneurial style with managers. Growing a successful start-up requires an entrepreneur to expand the number and types of employees because he or she can no longer do everything.

A successful serial entrepreneur stated it this way: "[We] entrepreneurs tend to think we know everything. And the quicker we recognize that we don't and we open up our ears and eyes instead of just our mouth, things start going well."

Many entrepreneurs learn to delegate only when they have to. At some point they cannot physically do all of the tasks the business needs: finding, selling, and servicing customers, delivering the products or services, and tending to the myriad administrative tasks. So, entrepreneurs are forced to change and to delegate. Few do this willingly or easily.

The threshold questions entrepreneurs face when growing their businesses are What tasks do I delegate? and To whom do I delegate? This leads to the next question: How do I delegate?

How to Delegate?

A thoughtful, successful entrepreneur talked about delegation this way:

I don't think that learning to delegate is a linear process. You have to delegate. Then you do delegate and you find that some things fall apart. Then you gather them up, pull them back in towards you and fix them and then start the process all over again.

It is difficult for many entrepreneurs to accept that others may get the job done differently than they would have. Part of accepting the need for delegation is acknowledging that what comes naturally to you may have to be learned by others who will make mistakes. How one reacts to these inevitable mistakes will either enable future learning and employee growth or it will hinder it by making people timid about trying new approaches or making decisions. Delegating involves patience, teaching, correcting, and trusting others. Another entrepreneur who built a successful service company stated, "It (delegation) is baptism by fire. You start looking at the fact that if you don't let go, you will lose."

Delegation transforms an entrepreneur into a manager. Successful entrepreneurs have made this transition by learning to "trust but verify"; having daily team meetings to set daily priorities; and having a short 10- to 15-minute team meeting each day teaching a key point. Although implementing the right processes and measurements is crucial, the most important lesson for the entrepreneur is learning to accept the reality that those to whom he or she delegates will make mistakes. Using those mistakes as opportunities to teach rather than punish, unless the same mistake keeps occurring, is a key factor in creating an engaged employee and a high-performance environment.

Successful delegation is directly related to having processes in place. To delegate you need processes for others to follow. And successful delegation requires implementing measurements. Having metrics on important activities of the business serves as an early warning system. The right metrics expose defects, variances, and discrepancies. Learning how to delegate and implementing the appropriate processes and measurements are all necessary for an entrepreneur to evolve from doer to manager.

For the initial step in this delegation process, some entrepreneurs chose an outstanding employee to promote to team leader or manager position. They then engaged the employee in writing the key steps, instructions, and tasks necessary to accomplish the job that the employee now was going to be responsible for. Next, they gave the employee responsibility for the task of communicating that to other employees. Then they frequently checked on the progress until they were convinced that the employee could execute the task appropriately and consistently. Frequent checking was then reduced to sporadic checking as the employee earned the trust of the entrepreneur.

What Tasks Do You Delegate First?

What tasks do you choose to delegate first? That depends on the business. But since successful delegation involves a process of both teaching and trusting, one should start with easy, non-critical tasks and work toward delegating more responsibility and more complexity. Some general observations were that entrepreneurs kept control over finances, quality, and customer relationships until they had to delegate them. But even then they maintained rigorous oversight on those three critical areas.

When Do You Start Delegating?

Although it is hard to come up with consistent rules of thumb about when entrepreneurs should delegate substantive tasks to other managers, the range seems to be around 10 employees. Of course, even before that some general delegation occurs, but as a business grows, delegation involves more differentiated tasks and the entrepreneur losing physical oversight of the tasks being done. At around 10 employees an entrepreneur needs to designate a person or persons as managers, which creates structure.

CLASS DISCUSSION QUESTIONS

1. Who is the best manager you have worked for or have been associated with? Why?
2. Who is the worst manager you have worked with or have been associated with? Why?

Learning to Lead: Managing Managers

After learning to delegate, the next big transition for entrepreneurs is learning how to manage the managers chosen to help run the business. Managing managers means the entrepreneur is evolving into a leader. Most entrepreneurs in my study had between four and eight direct reports—individuals who reported directly to them. Learning how to manage these people individually and as a team required most entrepreneurs to learn new skills and become more emotionally intelligent. This process of learning to lead changes both the "what" and "how" of what entrepreneurs do daily. Much more time is spent relating, listening, and engaging direct reports in meaningful conversations, including getting buy-in to both short-term and long-term goals. It also required teaching, correcting, giving feedback, and sometimes having difficult conversations. This new menu of work is hard for many entrepreneurs because it takes emotional engagement, self-management, patience, and a lot of time. Many entrepreneurs found this "people stuff" much harder and more emotionally taxing than their past activities of selling products or services to customers, making the products, or delivering the services. This does not come naturally to many business people.

One entrepreneur described the change in focus this way:

As you push decisions down you have to spend more time in alignment and prioritization making sure people are focused on the right thing, that they are communicating well and getting along, and that they've got the requisite skill sets to do what needs to be done.

Many entrepreneurs told me this "emotional" people-focused management was the reason why so many entrepreneurs fail as leaders and must step aside so the business can continue to grow. This transition to becoming a leader who manages managers creates questions of how involved the entrepreneur should be in the details of the growing business. How do you verify and check on your managers without conveying to employees that you do not trust the manager? When and how do you disagree with a manager's actions? How do you prioritize or decide where you will give managers leeway? What elements of the business are non-negotiable? How does an entrepreneur discover the optimal way to train and communicate with each manager?

These management-related questions are qualitatively different from the business questions concerning quality, financial metrics, logistics, sales, and production. As the entrepreneur's role changes with business growth, many miss the daily direct customer contact and practicing their craft. In fact, many became entrepreneurs because they did not want to be managers removed from customer contact. Growth can create a major tension for such entrepreneurs. How can an entrepreneur continue doing what he or she enjoys doing when growth requires a shift to managing people and processes and implementing controls?

The people part of building a business is a significant and essential part of business growth. Learning and developing one's teaching, managing, and leadership skills emerges as mission-critical needs to continue growth.

These transitions from manager to leader were summarized by a serial entrepreneur this way: "It takes one set of skills to run (manage) a company and it takes an entirely different set of skills to grow (lead) a company." These personal transitions for the entrepreneur present to many a big personal growth challenge. It should be clear by now that, as one entrepreneur so aptly stated, "businesses do not grow, people grow."

Effectively, to grow a business the entrepreneur has two choices. Either the entrepreneur must be a good enough manager and leader to inspire and receive high performance from his or her employees, or the entrepreneur has to remain a functional specialist and find someone else to manage the people.

From Leader to Coach and Mentor

As the entrepreneur learns to lead, teach, and build managers, he or she will have learned that each manager is a unique individual with strengths and weaknesses, needing an individualized approach to foster his or her personal growth. In other words, the leader must develop a repertoire of skills to be able to communicate with and teach each manager individually so as to be most effective.

As those managers develop and learn, they each will begin their own personal journey from manager to leader. As the business grows, each entrepreneur will have an increasing number of direct reports to manage and to develop into leaders. These managers will need to learn to be leaders. These cascading personal transitions are never-ending if growth continues.

Nurturing the transitions of the managers to increasingly responsible roles requires entrepreneurs to adopt a new way of interacting with their direct reports. At this stage, what is required is to be a personal mentor and coach for each direct report, so entrepreneurs must learn to maintain high accountability for results while at the same time serving as a trusted advisor, helping the direct reports deal with their leadership challenges. This mentoring role requires a deeper emotional engagement characterized by emotional vulnerability and honesty in order to ensure the trust of the developing manager, and his or her belief that the mentor truly has the manager's best interests at heart. The quandary here is that although developing a trusted mentoring relationship is important, it is complicated by the fact that the entrepreneur mentor can fire the mentee. The entrepreneur has to continue to do what is right for the business. Understanding and acknowledging this tension is critical to an effective coaching relationship.

One entrepreneur told me that he thinks many companies quit growing not because of the challenges of financing growth but because entrepreneurs often lack the interest and skills needed to address employees' personal needs and tire of mentoring members of the management team. He stated, "No one told me I'd be more a psychologist than a businessman!"

Evolution to a coaching and mentoring role requires the entrepreneur to move toward becoming a leader whose mission is to help others to be all they can be. As an entrepreneur told me, "When I started four years ago, I did everything. Literally, I touched it, did it, wrote it, fixed it. And now I do nothing like that. Today I have to learn how to be the CEO of a 65-person organization." To do this he spends every Monday and Tuesday in meetings with his direct reports individually and, when needed, as a group. In addition, he noted, "I have to constantly educate myself and reinvent myself to keep up with the business."

Jeff Bowling of The Delta Companies talked about coaching this way:

> My challenge as a leader was to transform away from performance management and metrics management to this more intangible thing of *leadership*, trying to increase people's capacities, or else they've got to "get off the bus," to quote Jim Collins.

From Specialist to General Manager Back to Specialist

Another transition an entrepreneur makes as the business grows is related to what business functional areas (sales, marketing, finance, human resources, or operations) the entrepreneur opts to focus on. During the start-up phase, infancy, and adolescent stages of business growth, the solo entrepreneur acted as a general manager involved in all functional areas whether or not he or she had experience in those areas. Why? Out of necessity. When more than one entrepreneur was involved in the start-up, they may or may not have overlapped in the tasks they performed. In either case, as the business grows and good management teams are built, many entrepreneurs can choose to spend more time in the functional area they enjoy in addition to their leadership role. The trajectory for those entrepreneurs is from specialist to generalist and back to specialist over the different business growth phases. This transition back to specialist generally happens after the "doer to manager" and "manager to leader" transitions. As the business growth continues, the entrepreneur either evolves into a coach and mentor, focuses on strategy, or installs someone else in that role and returns to being a specialist in the functional area he or she excels in.

From Me to Them

Related to these transitions is another major transition that happens with some entrepreneurs as their business grows. They find a new meaning in the business other than financial reward. For many entrepreneurs, growth for financial gain is no longer reason enough to deal with the challenges of continuing to grow. They find a new meaning in coming to work every day. They either focus on culture, being a builder of leaders—giving employees opportunities and education so they can be and do more, or they align the business with a community or charitable mission. Such examples can be found in the "Defender Direct, Inc.: A Business of Growing Leaders," "Mellace Family Brands, Inc.: Building a Socially Responsible Enterprise," "Trilogy

Health Services, LLC: Building a Great Service Company," "Room & Board," and "Leaders Bank: Creating a Great Place to Work" cases.

As an example, Dave Lindsey of Defender Direct described his personal transition this way:

> It's been a humbling learning [experience] for me as a business owner. It's not about having a better plan or a widget. It's about helping your employees, because every time they grow, I grow. And that's what keeps me going, that's my calling in life—to build and develop leaders. . . . We don't want to be in the business of buying and selling businesses. We want to be in the business of growing and developing leaders. We have a platform to do that. So that's what my goal is.

Voluntarily Stepping Aside as CEO

In a few businesses in my study, the entrepreneur realized that he or she did not have either the skills or the emotional makeup to take the business to the next level of growth. In all those cases they brought in an outsider to run the company. The entrepreneur then either became the CEO in name only, returning to working as a functional specialist, or became the chairman/CEO with a president or chief operating officer reporting to him or her. The latter occurred in about 15% of the companies studied.

Defender Direct, Inc.

Defender Direct is a good example of how an entrepreneur grew as his company grew. As you read the "Defender Direct, Inc.: A Business of Growing Leaders" case, focus on how Dave Lindsey's role changed as the company grew and how he evolved as a leader.

CASE DISCUSSION QUESTIONS

1. What do you think Dave means when he states, "Businesses don't grow—people do"?
2. What do you think Dave means when he states, "Build a culture on purpose, not by accident"?
3. Why did Dave want to build a business that could be "McDonaldized"?
4. Explain how Defender's business model of simplicity was scalable.
5. What is the "Circle of Life"? Why is it important?
6. How did Dave evolve his business model?
7. "Businesses don't grow—people do." How did Dave grow? How did Dave's growth enable the business to grow?
8. What do you think Dave meant when he said, "Focus Equals Growth"?

CASE
STUDY

DEFENDER DIRECT, INC.: A BUSINESS OF GROWING LEADERS

Defender Direct, Inc. (Defender), headquartered in Indianapolis, Indiana, was a privately held company that sold and installed ADT security systems and Dish Network Satellite TV to homeowners in the United States. President and Chief Executive Officer (CEO) Dave Lindsey started the business out of his home in 1998, making the transition to entrepreneur from new-product development at Medeco Security Locks, Inc. He used $30,000 of his and his wife's personal savings to fund the start-up, which he called Defender Security Co.

From its humble beginnings in the Lindseys' spare bedroom, Defender became one of the largest security and satellite dealers in the Midwest, experiencing an average annual growth rate of 60% over 10 years. In 2008, Defender generated $150 million in revenues and ranked 387th on the *Inc.* 500 list of America's Fastest-Growing Companies. With 1,500 employees, the company had a national footprint of 120 offices in 40 states.

Defender's stellar growth was fueled by an aggressive direct-marketing focus and national expansion, but Lindsey, who was fond of saying that "businesses don't grow—people do," credited the Defender culture, which fostered continuous employee development. He elaborated:

Defender has grown faster than its peers not because we are better at selling and installing security systems but because our people have grown. Our sales have doubled because the capacity and talents of our leaders have doubled. A few years ago, we stopped trying to double our business and realized the way to grow was to double our team members' enthusiasm, optimism, and skills. Send people to seminars, leadership conferences, and self-help programs. Build a culture on purpose, not by accident.[1]

The Founder

Lindsey was born in 1969 and grew up in the Midwest. He graduated with honors from Indiana University with a BS degree in Business Finance and an MBA in Marketing and Finance. After graduation, he worked for various companies in the lock and door hardware industry and became interested in security systems. A turning point for Lindsey came when he was passed over for a promotion while working for Medeco Security Locks, Inc., in Salem, Virginia. "We're going to start a business," he said to his wife, "because I don't want to ever be in this spot again, where it's office politics controlling my career."

Case Study UVA-ENT-0115 © 2009 by the University of Virginia Darden School Foundation. This case was prepared by Senior Researcher Gosia Glinska and Edward D. Hess as a basis for class discussion rather than to illustrate effective or ineffective handling of an administrative situation.

1. "Defender Security Co." *Indianapolis Business Journal*, September 15, 2003.

At Medeco, Lindsey had been involved in a program called Medeco Business Advantage—a 2X Strategy to Grow Your Business, a set of business processes inspired by Michael Gerber's best-selling book *The E-Myth: Why Most Businesses Don't Work and What to Do About It*. According to Lindsey, "It was a way for a mostly traditional type of locksmith to double their business, using the 2X process and then up-selling. We would teach it to our locksmith dealers, and I saw it work and decided, 'I've always wanted to own my own business, why not buy a locksmith shop, double it, and create value?'"

Opportunity Knocks

Lindsey and his wife started looking for a locksmith business to buy, but after finding none at a price they were willing to pay, they moved to Indianapolis. "That's where my family was and my support structure, and where I really wanted to be permanently," said Lindsey. He reflected on his days as a freelance locksmith:

I began changing locks and installing deadbolts, which was pretty horrible because every psychological test I've ever taken says that me and a power drill should stay as far apart as possible. I have some great stories about taking out my friends' locks and not being able to put them back on. . . . So that's how I began, pretty ugly, and my intention was to never do installation, because I'm not technical. But I had to get out and learn.

While his wife took over the role of a family breadwinner, Lindsey researched the security industry. "I was, like, if someone needs a lock, maybe they want an alarm system? And in the mid-90s the alarm industry really exploded." Lindsey jumped at the opportunity when ADT Security Systems and other brands began offering $99 start-up packages for homeowners, making home-security systems more affordable to a wide group of consumers. "We wrote a business plan, got ADT to take a chance on us, and began as an ADT Authorized Dealer. We never looked back. I never did another lock job once we signed our ADT contract."

Learning the Ropes

For his first three months as an ADT Authorized Dealer, Lindsey focused on meeting the sales quota. Failure to sell 15 systems per month not only could lead to problems for the business but also could result in a financial penalty, which would have swallowed much of the Lindseys' start-up capital. A devotee of the principles Gerber laid out in *The E-Myth*, Lindsey said he "was looking for that Gerber-type of repeatable system, something that could be McDonaldized."

Lindsey took advantage of a sales-training program offered by ADT. "The Dealer Program I came into was 90% door-to-door sales," he said. "ADT was teaching us to knock on doors. They threw me in a van with a bunch of other guys and put me on the street, and I'd sell ADT systems door-to-door."

The day that Lindsey, who had never sold an ADT system before, made his first sale within a couple of hours, he "saw it work." He immediately called his wife to tell her he was going to buy a 15-passenger van. He recalled:

I had seen a repeatable process, which involved a van; when you go door-to-door you have to have that team environment—when you drive together in one car, you've got to pick the people up so they can't leave, until they get a sale. When everybody drives individually, they end up getting back in their cars and leaving.

During the first month of knocking on doors, Lindsey sold six security systems and fifteen during the second month, with the help of a friend. It was cause for celebration because they had met ADT's monthly quota. The third month was even better; with first hires onboard, Lindsey and his team sold 30 systems.

The ADT Sales Contest

By September 1998, Lindsey had assembled a team of 10 salespeople. "I really wanted to start the team out with a bang," he said. "I needed a catalyst, a point of focus." ADT's sales contest with its $15,000 prize was exactly what Lindsey needed to fire up his team. "Each dealer's quota was based on the previous three months' sales," he said. "I believed we had a great opportunity to win since our previous three months' quota would be only 17 units." The team launched a sales blitzkrieg. As Lindsey recalled:

My living room was converted into our Sales Meeting War Room. My artwork was covered up with a makeshift sales board, and my entertainment center became an employee mailbox system. Administrative paperwork was handled from my back bedroom, complete with a board stretched out on the bed to form a desk, a computer, and a borrowed fax machine. Side meetings and training sessions were held on the front lawn. We were entrepreneurs, making the rules up as we went. We had no fear and knew we had a great product and wanted to meet as many people as possible. We went out together each day, feeding off each other's energy.[2]

One day in mid-September, while his sales team was gathered in his living-room, Lindsey went to the back bedroom to call ADT's headquarters to find out how his team ranked among other ADT Authorized Dealers. His surprise turned to shock when he learned that, as a new ADT Authorized Dealer, Defender had its sales quota increased from 17 to 45. Shaken, Lindsey weighed his options.

What happened next was what Lindsey referred to as "an inflection point in the company" and "the moment of truth" for him as a leader. He took a few minutes to compose himself and went back to the living room to face his sales team. He candidly related the news about the quota and then spent a few minutes rallying his troops. "We're going to blow through this," he said.

---

2. Excerpted from the Defender Direct Web site.

With 45 sales already under its belt and two more weeks to go, Defender still had a shot at winning the contest. "We took it up a notch or two during those last two weeks and worked long hard days," Lindsey said. Defender's installation crew tripled its capacity to make sure every system Defender sold got installed the next day. By the end of September, with 142 systems sold and installed, Lindsey's sales team was 316% above its quota and 835% above its three-month historical average.[3]

In snatching the top prize in the sales contest, the upstart company had defeated hundreds of other ADT Authorized Dealers from across the United States. "September was crazy," Lindsey said. "After four months of knocking on doors, we had a system, and we knew what we were doing. Soon after, we sold 200, 300 systems, and we ran pretty quickly to the 600 range a month. And it kind of skyrocketed from there."

The Entrepreneurial Mindset

During its first few months of operation, Defender subcontracted all systems' installations. "You know the old adage, nothing happens until a sale happens," Lindsey said. "So we focused on creating demand." In September, when sales numbered 142 systems, however, Lindsey hired his first installation technician. At the beginning, Defender hired technicians with minimal industry experience, who were able to handle a wireless alarm system that was relatively easy to install.

At approximately the same time, Lindsey hired his first sales manager, who took over driving the van with the sales team, freeing up Lindsey to "get the paperwork done to support this," as he put it. "I was able to stop and go back and put some processes in place." He reflected on the early building of the business:

We kept in mind Gerber's three roles in a business: the entrepreneur's job is to create the process, the manager's job is to assure the process is used, and the technician's job is to follow the process and use it. And that has dominated my thoughts for the past 10 years. Every time we're trying to grow something, we are very clear about who is playing these roles, and we make sure somebody's doing each of these. In the beginning, I played all those different roles, but I was conscious that I was ultimately the entrepreneur, and for the first three our four years all I did was build processes.

Thinking Big—With a Clear Focus

In November 1998, Defender opened a second office and sold 125 systems the first month. Lindsey's sales team pledged to open a new office every 90 days, and Defender ended its first year of operation with four offices. As Lindsey said, "We lived, and still do, by Gerber's tenet—'big business is just a small business that thought big.'

---

3. Defender Direct Web site.

And we wanted to be much bigger. In those days we'd always remind ourselves that it's not okay to put a mom-and-pop system in place, because that's just going to keep us small forever."

Looking for ways to grow his business, Lindsey considered expanding into the commercial security market, but after some thought, he decided that the residential market would be Defender's staple. "We weren't so much a security company as a home market and installation company," Lindsey said. "We found another product that could be marketed in a mass way and be installed in homes."[4] That product was satellite TV, which Defender added to its offerings in 2001 and with it quickly became one of the top Dish Network dealers.

Since making the decision to concentrate on the residential market, Lindsey stayed on course and steered his company away from potential distractions. "We have a saying posted all over our offices—Focus Equals Growth." He elaborated:

Today we still only have 13 part numbers in our inventory room, the same 13 we had 10 years ago. We have not added things. We keep doing more of the same better, trying to McDonaldize it. We understood focus as the goal early on, constantly using an ABC format to prioritize. I coach all of our new leaders, "We don't pay you to get everything done—we pay you to get the most important things done."

Defender's "Hedgehog Statement"

For help in knowing on what to focus each day, Defender employees turned to what the company called its hedgehog statement—"We are best in the world at customer acquisition for top brand-name products and services that target homeowners."[5] The Hedgehog Concept was one of the principles of greatness outlined in Jim Collins's 2001 best-seller *Good to Great.*[6] As Collins's research indicated, great companies refused to do anything that did not fit with their Hedgehog Concept, and they made as much use of stop-doing lists as to-do lists.

Lindsey cited Collins as one of his biggest influences and made his employees read his book; they even read whole chapters out loud in the office. Having spent five years discovering its hedgehog concept, Defender leadership used it as a frame of reference for all its decisions. As Lindsey said, "We really pride ourselves not on our to-do list but on our not-to-do list. And we have found that the more we say 'no' to things, the more we grow."

---

4. Terri Greenwell, "*IBJ*'s Fastest Growing Companies," *Indianapolis Business Journal,* September 17, 2007.

5. Defender Direct Web site.

6. Jim Collins, *Good to Great: Why Some Companies Make the Leap . . . and Others Don't* (New York: Harper-Business, 2001).

Defender's "Circle of Life"

Another practical tool, which Lindsey and his leadership team used on a weekly basis, was the so-called Circle of Life (Exhibit 5.1). It was a visual representation of their understanding of how the business worked. "Imagine a clock face," Lindsey said. "Twelve o'clock is marketing, three o'clock is sales, six o'clock is installation, and nine o'clock is admin and finance. It used to be just sales, door-to-door, but it all starts with marketing. So I spent my energy on really ramping it up over the last five years."

Whenever Lindsey noticed a bottleneck in any of the four areas of the circle of life, he would focus his full attention on that particular spot to alleviate the bottleneck. He elaborated:

First, I'd work with marketing until we had enough leads. But we didn't have enough sales-people, so I'd jump over to sales, and make sure we closed all the leads until we didn't have enough technicians. Then, I'd go down to installation and make sure we're getting all the systems installed, and it would flow back up, and then we'd have a paperwork backup, so I'd make sure ADT was paying us. And then as soon as that is all released, we say that the money flows around that. Marketing takes a dollar and starts at 12 o'clock, and you hope that two dollars come up when you spin around the circle. So then I'd go back to marketing and say, "Okay, we've got some more marketing programs: let's go." And I just kept running around that circle. The faster you spin the circle, the faster we grow.

I've had my direct reports say to me, "You're focusing on my part of the circle right now. You've been to my office every day this week," and I'm, "Yeah, I'm going to be in your part of the circle until our install rate or our backlog is down." Today, I'm backing up from that a little bit as I'm changing my role.

To keep a close eye on his business's financial performance, Lindsey used a score-card, which he had introduced a year after starting Defender. "It's a concise Excel spreadsheet," said Lindsey, "with weeks' and months' worth of history and then this week's numbers, like, what's the close rate? We want to get that scorecard more auto-mated, and we want that to be a live dashboard." Lindsey held weekly Friday meetings with his direct reports, during which they thoroughly reviewed all metrics on the scorecard. The meetings started in the afternoon and lasted more than four hours.

Financing Growth

All entrepreneurs know that funding growth is an expensive proposition and that access to capital is one of the biggest challenges facing start-ups. Defender had an advantage in that area because of its business model, which involved acquiring new customers and then "selling" them to ADT and Dish. "They cash us out up-front," said Lindsey. "We sell the contract, which is a three-year agreement that has a value, just like a bank sells a loan. It has always kept us cash rich, and we've been able to fund all this growth without any debt." In addition, Defender pulled in regular revenue from installation and monthly monitoring services.

But the company experienced its share of bumps in the road. About a year into his entrepreneurial journey, Lindsey struggled to make payroll. At a family dinner, he wanted to forget about work but could not stop thinking about it. "I remember my dad and I made eye contact," Lindsey said. "I just broke down crying, telling him how stressed out I was. So that's early on, just cash flow and understanding. You've got all these people believing in you, and you're trying to have that initial confidence just to get the ball to roll." Lindsey elaborated:

It got really ugly, and that led us to getting into Dish Network Satellite TV in addition to ADT. So, luckily, things righted there. But that was huge; we had one year of negative growth in 10 years, and that was that year. It was really just about holding things together. I remember I had everybody in the company on speakerphones, giving them a speech, "We're going to get through this, and these are the three or four things we're going to do." That was probably the biggest time I felt like a general of an army.

The Evolution of the Business Model

For the first three years, Defender's sales force consisted of "full-commission door-knockers," as Lindsey put it. "It was a great way to start, because there's no marketing, and you're only paying someone when the sale is made. Then we realized we could set appointments instead of knocking on doors, and we became 100% telemarketing-based."

Around the time Defender was transitioning to telemarketing, an acquaintance of Lindsey's introduced him to Marcia Raab, owner of a small call center in Indiana. Defender soon became Raab's exclusive customer. "She did a great job, was such a servant to our business—she really did it at an exchange rate with us," said Lindsey. "Terrific marketing and sales person. She grew the 20-person call center to 200 people in two centers, and she owned that."

Defender eventually bought Raab's call centers, and Raab became Defender's vice president of sales and marketing. "She was an absolute dynamo," said Lindsey. "She started coming to our staff meetings, when she was our outsource partner with her own call centers, which she ran like a division of ours. And then we formalized it and put her in the VP spot."

The telemarketing operation had to be scrapped in 2001, with the introduction of the "no-call list hit," as Lindsey named it, which allowed consumers to put a stop to unwanted telemarketing pitches. "So, we reinvented the business for the third time,"

Lindsey said. "Now it's 100% direct mail and the Internet, so our call centers handle only incoming calls."

Defender's call center kept growing, reaching more than 400 sales and customer-service agents in five contact centers located in Indiana and Ohio. The sales agents handled inbound calls from potential customers, who responded to Defender's newspaper ads, pitches on the Internet, or direct-mail offers, while customer-service agents handled the calls from existing customers seeking support. "The inbound agents who are taking calls from prospective customers are paid minimum wage plus heavy commission," said Lindsey. "And with those people we have a fairly high turnover. You have to hire four or five to get one who's good."

Lindsey's Biggest Challenges

From the time Lindsey launched his own business, he had been challenged to continually evolve his relationship with the company, transforming himself from a door-to-door salesman to sales manager to controller to regional manager to president and CEO in 10 years. As he reflected on his changing role,

My biggest struggle has been constantly reinventing my relationship to the business. You go from a business that's in an extra bedroom to 200 employees nationwide, $150 million in sales, and that is a huge challenge in itself, both in terms of process, skill, and psychologically. Every year I say to my wife that I have to reinvent my relationship to the business. It started with hiring the first sales manager to go take these guys to knock on doors for me, to then jumping to be an admin lead and putting someone else in my place. I feel like I kept filling a hole and then leaving somebody behind. Then taking it from being in Indianapolis to being a regional presence and all the skills it takes. And today I'm evolving even more into being—I think of it as a chairman, a shareholder, investor, as well as business strategy and new products.

Managing People

As Lindsey's relationship to his business evolved, so did his management philosophy. At first, he found it hard to delegate. "It was hard to release control," he admitted. "At one time I thought I could do it better than anybody else. All it took was to hire a couple of people and understand they could do it better than me."

After six months of driving a van with his door-to-door sales team, Lindsey found a sales manager he trusted who eventually became the number one ADT sales rep in the country and rose through the ranks to become vice president of sales. Similarly, the first installation technician Lindsey hired grew to become Defender's vice president of installation. When Defender was generating $20 million in revenue, he was in charge of installation for the whole company. "When the job started to outstrip him, he was put into a regional role, which was still almost a $10 million region," said

Lindsey. "I always say to people whose jobs outstrip them, 'You still have the same level of responsibility or more.'"

As a manager who never had much tolerance for mistakes, Lindsey described himself as a proponent of tough love. "I kind of manage with a Bobby Knight–type[7] of mentality with my direct reports," Lindsey said. "I've always said I need people with thick skin who themselves do not tolerate mistakes."

By 2008, Lindsey had four direct reports: chief operations officer (COO), chief marketing officer (CMO), chief information officer (CIO), and chief financial officer (CFO).

COO John Corliss, whom Lindsey had met at Medeco, came onboard in January 2006 as Defender's CFO, a position he held for a year. As the COO, Corliss was responsible for the company's customer service, human resources, and installations departments. Installations included all field installation technicians, who were full-time Defender employees working in 120 installation locations around the country. In 2008, Lindsey made him partner in the business.

Marcia Raab, a Defender employee since 2001, was promoted from vice president of sales and marketing to CMO and in 2008 became a partner. She was responsible for managing the planning and purchasing of all Defender marketing programs as well as overseeing the operations of Defender call centers. Lindsey said, "Marcia is the drumbeat of the organization, and as fast as she beats that drum, the rest of us dance."

Bart Shroyer, the CFO, came onboard in 2007. He was responsible for all accounting, funding, and financial management for Defender. Shroyer, who had a breakout year in 2008, was made partner in 2009.

Gregg Albacete, the CIO, joined Defender in 2007. He was responsible for building and maintaining systems, databases, and the IT infrastructure that supported and extended Defender's business model.

Finding the Right CFO

Among the many challenges Lindsey faced while growing his business, one of the toughest was filling the CFO position. At first, Lindsey "gave a box of receipts to an accountant," as he described it, but nine months into his contract with ADT, Lindsey's wife took over the accounting function of the business. A few months later, with the help of QuickBooks accounting software, Lindsey said, "She came on full-blown," and continued in the CFO role for five years, until the arrival of the Lindseys' third child, when she became a full-time stay-at-home mom. Then, her assistant, who "grew up in the business," took over.

---

7. Bobby Knight, the coach with the most career wins in men's collegiate basketball history, led the Indiana University men's basketball team to three NCAA championships between 1971 and 2000.

Lindsey admitted that he has had "four to five people" in the CFO position since he started Defender. "It was the hardest job to fill," he said. He elaborated:

Our average growth rate was 60% a year for the last 10 years. So you hire a bookkeeper, then you need an accountant, and then you need a controller. I didn't shoot far enough ahead. The problem was, when I tried to shoot ahead, I got real schmoheads. CFOs are all by nature pretty conservative people. They are sharp guys, not looking for a $10 million business to work in. The only person who wants to be CFO in a $10 million business says, "Well, I'll just start my own business. I'm not going to work for this guy, take on his risk." So I got a couple of screwballs, who didn't seem that way when I interviewed them. Once we got to $50 million plus, it was a lot easier to attract people.

Defender's Culture

Lindsey attributed Defender's success to its culture, which he built around each employee's personal growth. Describing it further, he said, "Another word is 'terrific.' We talk about being terrific every day, and we choose to be that way."

Lindsey was continuously learning and growing, and he encouraged his employees to do the same, sending them to various self-improvement seminars, such as Dale Carnegie Training and Ed Foreman's Successful Life Course. "We coined a saying, 'Businesses don't grow—people do,'" said Lindsey. "I don't want this to become a cliché around Defender because it's been our secret sauce. All of us had to grow. We've accomplished this reinvention through good books and good tapes and networking with good people" (Exhibit 5.2).

Over the course of 10 years, Lindsey reinvented Defender's business model three times, reinvented himself and his role, but, most important, he redefined the purpose of his business, which had evolved from making money to growing people. "Our growth plan is that you have to reinvent yourself this year," Lindsey told 1,500 Defender employees at its annual Self-Improvement Day, held in April in Indianapolis. This companywide commitment to personal growth and continuous reinvention was the linchpin of Defender's corporate culture, and Self-Improvement Day provided an opportunity for reaffirmation every year.

Lindsey was particularly proud of Defender Advantage, the company's four-year initiation program into the Defender culture, during which employees received leadership training, participated in the company's book club, and traveled with their families on mission trips abroad to work as volunteers.[8] In addition, newly hired installation technicians attended Defender University, a complete training program that prepared them to be successful in the field. Part of the Defender University's curriculum was Corporate Culture Day, during which all new hires listened to Defender's

---

8. *Inc.* 500/5000 Fastest-Growing Private Companies in America, 2008, Defender Direct, Inc.

senior managers, including Lindsey, via satellite. The main purpose of Culture Day was to drive the following message: "We are asking you to work harder on yourself than on your job." On Culture Day all new hires were also given the Defender Leadership Advantage Board, which charted the path of their growth (Exhibit 5.3).

Besides focus and drive, Lindsey listed forgiveness as one of his greatest strengths as a leader. As he told his staff, he believed that their "ability to forgive each other really built a culture around here. It's the glue that allows us to stay at this breakneck speed." Lindsey, who described himself as a "student of leadership," stressed that his "basic belief in forgiveness comes from [his] Faith and having learned from Jesus, who was a servant leader." Still, when reflecting on his entrepreneurial journey, Lindsey always emphasized the lesson of continuous employee development:

It's been a humbling learning [experience] for me as a business owner. It's not about having a better plan or a widget. It's about helping your employees, because every time they grow, I grow. And that's what keeps me going, that's my calling in life—to build and develop leaders. . . . We don't want to be in the business of buying and selling businesses. We want to be in the business of growing and developing leaders. We have a platform to do that. So that's what my goal is.

Exhibit 5.1   Defender's Circle of Life

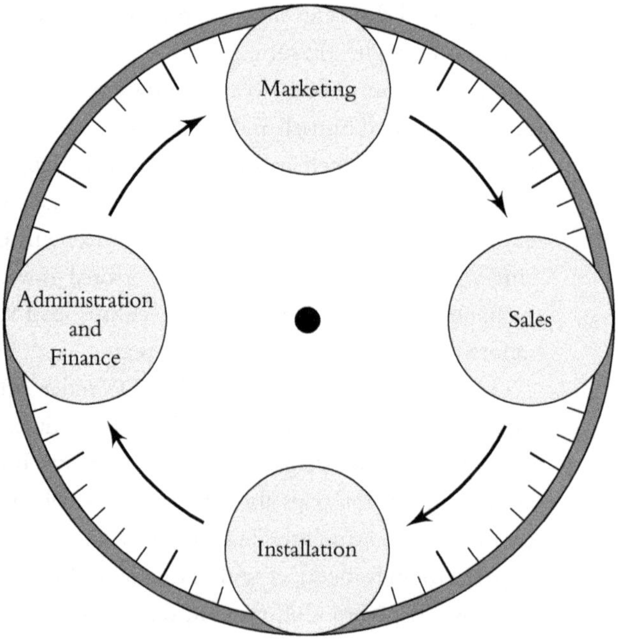

SOURCE: Courtesy of Defender Direct.

Exhibit 5.2   Defender's Culture

At *Defender Direct, we are about being the best!* We have founded ourselves on the principle that we can be the best in the world at customer acquisition for top brand-name products and services that target homeowners. It doesn't stop there. It has infiltrated throughout our entire company.

We have the best employees! We have the kind of employees that are constantly working on themselves and building themselves into leaders. At Defender Direct, you will find people that are always striving to set and meet new goals. That is why we are always promoting people from within. Our four passions act as a roadmap for making our people the best they can be, and they really take it to heart.

We work with the best products! As a Dish Network dealer, we are one of the top-five dealers in the country. For ADT, we are also a top dealer. How do we do that? By working with the best products in the industry and products we believe in. Our employees are some of our best customers! At Defender Direct, customers will find that we do our best so we can be the best! We strive for excellence and that is what customers get each time.

Defender Direct is the best in the world at customer acquisition for top brand-name products and services that target homeowners

Rewards and Recognition

- *Annual Superstar Celebration.* Every year we celebrate our employees' accomplishments by taking them on an annual trip. For 2008, we took 278 employees and their guests to Cancun, Mexico. Past trips have included trips to Jamaica and the Bahamas. Our superstars are what make us what we are, and we want to celebrate that with a trip that lets them know how much we appreciate their dedication and commitment to achieving their goals.
- *Defender Family Day.* Each Labor Day, we invite our employees and their families to spend time with us for some fun and sun, our treat! Past events have taken us to Indiana Beach and Six Flags Kentucky Kingdom. It's a great way to celebrate the last hurray of summer.
- *Sales Contests.* We understand that our sales team is a key driver for our success. We have weekly contests and awards for our sales team to keep them working on hitting and breaking new records. This year we even gave away a car!
- This is just a small list of the many things we do to reward and recognize our employees' dedication and hard work. We are always coming up with new ways to reward them for all they contribute. We put this as a high priority on our to-do list.

Training

- Every technician we hire attends Defender University, a complete training program that gets them ready to be successful in the field. We have had some of the top techs in the industry come out of Defender University, and we continue to expand the size of our classes every month.
- We are always looking for opportunities to send our employees to training and seminars, so that they are continuously developing and working on themselves. Programs include the Dale Carnegie Training Program, Ed Foreman's Successful Life Course, and much more. We believe in self-improvement, and we are always looking for ways to help employees do just that.

Additional Perks

- Extensive library with books from great authors such as John Maxwell, Jim Collins, and Jack Welch.
- Corporate-sponsored Weight Watchers program to help employees achieve personal weight-loss goals.
- Corporate chaplains
- Much More!

SOURCE: Adapted by the case authors from the company Web site.

Exhibit 5.3   Defender Leadership Advantage Board

SOURCE: Courtesy of Defender Direct.

List of Relevant Cases

Better World Books

Defender Direct, Inc.: A Business of Growing Leaders

Edens & Avant

Global Medical Imaging, LLC

Jeff Bowling at the Delta Companies: From Baseball Coach to CEO

LG Investments, LLC: A Family Business in Generational Transition (A)

LG Investments, LLC: A Family Business in Generational Transition (B)

LG Investments, LLC: A Family Business in Generational Transition (C)

LG Investments, LLC: A Family Business in Generational Transition (D)

Room & Board

Students Helping Honduras

Author's Commentaries

The following commentaries evolved from my consulting work and a course I designed and taught at Goizueta Business School at Emory University, titled "Entrepreneurial Leadership."

"Silver Bullet of Leadership"[9]

Leadership is part science and part art. Leadership is subjective, emotional and yes, hard work. There are over 200 definitions of leadership and various models of leadership: traits or personality; situational or context; Level V; transformational; authentic; and servant leadership.

Leadership is the convergence of heart, soul, intellect, and action. Leadership is the result of what you believe, value, and do. Authentic leadership happens when there is harmony among what you value, what you think, and what you do. Those actions must be for good and moral objectives.

We know that size, looks, gender, nationality, pedigree, ethnicity, and charisma do not either qualify or disqualify one from being a leader.

Leadership skills (listening, writing, speaking, empathizing, and self-discipline) can be learned. But what really matters is what is in your heart:

- YOUR CHARACTER;
- YOUR VALUES; and
- YOUR ATTITUDE.

And how you express them, through your actions, counts!

Learning to be a Good Leader is a life-long pursuit. You will get better as you

1. Experience life;
2. Lead and learn;
3. Become emotionally more aware and secure;
4. Learn not to focus on "me"; and
5. Truly adopt a servant-leadership approach.

What precludes you from being a good leader?

- Laziness;
- Arrogance;
- Lack of self-discipline; and
- The wrong focus, attitude, motivations, or value.

Good leadership is a constant, ongoing battle—inside a leader—between

- Selfishness ("me") vs. Altruism;
- Self-absorption vs. Emotional Maturity;
- Insensitivity vs. Sensitivity;
- Laziness vs. Disciplined work;

---

9. Edward D. Hess, "Silver Bullet of Leadership," *The Catalyst*, November 2004.

- Insecurity vs. Confidence;
- Arrogance vs. Humility;
- Charisma vs. Authenticity;
- My Way vs. Accepting Other Ways; and
- Group Think vs. Intellectual Honesty and Debate.

Unfortunately, most people want to be leaders because of what leadership brings to them:

- More pay;
- More power;
- More prestige and status; and
- More opportunity.

Unfortunately, great leadership is not about what you get—it is about what you GIVE! Leadership is not about what you take—it is about what you give.

LEADERSHIP IS NOT ABOUT YOU!

LEADERSHIP IS ABOUT THEM!

LEADERSHIP IS NOT ABOUT WHAT IS IN IT FOR YOU!

LEADERSHIP IS ABOUT HOW YOU CAN HELP THEM!

You see—the Silver Bullet of Leadership is YOU!

And only you can approach leadership with the right mindset, the right attitude, the right motivations, and yes, the right values. I submit that you can be a good manager while focused on yourself, but you cannot be a good leader.

Leaders serve! Good luck on your leadership journey. And thank you for reading my commentaries over the past two years.

"What Do Good Leaders Actually Do? (Part I)"[10]

Leadership is what business people talk about. Leadership is what academics write about. But, in my not so humble opinion, there is too much focus on leadership theory and not enough focus on actually leading. What do good leaders actually do?

There are over 200 definitions of leadership. Modern theories of leadership include traits, transformational, situational, adaptive, motivational, spiritual, and servant leadership. Major leadership centers include the James MacGregor Burns Academy of Leadership, the Jepson School of Leadership, The Kravis Leadership Center, The Center for Creative Leadership, and The U.S. Army Center for Leadership.

---

10. Edward D. Hess, "What Do Good Leaders Actually Do? (Part I)," *The Catalyst*, September 2003.

Leadership theory is based on economics, psychology, sociology, ethics, philosophy, and religion. But leading is doing. Leading is acting. To lead effectively, leaders need (1) the right attitude; (2) a heightened sensitization to the impact of their actions and inactions; and (3) to manage the daily details of leading. If your objective is to lead, you need to prepare to lead, plan daily to lead, and then do it.

I. The Right Attitude

What kind of attitude do you need to lead? I believe attitude is dependent on your motivation. Why do you want to lead? Most people want to lead for the wrong reasons. Most people want to lead because leadership translates into more pay, more status, and more perks. People who lead for those reasons probably will be focused on keeping their job—not on leading and helping others. Leaders who lead for the wrong reasons may be less open, less honest, and less trustworthy than leaders who lead for the right reasons. Think about it—how would you react to a leader, boss, or manager who said, "I am here for myself. I need your help so I can keep my job and make more money than you do." Or, "My main motivation is me—my advancement and my job."

What is the right attitude? What are the right values? One should want to lead or one is chosen to lead because the expectation is that you will act in others' best interests so as to make a meaningful contribution to the achievement of your organization and your followers' goals. Leaders help organizations and employees find meaning in accomplishing something that is important to them. Leaders help. Leaders serve. Leaders coach. Leaders mentor. Leaders teach. And leaders think about, plan, and prepare to do this through hundreds of little daily acts, all of which when taken together constitute leadership.

The right attitude is not a "me" or an "I" attitude. It is a "you" attitude. I want to lead because I want to help you achieve. I want to lead because I believe I can make a positive contribution to this company.

Many leaders get promoted to leadership positions because of outstanding past performance. Many are not prepared to lead. Many are not trained to lead. Many are not emotionally ready to lead. Figuring out whether you truly have the right attitude is work—thinking about yourself, your motivations, and your reasons for wanting or accepting a leadership position. This is not psychobabble. I submit that good, effective leaders have the right attitude. They are focused on their people for whom they are responsible—not themselves. Good leaders get the right attitude every day. Eventually, it becomes part of them and second nature.

II. Sensitization to Your Impact

Followers are very observant of leaders. Followers notice and react to your tone, your moods, your intended and unintended messages evidenced by what you do, what you do not do, what you say, what you leave unsaid, your smiles, your frowns, etc. Followers have expectations about leaders from how they should dress to what kind of role model you should be.

Being a leader is like being on stage all the time. Good leaders understand and accept this responsibility. They understand that their every word and act has impact. Leaders understand that followers look for cues and meaning, and evaluate them for consistency, reliability, and trustworthiness. Your employees notice how you treat the waitress at lunch, how you speak about former employees, how you treat your spouse, what kind of jokes you allow, and how you react to bad news. Employees are also sensitive about how you respect them and their time.

One personal example: In one of my prior leadership positions, I was consumed one morning with a business problem. As I was walking down the hall, I noticed a bright young employee. I saw him but being self-absorbed and consumed by my problem, I did not speak to him; I just nodded. An hour later his supervisor came to see me—panicked. This young star—an "A" player—took my silence as evidence that I—the boss—did not like him. So he needed to start looking for a job. Wow, an unintended, very bad message resulting from my lack of sensitization and my lack of focus on my people.

III. Leaders Manage Themselves—The Daily Details of Leading

Good leaders know that being a leader takes preparation every day and that it does not come naturally to most people. You have to work at leading. Leading is an active process. You do not just do it. It doesn't just happen. You have to actively engage yourself in thinking about leading—the what you will do—when—and with whom.

Good leaders focus daily on key objectives and values and on what people, teams, or functions need the leader's input—the who, what, why, and where. Leaders are constantly processing information and reassessing where their focus is needed. Who needs help? Who is on target? Who is behind? Why? Who needs be to "hugged"? Who needs to be "kicked in the butt"? Who needs a thank you? Leaders survey their operations and spend time daily on those people, products, and customers where they can make a positive impact.

Good leaders think about how people react to them and seek better ways to make their points clearer and more direct. Leaders live leading. Leaders work at it until they get it right. Leaders are engaged in the process of leading and understand that leading is more than image, style, or charisma. Leading is the little actions—the details—the what you do from the moment you get to work to the moment you leave work.

Leaders stay focused on their most important goal or objective:

"How Can I Make a Positive Impact Here?"

Leaders see mistakes, problems, or issues not as negatives, but as opportunities—opportunities to make a positive contribution—opportunities to teach, to help, to mentor, and to lead. Leaders also seek out opportunities to make their points—to emphasize key values—to emphasize over and over again what is important. Leaders focus on and manage the daily details of leading. Leading is acting. It takes preparation, planning, and thinking about the who and the what you need to focus on and the why. Leaders plan what they need to say, to which people, when, and why.

Conclusion

Leading is an art—not a science because it involves people. People with emotions, fears, hopes, dreams, jealousies, rivalries, etc. Leading is not theory. Leading is doing and being. Good leaders work daily at leading. Good leading means

1. Having the right attitude each day;
2. Becoming more sensitive to the intended and unintended impact of your actions; and
3. Preparing to lead each day down to the minute details of who, what, where and why.

"What Do Good Leaders Actually Do? (Part II)"[11]

In September, we discussed that good leaders (1) understand themselves and their motivations; (2) learn to be very sensitive to the impact they have on people and how followers observe, notice and calibrate their leader's consistency and reliability—whether they walk the talk; and (3) manage the minute daily details of their leading—the who, what, why, when, and where of leading.

This month I want to talk about three additional attributes of good leaders:

4. Good leaders STAY GROUNDED;
5. Good leaders STAY FOCUSED; and
6. Good leaders ENCOURAGE DIFFERENT VIEWS.

I. Staying Grounded

Good leaders stay grounded; they are into the details of their business and are on the "front lines." Good leaders do not lose touch with customers or their employees.

Good leaders understand the fragility of success and how their success results from the outstanding performance of their employees. Success does not go to a good leader's head. Good leaders resist and fight arrogance, hubris, and the trappings of success.

---

11. Edward D. Hess, "What Do Good Leaders Actually Do? (Part II)," *The Catalyst*, November 2003.

Too many business leaders spend too much time talking and dining with consultants, investment bankers, lawyers, and accountants. You did not become successful that way and you will not stay successful that way. You must allocate a significant portion of your time to being on the front lines—getting the facts first-hand, assessing the market, assessing customer needs and complaints, and assessing the competition first-hand. And yes, talking with your employees and getting their ideas on how to do things faster and better.

In the high growth days of Wal-Mart, Sam Walton sent every executive out into the field four days a week to learn first-hand what was selling, who was buying, and how store leaders were being innovative. Good leaders are in the field often, eat with the "troops" often, and never lose sight of the fundamental fact that business is really pretty simple—meeting a customer's needs through highly motivated employees. Good leaders understand that they have two constituencies they must serve: employees and customers.

II. Staying Focused

Sydney Finkelstein of Dartmouth Tuck School of Management in his new book *Why Smart Executives Fail* details the findings of his research which shows that the failure of most businesses is a result of one of four major business change efforts:

1) A major new venture; or 2) A M&A transaction; or 3) A major change effort; or 4) New competitive challenges. The four events named above increase your chance of failure greatly. Good leaders understand the risks and difficulties of major change. Good leaders understand that some of these big deals or change efforts result from executive boredom. Opening that geographic expansion—diversifying your business—buying a company—entering into a big joint venture—is in many cases nothing more than a way to escape executive boredom and to do something exciting and challenging.

Good leaders face the facts; they know that running an operationally efficient and excellent business means repetitive execution, and repetitive execution can be boring. Good leaders keep themselves and their people focused and find a way to make the daily repetitiveness fun. The job of a good leader is to make work fun and meaningful.

III. Encouraging Different Views

Finkelstein, in his book *Why Smart Executives Fail*, also states that business failure results from "flawed executive mindsets that throw off a company's perspective of reality" and because of "delusional attitudes that keep this inaccurate reality in place."[12]

---

12. Sydney Finkelstein, *Why Smart Executives Fail and What You Can Learn from Their Mistakes* (New York: Portfolio, 2003).

Businesses generally are built by people with similar values and views. In the recruitment process there is a strong bias to hire someone you like—someone like you.

Good leaders understand that diversity of experience and diversity of opinion are good—a good test of reality. Good leaders create an environment where critical debate can occur. Good leaders test their views of reality often.

As Bossidy and Charan stated in their book *Execution*, "You need robust dialogue to surface the realities of the business."[13]

I have told several CEOs that they should hire an Executive VP of Reality Therapy whose job would be to debate, test, and critique the underlying key market and business assumptions and to make sure the CEO is getting a complete and realistic picture of the market, customers, competitors, and his own organization.

Good leaders encourage critical debate and good leaders reward the courageous offering of well-reasoned differing opinions. Good leaders continuously test their views of reality.

---

13. Larry Bossidy and Ram Charan, with Charles Burck, *Execution: The Discipline of Getting Things Done* (New York: Crown Business, 2002).

6 The Challenges of Building an Effective Management Team

Anonymous Quotes from DPGC CEOs

"I have yet to be successful in putting somebody (manager) on a different seat on the bus and their ego being able to handle it."

"80% of the people who started with me are no longer here because they could not grow with the business."

"You have to dump stars who are not nice."

"One negative person can impact five, ten, fifteen people in a small company."

"My biggest mistakes were hiring too quickly and firing too slowly."

Multiple Hiring Mistakes

My DPGC research produced several surprising findings. One was the difficulty entrepreneurs had in hiring the right people for their management team. In fact, multiple hires—as many as four or five—were sometimes necessary to find the right person for the positions of chief finance officer, human resources officer, chief sales officer, and chief technology officer. This extraordinary inefficiency wasted time, money, and opportunities and generated stress for the entrepreneurs and their employees.

This pattern of multiple hiring mistakes can be traced to

1. Poor hiring processes and inexperience in evaluating candidates' technical competencies;

2. Inexperience in evaluating whether individuals would fit into the business culture;

3. Underestimating the difficulty that managers with big-company experience had transitioning to an entrepreneurial environment; and

4. Failing to understand the importance of team play.

Management Team Dynamics

A second surprise was the difficulty entrepreneurs had getting good managers to work well together and have constructive conversations rather than engage in corporate politics and gamesmanship. To foster constructive team dynamics, for example, two firms had to hire executive coaches or psychologists to work with the management team. This led one entrepreneur to state, "You have a choice, either build a star culture or a team culture." Related to getting managers to play well together and drive results was the challenge of getting their compensation right. It took several iterations for many businesses to find the right balance between rewarding individual results and rewarding team or company results. Likewise, many entrepreneurs experimented with how frequently to pay bonuses.

Upgrading the Management Team

Consistent with the recurring themes of change and evolution, the third finding was that companies frequently had to upgrade their management teams as they grew. Often managers who operated effectively at one revenue level of the business were unable to effectively manage at a much higher revenue level. The jobs simply outgrew their skills. The need to upgrade managers to fit the expanding job demands was gut-wrenching for many entrepreneurs, since the now ineffective manager had often had a successful history with the business but was now in over his or her head. Such cases presented personal and cultural tensions between the value of loyalty and the need for effectiveness. This was particularly difficult when the ineffective manager failed to transition back to a non-managerial role or to a lower-level management position. This caused tensions with employees too because many of them were comfortable and liked their manager, who was now going to be replaced by, in most cases, an outsider. Management of this dynamic was often overlooked by many entrepreneurs.

Whom to Hire First?

When an entrepreneur can no longer manage the business alone, he or she must then decide what skills to hire first. Circumstances will determine whether the answer to that is a finance, sales, HR, technology, or operations person.

CLASS DISCUSSION QUESTIONS

1. How would you decide whom to hire first?

2. What key factors should be considered?

3. If you did not have experience in that functional area, what steps would you take to minimize that hiring risk?

4. How would you evaluate the ability to be a team player?

5. How would you balance giving the recruit an attractive compensation package so as to entice him or her to join while wanting them to earn their rewards?

Assessment of Competencies

In my study many entrepreneurs chose to hire someone with functional experience and skills complementary to their own. For example, if an entrepreneur's strength was finance, then he or she hired a salesperson or an HR person. If the entrepreneur's strength was sales, then he or she hired a finance person. This decision heuristic, however, led to unanticipated shortcomings in the entrepreneur's ability to evaluate competencies outside of his or her specialty area. For example, how would one without a finance background evaluate the competencies of an experienced finance person in the first place and, further, how does he or she subsequently evaluate that individual's proposals and work when they are on the team?

Another pattern in determining whom to hire was assessment of the critical business need. Was there a need for more revenue or more process? If it was more process, entrepreneurs hired either a finance or HR person. If it was more revenue, they hired a senior salesperson.

Hire for Current Needs or Future Needs?

Many entrepreneurs also struggled with whether to hire someone who had helped another entrepreneurial company scale or to hire a person with experience in a much bigger company but who had no scaling experience. The results here were mixed. Some entrepreneurs brought in people with too much experience too early. Others hired people from companies slightly bigger and found the person could scale a little but not 3X or 4X. Several found that people making their first switch out of a big company had difficulty in adjusting to an entrepreneurial environment.

Many found it particularly challenging to attract good, experienced managers during their expansion, or as one entrepreneur called it, the "adolescent" stage. As a result, many entrepreneurs had to rely on younger, inexperienced managers with the drive and passion to learn on the job. Many had success by hiring people they already knew well from prior working experience. Others had success hiring those with big-company experience who had also at least one successful experience with a growing entrepreneurial company.

One entrepreneur stated, "We made mistakes hiring people whom we did not know well or who were not part of our network. Other mistakes were hiring people who gave us all the right answers but could not check their egos at the door."

One entrepreneur who built a successful national franchise stated his experience this way:

But as we started to go out and look for execution, we found out that no one really has any magic. I mean, magic is understanding your business, understanding your customer, understanding where you want to go, and being very passionate about it.

Hiring Processes

Many entrepreneurs learned best hiring practices from the book *Topgrading: How Leading Companies Win by Hiring, Coaching, and Keeping the Best People* by Bradford Smart.[1] Commonly used good hiring practices aim to mitigate the natural inclination to hire people like oneself. Especially in a growth business the tendency is to rush into a hiring decision because of the urgent need for more help. One lesson that came through clearly was to hire slowly (and fire quickly).

By bearing the financial and other business consequences of making sometimes frequent hiring mistakes, entrepreneurs learned the practical necessity of installing processes to put management applicants through a rigorous interview schedule, with multiple grading reviews by senior managers as well as other relevant line employees. There was considerable variability in the approaches taken, but all involved a more systematic review of the likely fit of an employee with the business culture. For example, one consulting company's response to hiring mistakes was to require that all six senior executives interview every hire regardless of the level of position. Further, to protect the culture, unanimous agreement on every hire was required as well.

Other companies chose to interview applicants in teams to get multiple views about the applicant's answers and behavior. Many used behavioral interviewing techniques, asking applicants to describe challenges faced and their responses or providing hypothetical situations for applicants to deal with. The goal of these techniques was to get past the "marketing ballet" between the interviewee and the company. Both of the examples above of having multiple interviewers were designed, in part, to ensure a cultural fit. Yet another entrepreneur made the need for cultural fit explicit by

---

1. Bradford D. Smart, *Topgrading: How Leading Companies Win by Hiring, Coaching, and Keeping the Best People* (New York: HarperCollins, 2005).

grading each management applicant on the basis of his company's cultural scorecard. In some cases, entrepreneurs found that hiring mistakes lessened if one hired people known to trusted advisors or other managers. By this route, the likelihood of the candidate both having the substantive skills and fitting into the business culture was enhanced. Assessing cultural fit and fit with the existing management team, when done well, was a time-consuming process. To do this, many companies found that multiple interviews of the candidate over a period of time by different people was required in order to get a good feel for a person and his or her values. These interviews included meetings outside of the workplace over dinner or at social events. Last, frank discussions were held concerning what behaviors were expected of a member of the management team and what behaviors would not be acceptable, including how one should treat employees.

In addition to the challenge of getting a good cultural fit, many entrepreneurs found it difficult to evaluate technical proficiency outside their functional area of expertise. This was especially true in the areas of finance and technology. They were able to solve this problem by either using highly competent specialized executive recruiters or enlisting a third-party functional expert to grade the technical expertise.

CLASS DISCUSSION QUESTIONS

1. What was the best hiring process you have participated in? Why?

2. What was the worst hiring process you have experienced? Why?

3. Have you ever taken a job and learned afterward that it was a mistake? Why? How did this happen?

Realistic Expectations

Context is so important in hiring. A growth company needs to have management expertise and experience. The need is generally urgent, and the risk of hiring the wrong people is particularly high because many entrepreneurs have little experience in hiring those with the appropriate skills to take the business to the next level. In addition to these skills, the candidate should have an appreciation, at least, of an entrepreneurial business as well as a broader understanding of what it takes to grow and develop a business. Many entrepreneurs fail to understand the weightiness of these early hiring decisions. As one stated, "It takes one set of skills to start a business and a different set of skills to grow a business."

One's approach to the hiring processes should maximize a good fit and minimize surprises for both the company and the interviewee after the hire. It takes time and several interactions with the candidate to achieve this. Almost every entrepreneur in my study that was scaling his or her first company and who hired managers they did not know well found this process surprisingly difficult and fraught with error.

Management Team Dynamics

Every new management-level hire creates multiple new interpersonal relationships among management team members, introducing change into an existing team. The need to attend to management team dynamics was a surprise and a major challenge for most entrepreneurs. And it was time consuming.

Unfortunately, many entrepreneurs lacked the interest or natural inclination to manage the interpersonal dynamics of the management team. Managing team dynamics and interpersonal dynamics takes emotional intelligence, the ability to understand each team member as an individual, and the ability to tailor the right message in the right way so as to get the right result. Many entrepreneurs were clueless in the beginning about how to do this or even the necessity of doing this. It took time away from what many entrepreneurs thought was the important stuff. But, in reality, this was the important stuff.

Having difficult conversations, holding team members accountable for results, and dealing with responsibility and compensation issues proved difficult. In the best of these cases, entrepreneurs accepted the need to do this as well as their own limitations and hired outside executive coaches or psychologists to teach the management team how to work well together. Most entrepreneurs also based a meaningful part of each manager's incentive compensation on team performance and company financial results rather than only individual performance.

Having learned from prior mistakes, one serial entrepreneur knew he wanted to foster direct, open conversations among team members. As he said, "I want a stab-me-in-the-chest culture not a stab-me-in-the-back management culture." Another entrepreneur said that he taught his managers that *respectful* dissent and disagreement were expected. What was critical was the management learning to deal directly and honestly with issues.

Fire Quickly

No entrepreneur in my study reported that he or she made a mistake by firing someone too quickly. To the contrary, most said that their biggest mistakes were firing too slowly, in hopes that the person would improve or that they could teach the person to be what was needed. Unanimously, entrepreneurs reported erring on giving a poor fit too much time in a position and making their biggest managerial mistakes by not firing faster. Having the wrong person in the job was costly in time, personnel dynamics, lost opportunities, and finances.

Entrepreneurs were constantly conflicted on the issue of firing someone who was not working out. Were they being fair? What message would it send to the organization? Could the person fit somewhere else in the organization? Some of this hesitancy to fire can be traced to the unpleasantness of the act of firing and the resulting bad feelings, debates about performance, or even the potential of legal actions. But hesitance can also result from the entrepreneur not wanting to admit that he or she made a mistake. Likewise, sometimes the hesitancy is rationalized by thinking one is too busy now to do it, so it is better to postpone it to a slower business time, which in some cases never really happens. In the meantime, the person continues to be a poor fit for either their job or the organization as a whole, infecting the organization and causing a risk for more damage.

Upgrading the Management Team

Another challenge for most entrepreneurs was the need to upgrade the management team as the business grew. Many found that their managers could "not grow as fast as the business grew." For many businesses, the need to upgrade the management team was not a one-time event. As the business grew to different levels of revenue, often greater experience and sophistication were needed in the areas of finance, HR, technology, and sales than could be provided by those who had performed well in those roles in earlier phases.

The need to upgrade caught many by surprise. It was not planned for, nor even contemplated. Because of this, in some cases entrepreneurs made the wrong hiring decisions by hiring people who had little or no experience in scaling a business to 3X or 4X. That is, the skill and experience level of the hire was exceeded too quickly. The limitation here in some cases was money—how much experience the business could afford to invest in with one hire at that time. This required a tough balance that was thought about more in hindsight than foresight by many first-time entrepreneurs.

In finance, a frequent progression was for businesses to move from having a part-time accountant to a full-time controller to a vice president of finance to a CFO as they grew. When they reached the need for a CFO, many had to find someone more sophisticated in the skills they needed, hiring someone who had been through revenue growth levels beyond where the business now was.

For HR, companies generally progressed from a single general administrative person to a junior full-time HR person to an HR person with experience with a much bigger company. In sales, it was often the case that a good salesperson does not necessarily make a good sales manager. A good sales manager at a certain revenue level cannot necessarily make the transition to a good vice president of sales at a much higher level.

These transitions were difficult because often the incumbent had done a good job earlier in the company's growth. Now, however, that individual was eased out and another, more senior hire was his or her replacement. Understandably, this loss of position status was hard for many incumbents to accept, and if not managed well impacted other employees' morale, especially those that reported to the now-displaced incumbent.

Entrepreneurs learned that morale was fragile and that in some cases the incumbent had to leave the company.

Many entrepreneurs were unprepared for the interpersonal challenges raised in this chapter of getting the right people in place to successfully grow a company and those challenges addressed in Chapter 5, which addressed the need for entrepreneurs to change their role(s) in the business and manage the managers. Many had never thought deeply about how most businesses are really nothing more than groups of people learning how to work together to produce something of value to sell to other people. Many entrepreneurs found that building a management team was an ongoing process with new team dynamics emerging with the addition (or subtraction) of team members.

Global Medical Imaging, LLC

Global Medical Imaging is a good illustration of how both the entrepreneur and the business evolve and change as the business grows. Ryan Dienst, the CEO, explains how he had to change, how he installed processes, the challenges of building a management team, the tension of investing in infrastructure ahead of growth, and how the business modeled expanded to include service offerings.

CASE DISCUSSION QUESTIONS

1. What role did prior industry experience play in helping these founders avoid start-up failure?

2. Why did Scott and Ryan make good partners?

3. What are the 10 key take-aways about growing a business that you learned from this case?

4. How is managing a business with seven employees so different from managing one with thirty-five employees?

5. Why did GMI experience so many people issues? What did they learn in the process?

6. What commonalities do you find in the Defender Direct and Global Medical Imaging cases?

GLOBAL MEDICAL IMAGING, LLC

The Charlotte, North Carolina–based Global Medical Imaging, LLC (GMI), has sold and serviced medical ultrasound equipment in the United States and internationally since April 2002. Managing partners Ryan Dienst and Scott Ray used $25,000 to launch their company.[2] Profitable from the start, GMI pulled in about $2.4 million in revenue the first year and $4.5 million in 2003.[3] Within six years, GMI had 64 employees and made $17.8 in annual sales.

The founders had a vision that met a market need, and the company they brought to life grew exponentially. Although they managed to avoid cash-flow problems, finding the right talent for their growing business was not easy. Describing the hurdles they had to overcome, Dienst said, "The number one challenge that we've always had is time and talent. The opportunity has always existed; it's having enough time and talent to be able to pursue it and execute against it."

Like most entrepreneurs, the founders at first kept up a frantic pace that did not allow time for them to effectively manage human resources, until a series of hiring mishaps forced them to take a hard look at the way they expanded their workforce. They realized that having no formal hiring process was a recipe for disaster, so they focused on bringing in the right people and putting them in the right positions. Dienst explained:

If you've got the wrong people in the wrong seats, no amount of rules or processes will get the right behavior. The right people in the right seats will overcome any problems; they'll put in any processes you need, they'll fix any issues you have, because they're the right people. Focusing on that early on can save the organization a lot of money and accelerate growth.

Meeting a Market Need

Ray was born in Boone, North Carolina. As the son of a builder, he grew up "driving nails."[4] While a student at the University of North Carolina (UNC) Chapel Hill, Ray turned building lofts for dorm rooms into a profitable business. After graduating with a bachelor of science degree in biomedical engineering, he moved to Charlotte, where he worked selling ultrasound machines for General Electric's medical systems division. In 1995, Ray took a job as general manager for Imaging Associates, a Charlotte vendor of used ultrasound equipment.

Case Study UVA-ENT-0143 © 2009 by the University of Virginia Darden School Foundation. This case was prepared by Senior Researcher Gosia Glinska and Edward D. Hess as a basis for class discussion rather than to illustrate effective or ineffective handling of an administrative situation.

2. Kathy Brown, "Sonic Was the Tonic for This Fixer-Upper," *Business-North Carolina*, November 1, 2005.

3. Lindsay LeCorchick, "Imaging the Possibilities," *Greater Charlotte Biz*, December 2004, http://www.greater charlottebiz.com/article.asp?id=477.

4. Brown.

During these years, Ray witnessed the consolidation of the ultrasound-manufac-turing industry, as large original-equipment manufacturers (OEMs) such as Siemens and Philips bought up the smaller ones. As the OEMs grew larger, however, they became increasingly focused on making a profit and less on performing personalized service. "That's the opportunity that's been created for us," Ray said. "To fill in that vacuum they've created and be more responsive, faster, and more cost competitive. Ultimately, to just provide a higher level of customer support and service that isn't currently part of this industry."[5]

Working with his brother-in-law Dienst, who had an MBA from UNC's Kenan-Flagler Business School, Ray developed a business plan for a company that offered not only the cost-effective solution of selling reconditioned ultrasound equipment but also "maintenance and service contracts, warranties, system upgrades, leasing, and trade-ins."[6]

At the time Ray launched GMI in 2002, Dienst was still a partner at Dienst Cus-tom Homes, but he made the painful decision to leave a successful company that he loved and had helped build. In January 2003, Dienst joined GMI to focus full-time on business management and finance. Ray was the "sales-and-relationship guy," and although he had started GMI, the two men were managing partners and split owner-ship of the company 50-50.[7]

GMI's Business Model

At first, the two entrepreneurs sold reconditioned ultrasound machines mostly to doctors in private practice and small clinics, but eventually they entered the hospital market. Dienst explained:

Our first market was the small, private-practice doctor's office, your nine-to-five cardiologist, ob/gyn, and urologist. It's the doctor who writes his own checks and makes his own money off that equipment. Our other customer was the director of biomedical or clinical engineering in a hospital, who is in charge of finding more cost-effective ways to service and support the ultrasound equipment in the hospital facilities.

A Value-Added Distributor

As the population aged and doctors needed better diagnostic equipment, demand for ultrasound machines grew; however, purchasing new units that cost between $20,000 and $120,000 was an expensive proposition. The entrepreneurs decided to offer reconditioned machines as an appealing alternative; these machines looked brand new, performed as well as new ones, and had an initial cost of 20% to 50% less than

---

5. LeCorchick.

6. Brown.

7. Brown.

comparable new units. "We're primarily in the aftermarket, so we're a value-added distributor," Dienst said. "About 60% of our products are reconditioned—we do that in-house—and about 40% are new or demo products that we distribute and service. We do not manufacture."

According to Dienst, GMI's freedom from manufacturing obligations contributed to its success. "It allows us to be responsive to what the market's needs are rather than what we are restricted to sell or stock in inventory," he said, adding that, as a distributor rather than a manufacturer, GMI could "focus on getting our customers the best products for their needs, instead of pushing a product or solution that may not be ideal."[8]

GMI bought used and off-lease equipment as well as overstocks of new ultrasound-diagnostic equipment. The machines were brought to GMI's Charlotte warehouse, where in-house technicians inspected and then reconditioned them, so the repainted and repackaged machines looked brand new when they were delivered to customers.

From day one, the entrepreneurs implemented a number of quality-control processes in GMI's reconditioning facility. "We've had a continual process improvement as we've gone along," Dienst said. "We've always been focused on checklists and how we run the business, so that if you had problems you could look back and say what happened, why that issue occurred, and modify your checklist to catch it the next time."

A Field-Service Unit

GMI's business model kept evolving. Constantly looking for new revenue streams, in 2004, the founders added a service component to their core business in the form of a field-service business unit. GMI's field-service engineers, with an extensive network of third-party technicians, provided warranty and service-contract support for all systems GMI sold throughout the country.

"Service was an opportunity for us," Dienst said. "Ultrasound equipment breaks. We've got the right technicians, software, and customer service reps to open trouble tickets, manage those calls, get the parts out, and get the customer back up and running." In addition to generating far higher margins than equipment sales, the service contracts helped the company develop long-term relationships with customers.

Further Expansion

The company expanded the breadth of its offerings by adding financing solutions with in-house leasing and a Trade-Up program that guaranteed customers cost-effective upgrades. Consistent with their mission to "lower the cost of high quality health care,"[9] in 2008, the founders set out to penetrate a new market segment: training. By

---

8. Michelle Said, "Global Medical Imaging," *24x7*, May 1, 2006.

9. GMI Web site.

teaching hospital technicians how to take care of the imaging and ultrasound machines in-house, GMI helped hospitals save 40% to 60% of their maintenance budget.[10]

Business Infrastructure

With Ray driving sales, Dienst focused on building a basic business infrastructure that was scalable and capable of providing ongoing support for the growing company, enabling the entrepreneurs to make more effective decisions. "We had the luxury of being able to build processes as we've gone forward," Dienst said. GMI's ultrasound-service business was an area where investing in the right technology to create infrastructure made a big difference.

Dienst said that he "wrote up a scope of what exactly we needed to run that business," and he outsourced writing code to a software company. "Putting that software package in place has had a huge impact on our business," Dienst said. "We've got the right platform now and have the data necessary to make good decisions and run that business. It's doubled our margins, increased our visibility, and cut our time managing service calls by 100%."

Several instances of employee theft early on had forced the entrepreneurs to take a hard look at the way they managed inventory. Dienst thought it was fortunate that "we haven't had anything that was major—any big public issues that compromised our brand." He continued:

It's better to have those problems when you're a $10 million company than as a $20 million company, just due to the size of the problems. And it gets you focused on putting the right processes and procedures in place to eliminate that early on; it forces you to really improve your cycle counts, and your inventory-flow practices.

Dienst acknowledged that as far as technology and putting the right processes in place, GMI had invested ahead of the growth curve. "We've overinvested, meaning we could have made more money getting to where we are if we hadn't spent as much time and energy on making sure we had the processes to do it right," he said. Reflecting on what he could have done differently; Dienst said that he "could have invested a little more slowly." Nonetheless, Dienst believed that it was money well spent, and that "it will certainly pay off in the long run." He continued:

We've been business builders rather than just trying to make the maximum amount of money in the shortest amount of time. A lot of our competitors have made a lot more money in the last five years than we have. But we have an incredible brand reputation, an incredible platform, and we have the ability to become a $100 million company.

---

10. Kaihan Krippendorff, "Save Your Clients Money—What Could Be More Economic?" *Fast Company*, May 28, 2009.

Growing Pains

From the start, GMI experienced stellar growth. As far as financing was concerned, "We have always done it with our own money and with lines of credit. Pure bank debt," Dienst said. While funding growth did not seem to be a problem, the increasing pace of change forced the entrepreneurs to start learning how to let go and lead, rather than supervise and control. They also realized the importance of delegating to the right people.

Rule of Seven

"Businesses grow in sort of a rule of seven," Dienst said. "There's the 1 to 7 employees [stage], the 7 to 49 employees [stage], and then the 50 to 350 level." According to Dienst, because of Ray's talent for driving sales, GMI grew to the stage of seven employees "real quick."

Each stage of business growth had its own unique challenges. At the first stage, communicating with the GMI employees was effortless, but as its workforce grew, Dienst understood that the old way of doing things would have to change. He explained:

You're doing stuff, you go to lunch every day, and you're all on the same page, and everything's easy. After you cross over that seven-person line, it starts to get tough again, because you've got too many people doing too many things to know every detail about everything. So you start building an organizational structure, with people having ownership in parts of the organization they're in charge of.

Delegating responsibility presented new challenges. The employees hired at the first stage of the business were not always equipped to grow with it, often lacking the skills to manage others. Dienst said, "You've got an inflection point at that 7- to 10-person range, where you have to start putting people in charge of parts of the business." He continued:

Typically then you get your phase-one management team in place over the 10-to-25-employee range. And then things start to grow again, because you're getting some synergy, you're gaining some leverage; you're back focused on creating revenue rather than putting out fires and managing the process.

Dienst identified the next inflection point as the 45- to 55-employee range, when the demands of growth outpaced the skills of the phase-one management team. To take the company to the next level, Dienst found it necessary to "reshuffle the deck and bring in new talent." At this point, the employees who were unable to grow with the company or become top performers—the C players—were moved to lower-level positions, where they could be A players. As Dienst said, "They're C players as managers, but they're A players if you can get them back to what they were originally hired to do."

When employee headcount at GMI topped 50, the founders were able to afford a "different level of talent," Dienst said, and he revealed that GMI brought in a professional management team that had the capacity to get the company to the level of 300 employees.

Hiring Under Pressure

At first, during periods of rapid growth, Dienst and Ray were under pressure to fill open positions quickly. "Rather than critically interviewing and making sure we're hiring the right person, [we] often started recruiting bodies," Dienst said. In his experience, this time constraint, combined with ineffective job-screening methods, led to frequent hiring mistakes early on. "It's not having a defined hiring process, not doing enough on the profiling standpoint," he said. "And the hiring process was more of a sales job on candidates about how badly we need them rather than us critically analyzing a candidate's abilities for the role."

In 2004, the start-up had an especially strong year, characterized by explosive growth. But Dienst told a cautionary tale. "You bring in 20 people for really fast growth over six months, and if 10 don't make it and you've got to let them go, that's extremely costly." Dienst said that hiring too fast in 2004 resulted in significant turnover at GMI in late 2005 and early 2006.

Topgrading

After a few years spent hastily filling positions, Dienst and Ray became more disciplined about the hiring process. "We became aware of the high cost of turnover and poor hiring and what that does to the organization," Dienst said. He dealt with the issue first by attending HR conferences and seminars and reading about the hiring process. Then he read a book by the industrial psychologist and consultant Bradford Smart that made a big impression.[11] The eponymous hiring method Smart had developed was a rigorous executive-grading process that helped CEOs (including GE's Jack Welch) recognize superstars or A players, redirect or retrain B players, and weed out the underachievers or C players who failed to prevent or fix problems. According to Smart, a hiring mistake at any level typically costs business owners more than the employee's original salary.

From late 2006 and into 2007, the entrepreneurs implemented significant changes to GMI's hiring and employee-ranking processes. They embraced Smart's rigorous

---

11. Bradford D. Smart, *Topgrading: How Leading Companies Win by Hiring, Coaching, and Keeping the Best People* (New York: HarperCollins, 2005).

in-depth interviews, meticulous reference checks, and other hiring techniques to identify top players. They also used Smart's following performance-review tools:

We try to be a lot more structured and strategic in our hiring now, with a good hiring process, and multiple people doing interviews. We do a lot of personality profiling. We are very focused on top grading and force ranking our employees as As, Bs, and Cs, giving them quantifiable performance rankings, and trying to make sure we are getting the bottom 10% and 20% out of our organization and refilling those spots. It was a lot of learning, and just getting really focused on maximizing the effectiveness of our hiring, on-boarding, and training practices, and getting the wrong people out.

The changes to the hiring and employee-ranking processes produced immediate results. After the performers at the bottom of the company were let go, GMI was "much better and much more productive," Dienst said. "I think [it's] the biggest reason why we're, again, growing very quickly and very profitably." He continued:

We went through a stage where we brought in a lot of folks, and we got the wrong people in the wrong seats. We took too much time leaving the wrong people in the wrong seats, so when we finally got serious about cleaning them out, everything got better and smoother and faster again. You're better off being a 30-person company than a 40-person company if you get the wrong 10 out of there.

In 2008, 18 of the 64 GMI employees worked as revenue-generating sales reps. The general and administrative staff—HR and accounting—numbered 12 employees. Dienst identified the rest as "the technical people in our organization that manage service issues and recondition the equipment and repair broken parts."

Building the Management Team

That the founders took more time to fill positions at the top was reflected in the results. "We've gone a little slower, a bit more focused in hiring those key people, and we've had more turnover in the middle than at the top," Dienst said.

In 2006, the founders brought in a bank consultant with a "big-business background," Dienst said. After looking for someone who could grow with the company, Dienst explained that "we overhired to get the right caliber of person. It's a guy who has exceptional talent, who has the ability to be the general manager of this business with its 100-plus employees."

The role of CFO was usually one of the hardest to fill, but fortunately, Dienst had the skill set, experience, and education to take on that role. From his experience managing a custom-home-building business, he understood the importance of monitoring financial information and managing cash flow. Therefore, from the start he had invested in the technology to develop effective controls and balance at GMI. He explained:

We have always believed very heavily in software, and we've always been on good business packages. We haven't gone the QuickBooks route or anything like that. You need the data, and you need that core software package to be able to get the information you need out of your business to run it. My previous experience growing a business, my MBA, have helped us always be pretty well off there.

Having tight financial controls was important in any start-up, where cash was a scarce resource, but it was especially critical at GMI where, as Dienst pointed out, "I can't tell you what our sales are going to be like next month. We're a month-to-month transactional business, so we're always impacted by good months and bad months and cash flow."

Building the HR Function

In hindsight, Dienst recognized the importance of finding and cultivating talent from day one. "I think that strategic HR early on is pretty critical," he said. He admitted he should have brought in a "very overqualified HR person earlier to make sure we didn't have the cost of hiring mistakes and lack of on-boarding processes and those kinds of things. The cost of those mistakes is so high that you could afford a rock-star HR manager."

The HR manager, who had been with GMI since its launch in 2002, was unable to grow with the company and was let go in 2007. "Those are painful changes, when you have somebody who was with you from the start," Dienst said. The position was filled with an internal candidate, who also served as controller. "We've identified somebody with the skill set who fit that role well. We hired for personality, ability, and the things we thought we needed rather than hiring a traditional HR person," Dienst said.

Compensation

The two managing partners had always owned 100% of the business. Only one member of GMI's eight-person leadership team had been offered equity, but, in 2008, the founders started looking into creating a stock-option pool for a few long-time employees who had contributed significantly to growing the business. "We need to find ways to retain them above and beyond just compensation," Dienst said.

Senior management's compensation consisted of a base salary, which was set at a market or above-market level, and a bonus tied to performance. To rate his key managers, Dienst used a comprehensive scorecard listing the skills and competencies that were important to the company at each particular stage of growth. "We've had quarterly scorecards, we've had annual scorecards," Dienst said. "Right now, we've got a six-month scorecard, which is about as far as we can accurately forecast and set goals."

GMI's balanced scorecard consisted of a mix of financial and "soft" metrics, such as teamwork that changed as the company grew. Members of the eight-person leadership team had an opportunity to earn a bonus up to 30% of their base salary. Dienst said, "They have a team-based card that's dependent upon the overall performance of the business, so our repair manager is tied to the same metrics as our sales manager." He continued:

Twenty percent of their 30% bonus is based on the overall performance of the organization. So, hopefully, they're breaking down barriers and working together. They have another 10% balanced scorecard that gets to be tactical within their specific area of impact. . . . That 10% is in their control so that they feel like they've got complete ownership of that 10% of their scorecard.

The Art of Time Management

For Dienst, who was in charge of day-to-day operations from day one, time was a scarce resource. Understandably, he tried to focus on areas that had the greatest impact on the fledgling business. "If you have 20 fires burning, it's knowing which ones are going to impact money, profitability, cash flow, and customer satisfaction and running after those things first," he said. Even though Dienst did not have a "great process," he had a lot of task lists and a set of priorities. "It was walking in and saying, 'Come hail or high water, I'm going to get these three things done today and, hopefully, these other 10 as well,'" he said.

Dienst recalled that in the early stages of building a business, when he was busy putting out fires, he also looked for the "right trends, where you can make a decision that allows you to fix something that would have a big enough impact, so it's worth the effort of fixing it once and for all, with a process change, or people, or whatever else."

Although getting caught up in the minutiae of running a business was easy, Dienst understood the importance of finding the time to step back from the daily grind to look at the big picture. He continued:

You always try to make sure you're balancing, as best as you can, the amount of time you spend working *in* the business versus working *on* the business. You make sure you're getting out of the office, which is the only time to think about working on the business. Because every day you walk through the front door of the office, inevitably, you're going to get pulled into working in the business and not on the business.

As GMI at times grew more than 400%, Dienst, Ray, and the rest of the organization had to constantly reinvent their roles and priorities and readjust their schedules.

According to Dienst, "It's been constant improvement, not only on the personal level but on the corporate level and how we restructure roles." He added:

I got to the point that I couldn't manage a $17 million business the same way I managed the $12 million business. Because of the pace at which we grow, about every six months we're almost a new organization. We have to redo our meeting schedules and our meeting rhythms and how we're communicating to make sure we're always addressing where we are as an organization.

In mid-2008, Dienst again revised his meeting schedule to better fit his role. The first two days of the week were devoted to internal meetings with the heads of those business units that added the most to the company's bottom line at a particular phase of growth. "I spend one hour with no phone, no BlackBerry, no computer, with each of the key managers, focusing on that impactful part of the business," Dienst said. He tried to keep his calendar free on Wednesday, Thursday, and Friday, to have time "to be able to do business development, travel, and meet customers, and do projects, and all of the other things I need to move it forward."

From Doing Everything to Delegating

Early in the game, Dienst and Ray were in total control of GMI, taking care of every detail and managing every area personally. Now, Dienst found it difficult to let go and allow others to take ownership of parts of the business he had nurtured from the start. As he recalled, "When I started with Scott, and there were four of us, you did everything. Literally, touched it, did it, wrote it, and fixed it." Dienst acknowledged that his transition from doing to managing had been painful and that learning to delegate "had been very hard."

"I don't think that learning to delegate is a linear process," Dienst said. He added that, at some point, he realized that there were not enough hours in the day and that he had to delegate. He described the process:

You delegate, and you find things fall apart, and you reach out and you gather them up and you pull them back in. And then you get to the point of pain again that you know you have to delegate and you push it back out. And it falls apart in different places, and you pull some of it back in. And you just keep figuring out where and how you go through that process by sort of hitting points of complexity in your personal operation, that you have no choice but to delegate. If you delegate out 10 major parts of your day, and six people grab that and are doing great, and maybe four of the folks aren't the right people, you grab those four things back, but at least you got rid of six.

The Strategic Coach Program

What helped Dienst switch from managing everything to delegating was Strategic Coach, a recognized organizational development program that encouraged successful entrepreneurs to stick to the three or four tasks they performed extremely well and delegate the rest. A crucial component of Strategic Coach was identifying these three or four unique abilities with the help of the Kolbe psychometric-profiling test; once these abilities were identified, entrepreneurs partnered with others with the same abilities.

It took Dienst and Ray two years to identify their skill sets and abilities. As Dienst described it, part of the Strategic Coach program was determining "how to maximize the amount of time you spend on that unique ability, because you're going to amplify your impact on the organization if you do what you do better than anybody else. And everything else that's outside of that unique ability, you've got to get off your plate."

When Dienst and Ray recognized their strengths, it was beneficial to the company. For example, in 2008, after Ray realized that his sales talent did not correlate with being a sales manager, a seasoned national-sales manager who was a better fit for managing a sales force was brought in. Dienst continued:

Scott's unique ability is giving customers the confidence to make commitments to do business with us. He needs to be out, talking to customers and closing business, and not managing a sales force. That's not his skill set. Now Scott is out, selling more than he ever has, driving revenue and transactions, and having as much fun as he's ever had.

The national-sales manager built an outside-sales model for GMI. "We now have outside reps, and we're growing that pretty aggressively," Dienst said. With a strong executive team in place, the founders felt comfortable focusing on hiring more revenue producers. Dienst explained:

We're trying to go from $17 million to $24 million this year, and then our goal is to get to $100 million in three years. I've spent the last six years focusing on building the backend processes, writing the software, getting everything in place so that we've got a scalable platform and the right technical and service people.

The Evolving Leader

One of the key factors in achieving stellar growth had been the two entrepreneurs' ability to continually evolve and change their management styles to meet the needs of the business at different points on the growth curve. In 2008, Dienst said:

Personal transformation is amazing in the growth of all of these businesses. Today I have to learn to be a true CEO of a 60-person organization. I've had to restructure my meeting schedules, I've had to restructure my management style, I've had to find different ways to impact the organization that are drastically different than two or three years ago.

Dienst's statement that "fast-growing businesses outgrow people quickly," came from his experience and understanding that, just because they had successfully launched a business, entrepreneurs were not immune to becoming irrelevant. Dienst emphasized the importance of constantly having to "read, educate yourself, and re-invent yourself." He explained:

If you can't keep up with the business, you may not get fired, but you're either going to go out of business because you make some critical mistakes, or you're going to stop growing because the business gets to the point where with your current management style, processes, and leadership abilities—it can't get any bigger. After businesses make it for three or four years, they hit a ceiling. And the ceiling is not the ceiling on the business or the ceiling on the opportunity; it's the ceiling on the entrepreneur as the leader of that business.

Dienst, whose career advice was "work hard every day, and have a quest for knowledge, talk with smart people, read books, listen to CDs, and make sure you are learning every day,"[12] set the bar higher for himself in terms of professional growth. He expected no less from his management team. "If people aren't willing to do the same, if managers that have been with you for two or three years can't keep up, you're going to outgrow them, and they're going to be gone." He continued:

Business is a game like baseball or golf or anything else. I enjoy being a student of the game, and reading, and learning, and going to conferences, whether it's building custom homes or selling or servicing medical equipment. A good entrepreneur can be a good entrepreneur in any industry because if you're a student of the game, the rules and the lessons are very much the same. And that's the fun part about it.

GMI's success proved that, with Dienst running the business as de facto CEO and Ray making the sales, its leaders were "the right people on the bus, in the right seats."[13] Dienst once described his goal as "growing a business to the point it has outgrown me and needs smarter, better leadership to continue to succeed.[14] Considering his passion for learning and continuous improvement, that goal could take longer to achieve.

List of Relevant Cases

Better World Books

Defender Direct, Inc.: A Business of Growing Leaders

Freedom Technology Services

Global Medical Imaging, LLC

James Abrams @ Clockwork Home Services, Inc.: Lessons from a Serial Entrepreneur

Jeff Bowling at the Delta Companies: From Baseball Coach to CEO

Motor City: A Disruptive Business Model (B)

Sammy Snacks (A)

SecureWorks

---

12. "Entrepreneurs Talk About What They Do and Why They Do It," *Charlotte Business Journal*, October 6, 2006.

13. Jim Collins, "Good to Great," *Fast Company*, 51, October 2001.

14. "Entrepreneurs Talk."

7 Culture—Creating a High-Performance Environment

Anonymous Quotes from DPGC CEOs

"You can build a star culture or a team culture."

"If you are in it just for the money you'll never succeed."

"If growth is the primary objective it is going to be very hard to keep people aligned and motivated."

"But being a great place to work takes work—it takes positive effort to keep it going."

"The big danger as you grow is how do you keep true to who you were?"

In Chapter 3, we learned from my public company growth research that consistent high-growth companies generally had highly engaged employees dedicated to constant improvement. We also learned that there is significant academic research that finds that highly engaged, satisfied employees impact customer satisfaction positively.[1]

---

1. Kim S. Cameron, Jane E. Dutton, and Robert E. Quinn, eds., *Positive Organizational Scholarship* (San Francisco: Berrett-Koehler, 2003); Jane E. Dutton, *Energize Your Workplace: How to Create and Sustain High-Quality Connections at Work* (San Francisco: Jossey-Bass, 2003); James L. Heskett, W. Earl Sasser Jr., and Leonard A. Schlesinger, *The Value Profit Chain: Treat Employees Like Customers and Customers Like Employees* (New York: Free Press, 2003); James L. Heskett, W. Earl Sasser Jr., and Leonard A. Schlesinger, *The Service Profit Chain: How Leading Companies Link Profit and Growth to Loyalty, Satisfaction, and Value* (New York: Free Press, 1997); Edward D. Hess, *The Road to Organic Growth* (New York: McGraw-Hill, 2007); Edward D. Hess and Kim S. Cameron, eds., *Leading with Values: Positivity, Virtue and High Performance* (Cambridge: Cambridge University Press, 2006); Edward D. Hess, "Organic Growth: Lessons from Market Leaders" (Working paper, 2007); Charles A. O'Reilly III and Jeffrey Pfeffer, *Hidden Value: How Great Companies Achieve Extraordinary Results with Ordinary People* (Boston: Harvard Business School Press, 2000).

Previous chapters have emphasized that private company growth inevitably represents change. Growth alters the number, and often types, of employees; necessitates an increased number of rules, controls, and processes; adds managers and functional specialists; and requires entrepreneurs to grow personally and professionally. These changes demanded by growth evolve as the business grows and new employees join and others leave the business. As the business continues to grow, additional people, processes, and infrastructure are needed. And, in many cases, new and often different types of managers are needed to orchestrate the needs of the growing business. The changes in personnel, processes, and infrastructure all contribute to major shifts in the interpersonal dynamics in the business. These changes are always challenging, sometimes tumultuous, and, occasionally, catastrophic if not handled well.

The Glue

What binds people together during the continuous changes that mark a company's growth? What is the glue? What business environments inspire employees to work hard and continuously improve rather than view their jobs as merely a means to a paycheck? What employee behaviors do an inspiring business environment encourage or discourage? What behaviors should be encouraged or discouraged? What are the rules of interpersonal engagement in the workplace?

One source of answers to these questions is the business culture. Culture encompasses the written and unwritten rules, beliefs, and values that a business aspires to and actually embodies in the daily behaviors of its employees with each other, suppliers, customers, and the community. Culture is not a neutral concept. Some business cultures can foster high employee engagement and high performance, and others can be corrosive to the very aims a business hopes to achieve. The power of culture was discussed in Chapter 6, which described several CEOs learning that cultural fit was a critical element in hiring the right people, with some going so far as to evaluate applicants with a cultural scorecard. Many CEOs understood not only the importance of culture but the fact that they had the responsibility for building and maintaining the culture that they wanted. Good cultures do not just happen; they take constant work and upkeep.

CLASS DISCUSSION QUESTIONS

1. In Chapter 1, you read the "Eyebobs Eyewear, Inc." case, which described how founder Julie Allinson created a unique cultural environment. Please describe it. How does the Eyebobs culture promote employee engagement and performance? Would that environment be a good fit for you? Why or why not?

2. Chapter 2 described how Dennis Lee and his partners created a very different culture at Octane Fitness. Please describe it. Would that environment be a good fit for you? Why or why not?

3. Chapter 3 discussed how John Gabbert built his "relationship culture" at Room & Board. Would it be a good fit for you? Why or why not?

4. How would you describe the SecureWorks culture? The Defender Direct culture?

Culture and High Performance

What is the relationship between culture and high performance? The research on high-performance organizations has consistently linked high employee engagement to high performance. High employee engagement generally results from employees having an emotional attachment to the organization that is more meaningful than just having a job. Creating that type of employee emotional engagement can result in high performance, loyalty, and productivity—all of which can drive excellent execution that results in both growth and satisfied customers. But those results just do not happen. They occur when organizations have meaningful purposes and values and are led by leaders who "walk the talk." These organizations constantly teach those values, and measure and reward behaviors that demonstrate those values while penalizing behaviors that violate those values.

High-performance organizations just do not happen. They have to be built.

It Is Not About the Entrepreneur

I discovered in my research that many entrepreneurs, in growing their businesses, at some point had to shift their perspective from a largely self-focused business perspective to one that encompassed a broader view of the business. This broader view included recognition of the importance of developing the skills and engagement of the people making that growth possible—the employees. The original motivations for the entrepreneur may have included a drive to make money, to build a business, or to be successful. At some point they realize that they need to attract and retain high-quality employees who will buy into a meaningful story that inspires them to work hard and grow the business. How do you build a great place to work? How do you build a culture that others will want to be part of? How do you create a work environment that inspires excellence and high performance? How do you make work meaningful for non-owners of the business?

The Awakening

Many entrepreneurs are passionate, driven people, comfortable in knowing that they can get the job done. As a company grows beyond the size in which an entrepreneur can have direct control over everything, however, a realization generally occurs that his or her continued success depends more on others than on him- or herself. That realization often comes after some bumps in the road, or even catastrophes, related to finding, hiring, training, and retaining good employees and managers.

Employees become the "end" rather than just the "means" to an end. This transformation in the entrepreneur's view comes about when he or she really understands that success depends on others and that such success is really fragile.

What Do Entrepreneurs Want?

Why do entrepreneurs start businesses? What do they want? The reasons are personal, but there are some commonly expressed reasons. Some entrepreneurs, like John Gabbert, start businesses because they want more control over their destiny or they get tired of conforming to someone else's business plan. Others see an opportunity to launch a different way of doing business and are not able to sell their employers on that vision. Entrepreneurs with a different business vision include the founders of Wal-Mart, Home Depot, and the company formerly known as EDS. Some entrepreneurs burn out on the dynamics of big-company politics. Others are forced to become entrepreneurs out of necessity after getting laid off. Some, like Dave Lindsey of Defender Direct, feel aggrieved after missing out on an expected promotion. Some, like Julie Allinson of Eyebobs, see a customer need and ask, "Why not me?"

Whatever the initial incentive for starting a business, most entrepreneurs have the goal of earning a living doing something they enjoy, and that provides personal validation and rewards. Many want the opportunity to flourish on their merits and not be impeded by inept bosses or corporate politics.

In many ways employees do not differ from entrepreneurs in what they want from their jobs. Many want to be associated with a "good" business—a business that produces good products and services that meets a valued customer need and a business that treats people fairly and honestly. Given that employees necessarily have bosses, the research shows that employees want to be respected and listened to by their bosses. In addition, they want to have some control over the content and execution of their jobs, the opportunity to excel, and to do work they feel good about and want to share with their families.[2]

What is a consistent finding is that money is not enough to motivate employees or to get them fully engaged in the business culture. High employee engagement cannot be purchased or dictated. Likewise, employee engagement cannot be promoted simply by aiming at the target of growth for growth's sake. One entrepreneur expressed that point this way: "Growth is not good enough. We are actually doing something

2. Marcus Buckingham and Curt Coffman, *First, Break All the Rules: What the World's Greatest Managers Do Differently* (New York: Simon & Schuster, 1999).

that is right. There is a mission behind it. There is value—something we care about that drives us." Another stated, "If you are in it for just the money, you will never succeed. But if you are in it because you love your product and you love your customer and you love what you do and you want to make them happy, you will never have to worry about wealth."

So, if financial incentives and business goals of growth are not adequate to foster a positive business culture and employee engagement, what variables are important? There are several.

The Manager's Behavior

First, employee satisfaction translates directly to employee loyalty, productivity, and customer satisfaction. Business research tells us that the number one determinant of employee satisfaction and engagement in a job is how the manager treats the employee. Does an employee's manager treat the employee with respect? Listen to the employee? Teach the employee? Care about the employee as a person? Help the employee advance? Review the employee's performance frequently and fairly? Not surprisingly, managers are more likely to act in those positive, enhancing manners if the entrepreneur treats the manager in the same manner. Building a business culture that promotes employee satisfaction is essential because as a business grows, most customers have direct contact with line employees, not with the entrepreneur. Many entrepreneurs learned the fundamental lesson that if you treat employees well, they will treat customers well.

Characteristics of High-Performance Cultures

The challenge for the entrepreneur and his or her managers is how to create the right environment to produce high employee satisfaction and engagement. Consistent with the *public* company research, my *private* growth company research found that "ownership," promotion from within policies, education and training opportunities, creating a "family" atmosphere, constant communication about the key values of the business, the celebration of success, consistent and fair reward and promotion policies, information transparency, living the values, and hiring for cultural fit helped create a positive business culture. The "Room & Board," "Trilogy Health Services, LLC: Building a Great Service Company," and "Leaders Bank: Creating a Great Place to Work" cases all illustrate some of these points.

My findings about the importance of fostering a positive business culture are consistent with the findings Collins and Porras discussed in *Built to Last*.[3] In fact, their

---

3. James C. Collins and Jerry I. Porras, *Built to Last: Successful Habits of Visionary Companies* (New York: HarperBusiness Essentials, 2002).

12 myth-shattering findings provide a good roadmap for any entrepreneur trying to build a business that can endure.[4] Consistent with my research findings regarding high organic growth public companies, Collins and Porras reported the preservation of many aspects of a small-company soul in a large-company body. Collins and Porras also found that successful growth was often accomplished by having highly engaged employees led by humble, passionate, home-grown leaders who, in many cases, were neither charismatic nor visionary.

It is important to note that building the right cultural environment is not a one-time accomplishment. Because business growth itself is a dynamic enterprise, crafting a positive business culture requires constant adjustments. As one entrepreneur stated, "But being a great place to work takes work. It's like being a homeowner. If you do not do anything to your house, it will fall apart. It actually takes positive effort to keep it going."

Culture, Values, Mission

Entrepreneurs try to create meaning and employee engagement by focusing on questions like the following:

"Why do we exist?"

"What do we do that is important?"

"What do we stand for?"

"How should we behave?"

"How are we helping our customers and employees?"

"How do we create a place that good people want to be part of?"

"What behaviors can we not tolerate?"

As discussed in Chapter 2, growth is more than an overarching business strategy. Successful growth requires an internal system that links consistently, seamlessly, and in a self-reinforcing manner a business's culture, structure, leadership model, HR policies, measurements, and rewards to drive desired behaviors that answer questions like those posed above.

Promoting a positive growth business culture cannot simply be an abstract goal. Businesses and their leaders have to lead by example and, yes, walk the talk. Easier said than done.

Many business people think that implementing high employee engagement policies necessarily requires that you be soft on employee accountability and performance. Not so. You can have both. Look at the "Room & Board," "Defender Direct, Inc.: A

---

4. Collins and Porras, 7–11.

Business of Growing Leaders," "SecureWorks," "Valley-Wide Health Systems, Inc.," "Enchanting Travels," "Trilogy Health Services, LLC: Building a Great Service Company," and "Leaders Bank: Creating a Great Place to Work" cases for examples of high performance; accountability; and a positive, engaging work environment.

Meaning, Fun, and Emotional Rewards

My research found three consistent areas that entrepreneurs focused on in building positive growth company cultures: meaning, fun, and emotional rewards. Identifying the meaning of the enterprise translated into finding a purpose in the business beyond making money. Non-financial elements of meaning included helping people, saving lives, making the world a better place because your product contributes to a healthy life, providing care to the sick, providing financial services to growing companies, or providing healthy and delicious foods to people with allergies. Meaning in the workplace also included non-employment-related activities such as collaborating in charitable projects, with the company organizing or supporting such efforts.

Incorporating fun into the business culture translated to the celebration of individual and group successes in business and life outside of work, as well as big events such as birthdays, anniversaries, and births. Such celebrations were found to build bonds among employees similar to the celebration of such events within a family. In addition, many companies also supported spontaneous ordering of pizza or ice cream, or barbecues and other get-togethers with employees and their families.

The importance of emotional rewards in the business culture was evidenced by efforts to showcase individual and group successes. This included formal recognitions for performance; acknowledgment for contributing to an effort; awards, gifts, and trips for jobs well done; education opportunities; promotions; and small gifts that said "thank you" and "we care about you." Some entrepreneurs evidently learned from their elementary school teachers the importance of gold stars in promoting performance!

"Ownership"

To attain high employee engagement employees need to feel like they "own" their job in that they have input into how it is done and some stake in the outcome. This feeling of ownership also has two corollaries. Employees want some control over their destiny in that if they work hard and perform according to the rules they want to be evaluated and rewarded fairly.

This feeling of ownership can be actual, through stock ownership or through incentive compensation, or virtual, through emotional rewards evidenced by awards, trips, education opportunities, and promotion opportunities.

Several entrepreneurs believed strongly that "if you want people to act like owners, then make them actual owners" of the business through the distribution of stock.

A few companies I studied gave stock ownership to 100% of the employees. Others gave an ownership stake to all managers. Others limited stock ownership to just a few people. Those that did not spread stock ownership broadly used virtual "owner-ship" mechanisms to make people feel like appreciated and valued members of the company, including annual rewards for achieving specific targets to semi-annual firm-wide holidays with spouses to a grand vacation destination with chartered planes taking the whole company to celebrate. Others built internal training and education programs and designed career paths for employees, showing them how they could progress to more responsibility and more compensation.

Hiring for Cultural Fit

As companies grew and maintenance of the positive business culture became a prior-ity, many entrepreneurs formalized a process to hire for cultural fit. The mechanism for assessing "cultural fit" varied, but some created a cultural scorecard or required top management, who served as protectors of the culture, to approve all hires. Others tried to limit new hires to those recommended and vouched for by current employees.

Even with such efforts aimed at ensuring a "cultural fit," hiring mistakes some-times were made. Entrepreneurs often learned the hard way that employees that do not fit culturally can rarely be retrofitted, and that the best course is to recognize the bad choice and rectify it quickly.

The importance of identifying and remedying a poor employee choice quickly should be emphasized, and business policies should be tailored to ensure this hap-pens. In fast-growing companies some entrepreneurs graded managers on employee satisfaction and retention, which were viewed as critical to promoting a positive busi-ness culture. However, if employees were terminated within six months of hiring, suggesting the recognition of a poor "cultural fit," those terminations did not count against the manager's employee retention numbers.

CLASS DISCUSSION QUESTIONS

1. How do you hire for cultural fit but not end up with the negatives of group think?
2. How do you hire for cultural fit but still encourage differences of opinion and input?

Measure Positive Behaviors

Measurements of employee performance are critical but challenging for entrepreneurs in growing companies. Entrepreneurs must continually define and redefine what be-haviors are desired to drive value and make the business a great place to work, craft useful measures of those behaviors, and provide feedback and rewards to employees. This is an iterative process of trying to be more and more granular in promoting the specific elements of employee performance. Not only must the entrepreneur and his or her management team be able to identify and reward employee behaviors, it is important that the basis for identifying good and bad performance as well as the standards for promotion, awards, and bonuses be clearly defined, transparent to employees, and both fairly and consistently applied.

Information Transparency

Many companies routinely fully disclosed to all employees the business strategy, annual goals, and financial results in the belief that a better understanding of why their job was important and how it fit into the business strategy would lead to greater employee engagement.

Meaningful feedback; training and education opportunities designed to help employees advance; and transparent, consistent, and fairly applied performance measures built trust. This trust was reinforced by constant honest communications, keeping employees informed of the business's successes, challenges, and failures.

Service Companies

While having a positive business culture is important in all businesses, it is particularly critical in service businesses because success is usually dependent on employees' direct, one-on-one interactions with customers. What we do know from the research cited earlier is that satisfied employees make for satisfied customers. This result is understandable because people that are satisfied in their jobs project that to others and it is contagious and uplifting. It leads to better performance and customers enjoying doing business with you.

Because the information is more publicly available, most examples of culture that lead to high employee engagement, loyalty, and productivity are public companies. Companies such as Southwest Airlines, Costco, Starbucks, Whole Foods, Levy Restaurants, Best Buy, UPS, and Sysco have different but high-performance-enabling cultures. The lack of private company information does not denigrate the importance of building a private company culture that generates high employee performance. The private organizations I studied, including SAS, Chick-fil-A, Patagonia, Room & Board, San Antonio Spurs, and the United States Marine Corps, also have high-performance-enabling cultures.

CLASS DISCUSSION QUESTIONS

1. What was the best organization, club, or business entity you were ever associated with? Why was it the best? Describe its culture.

2. What was the worst organization, club, or business entity you were ever associated with? Why was it the worst? Describe its culture.

Behavior Is Key

Entrepreneurs learn that to successfully grow their business they need to enlist others in their journey. Eventually they also realize that money is not enough. A business needs a "soul," in that it needs to be a meaningful organization. Culture helps define that meaning and sets boundaries for behavior. But words alone are not enough. The entrepreneur must exhibit behaviors on a daily basis that reinforce the values and meaning he or she wants to create. Employees watch the manager, leader, and entrepreneur as role models. Granular behaviors send messages both good and bad.

Entrepreneurs have to become very sensitive to the impact they have on others and on the emotional environment daily. One entrepreneur told me that every day is "show time" in that he learned that he was on stage every day and he needed to behave accordingly. This takes self-discipline, self-management, and sensitivity. Again, people skills are so critical to growth.

Leaders Bank: Creating a Great Place to Work

Leaders Bank set out to build a differentiating business model based on empowering employees to serve its customers. In order to achieve that result the management had to create a great place to work. As you read "Leaders Bank: Creating a Great Place to Work," please focus on the following questions:

CASE DISCUSSION QUESTIONS:

1. What did Leaders Bank (Leaders) sell? Is it a commodity?

2. How did Leaders' "culture of respect" make money for its shareholders?

3. What is Leaders' customer value proposition? What are the necessary conditions for the Leaders business model to be successful?

4. How did Leaders achieve high employee engagement?

5. How did Leaders manage the risk of culture dilution as it grew?

6. What message was sent to employees by the "open book" policy?

7. How did Leaders structure its hiring processes to protect its culture?

8. What employee benefits programs did Leaders implement? Why? How did Leaders justify the added costs to the shareholders?

9. How did Leaders review performance and improve leadership skills?

10. Is the Leaders "people model" transferable to a non-banking business? What kind of business? Why? Are there businesses in which the Leaders "people model" will not work? Please explain why.

LEADERS BANK: CREATING
A GREAT PLACE TO WORK

Leaders Bank (Leaders), headquartered in Oak Brook, Illinois, provided commercial, industrial, and real-estate lending, as well as treasury-management and retail-banking services for privately held businesses and their owners. The bank was founded in 2000 by five industry veterans—Patrick Kelly, James Lynch, Steven Schuster, Laura Mc-Grath, and Gordon Fitzsimmons—whose vision was to create a personalized banking experience for entrepreneurs and small businesses.

In an industry fraught with mergers and acquisitions and the resulting depersonalization of service, Leaders offered a refreshing alternative. As its name implied, the bank treated its customers and employees as leaders, focusing on their strengths and professional competencies and on developing long-term relationships based on communication and trust. The bank's officers were given the authority to take risks and make autonomous decisions, which resulted in the customized solutions and fast responses that business owners valued.

In addition, because of a workplace culture centered around respect, Leaders kept its employee turnover rate close to zero; consequently, its clients were able to work with the same banking professionals, who understood their businesses and goals. Therefore, it was not surprising that in a 2005 independent customer survey, Leaders received an overall satisfaction rating of 94%—no small feat considering that few financial institutions could claim a client satisfaction rating above the 75% industry average, reported by the American Customer Satisfaction Index.[5]

With CEO Lynch at the helm, the number of Leaders' employees grew within eight years from 9 to 72, and three new banking centers were established in the Chicago area. Revenues grew 85% in three years, reaching $30.5 million by 2007. The bank's holding company, Leaders Group, Inc., saw its assets balloon from $37 million in 2000 to $646 million in 2008 (Exhibit 7.1).

In 2008, during the most challenging economic environment in decades, *Entrepreneur* magazine ranked Leaders number 51 on its list of the Hot 100 Fast-Growth Businesses in the United States. The company also won Chicago's 101 Best and Brightest Companies To Work For award three years in a row and was a finalist on the *Wall Street Journal's* 2008 Top Small Workplaces list.

Case Study UVA-ENT-0128 © 2009 by the University of Virginia Darden School Foundation. This case was prepared by Senior Researcher Gosia Glinska and Edward D. Hess as a basis for class discussion rather than to illustrate effective or ineffective handling of an administrative situation.

5. "Leaders Bank Demonstrates How Deeper Relationships Help Private Businesses," Leaders Bank press release, 2009.

By building a strong culture that fostered high employee engagement and loyalty, the bank was able to thrive in good times and weather the bad ones. Reflecting on the bank's success, Lynch said:

[We've] stuck to our model, communicated effectively, and made Leaders Bank a great place to work every day. . . . We put our employees in a position where they can utilize their strengths, and we make sure they are supported well. This approach nurtures personal job satisfaction, which translates to low turnover and high levels of employee and customer satisfaction.[6]

Starting Out

The founding of Leaders coincided with a slowing of the U.S. economy in the second half of 2000 that ended the banking industry's string of eight consecutive years of record annual earnings. When Leaders opened its doors in 2001, the economy was showing signs of the first recession in a decade. Then came the terrorist attack on 9/11, and the stock market plummeted. The Federal Reserve feverishly slashed short-term interest rates to the lowest level in four decades.

Reflecting on the bank's early days, Steve Ritter, senior vice president and director of human resources, thought that market conditions had always been among the biggest challenges facing the company. Ritter said, "Certainly, in the first few years of our operation—2001 and 2002—there were a number of Fed rate reductions similar to what we've experienced in 2008." Ritter continued:

But because we are focused on the low end of the middle market our typical customer is an entrepreneur, a small business owner; that's a customer who often doesn't make the radar of a big bank anyway. In some ways, this economy makes our niche customer the perfect customer, because these are folks who are being challenged to grow their businesses as well. So there we were in 2000, a de novo bank with a vision of treating employees well and treating customers well. And there were businesses out there, looking for someone just like us.

Building a Strong Foundation with a Common Thread

James Lynch had wanted to build a bank around a culture with the vital elements of respect, leadership, quality, partnership, communication, and integrity (Exhibit 7.2). Ritter emphasized that Lynch started to lay the foundations for that culture long before his bank opened its doors in 2001. Ritter explained:

When Jim began looking for investors to start the bank, he was selling that vision about the way you treat others with respect as part of what he wanted people to understand would grow. Similarly, when he started looking for partners for the executive leadership team, he looked for

6. "*Entrepreneur* Magazine Ranks Leaders Bank as One of the Hot 100 Fast-Growth Businesses in the U.S.," Leaders Bank press release, 2008.

people who got it. Respect, transparency, communication, partnership, and integrity were the values that people had to live and embrace on a day-to-day basis. And as diverse as our team was, Jim's vision resonated with all of us—it was our common thread.

Because the modus operandi at Leaders had always been inclusion and participation, the defining elements of the workplace culture were fine-tuned by the employees themselves, mostly during leadership retreats conducted and described by Ritter: "We sat in retreat session after retreat session and hammered out the mission and the philosophy and the values." Ritter continued:

The rule was to challenge every word, and we did not move forward on the definition of these things until everyone in the room was comfortable that this is what we live and this is the way we behave. So there's a real values-in-action model to what we do because when that is what defines your culture, then any kind of its violation stands out in a big way.

To ensure that the human factor did not get pushed to the sidelines and the culture did not get diluted as the organization grew, Lynch invited Ritter to join the company's senior leadership team, whose members, besides Lynch, included the chief financial officer and chief credit officer. Since the company's inception, Ritter had conducted leadership retreats, team-building workshops, and career-path coaching sessions to help employees discover their strengths; he was also responsible for the most of the company's recruitment efforts, in addition to presiding over a three-person HR group.

A Culture of Respect

In an effort to recruit and retain top talent, Lynch and other Leaders executives worked hard to foster a corporate culture in which employees felt appreciated and were rewarded for exceptional performance. Lynch remarked that "employees need to believe they are valued and that the quality of the work they do makes a difference." He continued:

Those who don't feel valued or respected are more likely to go off and seek greener pastures. . . . A sincere compliment for extra effort or a job well done takes nothing away from the bottom line and pays big dividends, especially for smaller companies, which are generally less able to afford the time and cost of hiring and then losing an employee. It's also important to routinely acknowledge workers as individuals with a smile, a handshake, a pleasant comment. And we always make a point to remember their birthdays.[7]

Viewing Employees as Leaders

Lynch attributed his company's success in large part to its unique philosophy of treating employees and customers as leaders. "Because we view our employees as

---

7. Jim Lynch, "Appreciation Ranks High with Employees," *Bank News*, July 1, 2001.

being leaders themselves," Lynch said, "we give them the authority to make decisions without always having to check with their superiors. In staff meetings, we consider all ideas good ideas."[8]

Maintaining a healthy equilibrium between employee empowerment and internal controls can be a tough balancing act for many companies. While Leaders' employees were encouraged to take risks on behalf of their customers and were empowered to make their own—sometimes fast—decisions, the company's top management ensured that controls were in place, but that they did not stifle employee decision making or entrepreneurial spirit. According to Ritter, "The balancing factor is a sense of shared accountability." Ritter continued:

If somebody wants to bend the rules on behalf of the customer, they know how far they can go. The underpinning of everything we do is the credit quality, so there are parameters that people don't spread beyond. They hear what kinds of deals are being negotiated in the pipeline meetings every week, and they understand what our norms are. The fact that our CEO has a strong lending background and is involved in every deal establishes an unspoken set of parameters based on loan policy.

To encourage employee commitment to the success of the business even more, top management implemented a Leaders stock-purchase plan so that 75% to 80% of the employees had ownership in the organization through stock ownership. "We want everyone to function like an owner of the organization," Ritter said.

Open Communication

An important factor in employee empowerment was communication, which Lynch described as an "open, two-way street." Because he believed that some of the best ideas for improving operations, cutting costs, and gaining efficiencies came from front-line employees, he stressed the importance of soliciting their continuous feedback in meetings and with company-wide surveys. Lynch also valued employee feedback about organizational health and culture and suggested asking employees, "What can be done to make this a better place to work?" He gave employees the option of making suggestions anonymously and advised implementing the best ideas immediately. "Employees will notice and appreciate a sincere, ongoing effort to improve the work environment,"[9] he said.

Leaders employees participated in a confidential survey twice a year. "It is designed to measure the kind of distress that you would expect to see in organizations that are growing and changing," Ritter said, and explained that the survey asked for feedback

---

8. Milton Zall, "Empowering Employees," *Independent Banker*, January 1, 2002.

9. Lynch, "Appreciation Ranks High with Employees."

in the areas of leadership, vision, collaboration, communication, commitment to excellence, morale, learning, and how well the company managed change.

The top management at Leaders treated employee feedback as a call for immediate action. "Whenever the aggregate data rises above even the smallest measurable level of distress, we get together as a group and plan around that," Ritter said. He remembered the time when the company experienced an intense growth spurt, going from 33 to 47 employees in six months, and survey data indicated concern about company-wide communication. Ritter continued:

We added dinners with the CEO, breakfast with the board of directors, an employee newsletter, and a couple of different summer events, and the number went down to nearly zero within six months. We're proactive about getting folks' opinion about the strength of the organization, and then we address these things before they have a chance to take root and influence our culture.

Part of the company's open-communication policy involved financial transparency. The details of the company's financial performance were shared with all employees on a monthly basis during staff meetings. In addition, "the company newsletter has a performance dashboard in the corner that shows what our gross level is, what the return on equity is, tracking the major financials month to month," Ritter said. "So that's as open-book management as we can get." As Ritter explained, the data on how individual lenders were doing relative to their targets was not available to all employees, but individual contributions were transparent within each team.

On those rare occasions when employees did not live up to the company's high expectations in terms of performance or upholding its cultural values, they were asked to leave; however, the terminations did not have a negative effect on employee morale precisely because of the company's emphasis on open communication. Leaders' management worked hard to convey what was expected of its employees and made sure they understood how their individual contributions affected overall company performance. Ritter explained:

Whether you're a bank teller or a chief credit officer, you know what it is about your work each day that moves the needle of the organization in some way. And everyone experiences a collective responsibility for linking all those strengths and talents together to achieve successful results. When someone isn't holding up their end of that shared responsibility, everyone understands that it's costing the rest of us money.

Recruiting—The Culture Fit

Lynch gave Ritter a mandate to screen out prospective hires who did not share the company's values. From the beginning, "Jim wanted to have a threshold of culture evaluations on the front end of every interview," Ritter said, admitting that some of that evaluation was subjective. "We talk about what's important, the way we treat people, and what our values are, and we see pretty quickly whether people get that or not." Nevertheless, whether a job candidate realized it or not could make or break an interview. Ritter explained:

While there is a technical aspect of evaluating a prospective employee, there has been a culture-fit evaluation on every single hire from top to bottom, including very experienced, high-level people. And if I give the culture-fit a "thumbs down," that decision will be respected. It has only happened a handful of times, but when we miss the mark on the subject of culture in the recruitment process and the person gets on board after having had a good interview but they don't fit, it becomes evident to everyone in a short time. And, generally, Jim will stand up as the CEO and apologize to the entire organization for missing that one.

A typical interview process for a mid-level job candidate started with a culture-fit screening with Ritter, followed by an interview with the leader and select members of the team that had the job opening. Ritter described the second interview as "a team screening for technical ability and fit with the team." The last leg of the recruiting process involved a leadership interview with a member of the executive team—often the CEO—"to kind of embrace the fit," Ritter said.

Leaders viewed the job interview as an opportunity to present the best features of the company to a candidate. For that reason, Ritter and the HR team tried to ensure potential hires had a chance to meet Lynch. Ritter said:

We really want people to hear the Leaders Bank story from Jim's perspective since he started it. So to the extent that we are measuring the candidate, we know that the candidate is measuring us, too, and we want them to know fully what the culture is about and what's expected of someone who works here. And Jim does a wonderful job relating that. He also has a real good assessment competency for understanding whether people fit our culture or not.

Benefits Package

To attract and retain talent, Leaders offered its employees an attractive benefits and compensation package. "We are very attentive to the compensation surveys for our industry and our geographic area, and we pay people competitively," said Ritter. He added that the company offered a "better-than-competitive" benefits package with medical and dental coverage. "We've got a very strong 401(k) with an employer match. But all that is typical," Ritter said.

Less typical were other job perks—such as the ability to adjust hours—designed to cultivate healthier work and home environments for the staff. "A corporate culture of respect means also helping workers succeed as individuals in their private lives," said Lynch.[10] He acknowledged that because Leaders was aware that the number of employees taking care of elderly family members or small children had increased, it encouraged flexibility in scheduling whenever possible. "It is not difficult

---

10. Lynch.

to accommodate an employee who has a family emergency or occasional daytime appointment, and we've found that the modest inconvenience is greatly offset by the loyalty and goodwill such gestures tend to generate,"[11] Lynch said. The company was particularly attuned to the needs of Leaders employees who were single parents.

The Wellness Program

A fringe benefit that attracted the attention of the Society for Human Resources Management, which listed it among its best practices in January 2007, was the company-sponsored wellness program. Every year, Leaders designated a pool of money—$1,500 per employee—to encourage its work force to make healthy lifestyle choices. Ritter explained how the program worked:

You can earn these dollars by lifestyle changes, such as quitting smoking or losing weight. You can earn these dollars by getting your annual physicals, your dental cleanings, or through fitness/health-related things. People are getting immediate financial rewards for their choices to be healthy, and then they can cash in the money they make on a monthly basis for any numbers of things. They can hire personal trainers, buy exercise equipment, get wellness coaching, health club memberships, or nutritional consultations. They can even buy things like musical equipment or iPods to help them relax.

Since being implemented in 2005, the wellness program had shown measurable return on investment. In 2007, Leaders' employees used only 31% of their available sick-leave time. "Basically, they're leaving seven out of ten days on the table each year," Ritter said. But he added that the program also had less tangible benefits. "There're some obvious positive things that have happened in terms of morale and vthings like that," Ritter said.

Part of the wellness program included an annual health-risk assessment for everyone, which Ritter credited with detecting potentially serious medical problems facing two Leaders employees early on. "In addition to gathering aggregate return on investment data from better wellness, we've had a couple of good catches with folks who were closer to major medical issues than they thought they were," Ritter said, referring to the health-risk assessment. "Their participation in the wellness program saved them a lot of medical trouble."

Training and Education

Aware of the high cost of recruitment and training, Leaders took great care in finding the right person for the job in the first place and then spared no effort to engender employee loyalty. According to Lynch, one of the best ways to ensure that the most talented and valuable employees stayed with the company was to offer them the kind of support that helped them succeed in their jobs. "We are always inviting people to

11. Lynch.

sit down and have discussions about how their natural strengths fit their career path, and how we can grow and develop them," said Ritter.

Leaders' employees did not only receive training at the beginning of their employment when they developed an annual training plan with their supervisors. In addition, they learned new skills by attending conferences, seminars, and workshops, or took advantage of a tuition reimbursement program to take courses that increased their professional capabilities.

Focus on Individual Strengths

Lynch believed that the key to unlocking employee potential was to see them as individuals with unique strengths and weaknesses. All senior staff at Leaders was required to read the management book *First, Break All the Rules*,[12] which recommended that companies take advantage of people's strengths by placing them in areas where they could succeed, instead of merely identifying their weaknesses and working to overcome them. Lynch elaborated:

Take, for example, someone good at organization but lacking interpersonal skills. We would not expect that person to do well in sales; we would place the individual in an operational support position, where he or she would have the opportunity to excel, and provide one-on-one support to mitigate weaknesses.[13]

Employees at Leaders used the Gallup Organization's Web-based StrengthsFinder Instrument to pinpoint their five signature strengths, which were then analyzed during so-called strength sessions, which were part of the performance-evaluation process. "We look at the StrengthsFinder results, and we tie it to people's career-path plans," said Ritter. "We make sure that we grow and develop people in a way that's aligned with their natural strengths and competencies."

Performance Evaluation

The performance evaluation process at Leaders ensured that all employees got the training they needed to improve their performance. Even though official performance reviews at Leaders took place once a year, in many cases performance evaluation was a year-round process. "Often, the learning goals that come out of the evaluations are things that you follow up on an ongoing basis," said Ritter.

To get a comprehensive look at how its officers and executives were performing, the company implemented the 360-degree feedback review, which included feedback from three co-workers—one selected by the individual's supervisors and two selected by the employee being evaluated. In addition, an employee was evaluated by his or her supervisor and also submitted a self-evaluation. "All that feedback becomes

12. Buckingham and Coffman.

13. Lynch.

a written document, and then we associate a merit increase with that depending on the performance," explained Ritter, adding, "We track it throughout the year to make sure that we're moving in the ways that we agreed to move."

Leaders also used the 360-degree feedback system, part of a leadership competency tool developed by Lominger International, to evaluate its executive team. "It's a three-year cycle where we all get 360-degree evaluations through Lominger," said Ritter. "We all receive executive coaching on a monthly basis. And then the cycle ends with another 360-degree to measure our growth."

Monthly executive coaching was a huge cost commitment, and Leaders decided to implement a more cost-efficient model by investing in the training and certification of a team of internal coaches who would provide professional coaching to everyone in the organization. "The research supports the fact that your return on investment is much greater when you can get coaching into the organization internally as opposed to hoping that coaching of the executives will trickle down," Ritter said.

Celebrating Success

While Leaders understood that one of the ways to keep the enthusiasm and emotional engagement of its employees consistently high was to honor their achievements, "the fact that we've been the recipient of a sequence of awards also helps," said Ritter. "Recognitions have been coming in regularly enough that it gives us reason to stop and celebrate" (Exhibit 7.3).

Keeping the morale high and energy up was a day-to-day effort that Leaders' management took very seriously. When the bank surpassed $500 million in assets in early 2008, Leaders' top management decided to treat its entire work force to a White Sox game, renting a luxury sky box at U.S. Cellular Field. "Putting everyone in one bus and driving downtown together, singing karaoke, and going to a ball game was a nice way to celebrate that. We try to recognize, acknowledge, and celebrate whenever we can."

Investing in Workplace Culture and Measuring ROI

Such fringe benefits as the wellness program, various companywide initiatives, and dinners with the CEO were designed to create a strong workplace culture at Leaders, but they were not cheap. To justify the expense to the board of directors, Ritter and his team demonstrated the impact of workplace culture and retention on Leaders' bottom line. "When we took the subjective, soft, philosophical approach to culture and translated that into metrics and numbers that affected shareholder value by virtue of retention, the light bulb went on and the board understood it," said Ritter.

Ritter and his team first looked at the data from a company-wide employee survey conducted by the Best Places to Work organization. Most Leaders employees (97%) had responded in the affirmative to such statements as "I would invest my own money in this organization"; "Senior leadership models the organization's values"; and "I know how my job contributes to the organization's success." Next, Ritter's group identified the concrete, measurable results of having a strong workplace culture: a 4% turnover rate in 2006 versus a 30% industry benchmark and the 30% of unused available sick days. "Then, we did a little exercise," said Ritter. He explained:

If you look at 4% retention in an industry that experiences 30%, if half of those people were business developers, what would be the cost to an organization and what would be the impact on shareholder value? We made an assumption that the average business developer is making $120,000 and he's got a $12 million annual loan target, and we lose 4% of those versus the industry's 30%, and there's a vacancy rate of 90 days to get them replaced. And so we calculated a little bit of recruitment expense and then we looked at the opportunity costs that that person is not making 25% of their target because they were gone for three months and you can multiply that by a 2.48% average yield on a current loan. The opportunity cost is about $75,000, and there's another 30-odd thousand dollars in recruitment and training expense. And so we calculated the turnover costs conservatively at $111,000. Now the ROI Institute says that a business developer's turnover cost is about 125% of annual salary. So we're going slightly under—about 95% of annual salary. We said, "Leaders Bank's losing two business developers at a 4% turnover costs the bank $222,000." And if it were six business developers and a 30% impact, that would end up costing $445,000, and saving nearly $300,000. If you multiply our earnings, our number of shares, it ends up being nearly $3 a share that it earned the shareholders by virtue of maintaining good, solid retention and low turnover.

Managing Growth

With the opening of three new banking centers in the Chicago area in 2008, the company started experiencing the challenges associated with organizational growth; however the Leaders executive team and the HR group worked to identify and address problems before they grew roots. To ensure that the culture was strong in all Leaders' locations, "we are trying to have as much leadership team visibility in all locations as is humanly possible," Ritter said. He and his vice president of HR visited all bank centers regularly. Each location had an HR person, a compliance person, trainers, and access to the leadership team. In addition, instead of having one company-wide staff meeting every month, each location had its own with an agenda especially tailored to each group.

Ensuring that the bank's employees had access to the members of the leadership team was particularly important because as Ritter said, "We are modeling the culture from the top down." He continued:

We know that our behavior has to model mutual trust, inclusion, ways to take risks, conflicts being invited and addressed rather than avoided, accountability, inviting and welcoming feedback, direct communication, group interest versus individual interest. We know that if we take care of those things and model it from the top, that's the way the teams will behave as well.

Exhibit 7.1   Leaders Bank: Creating a Great Place to Work

2000
- Founding of Leaders Bank
- 9 employees
- $37 million in assets

2001
- $88 million in assets

2002
- $127 million in assets

2003
- $148 million in assets

2004
- 20 employees
- $242 million in assets

2005
- 30 employees
- Exceeded $300 million in assets

2006
- 48 employees
- Compounded annual growth rate of 35%
- $382 million in assets

2007
- 58 employees
- $425 million in assets

2008
- Opened Hoffman Estates Banking Center
- Opened Naperville Banking Center
- 70 employees
- $646 million in assets

SOURCE: Leaders Bank Web site.

Exhibit 7.2   Vision, Values, Mission, and Philosophy

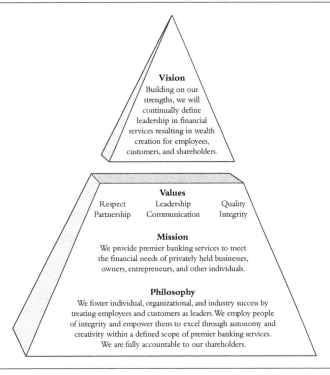

Vision
Building on our strengths, we will continually define leadership in financial services resulting in wealth creation for employees, customers, and shareholders.

Values
Respect   Leadership   Quality
Partnership   Communication   Integrity

Mission
We provide premier banking services to meet the financial needs of privately held businesses, owners, entrepreneurs, and other individuals.

Philosophy
We foster individual, organizational, and industry success by treating employees and customers as leaders. We employ people of integrity and empower them to excel through autonomy and creativity within a defined scope of premier banking services. We are fully accountable to our shareholders.

SOURCE: Leaders Bank Web site.

Exhibit 7.3   Awards and Recognitions

2003
• Winner of United Way Campaign Platform Award

2006
• Voted No. 1 small/medium-sized company in the Best Places to Work in Illinois award program

2007
• Winner of Chicago's 101 Best and Brightest Companies to Work For
• Ranked in *Entrepreneur* magazine's Hot 500—America's Fastest-Growing Businesses

2008
• No. 51 on *Entrepreneur* magazine's Hot 100 Fastest-Growing Businesses in America
• Finalist of *Wall Street Journal*'s Winning Workplaces' Top Small Workplaces 2008
• Winner of Chicago's 101 Best and Brightest Companies to Work For

2009
• Winner of Chicago's 101 Best and Brightest Companies to Work For

SOURCE: Leaders Bank Web site.

List of Relevant Cases

Defender Direct, Inc.: A Business of Growing Leaders

Jeff Bowling at the Delta Companies: From Baseball Coach to CEO

Leaders Bank: Creating a Great Place to Work

Mellace Family Brands, Inc.: Building a Socially Responsible Enterprise

Room & Board

Students Helping Honduras

Trilogy Health Services, LLC: Building a Great Service Company

Author's Commentaries

The following commentaries deal with the relationship between leadership, creating a high-performance environment, and high employee engagement.

"Entrepreneurial Leadership: Why Should Anyone Follow You?"[14]

My MBA students spent the Spring studying leadership. Their journey took them from Jack Welch to Sam Walton to Howard Shultz to The Ritz Carlton Corporation to Chick-fil-A Company to Presidents Nixon, Ford, Reagan, and Clinton and to General Harold Moore and the U.S. Army. Along the way, we talked about Greek philosophers, Hitler, Gandhi, and Machiavelli. We studied two movies—"We Were Soldiers" and "Changing Lanes" and debated at length whether the ends justify the means or whether how you play the game is more important.

We focused on several questions:

1. Why should anyone (employees or customers) follow you?
2. What are the roles of personality, charisma, timing, context, situation, and adversity in leadership development?
3. Why do some companies achieve consistent execution excellence?
4. What really motivates employees?
5. How can educated young managers understand and lead hourly employees?
6. What is the relative importance of strategy, structure, people, and process in building a great business?
7. Why is execution so hard?
8. How do you make repetitive, boring jobs fun and meaningful for employees?
9. What is the relationship between an entrepreneur's personal values and the business culture?

---

14. Edward D. Hess, "Entrepreneurial Leadership: Why Should Anyone Follow You?" *The Catalyst*, June 2003.

I believe that principled or values-based leadership is the most important element in building a world-class sustainable business. Unless suppliers, customers, employees, and lenders trust and believe in you, you will fail. Leadership is a daily job—it is hard, fun, meaningful, and challenging.

What is leadership? There are over 200 definitions of leadership. Some people cannot define it but know it when they see it. Let us start with what leadership is not. We considered leadership is not about perks, money, power, adulation, and ego fulfillment. We concluded the following.

1. Leadership Is a Trust Relationship

If operational excellence is your goal, if consistent high-quality customer satisfaction is important, if employee loyalty and enthusiasm are important, employees have to trust you and believe in your goals. Trust is earned—not bought. Part of trust is respect. Trust is respect for your values—that you will act in the best interests of your followers and not solely in your self-interest. Trust is earned drop by drop but lost by the bucketful. The essence of a leadership relationship is trust between the leader and the followers and vice versa.

2. Leadership Is Honest, Two-Way Communications

The execution of leadership on a daily basis is through honest, direct two-way communications with employees and customers. Employees want to know what the objectives are; how what they are doing contributes to those objectives; how the business is doing; how they are doing; how they can improve. To be effective, communications need to be direct, concise, two-way and repetitive.

To be a good leader, you must be a good listener and understand people and their emotions and motivations. Two-way communication gives employees respect and sends the message that he or she is a valued member of the team.

3. Leadership Is Teaching and Learning

Fundamentally, to build a sustainable business you have to teach your employees and your managers what is important, what are acceptable standards, why what they are doing is meaningful, and how each person can develop to be all they can be.

Leaders lead by teaching, critiquing, and setting standards of conduct and performance. Leaders help people improve and learn. At the same time, leaders learn from their followers. They encourage different opinions and suggestions in order to instill a sense of ownership in the end result and to get the best results.

4. Leadership Is Helping People Be All They Can Be

A paycheck alone will not, in most cases, achieve operational excellence. Employees are human beings, too. Human beings thrive on recognition, thank you's, and pats on the back, if earned. Emotional rewards are as important as tangible rewards. As importantly, people want to be part of something bigger than themselves and something meaningful. They want their job to be important in some way. People want to belong to and be part of something that is viewed by others as good and meaningful.

It is a leader's job to create that meaning and to treat his followers with dignity and respect, to make them feel like they have a stake in building something special, and to help them advance and prosper.

5. Leadership Is Courageous Acting

Leaders act. Leaders never ask their followers to do anything they would not be willing to do themselves.

Leaders have the courage to make the tough decisions. Leaders confront reality. Leaders respect differences of opinion and debate. Leaders learn, adapt, adjust, and, most importantly, they make the tough decisions and act in the best interests of the whole enterprise—not just in their self-interest.

6. Leadership Is Harmony Between What You Do and What You Say

Gandhi stated, "Happiness is when what you think, what you say, and what you do are in harmony."

Or stated another way, leaders walk the talk. Leaders are loyal to their values and standards. Leaders understand that employees watch their actions, their moods, and how they treat others, in order to help determine a leader's consistency, reliability, and trustworthiness.

Hypocrisy, inconsistency, and dishonesty will kill your corporate culture and decrease your chances of operational excellence.

7. Leadership Is "Washing the Dishes Often"

Leaders are not seduced by the perks of leadership. Good leaders do not forget they are only as good as their followers and they are there to serve their followers. Good leaders are humble, and understand the role of luck, education, opportunity, and birth in their success. Leadership is an attitude—an attitude of serving others. Good leaders never, never forget to honor and respect the menial, repetitive tasks done by others.

Good leaders eat with the troops. Good leaders wash the dishes. What do I mean by that?

When Dan Cathy, president of Chick-fil-A, came to talk to my class he shared with them his rule at operating at both the 80,000-foot level and at the 5-foot level and told them how at a new store opening recently in Florida, he washed dishes for two hours the night of the opening. That is a humble leader. Think of the message he sent to his employees. That is leadership.

Like many things in business, the concept of leadership is not difficult to understand. What is difficult is the execution—execution day in and day out.

Leaders must focus on their followers—not themselves. A leader's focus is not I or me but we. What have you done today to show respect for your followers? What have you done today to help them learn, be better, and grow? What have you done today to help them do their job better?

Leaders understand the most important five words in a customer or employee relationship are "HOW MAY I HELP YOU?"

"Are Your Employees a Means to Your End?"[15]

Your true beliefs and attitudes about your employees will ultimately increase or decrease your probability of building a sustainable high-performance business. Let me repeat, even more directly to get your attention, the amount of money you will make depends in large part on how you treat your employees.

Your first reaction will be "Well, I am fair," "I do pay well," "I pay market," and "My benefits are market." Money and benefits are not enough by themselves. Money will not buy loyalty or sustainable high performance. Employees want respect, dignity, to be listened to, to be treated as important, to be valued as someone with something to contribute, and they want you to be fair, honest, and trustworthy. Last, employees want their work to be meaningful and to feel they are part of something special. Your first reaction may be "who needs this touchy-feeling stuff?" Or, "Those feelings are the province of family, friends, and church." Think again!

You can read all the leadership, management, or motivational books you want, but unless you truly believe that your job as a leader is to serve your employees, you will not act accordingly or consistently.

The Prevailing View

Unfortunately, in the business world, the prevailing view is that employees are assets to be managed and controlled—assets which are disorganized, undisciplined, and lazy unless a good manager uses "tuff-luv" to bring order, discipline, and standards to bear. In this model, leaders must be strong, all-knowing role models for the followers. Command and control, charisma, strength, and toughness are key components.

Results, numbers, and shareholder value are the key drivers. This leadership philosophy is rooted in history and philosophy, and underlies the historic command and control management theory which has dominated U.S. business since the days of the automobile assembly lines. I suggest that you can build a high-performance organization with high standards and with GREAT results with a different model.

Servant Leadership

A different leadership model is growing which is based on values-based or servant leadership. This model states that if you treat employees with respect, dignity, and trust they in turn will give the same back to you and be excited about contributing

---

15. Edward D. Hess, "Are Your Employees a Means to Your End?" *The Catalyst*, May 2004.

in a meaningful way to the business. This model values employees as people worthy of dignity and respect; values and seeks their inputs; gives meaning to their work so they can be proud of what they do; and changes work from being simply a job that pays the rent to something more meaningful.

Think about this. When have you performed at the top of your game? What job experiences were fun, exciting, and meaningful? Under what conditions do you look forward to going to work??? I bet it is when you feel like you have impact; when you feel like you are contributing to something important to you; when you are with good teammates; when your contributions are valued by others and you are told so; when your input is sought, respected, and taken seriously; when you trust your boss; and when your efforts stand for and represent more than making money. Why do you think your employees feel differently than you feel?

Your challenge as a leader and business builder is to create those same feelings in all of your employees. And you cannot do this unless you have the right attitude and belief about your employees as people. THEY ARE NOT A MEANS TO YOUR END ($$$$); THEY ARE THE END RESULT.

Being hard-nosed business people you ask—well, who does it this "new way"? In my judgment, Synovus Financial Corporation, Chick-fil-A, Southwest Airlines, and Starbucks, and Charles Brewer did it at Mindspring and Horst Schulte did it at Ritz Carlton.

Let me quote from Jimmy Blanchard's (chairman of Synovus) Letter to Shareholders in the 1998 Annual Report:

"But we are striving every day to make our workplace better for our team members, to make sure they know somebody gives a darn about them. It's the right thing to do. Our value chain begins with our people and our customers, and ends with value for you. Our shareholders . . . people respond when they know someone really cares about them and appreciate them. They just do."

Does it work? Yes; for example, check out Synovus's financial history yourself. Everybody from the CEO to the cleaning person wants to be appreciated and valued. On Sunday, March 14, an article in the *New York Times* said the great New York Yankee baseball manager Joe Torre almost quit because he did not feel appreciated by the owner. It is universal.

As I look back over my 33 years in the business world, my best bosses

1. Cared about me as a person and acted accordingly;

2. Helped me grow, achieve, and be successful;

3. Said "Good job" and "Thank you" often; and

4. Removed bureaucratic or political obstacles from my path.

They were there to help me be all I could be. They served me—not vice versa.
WHOM DO YOU SERVE?

8 Growth Thrusters
"Replication" and "Boosters"

How do private companies grow after they have survived the start-up phase? In the start-up phase, successful entrepreneurs create a customer value proposition sufficiently attractive to customers to generate enough profit to support both the business's capital needs and the entrepreneur's income needs. In other words, the entrepreneur reaches a revenue level of survival that varies by type of business. For our purposes, let's assume a net profit before tax of $500,000.

This chapter focuses primarily on how entrepreneurs grow *after* this start-up, commercialization, and stabilization phase. Post-start-up growth can come in two separate but overlapping stages. First, the entrepreneur can scale the business—the "replication" growth phase. Scaling is the primary way most entrepreneurial ventures grow to bigger revenue numbers. Second, profitable growth can occur through "boosters": improvements and innovations driving or creating new sources of revenue or from cost efficiencies and productivity.

Scaling: "Replication"

Ever since my first research project on high organic growth public companies I have explored the concept of how businesses scale. How do they get big quickly in a cost-efficient and profitable way? I first used the term *replication* in 2004 to describe the process of consistent high-quality execution of replicating a process or business model. I thought successful replication was the key to fast growth.

The requirements of successfully scaling bring together all the themes of this book. Scaling requires planning, processes, and more people, and it requires change and, in some cases, business models must evolve to make scaling easier. By necessity, scaling requires decisions about what to do yourself and what to outsource. Those decisions impact quality, control of the customer relationship, and capital considerations. Scaling means doing what you are doing now but in much bigger volumes—replicating many times over what has worked in the past. Scaling volume requires you to scale production and sales without losing quality and financial controls. Increasing volume may involve adding a large number of employees quickly, which may stress your culture and quality standards.

Planning to Scale

Entrepreneurs can scale *ad hoc* reactively or they can proactively plan for scaling. Interestingly, first-time entrepreneurs in my study generally scaled, iterating as they went along, and those entrepreneurs with prior start-up experience approached scaling more methodically and proactively.

Planning for scaling a business requires many decisions and involves many variables: (1) What needs to be scaled in order to grow your business 4X? (2) What aspects of your business model are so critical that you must control them? (3) Is your business model a direct-to-consumer model or indirect? (4) How can you use technology to scale quickly and cheaply? (5) How does capital restrain your scaling alternatives? (6) If you need capital, what are your alternatives and what are the pros and cons of each alternative? (7) Are your current processes and people scalable or do you need to upgrade? (8) What parts of your value chain do you scale yourself, and what parts can you outsource? (9) What are the advantages and disadvantages of outsourcing from quality control, customer control, and capital investment perspectives?

What Do I Need to Scale?

Production

For a business to scale, what exactly has to scale? First, a business has to be able to produce consistent, high-quality products or services in a volume sufficient to accommodate larger and larger numbers of customers at the same time. How do you do that? Depending on the business, production is done by people and/or machines and aided by technology. A business can produce the goods or services in-house or it can outsource the production. Service companies generally utilize people to produce the service. Product companies generally use machines. To scale production you also need processes that, if followed, will consistently make high-quality products or services. In producing both goods and services a business generally should be looking for 99% on-time defect-free production.

To scale production in-house requires capital because the business must add people and/or machines and/or technology before realizing the financial gains from the scale-up. Further, if a business scales by adding people and/or machines it will need more space to house production. This, too, generally requires capital, and this capital is usually needed before the added production assets produce revenue.

If a business scales by outsourcing, capital is also needed, albeit usually a smaller amount of capital. If production is outsourced, the manufacturer generally will want to be paid upon delivery or, if using a foreign manufacturer, before shipping. Financing production growth complicates the scaling decision for most growing private companies because financing can be as concerning for an entrepreneur as maintaining quality.

Sales

Scaling production is not, in and of itself, growth. Scaling production generates inventory that must be sold. Selling must be scaled, too. How do you scale sales? Sales can be scaled through people, technology (e.g. the Internet), or outsourcing. The decision of how to scale sales depends on the type of business and, in part, on whether a business is selling to the ultimate user or to an intermediary who resells to the consumer. Selling can be scaled in several ways: building an in-house sales force, outsourcing sales to independent representatives or wholesale distributors, using the Internet or other media, opening more locations, or franchising.

Fulfillment

Scaling also requires delivering the product or service to your customer no matter whether you sell it directly or indirectly. Again, you can scale fulfillment of the customer's order by adding people, machines, and technology or by outsourcing it. Most of the product companies I studied outsourced manufacturing but kept control of fulfillment to ensure quality and to control the customer relationship.

Business Model

In addition to scaling production, sales, and fulfillment, the business model must scale. Scaling the business model was a challenge for several companies in my DPGC research. Evaluating whether the business model is scalable is critical because it is possible to build a profitable small business that cannot scale, or at least not easily. For example, a business may sell high-priced products or services that only a few people can afford. Scaling may be difficult because the potential market size is small or the customers' purchasing decision times are too long for the business to survive the wait. Sometimes, even with a good product, if the sales price is high, potential purchasers may have concerns dealing with a small company that may be relatively new in the marketplace. To scale, a business often has to change its pricing model to appeal to a broader marketplace, particularly when the product or service price is relatively high and the business's track record is relatively short. Lowering the up-front costs to customers may be essential to gain market share. Five of the private companies I studied had to change from a high-price purchase model to a smaller price rent or subscription model to attract customers.

Others had to modify their sales model from a retail model to a wholesale model because they could not afford to build a sales organization. The "Sammy Snacks" case is a good example of a business that expanded by shifting from a retail sales model to a wholesale model.

DPGC Companies

In my sample I found examples of a variety of scaling strategies. Mellace Family Brands and C.R. Barger & Sons, Inc., invested or raised capital to build their own manufacturing facilities. In contrast, Octane Fitness, Inc.; Eyebobs Eyewear, Inc.; and Room & Board outsourced manufacturing.

Almost all who outsourced manufacturing overseas also sold to intermediaries in volume, opting not to sell directly to consumers. By outsourcing production and selling indirectly, these companies lessened the burdens and risks of building manufacturing facilities and a large sales force. In addition, outsourcing both production and sales enabled most to scale without resorting to outside equity capital partners. There are several examples of companies in my study that relied on outsourcing to scale, including Sammy Snacks, Octane Fitness, Inc., and Eyebobs Eyewear, Inc.

Technology

Technology was a critical enabler of scaling for a few of the companies. "Better World Books"; "C.R. Barger & Sons, Inc."; "Enchanting Travels"; and four others in my study were able to scale because of technology. For example, C.R. Barger & Sons, Inc., used technology to drive production efficiencies, lowering costs and time to market. Enchanting Travels used the Internet to drive sales and technology to drive execution excellence and to monitor quality control.

The Chicken or the Egg?

Some entrepreneurs struggled with whether to scale production ahead of or behind sales. At issue was minimizing the risks associated with scaling. Service companies generally scaled behind sales, booking business opportunities and then expanding the service capabilities to meet the demand. The conundrum was more challenging for product companies who faced the question of whether and how to expend capital in expanding production capabilities. Those product companies that outsourced production minimized their short-term capital needs and could test the viability of their scaling plans by contracting for production. Those companies that chose to keep control of production, however, were forced to address the capital needs of production. These companies either built smaller facilities on the basis of the limited capital they had available, even if such facilities were likely to be inadequate if the scaling plans were successful, or raised equity capital to finance the expansion of production capabilities. Raising equity capital often complicated the scaling efforts, however, by generating a set of issues related to the company's governance and control, and the ultimate exit scenario for the equity partner.

Scaling Case Examples

The "Sammy Snacks" cases tell a scaling story. Sammy Snacks was a retail business that tried to scale first by geographical expansion. This geographical scaling effort failed for several reasons. First, the CEO/founder tried to operate a new geographic location sixty miles away from the company base. Second, the cost of the new location's lease was so high that operating deficits during the start-up phase of the second location exceeded projections and available capital. A new CEO was hired, and he cut costs and outsourced production, stemming the operating losses. He then moved to a wholesaling model to scale.

The "C.R. Barger & Sons" case is a success story of how a young engineer took a faltering family business making and selling septic tanks and scaled it by changing a commodity product into a value-added product; adding new sales channels; and expanding geographically via the Internet.

Other important scaling issues are raised by the following cases: "Room & Board"; "Defender Direct, Inc.: A Business of Growing Leaders"; "Eyebobs Eyewear, Inc."; "Octane Fitness, Inc: The Power of Focus"; "SecureWorks"; "Global Medical Imaging, LLC"; "Trilogy Health Services, LLC: Building a Great Service Company"; "Mellace Family Brands, Inc.: Building a Socially Responsible Enterprise"; "James Abrams @ Clockwork Home Services, Inc.: Lessons from a Serial Entrepreneur"; and "Valley-Wide Health Systems, Inc."

Cases having scaling decisions that need to be decided by both the entrepreneurs and students include "Students Helping Honduras"; "C.R. Barger & Sons, Inc. (B)"; "Motor City: A Disruptive Business Model (B)"; "3 Fellers Bakery"; "Hass Shoes"; and "Enchanting Travels."

"Growth Boosters"

Scaling a business generally involves doing more of what has made the business successful to begin with. It means selling more of the business's products or services to more customers in more locations. Scaling requires leveraging existing capabilities. Scaling, however, has its limits because the market for a particular product or service is not infinite. So what do private growth companies do when the capacity for scaling of a particular product or service is reaching its limits? To continue to grow, a business must explore "growth boosters."

Businesses that reach this stage of growth must ask the following questions:

1. What complementary products or services can I sell to existing customers?
2. Can I add non-complementary products or services that my customers need, are easy for me to add, and make vendor management easier for my customers?
3. Is there another customer segment that I can sell to that requires part of my existing offering? Can I go down market?
4. What can I do to generate more frequent purchases from existing customers? Can I create more reasons to purchase my products or services?
5. Can I add a new distribution channel?
6. Can I add net margin by focusing on cost efficiencies through technology?

"Growth boosters" are those activities that involve delivering products or services more efficiently, expanding the package of products and services offered to existing clients, entering new customer segments, or making it easier for customers to buy your products or services.

Identifying potential "growth boosters" is challenging because it requires entrepreneurs to think *strategically* in contrast to scaling, which requires primarily *tactical* thinking. Scaling involves finding a broader market for existing products or services. Identifying potential "growth boosters," however, requires an experimental mindset that tests new approaches, additional products or services, and other efforts to boost sales. Only after such trial and error of innovative approaches can successful "growth boosters" also be scaled. Scaling a successful business can take it only so far. Continued growth requires innovation, testing, and then scaling those "growth boosters" that work.

Types of "Growth Boosters"

What avenues should an entrepreneur explore in seeking potential "growth boosters"? Of course, there is no single answer but successful "growth boosters" include

1. New products;
2. Product upgrades;
3. Adding services;
4. New business processes;
5. New channels of distribution;
6. Changing the customer experience;

7. Pricing innovations;

8. Branding innovations;

9. Bundling or even packaging innovations;

10. Payment innovations;

11. Different guarantees; and/or

12. Expanding along the value chain to capture a new source of value from other value chain players.

Five of the fifty-four companies in my DPGC research that had reached limits to their initial scaling efforts were at the "growth booster" stage.

The Big Customer

Sometimes, a business is catapulted to a new level of growth by the entrance of a major customer for its product or services. Seven of the fifty-four companies in DPGC research got a major boost by landing a significant public company customer. The acquisition of a big customer certainly cannot be counted on and, occasionally, even when offered, a business opts to scale according to their previous business plan. For example, Eyebobs Eyewear, Inc., turned down a big customer to keep tighter control of its operations and still grew at a compounded growth rate of more than 50% for several years.

CLASS DISCUSSION QUESTIONS

1. What do you think the biggest risk is to scaling a service business?

2. What are the biggest risks to scaling a product business?

3. Which can grow faster? Why?

4. As firms grow from $1 million to $5 million to $10 million to $20 million in revenue, why are they able to grow faster as they get bigger?

5. Do you think future scaling challenges should impact what business an entrepreneur starts? Why?

6. What do you think the major restraints are in scaling a retail business?

7. Is it easier to scale a business that sells a service or product that has a short life-span? Why?

Enchanting Travels

Enchanting Travels has grown using a joint venture model in Africa and an organic model in Argentina. Its challenge now is how to grow more quickly by expanding into new geographies. It has a scaling challenge, and the case raises the issue as to whether it should franchise to scale more quickly.

CASE DISCUSSION QUESTIONS

1. What was Enchanting Travels' differentiating customer value proposition?

2. Should Enchanting Travels franchise its business model? Why?

3. Explain the following statement: "What made Enchanting Travels successful limited its growth."

4. What are Enchanting Travels' major growth risks?

5. The founders had an unusual philosophy of hiring. How does it contribute to their success and limit their success?

6. How can Enchanting Travels expand its business without opening new locations in new countries?

7. Do you think Enchanting Travels' business model is scalable? Why?

8. Would you buy this business? Why?

ENCHANTING TRAVELS

In the early days when we were trying to build a brand and it was imperative that every single guest who booked a trip with us had a wonderful time, focusing on the operations or the issues that would have a direct impact on guest feedback or the guest experience would be of prime importance to anyone who was involved with the company—an almost fanatical approach toward guest feedback. And one of the big challenges that we faced and we continue to face is continuing to do what we have done during the past five years. Every entrepreneur goes through that very difficult task. I would say that to be able to build people's skills and abilities you have to at one point take away the safety net and let them figure it out; if the issue or the problem at hand involves solving the problem yourself as opposed to giving someone an opportunity even if they may fail, you reach a point when that focus becomes investing the time and effort in getting that person able to solve the issue or problem rather than doing it yourself.

I think that mindset is the big difference between a small start-up and a larger high-growth company that needs to enable its people to grow and do things that you would have done. I think in the first year if you had asked me what our focus areas were, I would say that I was involved in creating our product, actually "doing" rather than "managing" operations and personally fixing what went wrong. Now, if you ask me what my focus would be, I would say that investing the time to teach someone or enable someone to fix something would be the focus rather than fixing it myself. And I think that is a point to reach when growing a company. Enabling people around you to do what you do and help you grow the company is a big thing, and one of the big changes we have seen in the last couple of years.

—Parikshat Laxminarayan

Founded in 2004 by Parikshat Laxminarayan and Alexander Metzler, who met during their MBA education at INSEAD, Enchanting Travels (ET) was an India- and Germany-based travel company. Its discerning clients, mainly from Western countries, were interested in visiting exotic destinations. ET had expanded its operations to East Africa and South America, growing by 100% a year its first three years, and by 30% to 50% in 2008–09. By 2009, ET employed close to 100 people on four different continents and had booked more than 4,000 travelers, mainly from the United States, Germany, the United Kingdom, and Australia.

ET's business model was based on (1) thoroughly knowing its customers in order to customize trips that met their expectations; (2) vertically integrating and controlling every aspect of the trips; and (3) seamlessly executing all operations. This business model differentiated ET from most travel companies that typically outsourced all activities involving clients after their arrival at a destination. ET's business model required that

Case Study UVA-ENT-0144 © 2009 by the University of Virginia Darden School Foundation. This case was prepared by Monidipa Mukherjee and Sanju Jacob of the Indian School of Business, under the supervision of Edward D. Hess, as a basis for class discussion rather than to illustrate effective or ineffective handling of an administrative situation.

its employees be highly engaged with customers and used extensive measurement and information systems to quickly identify problems that could be remedied without delay.

At this time, ET had the opportunity to further expand globally and offer customers a broader choice of destinations for their customized vacations. This opportunity created a new decision for Laxminarayan and Metzler to consider: Should ET continue to expand organically or should it consider franchising in order to gain first-mover advantage in more countries faster? The two entrepreneurs pondered the advantages and disadvantages of this decision.

Genesis of the Idea

The birth of the idea for ET was somewhat of an accident and a surprise. At the end of 2003, while a student at INSEAD, Laxminarayan had visited India with several of his classmates. During their travels around South India, one student commented that his impression of India turned out to be quite different from his mental picture of the country. Laxminarayan recalled, "That set me wondering why there was a gap between the perception that outsiders bear and what India can really be if promoted and presented in an excellent manner." He wondered if he was in the presence of a business opportunity.

Back at INSEAD, Laxminarayan and Metzler discussed opening an exclusive travel service as a potential business venture after graduation. Their research about this market was encouraging because the travel industry was fairly traditional. According to Laxminarayan, "If you take out the online space, it is very traditional in the way it works, and there were a lot of unnecessary players in the value chain that weren't adding much value." He continued:

We found out that a foreign tour operator who might be offering India as one of the many destinations often did not have an on-the-ground presence in India. So he would contact a consolidator in Delhi or Mumbai, who would then subcontract to a final service provider in the final destination or in the region that the trip was actually happening. So there were three to four, or maybe even five parties between the traveler and the actual experience, which we thought was completely unnecessary and not an efficient way of doing things.

Laxminarayan and Metzler's business plan was focused on streamlining the value chain so that ET would be the single point of contact for each customer during a trip. The entrepreneurs attracted 16 investors and raised almost half of the initial money for their start-up before their June 2004 graduation. They flew to India in early July and, as Laxminarayan said, "We pretty much hit the ground running and started from there."

The Partners

Laxminarayan had grown up in India but as an undergraduate studied finance in the United States on a tennis scholarship. Prior to joining INSEAD's one-year MBA program in September 2003, he managed several projects at Analysis Group, a consulting firm in Washington, D.C., that provided economic, financial, and business strategy consulting to law firms, corporations, and government agencies. An avid international traveler, Laxminarayan acquired his tourism experience from organizing informal trips to India, using his in-depth knowledge of the country's various attractions and regions.

Before attending INSEAD, Metzler had worked as a project leader in marketing and sales strategies at Monitor Group, a strategy consulting firm. "We both came from a consulting background, which is normally a very different skill set and profile when you look at successful entrepreneurs," Laxminarayan said. Metzler also had traveled extensively through India and shared a passion for that country with his partner. Laxminarayan described their relationship:

We have a very healthy partnership. And I think one of the key things we did early on was to sit down and have certain key agreements, not a sort of a contract but more a common understanding of each other's styles, each other's preferences, each other's strengths and weaknesses. This kind of open discussion has always helped us manage through challenging times in the relationship, if there were any. And we haven't had that many.

From the first day, the partners were conscious of how their roles were divided:

There is very little overlap in day-to-day operations. We have a clear split in terms of which team is managed by whom, and there is no ambiguity in an employee's mind as to whose team he or she belongs. I think it is very important to avoid unhealthy overlap. The only decisions we make commonly are corporate level and strategy decisions. But everything else on a day-to-day level is very separated and very split. And I think that is critically important to having a successful business partnership.

Early Challenges

At first, the big challenge for the partners was managing everything themselves. They started ET with a small team: two partners, two spouses, and one employee. The five of them were responsible for sales, marketing, and operations. The initial task of deciding on a location consistent with their model seemed daunting. They spent three months combing the length and breadth of India visiting every hotel they wanted to offer to their clients. They tested everything: drivers, activities, restaurants, and cars, in detail and with a level of quality control that was taxing. They did it because they were not going to work through intermediaries. Laxminarayan explained:

It wasn't as simple as going to Delhi and telling someone I am going to plan trips to Rajasthan so can you help me out. It was actually going to every small village and destination in Rajasthan, staying at and visiting every hotel that we wanted to sell and promote in our itinerary. I think just setting up the entire operation was a huge challenge early on.

Laxminarayan and Metzler decided that the biggest differentiator between a successful travel company and one that fails before it starts or shortly thereafter was in the execution. The five-member team had a tough first six months but managed to overcome the challenges. Laxminarayan said:

All entrepreneurial ventures have risk, otherwise they won't be entrepreneurial ventures, but I think it is not about feeling 100% sure about your business plan or that making complete sense. I think it is about having sound business logic, but then much more time should be spent on executing and actually pulling it off. So for me the appetite for risk is far more important than writing a business plan. The ability to pull off a successful operation and execute on a promise is much more challenging and important than having a very picture-perfect setup or picture-perfect brand or things like that.

Expansion

When ET opened in 2004, the plan was to operate in India. The partners had agreed that, while their customer base would be Germany and North America, the destination for customers would be India. But, by 2006, ET's success in India encouraged expansion. Laxminarayan continued:

Our India model worked very successfully, and we grew very well in the first two years. We then asked ourselves—what is it that makes us successful in India? Clearly, more than knowledge of India or the background of being Indian and our presence there, it was our concept of being able to master challenging destinations, the ability to tackle unreliability, lack of professionalism, lack of transparency, the ability to manage the entire operation in a challenging destination. And secondly the ability to connect with and basically understand the mind of a customer was our key strength and value proposition and what made us different and successful. And finally, and most important, our ability to provide world-class service from India at an Indian cost base made us very different from other travel companies.

ET also feared losing its customer base unless it offered more places for them to travel. Laxminarayan explained:

Our goal was to develop a customer base that sort of stays with us for 10 years or more and takes an exotic trip every year or two. Now we have had several people who have come back to India with us on repeat trips, but our kind of guests often have a list of six, seven exotic trips they want to take. So having a lifetime customer base locked in was one of the biggest drivers of our destination expansion.

East Africa

Enchanting Africa was started up in 2006 in Nairobi with the goal of selling and operating trips initially to Kenya and Tanzania. This was a joint ownership venture between ET and Florian Keller, a European national and management consultant, who had lived in East Africa and was familiar with business and life in Africa. This partner also had experience working with several large international companies that had expanded to Africa. Having a partner who lived in Africa and was knowledgeable about the country was thought to mitigate some of the risk of testing the waters outside of India.

The complexity of Africa presented a huge challenge for ET. In an area the size of India, there were 10 countries, with different laws, regulations, and ways of operating. Although ET maintained that one of the biggest differentiators of its model was its ability to offer world-class quality and service at an Indian cost base, the infrastructure challenges, such as no high-speed bandwidth and the lack of an affordable yet highly skilled and qualified labor pool to draw from, presented significant challenges.

In spite of the challenges, Africa was an attractive travel destination for Americans and Europeans. The ET team was convinced it could make Africa even more attractive to travelers if it could adapt its Indian business model to the African environment. By the end of 2009, Africa was ET's second-biggest destination, with ET offering tours in eight countries in East and Southern Africa. "We are fairly pan-African now, and we continue to grow. We have had challenges. . . . But we recovered and are on our way to building what I imagine is a second pillar of profitability in Africa," said Laxminarayan.

South America

By 2008, ET had incorporated and founded Enchanting South America, which focused on Argentina and Chile from its head office in Argentina. The main driver behind ET's expansion in South America was twofold—first, it was a destination that fit well with ET's concept and value proposition of providing a hassle-free experience of exceptional quality in a destination that was known to be difficult. Second, its proximity to the United States, its second-biggest customer market, made South America an attractive destination.

During the expansion to South America, the partners had to decide whether to hire and train a local manager and pay compensation or to enter into a joint ownership venture as they had done in Africa. Taking the first route required one of them spend several months in Argentina to get a feel for the market, set up operations, and hire and train local employees. They chose to build the business organically. Although they knew it would take several months to start ET in that region, they also knew that the end result would be a value proposition—the end-to-end control of the luxury travel business in South America that protected their brand. This gave those customers who had traveled with them to India or Africa the chance to explore South America and enjoy the same high-quality experience with the same reliable customized service they had received in other destinations.

Human Resources

The organizational structure of ET was linear, uncomplicated, and international in culture, with 90 employees from 14 nationalities working together across five countries. Most of them worked in India out of offices in Bangalore and Delhi, where there were employees from nine nationalities. According to Laxminarayan:

It is a very healthy and open environment because it is international, and it is not a very typically Indian hierarchical business. . . . Our entire recruiting model is hiring freshers without any past experience but with a lot of potential, lots of drive, and lots of intelligence that we can mould into careers rather than laterally hiring people with experience. . . . Of our 90 or so people, I think only three had any idea of tourism and travel before they joined us. So it was a conscious decision not to hire people from the travel industry.

Laxminarayan admitted that hiring without requiring experience working in the travel industry posed some risk. "Our training on basic travel skills takes more time, so all of this is a challenge, but I think it more than pays off by having someone who doesn't have any preconceived notions and can adapt easily to a different process." ET stuck with this hiring strategy to eliminate people who already had learned operating procedures that were not appropriate for the company.

Another crucial and unique part of ET's HR strategy was to hire foreigners from its customer markets (e.g., Germany, United States, United Kingdom, and other European countries) in India to further bridge the gap between a customer and the travel experience. This focus evolved into a truly multinational and multicultural team in each of ET's offices around the world.

Structure

At the top, Laxminarayan and Metzler managed in tandem as managing directors. Laxminarayan oversaw trip operations on the ground and the sales and marketing, PR for the company's English-speaking markets (United States, United Kingdom, Australia), while Metzler did the same for ET's European customers. Corporate strategy, finance, and new destinations were evenly split between them, with Laxminarayan in charge of South America and Metzler responsible for Africa with their partner in Nairobi and Asia.

In line with its horizontal management structure, at the second layer, seven functional managers with an average age of 32 supervised a team and managed finance and accounts, operations, marketing, customer management, and reservations.

To keep an international work environment, Laxminarayan and Metzler created an open structure that allowed numerous opportunities for employee growth, which was not typical of an Indian work environment. Because of this philosophy, ET had not lost a person to another company in the travel industry.

ET had a healthy and aggressive performance-linked bonus that was one of its big drivers. Because the company believed that incentivized performance was a fragile way to keep employees, it invested a lot of time in training and giving employees a sense of emotional attachment to the company. This enabled ET to retain people at a time when attrition was the biggest business challenge in India. ET's turnover in the first five years was 15% to 20%, but that number was reduced to just 5% in subsequent years.

The Business Model

One of the aspects of the business model that was clear to Laxminarayan and Metzler right from the beginning was its strong focus on only offering tailor-made travels and to never have catalogues with standardized itineraries. In order to pull this off and to efficiently create highly customized travel experiences for each guest, they implemented a highly flexible and tailor-made IT system to automate an otherwise hugely time-intensive activity of individual itineraries. They recalled an apt Michael Porter quote from business school: "Strategy is about being different and it means deliberately choosing a different set of activities to deliver a unique mix of value."

With this in mind, ET set up processes geared to offer high-quality tailor-made travels and a unique mix of activities to enable the company to clearly differentiate themselves from competitors and leverage competitive advantages in its market space. As Alexander Metzler said, "We feel that large tour operators would find it nearly impossible to copy our business model and processes given that their entire setup is geared and catered for providing standard packages and mass tourism."

The first differentiator in ET's unique business model of vertical integration was that it handled all operations from beginning to end. Then there were the various nationalities and cultures of the people working in its offices in India, with some often coming from the same places as the customers. In short, ET was an international organization in India; out of its 60-odd employees, 25% were foreigners.

The partners also invested heavily in training their employees about company processes and about India, a complex and diverse country. Getting the right people and building up their destination knowledge through training, test trips, integration with ET operations, and integrating customer-facing employees with operations was another characteristic that set ET apart. Laxminarayan explained:

If you ask our customers why they book with Enchanting Travels, this is what often comes up: "We felt very well taken care of, the quality of interaction was fantastic, the documents we got were fantastic, but most importantly, the person we were speaking to was really able to understand our needs and had a very good competence level on how to bring India alive in an itinerary that was a good fit with our personality and our needs at a very compelling value for money equation."

One of the most appreciated value propositions that helped guests feel comfortable was ET's guest management strategy of assigning a hands-on contact person to see to all the activities of guests during their stay at a destination. Carefully selected tour guides were independent contractors who went through a quality check and a training process that taught them ET's different concept and way of doing things. Tour guides who had worked with other companies underwent a stringent selection process, and ultimately approximately 80% of the guides worked solely for ET.

On average, the overall level of education, quality, sophistication, and skills was extremely low in the travel industry worldwide. Aware of this, ET selected well-educated, competent people to train. Although ET's salary costs were higher, it was able to provide American- and European-quality service in India. By hiring foreigners and Indians on the same professional level as European or U.S. employees, ET produced the same or better quality of work as a premier travel company located in Munich or New York City. And it was able to deliver that quality from Bangalore and Delhi.

Because ET was passionate about personally experiencing, testing, and validating all hotels and restaurants that it recommended to its clients, it also tracked feedback about every hotel in its portfolio. ET invested a lot of time and money in test trips to build a destination from the ground up because the possible bias of trip advisors and independent rating agencies made it important to verify that a destination was a tailor-made travel experience. This extensive, time-consuming quality control process made expansion to a new destination a major research project. Nonetheless, ET preferred to take this slower approach to growth to make sure that its system was in sync with its promise to give guests a trip to remember.

Pricing

Laxminarayan gave all the credit for the success of the ET pricing model to the absence of middlemen. He considered it "the most innovative factor of our pricing model." Explaining why ET was not completely positioned as a luxury travel company, Laxminarayan said:

We are not as expensive as Abercrombie and Kent, the world's leading luxury travel company but neither are we as cheap as a regular tour operator. We are somewhere between those two in terms of our price positioning. We believe we offer amazing quality at a price-competitive proposition. But obviously in order to deliver that quality, we can't be playing with very small margins, which is very risky.

The Road Ahead

Sowing the early seeds of Enchanting Asia, which would initially comprise Bhutan, Myanmar, Sri Lanka, and Nepal, and then slowly include Vietnam, Cambodia, Laos, and eventually reach the Chinese borders, was ET's main focus for 2010. Also in 2010, ET planned on growing Enchanting South America to harness the potential for Argentina and Chile and in a year or so expanding to Peru and Brazil. The focus in India was to scale up by exploring avenues for new marketing channels. Laxminarayan explained:

One of our big questions going forward is how to do China? We don't have the same comfort level as we would have in South America. In China, we are daunted by the challenge of what it would take to actually run an operation with Chinese managers or even with Western managers. We need to figure out the massive potentially viable business opportunity that China presents. Would we pull that off using Africa's [joint-ownership] model or along the lines of the South American [solely owned] model?

In Laxminarayan's opinion, "One of the big challenges going forward is how to get the managers to drive growth and independently manage initiatives as opposed to me having to spend several months setting up a new operation as I did with Enchanting South America in Argentina." He concluded:

Whether we can become the Google of the travel world (at a relatively smaller scale given our industry of course) is a question that will hopefully be answered in the coming years, but I am hoping that we at least emerge as the world's leading company for high-end tailor-made travels to exotic destinations with a global reach in terms of markets and destinations.

Growth Strategy

As the ET partners pondered how to expand to China, they wondered whether they should franchise the ET concept and operational model to other countries in South American and Asia.

List of Relevant Cases

Scaling Cases

3 Fellers Bakery

Defender Direct, Inc.: A Business of Growing Leaders

Enchanting Travels

Global Medical Imaging, LLC

James Abrams @ Clockwork Home Services, Inc.: Lessons from a Serial Entrepreneur

Mellace Family Brands, Inc.: Building a Socially Responsible Enterprise

Motor City: A Disruptive Business Model (B)

Octane Fitness, Inc.: The Power of Focus

Room & Board

Sammy Snacks (A)

Sammy Snacks (B)

Sammy Snacks (C)

Sammy Snacks (D)

SecureWorks

Students Helping Honduras

Trilogy Health Services, LLC: Building a Great Service Company

"Growth Booster" Cases

Better World Books

C.R. Barger & Sons, Inc. (A)

C.R. Barger & Sons, Inc. (B)

Hass Shoes

Valley-Wide Health Systems, Inc.

Author's Commentary

In some cases, in order to grow the business, the entrepreneur needs to raise private equity capital. That raises serious new issues of control, governance, valuation, and potential exit strategies for the private equity investors.

"10 Keys to Raising Growth Capital"[1]

I spent 20 years of my career on the private equity side of the investment world—as an agent and as a principal. I participated in billions of dollars of private equity investments. Accessing private equity is part science and part art. By science, I mean raising private equity is a process that can be managed like any other business process. And by art, I mean the feel of a deal—the emotional components of the chemistry, why people do a deal with each other—the motivations, the needs, the touchy-feely stuff. Raising private equity is not simply making and closing a sale.

In summary form, here are my ten keys to successfully raising private equity growth capital.

1. *"Scrub the Patient"*

Hire an independent, objective, experienced advisor whose first job is to critique your company and find all the "obstacles to sale"—problems that can come up in due diligence—and deal with the problems up front. Common problems are poor HR compliance, lack of audited financials, tax issues, incomplete legal formation documentation, inadequate financial personnel, unresolved lawsuits, IP issues, uncollectable receivables, etc. Every company has issues. I have never worked on a deal where the actual income was what the owner said it was. FIX THE PROBLEMS BEFORE GOING TO MARKET.

---

1. Edward D. Hess, "10 Keys to Raising Growth Capital," *The Catalyst*, April 2004.

2. *Target the Right Money*

Private equity investors can be categorized along three (3) parameters: (A) industries in which they will invest; (B) preferred dollar size of the investment; and (C) geographical preference. Find people for whom you meet all three qualification criteria. Then choose advisors (financial, legal, and accounting) who are high-quality institutional firms who have done deals with the people you have targeted. Choose the right advisors who can "nominate" you to join the private equity club. The right advisors legitimize you because it is assumed that they would not take you on as a client unless you were good.

3. *Where's the Beef?*

Investors are looking for growth stories and the management team that can execute—pure and simple. Why is your opportunity compelling? Why can you execute? Prepare a one-and-a-half-page Executive Summary and a ten-page Offering Memorandum. Remember the C's—be Concise, be Clear, and be Compelling. Avoid the D's—denial and defensiveness.

4. *Create a Competition*

Just like in high school, everyone likes to take the pretty girl or handsome boy to the dance. Create a competition. What do I mean by a competition? Have more than one firm bidding on your deal and keep the bidding alive until you have negotiated all the major financial, operational, control, and exit issues. Only through a competition will you get a market deal; only through a competition can you keep investors' pricing and valuations "honest." The key to a competition is getting the first major player to the table to talk and then using that player as legitimization—as "bait"—as an attractor—to bring in other players. Investors do care and do take notice of who their competition is.

5. *Keep the Leverage*

He who has the gold makes the rules. And you do not have the gold. Your only recourse to keep the game from becoming even more tilted to the money's advantage is by keeping your competition going as long as possible. Get bids and rebids and negotiate major deal points BEFORE signing an exclusive or a letter of intent. Once you sign an exclusive or a letter of intent, you have lost whatever leverage you had because you will lose the other interested parties and they will focus on other deals. And psychologically, does anyone like being someone's second choice?

6. *"Money Is Fungible"*

Money is fungible. What else can your new investor bring to the table? Suppliers? Customers? Relationships? What doors can they open? What companies have they invested in which can become customers or joint venture partners? And remember the key test: Would you invite the money partner over to dinner? Do you like the people? Everyone is nice and a good partner when everything goes well—check them out. What are they like when things go bad? Let me stress this point—It is easy to be nice and honest when things are going well. But business does not always go well. You will not do as well as you think. How is the money partner when the going gets tough? How have they reacted in the past? Find out!

7. Start Early

In the best of times—absent luck or an unusual circumstance—closing a money deal takes six to nine months from start to finish. So start early and avoid the vacation times of August and December 15th to January 15th. Do not be in a position of an investor finding out on due diligence that you are running out of cash. Remember the ole country saying of "Banks like to loan money to people who don't need it."

8. Avoid the Deal Killers

So once you have chosen a partner and have negotiated a fair deal, what can kill your deal? Surprises, lies, trying to retrade the deal, and "bad" attorneys. Who are the "bad" attorneys? Attorneys who see it as their mission to prove they are smarter than either you or the other side's attorneys and who try to impress you with how smart they are. Closing a deal is a difficult enough emotional experience without ego playing a big role. Every deal will "die" an unexpected death two or three times. Hire a good, experienced attorney who is a deal closer and who can advise you of the risks, quantify those risks, and allow you to make informed business judgments.

9. Find Someone Who Needs to Do a Deal

Ultimately, you need to find someone who for some reason personal to them needs to do a deal. Investors need to do deals for different reasons—figure out their motivations. But do not get cocky. I have seen investors walk at the closing table because of changes external to the deal—industry developments, macroeconomics, and their needs have changed. A deal is never, never done until the check clears.

10. Don't Forget the Business

Raising equity is a time-consuming effort and it requires you to focus on things other than the business. Who will cover for you in running the business? How can you minimize the loss of momentum, focus, accountability? Plan and prepare to spend half of your time on fund-raising efforts for six months. How will you do it?

Conclusion

Raising private equity successfully and efficiently is both a process management task and a sale—you are selling yourself, your enthusiasm, credibility, and ability to execute. Are you a good "horse" to bet on? If the answer is yes, pick the right team of advisors and go for it.

9

The Added Complexity of Managing a Family Business[1]

Family businesses are a major part of the U.S. economy. Eighty percent or more of all businesses in the United States are family controlled. Over 60 percent of the U.S. work force works for a family business.[2] By definition, family businesses are owned by families—groups of related individuals, each with their own unique mixture of values, history, and emotional relationships. Through the family business some families seek continuity, closeness, a sense of community, and belonging to something meaningful, As well, the business is a major source of family wealth. Although the issues raised in this chapter apply to family businesses of any size, they are of particular concern in multigenerational family businesses.

The Difference

What makes family businesses different from non-family businesses is the added complexity of family dynamics that affects how the business operates and makes decisions—in terms of both the processes and, often, the substance of the decisions. Families factor family needs, hopes, and fears into their decisions regarding the business. Family businesses are fraught with sibling or cousin rivalries, jealousies, and competition for parental love, approval, and financial favor. Family dynamics, the family's ways of communicating and making decisions, have the potential of adversely affecting the business unless they are proactively managed. This is the additional challenge of managing a family business.

---

1. This chapter was adapted from *The Successful Family Business: A Proactive Plan for Managing Both the Family & the Business* by Edward D. Hess, Copyright © 2006 Praeger. Reprinted with permission of the publisher.

2. J. H. Astrachan and M. C. Shanker, "Family Businesses Contributing to the U.S. Economy: A Closer Look," *Family Business Review* (September 2003): 218.

As a result, a successful Family Business Leader (FBL)—the chairman-CEO of the family business—carries the responsibility of managing not only the business but also the family. The preceding chapters stressed the importance of planning and process to manage business growth. Planning and process are just as important in dealing with the family dynamics found in all family businesses. Chapter 5 discussed how an entrepreneur must change how he or she manages as a business expands. When family businesses grow and the number of family members involved in the business either as employees or shareholders increases, the entrepreneur generally must change the usual ways of dealing both with the family and the family business.

Successful family businesses "do not let the family destroy the business or the business destroy the family." This is not always an easy maxim to follow, but planning for some inevitable decisions, anticipating potential areas of conflict, and providing a forum for educating and communicating with family members are necessary.

Rules of Thumb

I have found several rules of thumb working with and researching family businesses:

1. The chances of having a successful family business will be greater if both the business and family dynamics are *proactively* managed.

2. To manage a family business successfully, it is important to acknowledge that having recurring family issues that affect the operation of the business is the norm. For family businesses there is a complex interaction of family issues impacting the business and business issues impacting each family member differently. Family members have differing expectations about how financial resources of the business should be used based on their personal situations. The issues will change as the family expands and ages because family members' emotional and financial needs will change with their life circumstances. These issues, although challenging, are predictable. They occur in most family businesses and can be proactively managed to mitigate consequences potentially adverse to the business.

3. It is important to have a mindset that takes into account the differing, changing perspectives of the business, the family, and the non-family-member employees and shareholders, if any.

4. It is also important to establish a process of providing information and identifying and debating family business issues early, before they can derail important business opportunities.

5. That proactive family business management process (Process), which will be discussed later, should be based upon the principles of transparency, inclusiveness, fairness, respectful behavior, and frequent communications. The Process

should also reinforce the key values that are most important to the family. Identifying and agreeing on fundamental family values provides guidance in important decision making and can be a crucial aid in mitigating jealousies, rivalries, and financial self-interest. It is important to understand that the family and business are two dynamic, evolving, changing entities—each unique—each with their own history, challenges, strengths, weaknesses, opportunities, and threats. It is rare for a family and a business to be static. Something is always changing. Family members are aging—going to college, getting married, having children, buying homes, getting older, getting sick, and getting divorced. Likewise, the business is changing—new competitors, employees quitting, customers changing, and growing pains. It is this constant change—the evolution of the family as well as the business—that can undermine a family business's success if both are not proactively managed.

Multiple Stakeholders

Not only are the family and the business both evolving, dynamic entities, but each is made up of different, although overlapping, constituents or members. Family members include the founders of the business, family shareholders, their children, their grandchildren, and spouses, some of whom may work in the business. In addition, some family members may own stock in the family business while others may not. Adding to the complexity of managing a family business is that the business will likely have non-family-member employees and also may have non-family-member shareholders whose interests impact the business and the family. The complexity of the issues and the range of perspectives of individuals involved will vary with their roles in the family and in the business. It is this dynamic and these different perspectives that present the challenges of managing a family business.

Common Conflicts

Most family business conflicts involve either money or fairness. They generally can be grouped into one of the following five categories:

1. *Inter*-generational equity, financial, and control issues;
2. *Intra*-generational equity, financial, and power issues;
3. Family member favoritism or privileges versus arm's-length market business dealings;
4. Jealousies and rivalries between family members competing for recognition, love, and money; and
5. Succession issues.

Family Processes

To deal with these issues, FBLs need to understand that family business issues are inevitable, are normal, and will change as the business grows and as the family grows. To deal with these issues the FBL must utilize consistently applied or standardized processes to debate and decide issues on the basis of the fundamental principles discussed above. In deciding family business issues or resolving family business conflicts, the process of how that is done is as important as the answer or decision. In addition, successful family businesses need to formally create their own values statement that establishes the overarching goals of the family with respect to the business. And, to guide the interactions of the family in relation to the business, it is also important to develop a code of conduct that outlines what is expected of family members and what behaviors are not to be tolerated, as well as family business operating principles. These family business operating principles should include, for example, rules for employing family members and family members' use of business assets.

I was interviewed to be an advisor to a very successful fourth-generation Oklahoma family business with over 100 family shareholders. One of the board members asked if my approach to family business issues had changed over the years. I answered:

Yes, in the following ways. I have learned that one cannot manage family business issues in the same manner as most entrepreneurs manage their business; family business issues are complex and often with emotional undercurrents that are not obvious. When implementing a Process and encouraging family exchanges of information and ideas, it is likely that it will take time for people to get comfortable and understand other family members' perspectives. And, depending on the nature and magnitude of the business issues, it will also take time to reach decisions. In spite of the time needed to implement and maintain a proactive management of family business, it is worth it because it produces much better results than reactive management. Proactively dealing with issues can mitigate uneducated opinions, anger, jealousies, and greed. Ultimately, to ensure the long-term viability of the family business, the family has to believe and behave on the basis of the principle that business success and family harmony outweigh the financial or personal self-interest of any one family member.

The Mindset of the Family Business Leader

In many cases, FBLs have been entrepreneurs who have built the family business from the ground up. Entrepreneurs tend to be confident, strong-willed, dominant personalities used to overcoming obstacles and problems through perseverance, willpower, and focus. Many have built their successful business "doing it their way" and have not developed a business style well suited to managing families. Often, entrepreneurs are narrowly focused on business results, a characteristic that served them well in building the business, but such a focus can be inadequate in juggling the complex dynamics of a growing family business. Strong-willed entrepreneurs often view the family side of family business as a nuisance, at best. They fail to understand the potential harm to the business of unresolved family issues, believing that if the family would just sit back and let the entrepreneur handle the business, the family issues would just melt away. This hierarchical, and in most cases, patriarchal mindset generally will not work when there are adult children of the business founder(s) either working in or owning part of the business as shareholders. They will have strong interests in the business revenues, at least, and may have opinions about how the business should operate as well.

Once the business has evolved to include many family members—either directly as employees or indirectly as shareholders—these entrepreneurial, business-only approaches fail to work well in identifying or resolving emerging family business issues. One cannot send the family "down the highway"—you have family, the good and the bad, for life. The family goes home with you at night.

In managing family business issues, FBLs must continuously ask themselves two questions: (1) What is in the family's best interests? and (2) What is in the business's best interests?

FBL Skills

To be an effective FBL, the entrepreneur must become a servant leader serving the family and the business. This is the same as the concept introduced in Chapter 5, in which the entrepreneur evolves into being a servant of the business. Servant leaders must learn how to:

- Be sensitive and emotionally intelligent;
- Be open and listen with respect;
- Be patient and respectful with those family members with less business experience;
- Listen, educate, and build consensus; and
- Act in accordance with and teach family members the family values.

One of the biggest challenges for FBLs is realizing that dealing with family issues takes time—time to listen, time to think, time to educate, time to talk, and time to reach a decision.

Different perspectives will exist and have to be aired honestly, discussed openly, and sometimes hotly debated. The act of being sensitive to, acknowledging, and leading an all-encompassing family discussion about these different viewpoints is the act and skill of family business leadership.

It is the skills of sensitivity, empathy, listening, bringing out different viewpoints, building consensus, and ultimately making the hard decision—what is right for both the family and the business at this point in time and under these known circumstances.

Common Mistakes

Unfortunately, many FBLs make common mistakes when facing difficult family business issues. These include:

1. Avoidance—Avoiding, delaying, or believing family business issues will vanish on their own; and/or
2. Denial—Failing to accept or plan for certain realities—particularly those related to one's own limitations or mortality (including lack of skills sets and succession planning), or inability to candidly assess the abilities of their children to assume leadership roles in the business.

Avoiding family business issues frequently only delays the need to address them. Rarely do significant issues simply dissipate, and often they fester and the aggrieved party or parties become more entrenched and angry not only about the issue but also about how they are being treated.

More Money, More Problems

Family business issues usually involve money. But often, beneath the money issues are emotional issues of intergenerational or intra-generational equity or psychological needs of wanting to be valued, respected, and loved by one's family. Being ignored or dismissed makes a family member feel like a second-class citizen, particularly when the aggrieved party receives minimal economic benefits from the family business while other family members receive significant current economic benefits.

The FBL must anticipate life changes in the family such as sending children to college, marriage, divorce, or retirement. These life changes will ultimately have an impact on the business and the FBL must be proactive in resolving them. Although the FBL may think his younger son would make a fine successor, how would the other siblings, particularly the eldest son, react? When the FBL shows obvious signs of cognitive decline, who should raise the need for succession planning and in what forum? These emotional attachments make it more difficult for many family members to be as direct with each other about business needs, due to a reticence to hurt another's feelings as well as the desire to avoid conflict. The failure to address these decisions until a family crisis, however, often is magnified in a parallel business crisis as well.

A Proactive Family Business Management Process

In addition to a broad perspective of the family, a family business requires a different management process to manage the family side of the business. The main purpose of a proactive family business management process is to prevent or mitigate major family disputes that put the business at risk and disrupt family relations. Family business issues will arise frequently, but they are predictable and, in many cases, can be planned for so the adverse impact to the family and the business can be largely avoided. What should the FBL do to deal proactively with these realities?

What is needed is a Process—mechanisms and rules through which family members can:

1. Be educated, often, about the family business and its financial capacity and needs;
2. Have a forum to raise questions, concerns, and issues;
3. Discuss openly and understand family business issues from the different perspectives and viewpoints of all of the family members; and
4. Have a means for reaching consensus on what is in the best interests of both the family and of the business.

Any Process for family involvement that is adopted should take into account the underlying needs of family members to be listened to in a respectful manner and to have their views considered irrespective of age, gender, or business experience. In addition, the Process must be inclusive, transparent, and respectful of family members' input. And consistently used.

Inclusion

Fundamentally, for a proactive family business management Process to work, it must be inclusive. Inclusion means that every adult family shareholder, adult family employee, and their spouses should be included in the Process. The purpose of inclusion is to educate and communicate with all family members impacted by or involved in the family business about the status of the business, the role of individual family members in the business, and other issues that might affect their personal and financial interests in the family business. Inclusion promotes a better understanding of the operation of the family business and mitigates the potential of misinformation derailing family harmony. Excluding, or failing to include, those family members who do not work in the business or family members who live out of state results in a two-class system that often leads to misunderstandings, jealousies, and conflict that can undermine the business. The purpose of inclusion is to prevent or mitigate the likelihood of major family disputes.

Common client questions about initiating a family inclusion process include the following:

1. Should spouses of family members be included?
2. At what age should children or beneficiaries of family trusts be included?

Whether to include spouses of family members is an easy question to answer. The answer is yes. Even if the spouses are not shareholders, the answer is yes. Why should spouses be included? First, education about the business will lessen the impact of ignorance or rumors on feelings, judgments, and opinions. Spouses are going to have input either directly by participating in the Process or indirectly through pillow talk. Spouses can mitigate sibling jealousies or rivalries if they are treated with respect, provided information, and given the opportunity to be heard. Often when spouses are excluded and uneducated about the family business, they emerge as a major factor in pushing their family member spouse to seek more power, money, or prestige, fueling family strife.

Why is inclusion of family members difficult for many FBLs? Often family business leaders are knowledgeable business people, have founded the business or have been instrumental in its growth, and are wary of any "outside" input. Many are men with little patience, tolerance for differing points of view, emotional intelligence, or understanding for family members without business education or experience. Gender and generational biases may also be in play. Suddenly being asked to include daughters or grandsons on the family business board, or even in periodic family business meetings, for some, takes a major leap of faith.

Inclusion is not successful, however, if it is only perfunctory. Inclusion works to mitigate and preempt family disputes only when it is substantive and participants are given genuine opportunities to be heard and their input is respected and taken into consideration in the family business decision making. Having the FBL make major family business decisions and then informing family members or appearing to seek input *post facto* frustrates the purpose of inclusion. Attempts to limit inclusion to those family members working in the business or to family members with business or finance degrees are problematic, as is limiting broader family input to a *pro forma* approval. Inclusion must be genuine and broad to be an effective proactive family management tool.

Although my recommendation is for broad inclusion of family members, a frequent question is when children should be included in the family business education and communication processes. In many multigenerational family businesses stock ownership is held in trust for children or grandchildren. At what age should these beneficiaries be included? Clearly, when the trust beneficiaries reach the age of 18, they should be included in the Process and afforded full education, input, and communication rights regardless of the terms or powers of the trust agreement. However, there are many variations of including younger family members.

For example, one of my clients has over 200 family shareholders spanning four generations. Because of the financial success of the business and its investments, many trusts were established for estate planning purposes. They adopted the rule of 18 for full inclusion. But they went further and allow any beneficiary aged 15 through 18 to participate in the family education and communication process if they desire to do so. Why? Again, they have learned that the more family members know about the business, the less likely that rumors or misunderstandings can create false opinions or prejudices and feelings of unfair treatment.

So keep in mind the purposes of inclusion—to educate and to give people the opportunity to be heard and to mitigate to the extent possible misinformation fueling family disputes.

Information Transparency

Saying that all adult family members should be included in periodic forums to educate them about the business is fine as far as it goes, but what information about the business should the FBL provide? In general, the more information, the better. Inclusion works to tamp down counterproductive family issues only if family members (including spouses) are given adequate information about the business, including detailed operating financials.

That information should include all the details about any financial dealings between any family member and the business including salaries, benefits, perks, the purchase of company inventory, or the sale of services or products to the family business. Transparency means an open book. No family member shareholder should be surprised by the occurrence of, amount of, or timing of a financial benefit received by any other family member from the business.

Transparency in the financial dealings of the family business is a hard goal for many FBLs to accept for at least two reasons. First, knowledge is power, and some FBLs may be concerned about the wrong people—within and outside the family—knowing too much about the business. This knowledge might generate challenges to their nearly absolute control of the family business. In addition, transparency will expose any inequitable dealings with family members that have occurred. Second, many FBLs think giving detailed financial information to family members is simply a waste of time because many family members are not knowledgeable about the business or its finances.

Respectful and Frequent Two-Way Communication

Having a fruitful, proactive family management Process does not translate into providing only numbers or reports. Process is much more. In addition to educating family members about the business, it is important to provide a forum for two-way communication. Process requires explaining, teaching, and answering questions that can be elementary or complex. It also requires a respect for family input.

An inclusive, transparent, proactive family business management Process will not have positive effects if family members' views are not solicited and listened to with respect. People want their input and views to be respected, valued, and considered by the family. These discussions should be conducted with some basic rules of participation, such as the following:

1. All views should be listened to with respect;
2. People should not interrupt or characterize input as stupid, ill-informed, or immature;
3. Views should not be critiqued in a personally offensive manner; and
4. *Respectful* disagreeing or dissenting views should be encouraged.

The FBL must enforce the rules of participation and set the tone to encourage openness, respect, and good discussion.

In many cases, providing family members with substantive information about the family business and the opportunity to have their input respected and considered can prevent family disputes. It is simple in principle, but devilishly difficult for many entrepreneurs, business builders, and FBLs to execute. Execution takes commitment, discipline, focus, and an iterative improvement attitude. Proactively managing the family side of the business takes time, but it is an investment worth making in building a legacy business that survives beyond one generation. The education of and two-way communications with family members must be frequent to be effective. Many FBL clients find it intellectually easy to agree with the need for a proactive family management process but, for many, their immediate reaction is "okay, we will do this stuff every year at the annual meeting." Many believe they are already including the family. However, particularly as the family grows, an annual opportunity to be heard is inadequate.

The proactive family business management process should include frequent communications from the FBL to the family. In addition, communication from family members should be encouraged. How should this be done? There is no one-size-fits-all approach, but here are a few examples that I have seen:

1. Invite all interested family members to attend any board meeting;
2. Conduct a quarterly conference call with an 800 dial-in number for any interested family member;
3. Hold board meetings in the different cities where family shareholders live;
4. Routinely solicit questions from family members and respond in writing to all shareholders—irrespective of whether they asked the question; and
5. Adopt committee structures and populate the committees with family members not involved in the business on a daily basis.

There are many ways to give family members the opportunity to ask questions and have input, but what is important is that the FBL's actions are consistent with his or her words. "Walk the talk" is so important in this area. As I tell my clients, in most cases, the proactive family business management Process is more important than the format or ultimate answer to a family member's query. Although all views cannot be adopted, respectfully airing family members' ideas reinforces the notion that all are valued participants in the family business.

Yes, some family members will want a larger role, more power over family business decision making, and larger shares of the business. And some will have strong self-interests at odds with what is good for the family or the business. But these tendencies can be better managed proactively in an open, transparent process since "non-offending" family members will seek to uphold family stewardship values— what is best for the business and what is best for the family.

A Good Family Process

The essential components of good proactive family business management Process are, at a minimum:

1. Quarterly two-way communications to shareholders discussing business issues, financial results, and upcoming family issues;
2. Quarterly board meetings with open attendance;
3. Annual audited financial statements distributed to all shareholders with question-and-answer sessions;
4. Annual family and shareholder meetings where education and input are emphasized—not the type of two-hour meetings approving board elections, financials, and previous minutes of meetings often seen with non-family businesses;
5. The adoption and use of a Family Values Statement;
6. The adoption and use of a Family Code of Conduct; and
7. The adoption of consistently applied Family Business Operating Rules concerning family employment, compensation, dividends, stock ownership, stock buy-back plan, and stock transfer rights.

The larger the number of family shareholders, the more geographically dispersed family shareholders are and the more generations involved, the more important a good institutionalized proactive family business management Process will be. Institutionalizing this Process promotes consistency and fairly applied family business policies.

This Process is the HOW of building family trust and the family's commitment to the fundamental principle that what is in the best interests of the family and of the business outweighs, or is more important than, the financial self-interest of any one family member.

CLASS DISCUSSION QUESTIONS

1. What rules should a family consider concerning employment of family members?

2. Should family members be able to ask employees to do personal work for the family? Why? If so, under what circumstances?

3. Should family members be required to have pre-nuptial restrictions on their spouse's ownership of family business stock? Why?

4. Should family members owning stock in the business be restricted from selling that stock? Why? If so, under what circumstances?

5. Should family shareholders not working in the business receive dividends equal to the compensation of family members working in the business? Why?

6. How can an entrepreneur structure the family involvement in the business so the business passes to future generations?

7. When should a non-family member be made CEO of a family business?

Edens & Avant

Now let's look at the issue of succession planning and how one successful entrepreneur using the philosophy and principles expressed in this chapter made the hard decision between three very different potential CEO successors. How did he balance the various needs of his family, his employees, his shareholders, and his personal desires for the company to be institutionalized beyond his tenure?

CASE DISCUSSION QUESTIONS

1. Put yourself in Joe Edens's shoes. What are your key concerns about succession? Your goals? Whose (stakeholders) interests do you need to consider?

2. How did Edens's family history impact his views about succession?

3. Joe Edens hires you as his advisor. He asks you to outline the pros and cons of each of the three candidates. What would you tell him?

4. Whom would you choose? Why?

5. What process should he use to get buy-in from the stakeholders?

6. What process should Joe use to pass on the CEO mantle to the successor?

7. Which succession choice has the least risk? Which has the most risk? Why?

8. Joe can pick only one successor. He has three good candidates, all of whom he wants to stay with the company as employees or, in the case of the outside candidate, as a consultant. As Joe's advisor, he asks you how he can accomplish that goal. What would you tell him?

9. Role play being the outsider who, if chosen, has discussions with the son and loyal employee trying to convince them to work for him.

CASE
STUDY

EDENS & AVANT

In 2006, Edens & Avant (Edens) was the largest private owner of neighborhood retail shopping centers in the United States. The company's operations extended geographically from New England to Florida, with major regional offices in Boston, Washington, D.C., Miami, and Atlanta. Based in Columbia, South Carolina, Edens owned 140 shopping centers, employed more than 175 people, and had net operating income that topped $160 million. Its assets were valued at more than $3.5 billion, and it was developing over $1.6 billion of new shopping centers. Owned primarily by the Edens family, its management team, and three large institutional investors, Edens was a full-service real-estate development and management company involved in the design, construction, leasing, management, and rehabilitation of retail and retail-mixed-use properties.

Started by Joe Edens Jr. (Joe Jr.) in 1967, the business provided financial security for his family and its employees and made major contributions to the community; thus, Joe Jr.'s choice of his successor was a critical decision that concerned many people. He had three candidates under consideration.

Beginnings

Joe Sr.

Joe's father, Joe Edens Sr. (Joe Sr.), was one of 16 children born to a self-made wealthy Columbia cotton farmer, who, even though he had become wealthy as a cotton farmer, decided to switch to the more profitable area of peach farming. Unfortunately, before he was able to transition his crop, it was wiped out in a boll-weevil disaster, and the so-called entrepreneur lost his family's livelihood and entire fortune. He died a broken man. At the time of his death, his son Joe Sr. was only 10 years old, but he dropped out of school and went to work to support his family. Joe Sr. never returned to formal schooling but continued to learn, as he often said, "by attending the school of hard knocks."

In 1929, at the age of 17, Joe Sr. and his brother Drake opened their first produce stand in Columbia with $200 of their own money, a Mettler Toledo hanging scale, and their first batch of produce purchased from wholesalers. Joe Sr. spoke about the risk and fragility of the start-up in a speech he gave in 1954:

In the late twenties, with $200, a barrel of apples, and faith in God, my brother and I opened a small fruit store on Assembly Street in Columbia. Dealing only in fruits and vegetables and

---

Case Study UVA-S-0146 © 2007 by the University of Virginia Darden School Foundation. This case was prepared by Edward D. Hess as a basis for class discussion rather than to illustrate effective or ineffective handling of an administrative situation.

without any refrigeration, selling was our business from the very beginning. From the orchard in the mountains of Virginia, my brother Drake bought five carloads of apples; one car to be shipped each week for a period of five weeks. Early on the first day of the week, we were notified by the freight agent that we had five cars of apples on hand for our account. Needless to say that someone had made an awful mistake. With concerted effort, we began selling apples in dozens, bushels, pecks, and in every conceivable fashion. In nine days, we were successful in selling four carloads, and without question, every home in Columbia had an ample supply of apples for the winter.

Of course, we had sold the best first, including Delicious, Winesap, and other choice varieties. The last was a carload of Pippins, the little greenish-looking apple that in those days no one wanted. All of a sudden, the weather turned warm. Realizing that Columbia was well stocked, we began to try our luck in other towns, including Winnsboro, Chester, Great Falls, and others. After trying for two days, the customers I called on had all but convinced me that the product I was selling was no good and would not sell at any price. In fact, I began to wonder if the apples were poisoned.

I never shall forget when I returned to Columbia late Friday afternoon after a final try in Augusta, Georgia. The apples had become spotted, and in an old house near the freight station where the remainder [of the apples had been stored in a freight car], the bees had begun to swarm over the fruit. We were discouraged and almost defeated, but we knew that we must sell this last car that was the profit on the five cars if we were to remain in business. From greater powers, the solution to our problem came to us. By telegram, we ordered a cider press from Atlanta, Georgia, and by late Saturday night our precious cargo had been converted into cider—in fact, honey-flavored cider, something new for the day. On Monday morning, I went back over the same route where I had tried to sell the apples. With apples packed six gallons to the case, I sold every case in one day without any trouble, and realized far more than the apples would have brought at top price.

The Edens's fruit stand diversified and expanded when customers requested nonperishable items like flour and canned sardines. In 1931, it moved into a bigger 3,000-square-foot store. In 1932, a second store opened in Columbia, and by 1956, there were 38 stores in South Carolina. Over the next 25 years, what had started out as a small fruit stand in 1929 became Edens Food Stores, a business that included a bakery, a huge warehouse, and a fleet of refrigerated trailer trucks. Sales grew from more than $3 million, in 1945, to more than $16 million by 1956, establishing Edens Food Stores as a dominant grocer in South Carolina, with a business based on a culture of "That There May Be More For All." Employees were considered part of a family dedicated to "friendly and courteous service" and, as in many family businesses, Joe Sr.'s personal values became his business's core values (Figure 9.1).

Figure 9.1.   Core Values of Edens Food Stores

"Let's make it 1,000% for '47" —Joe Edens Sr. in 1946	
Loyalty	100%
Interest	100%
Dependability	100%
Reliability	100%
Energy	100%
Ability	100%
Character	100%
Cooperation	100%
Salesmanship	100%
Efficiency	100%
Total	1,000%

SOURCE: Courtesy of Edens & Avant.

In 1956, Joe Sr. and his brother merged Edens Foods with Winn Lovett—a Jacksonville, Florida, grocery chain—and received approximately $12 million in stock, a substantial amount of money at the time. Winn Lovett set up a division in Columbia called Edens Winn Lovett, which became Edens Winn-Dixie after merging with the Dixie Home Stores chain, headquartered in Greenville, South Carolina, in late 1955, and, ultimately, Winn-Dixie. Winn-Dixie wanted Joe Sr. to move to Jacksonville, Florida, to work in top management, but his family wanted to stay put.

So Joe Sr., a multimillionaire at the age of 44, left Winn-Dixie to enter politics and public service, becoming a trustee of both Emory University and Wofford College. He also became a political contemporary of Governor Strom Thurmond and the driving force behind changing the form of city government in Columbia, South Carolina, from a structure with concentrated mayoral power to a structure with power distributed between the city council and the city manager. Joe Sr. was constantly being asked to head fund-raising campaigns for local hospitals, churches, the YMCA, and other organizations. Still, he missed the business world and looked for new business opportunities. In 1957, he found the business he was looking for. It manufactured custom-made architectural plastics and aluminum products, hot new items that did not rust, which was important in the wet, humid southern climate because these products did not require frequent repainting.

From 1957 to 1967, according to Joe Jr., "The business went from one chaos to another—this business did not play to Dad's strengths. He was a terrific food retailer, but he was completely lost in the world of manufacturing." The result was that 10 years after buying the manufacturing business, Joe Sr. had depleted the millions he had made in the food business. Thus, history had repeated itself: like his father, Joe Sr. had accumulated wealth at an early age and then lost it.

Joe Jr.

It was into this heritage of individuality, entrepreneurship, risk-taking, and constant searching for success that Joe Jr.—the main character in this story—was born, in 1941. At the age of eight, he began working in his father's food stores 20 hours a week—seven-and-a-half hours after school on weekdays and twelve-and-a-half hours on Saturdays—for a weekly paycheck of $4.65. To maximize his earnings, he frequently carried grocery bags for ladies to their cars or homes. Very early on, while bagging groceries, he discovered and followed two fundamental business principles.

- Tips will be bigger if you are nice to the customers.
- You make the most money if you figure out which customers are big tippers and appreciate your prompt, competent, and courteous service.

Learning the food business from the ground up, Joe Jr. worked in the family food stores all through elementary and high school and six days a week in the summers. He was promoted from bagger to merchandise stocker and then to meat cutter by the age of 12. His father's admonitions about service, courtesy, friendliness, and quality were all taken in by Joe Jr., along with his family's strong Methodist beliefs. These values would drive his success as a cutting-edge innovator in the real-estate industry and as a builder of one of the biggest private real-estate companies in the United States.

At that time in small Southern towns, football was the dominant way for a boy to gain recognition while in high school. Joe Jr. was a good football player, scouted by 35 colleges and universities, and during his senior year his team won the state championship. But during that game, he suffered an ankle injury that ended any chance of his going to the college of his choice, as he could not rely on his mediocre grades for admission. Instead, he attended the Citadel at the same time his father's venture into the custom-manufacturing business had begun to "sink" the family emotionally and financially. Feeling guilty because he felt he was adding to the family's financial burden, Joe Jr. left the Citadel and returned home.

Homecoming for Joe Jr. was difficult because his father berated him for his academic failure. In a way, it was as if he were an outlet for his father's anger at his business failure that ended his reign as one of the town's financial, political, and charitable leaders. Desperate to earn money, 20-year-old Joe Jr. answered an ad in a Columbia newspaper that read: "Real Estate Salesman Wanted—No College Degree Necessary." He liked real estate well enough but was interested mostly because he had no college degree.

Joe Jr. worked one year at Boineau Realty, selling residential and some commercial real estate. In 1961, after only a year at Boineau, his father's sales manager recruited him to work in sales at his father's failing business, where he reported to the sales manager rather than to his father. After 18 months, because of his selling success, he was elevated to sales manager. Still feeling duty-bound to help his father, he spent the next five years trying to make his father's business work in spite of his distaste for manufacturing. In 1966, after a huge disagreement with his father, Joe Jr. finally left the business although he did not completely abandon his father.

During the time Joe Jr. worked in his father's manufacturing business, he bought old houses and fixed them up as rental units, primarily with 100% financing. By 1966, he had accumulated more than 300 rental units, and he gave his father all the equity created and income derived from the renovated homes. Then, backed by $500 drawn from a Banker's Trust credit card, Joe Jr. opened Joe Edens Realty. He bought some used furniture and, as the sole proprietor, rented an office for $225 a month. Unfortunately, his father's deteriorating health and failing business became such a problem that Joe Jr.'s cousin offered to support him if he would help sell or liquidate his father's business. When his father's business was sold 10 months later, Joe Jr. was able to return to his own real-estate business with no more capital than he had when he started.

Luckily, in the latter part of 1966, a serendipitous event took place that changed Joe Jr.'s personal and business life. He learned that Bi-Lo, a new food chain in Greenville, wanted to expand to Columbia. Driven by ambition and fond memories of growing up in the grocery business, he drove to Greenville to see Frank Outlaw, the CEO of Bi-Lo and a former executive with the Dixie Home Store chain. He had no appointment but he had a plan to sell Outlaw a site for a grocery store in Columbia. When he left Greenville later that day, he had a 30-day exclusive to find Bi-Lo its first Columbia site. He found what he thought would be a great site, but what Outlaw decided to do next was momentous. He told Joe Jr. that Bi-Lo was not interested in owning the site but in leasing it. He wanted Joe Jr. to build a shopping center in which Bi-Lo could lease a store. It was a change in plans that started Joe Jr. down a new business path.

Shopping centers had started to evolve in the mid-1960s, when grocery and drug stores wanted to reach new customers in new neighborhoods. But in Columbia at that time, there were only three neighborhood centers, which had been built in the late 1950s. In 1967, Joe Jr. built his first 75,000-square-foot shopping center, which included a Bi-Lo food store, drug store, shoe store, Dollar Store, and dry cleaners. The shopping center that began with an entrepreneur's unannounced call on the president of Bi-Lo Groceries was named Edens Plaza.

Joe Jr. reinvested whatever cash he netted from these shopping centers in the business. Still, he wanted to find a way to deal financially with the volatility of real-estate development. Remembering what he had learned as a child about the benefits of monthly dividend income—as a bag boy, he had bought food stock, which became Winn-Dixie stock that paid monthly dividends—he built a full-service real-estate company with third-party brokerage, leasing, and management in order to have a more reliable source of predictable monthly cash flow. He had set a goal of making $3 million by the time he was 34, and he reached his goal early, at age 33. He made his business a huge success during a time that was rocked by volatility and large surges in interest rates and capital sources. He dealt with it all—and built his fortune in spite of the 21% interest rates and the mortgage REIT and bank debacle of the late 1960s and early 1970s. Then he set a new goal: to expand his business into the first regional full-service real-estate company based in Columbia.

By the mid-1970s, Joe Jr. had built 38 shopping centers and had equity in those centers of more than $3 million. In 1979, he merged his firm with a leading brokerage firm, McTeer & Company, to form Edens & McTeer, Inc. Edens & McTeer was a success, growing along every dimension by doubling its managed projects and the square footage of new leasers and reaching a goal of constructing one new shopping center per month. By 1982, Joe Jr. owned 64 shopping centers in Alabama, Georgia, Mississippi, North Carolina, and South Carolina, along with eight office buildings in Columbia. Also in 1982, he brought in Dan Avant as a principal and changed the name of the company to Edens & Avant.

During these years, there were constant changes in the sources of real-estate capital and in the structuring of deals. The players kept changing and how deals were financed kept changing, and to survive in a capital-intensive business Joe Jr. had to be flexible, creative, and determined. He almost went under three times, but he refused to suffer the same fate as his father and grandfather and focused on figuring out how out to manage the risk created by high interest rates, changing financial sources, and intensifying competition. And he survived in spite of the 1970s syndication craze and its demise in the early 1980s, in spite of the savings-and-loan busts of the mid-1980s, and in spite of the real-estate depression that began in the late 1980s and lasted until the public REIT revival in 1992. When asked what drove him, he answered:

I was driven to be successful financially because being well off put you in a position to do things for your family and for others. When Daddy was in the food business, he would take us with him to New York City when he visited suppliers, and we went to Broadway plays, ate at the Stork Club, and it gave us broadening experience. And when he sold to Winn-Dixie, he dedicated himself to education and hospital fund-raising until his new business consumed him.

From 1978 to 1986, Joe Jr. took advantage of opportunities to liquefy a significant amount of his net worth and removed enough money from the business to place in family trusts so that finally, after weathering nearly 20 years of volatility and change in the real-estate capital markets, the Edens family had wealth to pass on to the next generation—unlike his father, with his unfortunate business investments, and his grandfather, with his boll-weevil disaster. In addition, he was very active in community service, philanthropic work, and politics. He served on the boards of several large South Carolina banks, as a member of the Board of Visitors of the Medical University of South Carolina, on the boards of the South Carolina Parks, Recreation, and Tourism Commission and the South Carolina Natural Resources Commission, as a trustee of the Hammond School, and as chairman of the Columbia Development Corporation.

Because he was raised to help others, Joe Jr. was not selfish in his success and was actively involved in raising funds for many Columbia charities, in keeping with his personal promise to help others. As he said, "I was never motivated to be the richest person in town; I was motivated to make a difference."

During the 1980s, Joe Jr. participated in the creation of state-of-the-art real-estate financing structures with Balcor and with WestPac Investors Trust of California. These innovations became wrap-mortgage financings as well as collateralized loans secured by groups of first and second mortgages. During the 1980s, he branched out to build suburban offices, apartment complexes, light-industrial facilities, and one of the largest Class A high-rise office buildings, a 320,000-square-foot Bank of America Plaza that opened in Columbia in 1989.

Industry Changes

Joe Jr.'s foray into real-estate product diversification, while successful, exposed him to big risks, and he found it hard to contain and control the costs of those projects, so he focused again on what he knew best: grocery-anchored retail centers. And then the real-estate depression of 1989–92 hit the industry and Joe Jr. hard. Traditional bank lenders withdrew from the markets. The savings-and-loan scandals crippled that industry and that source of capital, forcing Joe Jr. to scramble for new capital. He found a new lender and created a new financing structure with Protective Life Insurance Company of Birmingham, Alabama, financing $170 million.

Liquidity started returning to the real-estate market by 1993 through the public-debt-securitization marketplace, which arose out of the savings-and-loan bailouts, and through the reemergence of the public REIT marketplace, which began in the late fall of 1992 and burgeoned until August 1994. One of Joe Jr.'s competitors went public, but he knew his business did not have the management depth to go public, and he also knew he did not have the temperament to be CEO of a public company. By 1995, he was 54 years old, and, in his words, "My warhorse years were behind me. But I had to do something to find long-term capitalization for the business and for my employees." He decided he had to partner with a strong financial player "who could get along with [my] cornbread, collard greens, and black-eyed peas group."

When Joe Jr. looked back on his 37-year career, he believed it was partly the loyalty of his wife, children, friends, employees, lenders, and other business associates that had kept him in the game. "Many people helped me who had no obligation to do so," he said. He also thought people were loyal to him because he was "sincere in his actions and deeds." It was said that Joe Edens "never drank the entrepreneurial Kool-Aid" of being invincible and all-knowing. He was not selfish with his success. His humility was evidenced by his discomfort with accolades and by the fact that he had helped so many people and so many charities anonymously.

And yet, Joe Jr. also possessed skills that were unique for an entrepreneur. He had the uncanny ability to assess reality, face the facts, and take action. So, in 1997, Joe Jr. entered into the first of the three major transactions in which he sold part of his company to the State of Michigan Retirement Systems for $150 million. He knew that for his company to compete against the new public companies, he had to institutionalize and recapitalize the company with long-term money. He believed the industry would undergo major changes driven by technology; grocery-chain consolidation; and new retail formats, trends, and players.

Succession Planning

When he closed the Michigan investment deal in 1997, Joe Jr. was 56 years old and stepping down was on his mind. Therefore, he had started thinking about his successor for the company he had built, which now included more than 150 employees he considered family. He described his relationship with his employees: "I tried to instill in these people that they care about each other and to be there for each other when illness, death, or financial troubles arise. I tried to teach them that they can be better and if I critique them, it's because I care about them and want them to be better."

Joe Jr. reflected on how, from meager beginnings, he had achieved success with his company because, in his mind, he "was not the brightest penny in the purse." He attributed it to living his life as if it were his goal to do what was best for his family, his employees, and himself, and in that order. That meant two things: treating people with sincerity, honesty, and caring, and doing what he said he would do. As for picking his successor, "I knew I needed someone with a different skill set, different energy level, but who would appreciate our culture and our family." He also wanted someone who "was grounded and humble" and not a "what's in it for me" person. He visualized his successor as "somebody who would truly be color-blind and gender-blind—somebody who would have the passion and drive to make this company the best in the industry." But most important of all, he was concerned with what he called the "heart and soul" of the person.

Candidate Pool

Joe Jr. reflected on what successor qualifications were important—what skills or competencies the changing industry demanded. There were three candidates: his son, Joe III, his chief investment officer, who was like a daughter to him, and his investment banker.

Family Member

Joe Jr.'s 36-year-old son had begun his career in banking but joined Edens as a senior development officer. And he had done very well in his role of being responsible for developments, renovations, and expansions. Joe III understood the business, the company, the culture, and the respect required for both the employees and the family. As a member of the family, he had the love of his father, but he did not have experience with real-estate-capital markets. And Joe Jr. realized that family-business successions were risky. Many did not work out and had the high potential of destroying value. This reality raised the question whether it was best to sell the company, although that clearly was not his preference.

Loyal Employee

His chief investment officer, his most senior and trusted employee, had been the point person on the big financing with the state of Michigan. With more than 10 years' experience with the company, she had financing experience but not operating experience. Still, he promoted her to the position of president and chief investment officer to keep her in the mix of CEO candidates and, at the same time, safeguard the culture and values that were the foundation on which he had built the company.

The Outsider

The third candidate was his investment banker, 36, who had headed the capital-markets advisory team for Edens for the past five years. He lived in Atlanta, and had spent his entire professional career at Arthur Andersen. His strength was in real-estate-capital markets. His weaknesses were his lack of hands-on retail operating experience and experience in development. In the preliminary explorations, the investment banker had expressed reluctance to move from Atlanta to the smaller city of Columbia, and he had no interest in coming in as CFO during a transition year.

Time Is Up

Joe Jr.'s succession-planning time involved deep-down thinking and asking himself some hard questions. Was he ready to hand over the $500 company he had built into a multi-billion-dollar company? Was he willing to give up decision making after 35 years of being the chief decision maker? He worried about how his decision would be received by his employees, and he understood that they needed some reassurance that the fundamental values of the company would remain in place. He felt a great responsibility to his family and to his conviction not to endanger the family fortune as both his grandfather and father had done. He spent a lot of time thinking about how the transition should be made with the family, the employees, and his new pension partners. His journey had been interesting. But now he had to make a decision. He knew the buck stopped with him and only he could make it.

List of Relevant Cases

Appalachian Commercial Cleaners

Edens & Avant

LG Investments, LLC: A Family Business in Generational Transition (A)

LG Investments, LLC: A Family Business in Generational Transition (B)

LG Investments, LLC: A Family Business in Generational Transition (C)

LG Investments, LLC: A Family Business in Generational Transition (D)

Author's Commentaries

The added complexity of managing a family business is further illustrated in the following commentaries.

"Managing the Family Business: Golden Goose"[3]

Eighty percent or more of all businesses in the U.S. are family controlled. Over 50% of the work force works for a family business. Family involvement in a business adds an additional layer of complexity to the customary challenges facing business builders. There are books and articles which deal with the common family business issues of nepotism, succession, and equitable treatment of family members not in the business. Today, I want to share with you three lessons I have learned over the years in working with many family businesses:

1. Rule #1—Do not kill the Golden Goose;
2. An entrepreneurial management style will not work with family issues; and
3. Everyone needs their own sandbox.

1. Do Not Kill the Golden Goose

Building a successful family business is hard. Successfully passing it along to future generations is even harder. In fact, 70% of all family businesses do not successfully make the transition to the second generation.

---

3. Edward D. Hess, "Managing the Family Business: Golden Goose," *The Catalyst*, May 2003.

Difficult emotional issues arise in all family businesses: issues involving employment of family members, compensation of family members, equity amongst siblings, the cash needs of family owners not employed in the business, in-law issues, succession choices, and as importantly, the effect of all of the above on non-family employees and managers. Family issues are like waves in the ocean. They keep coming and coming and coming. As family members age, their perspectives, needs, and views of the business change. These changes interact with changes in the business to produce a nice unique gumbo of issues for every family business. Issues, which if ignored, can kill prematurely the golden goose.

A family business which produces enough profits to support many members of a family is a unique treasure and blessing to be appreciated by all. All family members need to understand what they have and how fragile it may be—not only do you have the risk of business factors but you also have the risk of family factors which can kill the golden goose. Family members need to be made aware of and sensitive to how they, yes, they can destroy the business as easily as the competition unless they learn to communicate and work through family issues.

Every family member that "feeds at the family business trough" has the duty and responsibility to understand the uniqueness and goodness of what exists and further has the responsibility not to hurt the business or cause serious strife out of personal self-interest. The good of the whole outweighs the greed, selfishness, or ego of the one. Pure and simple, paraphrasing General Douglas McArthur—duty, honor, and family. Family leaders have the obligation to educate family members about the realities and risks to the business from outside the family and from within the family. The family has to agree on certain inviolate values which all can ascribe to. These overriding values will help family members deal with business issues and family issues as they arise. Families need to meet and discuss values and goals, and reach understandings about those values and goals for both the business and the family.

2. A Different Management Style Is Needed for Family Issues

Managing family issues is different than managing business issues. Non-family member employees are easier to talk to, persuade, and direct than family members. You can be more objective about non-family members and issues. The common entrepreneurial management styles and process of quick decisions and taking charge does not work well with family issues.

The emotional aspect of family impacts decision making, impacts communication directness and honesty, and the carryover of family issues to the home—and in some cases, to the bedroom—makes it impossible to leave family business issues at the proverbial office. The emotional complexity comes not only from the participants' emotional baggage but also involves spouses, parents, and siblings. Every family has issues. Every individual has family emotional "baggage." Accept those realities and manage them.

An autocratic, quick-decision-making, handle-it-once-and-for-all entrepreneurial mentality does not work well with family issues. A different style and process is needed to lessen the risk of family issues destroying the business. And this different management style is hard for entrepreneurs to adopt successfully. It is contrary to their demeanor and way of operating. It is a style of openness, communication, listening, being empathetic, and having a forum or process of allowing all of the family emotions to be vented, heard, and discussed with resulting compromises again, again, and again. Family leaders need patience, listening skills, and dispute resolution skills. Or, they need to bring in a facilitator.

Listening, giving people the opportunity to be heard, and having a process whereby family members are educated about the realities of business are critical to managing the family. The process is as important as the results. Reaching the quick bottom line results does not work well in this arena. People have to go through their own process of dealing with their respective needs and wants relative to the family and the business. It is constantly evolving and never ending.

Family councils, family constitutions, and frequent family meetings do and can work to mitigate against the risk of killing the golden goose if and only if you have a process that is values driven and the family understands its duties and responsibilities toward the whole not just me, me, me. To do this takes time, emotional effort, listening, compromise, and leadership. Remember—you ignore family issues at your peril; they do not go away. You have to manage family issues differently and with a different style and mental framework than business issues.

3. Everyone Needs Their Own Sandbox

Many family businesses dissolve or split up because "everyone needs their own sandbox." Siblings or cousins want to show themselves and others they can make it on their own or they want control of what and how their money is spent. And so, you need to plan how to address this need for individual sandboxes. There are different ways that I have seen work:

1. Business Structure—Structure the business so that different siblings (assuming qualifications and training—remember the golden goose) have "their own sandbox" within the business whether that be a function, a location, or a product that they are responsible for. Give people the opportunity to be independent with specific non-shared responsibilities. Give them the burden of responsibility and leadership.
2. A Separate Investment Vehicle—Another alternative is to give certain family members their own sandbox in the form of a family investment or a venture capital vehicle separate from the business.
3. Separate Toys—Another alternative is to give each family member a meaningful amount of assets over which they have sole investment or spending control.

4. Invest in Them—Last, the business can invest in a new business of a family member either directly or indirectly through the purchase of services or products. I have seen this work well with in-law issues.

All four of these alternatives attempt to deal with individuals' need for autonomy and their need to prove to themselves and to others that they are worthy and good. In some cases, it is not the direct family member driving the needs or stirring the pot; it is the daughter-in-law or son-in-law. As stated above, an education process is a necessity for new family members—family values and the common good must trump individual greed and ego.

Your family business is your own unique multi-variant set of issues. Recognize that you have to spend time managing family issues, too. Good luck with your gumbo and remember rule #1—Do not let family issues kill the golden goose.

"Family Business Succession: The Duality Principle"[4]

Most family businesses do not successfully make it to the second or third generation. Estimates are that only 70% of the family businesses successfully make it to the second generation and only 10% to the third generation.

Two Major Life Changes

Intergenerational successions are major life changes for two people (and their spouses) and for the company—its employees and customers. To increase the probability of success of succession planning you should plan for not one, but two successions:

1. The choice, the training and the testing of the potential successor; and

2. The planned exit and moving on to something meaningful by the retiring leader.

Why Do Successions Fail?

Most successions fail for one or more of the following reasons:

1. You choose the wrong successor;
   a. He or she is not qualified or experienced enough;
   b. He or she is not respected by the employees and customers; or
   c. He or she is not respected or trusted by family members; or

2. The retiring CEO will not let go and undermines the successor; or

3. Other family shareholders who are employed in the business and who were not chosen as successor create major problems; or

4. Other family shareholders not employed in the business use this opportunity to force a stock sale.

---

4. Edward D. Hess, "Family Business Succession: The Duality Principle," *The Catalyst*, February 2004.

Five-Year Plan

Proper succession planning is a five-year process for both parties—the retiree and the successor. A successor, whether a family member or an outsider, has to earn the trust of the family, the employees, and the customers and be tested over time.

As important, the current CEO needs to plan his or her exit and "moving on" to something meaningful. Most business builders cannot all of a sudden do nothing—have no status—no place to go in the morning. The retiring CEO needs time to think, test, and create what he or she will look forward to in the next phase of their life—whether that is public service, charitable work, alumni activities, teaching, or politics. Most retiring CEOs need a new sandbox—somewhere else to go and play in a meaningful way.

So there are two successions going on simultaneously, a "succession-in" and a "succession-out"—two major life changes—both of which take time and planning.

Getting Started—It Is Not About You

In many cases, it is hard—no, very, very hard—for entrepreneurs and business builders to confront their mortality and to deal with giving up control over their "little baby." Yet only through proper succession planning can the "baby" successfully move on to its next phase of life. A failed succession can destroy the "baby."

Succession planning is a business builder's greatest duty—one of STEWARD-SHIP. Succession planning is a necessity to protect the family's source of wealth—the business. The CEO owes it to his spouse and family to do everything he or she can do to ensure that the family legacy survives and prospers. Succession planning is not really about you—it is about your spouse, your children, your employees, and customers. The hundreds of people who depend on you to do what is right for the business and for them.

Focus as Much on the Succession Out

To increase the probability of success two simultaneous successions need to be managed: The moving on of the older generation and the moving in of the younger generation or the non-family-member CEO.

Good Successions

I have worked on two successions in the past few years, both of which, thankfully, worked well—not because of me, but because of the people involved. One involved a succession from a 65-year-old second generation son-in-law to a 37-year-old third generation grandson; and the other involved a 62-year-old second generation to a 40-year-old outside (non-family-member) CEO.

In both cases, the new leader had industry knowledge, had worked with the business and the family for over five years, and had been tested thoroughly. Both of the new leaders had, over time, earned the trust and respect of family members (including those not chosen as successor) and employees.

Second, both retiring CEOs had something meaningful in their lives to move on to. One is working on environmental causes and the other entered public service. Both have stayed on their respective boards as chairman for the purpose of advice and council. These meaningful exits were well thought out and planned over time. The retiring CEOs took the time to find their "place" and transitioned over time. Good successions do not just happen. They take time and have to be managed.

PART II
Case Collection

Subject Matrix

	Business—Capital Needs	Business—Processes	Conflict Business and Family	Controls—Financial
3 Fellers Bakery		X		
Appalachian Commercial Cleaners: Family Dynamics Versus the Business			X	
Better World Books	X			X
C.R. Barger & Sons, Inc. (A)				
C.R. Barger & Sons, Inc. (B)		X		
Defender Direct, Inc.: A Business of Growing Leaders		X		
Edens & Avant				
Enchanting Travels		X		
Eyebobs Eyewear, Inc.				X
Freedom Technology Services				
Global Medical Imaging, LLC				
Green Copier Recycling: Entrepreneur Meets Private Equity		X		
Hass Shoes				
James Abrams @ Clockwork Home Services, Inc.: Lessons from a Serial Entrepreneur		X		X
Jeff Bowling at the Delta Companies: From Baseball Coach to CEO		X		X
Leaders Bank: Creating a Great Place to Work				
LG Investments, LLC: A Family Business in Generational Transition (A)			X	
LG Investments, LLC: A Family Business in Generational Transition (B)			X	
LG Investments, LLC: A Family Business in Generational Transition (C)			X	
LG Investments, LLC: A Family Business in Generational Travnsition (D)	X		X	
Mellace Family Brands, Inc.: Building a Socially Responsible Enterprise	X	X		
Motor City: A Disruptive Business Model (A)				X
Motor City: A Disruptive Business Model (B)				
Octane Fitness, Inc.: The Power of Focus				X
Room & Board				
Sammy Snacks (A)				X
Sammy Snacks (B)				X
Sammy Snacks (C)				X
Sammy Snacks (D)				
SecureWorks		X		X
Students Helping Honduras				X
Trilogy Health Services, LLC: Building a Great Service Company				
Valley-Wide Health Systems, Inc.		X		

Controls—Inventory	Controls—Quality	Culture	Customer Concentration	Customer Segmentation	Customer Value Proposition	Delegation	Differentiators
			X				
X							
					X		
				X			X
		X				X	
	X						
X	X	X	X		X	X	
				X	X	X	
			X		X		X
		X			X		X
		X					
		X					
	X	X				X	
							X
	X						
	X						
				X		X	
	X						
		X					
		X					

Subject Matrix, Cont'd.

	Distribution	Employee Compensation/Benefits	Employee Engagement	Entrepreneur's Growth
3 Fellers Bakery	X			X
Appalachian Commercial Cleaners: Family Dynamics Versus the Business			X	
Better World Books	X			X
C.R. Barger & Sons, Inc. (A)				
C.R. Barger & Sons, Inc. (B)	X		X	
Defender Direct, Inc.: A Business of Growing Leaders			X	X
Edens & Avant				
Enchanting Travels			X	
Eyebobs Eyewear, Inc.		X		
Freedom Technology Services				
Global Medical Imaging, LLC				X
Green Copier Recycling: Entrepreneur Meets Private Equity				
Hass Shoes				
James Abrams @ Clockwork Home Services, Inc.: Lessons from a Serial Entrepreneur		X		X
Jeff Bowling at the Delta Companies: From Baseball Coach to CEO				X
Leaders Bank: Creating a Great Place to Work		X	X	
LG Investments, LLC: A Family Business in Generational Transition (A)				
LG Investments, LLC: A Family Business in Generational Transition (B)				
LG Investments, LLC: A Family Business in Generational Transition (C)				
LG Investments, LLC: A Family Business in Generational Travnsition (D)				
Mellace Family Brands, Inc.: Building a Socially Responsible Enterprise		X	X	
Motor City: A Disruptive Business Model (A)		X		
Motor City: A Disruptive Business Model (B)				
Octane Fitness, Inc.: The Power of Focus		X	X	
Room & Board		X	X	
Sammy Snacks (A)				
Sammy Snacks (B)	X			X
Sammy Snacks (C)	X			
Sammy Snacks (D)	X			
SecureWorks		X		
Students Helping Honduras				
Trilogy Health Services, LLC: Building a Great Service Company		X	X	
Valley-Wide Health Systems, Inc.			X	X

Evolution of the Business Model	Family Business	Financial Transparency	Founder Succession	Founder— Two Founders	Franchising	Growth—Financing of Growth
	X					
X						
X						X
	X		X			
				X	X	
X				X		
X				X	X	
						X
		X				
X	X		X			
	X					
	X		X			
	X					
X				X		
						X
						X
		X		X		
		X				
						X
		X				
				X		X
						X
X						X

Subject Matrix, Cont'd.

	Good Growth Versus Bad Growth	Growth Decision Template	"Growth Boosters"	Growth Pace of
3 Fellers Bakery	X	X		X
Appalachian Commercial Cleaners: Family Dynamics Versus the Business				
Better World Books			X	
C.R. Barger & Sons, Inc. (A)			X	
C.R. Barger & Sons, Inc. (B)				
Defender Direct, Inc.: A Business of Growing Leaders				
Edens & Avant				
Enchanting Travels	X			X
Eyebobs Eyewear, Inc.	X			X
Freedom Technology Services				
Global Medical Imaging, LLC			X	
Green Copier Recycling: Entrepreneur Meets Private Equity				
Hass Shoes			X	
James Abrams @ Clockwork Home Services, Inc.: Lessons from a Serial Entrepreneur				
Jeff Bowling at the Delta Companies: From Baseball Coach to CEO				
Leaders Bank: Creating a Great Place to Work				
LG Investments, LLC: A Family Business in Generational Transition (A)				
LG Investments, LLC: A Family Business in Generational Transition (B)				
LG Investments, LLC: A Family Business in Generational Transition (C)				
LG Investments, LLC: A Family Business in Generational Travnsition (D)				
Mellace Family Brands, Inc.: Building a Socially Responsible Enterprise				
Motor City: A Disruptive Business Model (A)				
Motor City: A Disruptive Business Model (B)		X		
Octane Fitness, Inc.: The Power of Focus				
Room & Board	X			X
Sammy Snacks (A)				
Sammy Snacks (B)				
Sammy Snacks (C)				
Sammy Snacks (D)				
SecureWorks				
Students Helping Honduras	X	X		X
Trilogy Health Services, LLC: Building a Great Service Company				
Valley-Wide Health Systems, Inc.	X		X	

Growth Risks	Human Resources (HR)	Innovation	Leadership	Management Team—Building	Management Team—Upgrading	Manufacturing versus Outsourcing
						X
			X			
				X		
			X			
X				X		
X						X
	X			X	X	
				X		
X	X		X	X		
X	X		X			
			X			
	X	X		X		
X						
	X	X				X
X	X					X
X	X			X		
X						X
				X		
X						
	X		X	X	X	
				X		
X			X	X	X	
X				X		

Subject Matrix, Cont'd.

	Multiple Stakeholders	Planning	Prior Industry Experience	Prioritization	Private Equity
3 Fellers Bakery				X	
Appalachian Commercial Cleaners: Family Dynamics Versus the Business	X		X		
Better World Books			X		
C.R. Barger & Sons, Inc. (A)				X	
C.R. Barger & Sons, Inc. (B)					
Defender Direct, Inc.: A Business of Growing Leaders			X	X	
Edens & Avant					
Enchanting Travels		X			
Eyebobs Eyewear, Inc.					
Freedom Technology Services	X		X		
Global Medical Imaging, LLC			X	X	
Green Copier Recycling: Entrepreneur Meets Private Equity			X		X
Hass Shoes					
James Abrams @ Clockwork Home Services, Inc.: Lessons from a Serial Entrepreneur		X	X		
Jeff Bowling at the Delta Companies: From Baseball Coach to CEO		X	X		
Leaders Bank: Creating a Great Place to Work					
LG Investments, LLC: A Family Business in Generational Transition (A)	X				
LG Investments, LLC: A Family Business in Generational Transition (B)					
LG Investments, LLC: A Family Business in Generational Transition (C)					
LG Investments, LLC: A Family Business in Generational Travnsition (D)					
Mellace Family Brands, Inc.: Building a Socially Responsible Enterprise					
Motor City: A Disruptive Business Model (A)					
Motor City: A Disruptive Business Model (B)					X
Octane Fitness, Inc.: The Power of Focus		X	X		X
Room & Board			X	X	
Sammy Snacks (A)		X			X
Sammy Snacks (B)		X			X
Sammy Snacks (C)					
Sammy Snacks (D)					
SecureWorks				X	
Students Helping Honduras	X	X		X	
Trilogy Health Services, LLC: Building a Great Service Company			X		X
Valley-Wide Health Systems, Inc.			X		

Process Implementation	Process Improvement	Product Business	Scaling	Service Business	Social Entrepreneurship	Strategic Focus
		X	X			X
				X		
X		X	X		X	
		X	X			
		X				
		X	X			X
		X	X			
				X		X
		X				X
				X		
X	X	X				X
		X	X			
		X				
			X	X		
				X		
				X		
		X	X		X	
		X				
		X	X			
		X	X			X
		X				X
		X				X
		X	X			
		X	X			
		X	X			
				X		X
				X	X	X
			X	X		
			X		X	

3 Fellers Bakery

CASE DISCUSSION QUESTIONS

1. You are Susan Feller. Should you grow your business? Why?

2. What are the key questions that you must answer to decide question 1?

3. What are Susan's growth options? What are the pros and cons of each?

4. You are Susan Feller. How would you grow your business and why?

5. Growth can be good and growth can be bad. What does that mean with respect to this case?

6. Prepare an argument for why Susan should not grow the business.

CASE STUDY

3 FELLERS BAKERY

On a July morning in 2009, Susan Feller sat in the eating area of her retail bakery, 3 Fellers Bakery (3 Fellers), in Goochland, Virginia, with her son Mike, a recent MBA graduate of the Darden School of Business, and marveled about how, in just two-and-a-half years, she had been able to build a successful business by baking and selling gluten-free cakes and desserts. The gluten-free products that 3 Fellers made were now sold in 26 grocery stores, including 10 Whole Foods stores, on the Internet, and in her retail store.

In 2005, when Feller was a happily retired high-school guidance counselor, home-maker, and mother of three adult sons, she was diagnosed with celiac disease. Celiac disease is a disease of the small intestines that forced Feller to avoid eating or being exposed to a list of foods made with wheat, rye, most oats (unless grown in a gluten-free environment), or barley. But it was really the inclusion of flours, breads, pastries, and desserts on the list that got Feller moving toward starting her own business.

Feller loved to bake and make beautiful cakes for birthdays, weddings, and other special occasions. Now she found to her dismay that most store-bought gluten-free desserts did not even come close to tasting as good as what she baked at home. So, she spent more than a year learning how to make her own gluten-free pastry creations, which she knew tasted as good as anything made by the finest pastry chefs. Her secret ingredient was her own flour mix, the product of 12 months of trial-and-error experimentation. She tested her desserts first on members of her family and then on members of her gluten-free support group, the West End Gluten Intolerance Group. She discovered everyone loved her desserts, and several support-group members encouraged her to sell them.

Case Study UVA-ENT-0137 © 2009 by the University of Virginia Darden School Foundation. This case was prepared by Edward D. Hess as a basis for class discussion rather than to illustrate effective or ineffective handling of an administrative situation.

With no previous business experience or training, Feller decided to make the leap and started a business in her home in the spring of 2007. She baked in her kitchen until December 2008, when she bought and transformed a 2,400-square-foot house into a commercial bakery and retail store. By July 2009, the woman who had never even thought about becoming an entrepreneur now managed seven part-time employees. Feller handled new-product development, sales, and accounting. She also oversaw production, managed inventory, and ordered supplies. Her modified kitchen had two traditional stoves, two refrigerators, and four stand-up freezers, along with two professional bakery mixers and several small counter mixers.

Like most entrepreneurs of successful start-up businesses, Feller kept accounting records by hand and paid bills the week she received them even though her grocery clients paid her between 30 days and 45 days after delivery. She self-financed her business; she did not advertise; and she did not buy anything she could not pay for with cash. She had no computerized inventory or accounting system, no employee manuals, and no automated processes. She did have a Web site and many loyal happy customers.

When Feller started selling her products in the late spring of 2007, she set her prices after researching competitive prices, but she did not know her per-unit costs. She began selling in three Richmond gourmet and natural-food grocery stores and acquired new customers by repeatedly calling on them herself and giving them samples to try. In addition, in June 2007, she launched the Web site from which she sold her products and participated as an exhibitor at the National Gluten Intolerance Conference held in Richmond, Virginia.

In July of 2007, she began discussions with the Whole Foods store in Charlottesville, Virginia. By November, she was selling her gluten-free cookie dough in five Ukrop's grocery stores in the Richmond area. Her persistence with Whole Foods paid off when she was approved as a vendor for the Mid-Atlantic region and began selling in the Charlottesville store in June 2008. The Whole Foods Mid-Atlantic region comprised 35 stores located from New Jersey to North Carolina. By July 2009, Feller's gluten-free products were in nine of those Whole Foods stores, in Virginia and the District of Columbia, Ellwood Thompson's Natural Market in Richmond, and in 16 other grocery stores, including Ukrop's.

Along with her success starting her small business had come more opportunities than she ever had imagined, and as a typical entrepreneur she struggled with deciding which opportunity to undertake first.

Market

At this time, between 5% and 7% of the U.S. population suffered from gluten intolerance and struggled with having to eat gluten-free food. The producers of gluten-free baked breads and desserts faced the issue of having to produce these products in completely gluten-free environments. Thus, for gluten-free production, only gluten-free machines, equipment, utensils, and bowls were used to make gluten-free products. This led to the creation of many small gluten-free bakeries and several midsized gluten-free dessert companies that produced and sold frozen desserts in different areas of the United States. The market for gluten-free desserts became big enough to convince Betty Crocker to introduce gluten-free cake mixes. Even Budweiser's Redbridge gluten-free beer landed in grocery stores in the fall of 2009.

3 Fellers Products

If refrigerated, fresh 3 Fellers products lasted approximately two weeks. By experimenting, Feller created recipes for gluten-free products that could be frozen and when defrosted tasted as good as freshly baked ones, giving her the flexibility of selling both frozen and fresh products. Frozen gluten-free baked desserts had a shelf life of approximately four months, and 3 Fellers sold frozen chocolate-chip, oatmeal-raisin, and sugar cookie dough and frozen buttermilk slice-and-bake biscuits. Baked cornbread and six-inch chocolate, vanilla, carrot, and coconut cakes were also offered for sale. All of Feller's grocery customers carried her gluten-free frozen dough, and several of them also carried her fresh-baked cakes, pastries, and individually packaged desserts such as cupcakes, muffins, and pies. She planned to add cinnamon-raisin cake, mini-cupcakes, and baking-biscuit dough.

An additional outlet for 3 Fellers' gluten-free products was the retail store in the bakery, where custom orders were filled for a variety of cakes, brownies, scones, tarts, pastries, dessert bars, seven varieties of cupcakes, eight varieties of pies, four types of muffins, wedding cakes, banana bread, cinnamon-raisin buns, cheesecakes, and cakes for birthdays and other special occasions. Standard items such as gluten-free breads and rolls were always available.

Feller's research had shown that some bakeries sold gluten-free products that were not manufactured in a gluten-free environment and therefore risked contamination. All 3 Fellers' products were produced in the 100% gluten-free environment of the 3 Fellers' bakery kitchen in Goochland, where current space and equipment were operating at 70% of capacity, and from which products were delivered to each grocery store. All ingredients in these gluten-free products were natural, and only flavorings, fruits, and chocolate of the highest quality were used. Also, all ingredients were certified by the Gluten Intolerance Group of North America, which had higher standards than the gluten-free standards of the FDA.

Opportunities

In all Whole Foods' stores in the Mid-Atlantic region, 3 Fellers' products were approved for sale but were actually only sold to the 10 Whole Foods' stores located in the cities of Charlottesville, Richmond, Washington, D.C., and in Northern Virginia; however, there was a demand for 3 Fellers' products from other Whole Foods stores in the District of Columbia and Maryland. In the beginning, most stores sold just the gluten-free frozen products, but then Whole Foods requested the freshly baked cakes and other desserts to sell in its bakeries. At the rate 3 Fellers' sales were going, the demand from Whole Foods could soon exceed its current capacity to provide.

Feller's research had also shown the lack of competitive gluten-free frozen cookie dough or biscuit products on the market anywhere else in the United States. To expand into the national market, 3 Fellers would need to buy the equipment to produce, package, seal, and freeze-dry the dough in volume quantities to sell to such centralized national grocery chains as Kroger, Safeway, and Wal-Mart. In addition, many local bakeries that did not carry gluten-free products had approached Feller about selling her products in their retail outlets. Although this would require more distribution capacity, it would increase the 3 Fellers made-to-order business significantly.

Recently, Feller had been approached by two businessmen she knew by reputation. They had experience in the baking business and wanted to include her in building and operating a gluten-free baking plant. It would be a joint venture as the three of them would be partners in the baking business and use her recipes; her Goochland retail store would be excluded. This offer made Feller think about how she viewed her success:

I love baking and decorating cakes. I have found my passion. My bakery brings together the artist in me—I was an art major in college—and it's the guidance counselor in me—I enjoy helping people. You would understand if you could see the look of a 10-year-old boy upon receiving his first decorated birthday cake that he can eat that is gluten free.

Issues

Still, Feller faced some big questions: How big a business did she want to build? What was her "end game?" Did she want to build something for her children to take over? Should she focus on meeting the needs of Whole Foods first by expanding into all its Mid-Atlantic stores? Should she diversify her customer base? Should she try to be a first mover and go national with her cookie and biscuit dough by selling through big national grocery chains? How would she finance production expansion? Could she manage a bigger business? Her love was creating new recipes and producing beautiful great-tasting desserts but would growth take her away from that? Should she partner with someone? Should she outsource production? If so, how would she protect her trade-secret flour recipe? Should she open more retail locations? Should she wholesale her products to local bakeries throughout Virginia?

In other words, how should Feller grow her business?

Appalachian Commercial Cleaners:
Family Dynamics Versus the Business

CASE DISCUSSION QUESTIONS

1. For business purposes, should JJ fire Billy?

2. For family purposes, should JJ fire Billy?

3. Should other family members have a say in the decision? Who? Why?

`4. How will firing Billy impact the business? JJ? His daughter? His wife?

5. Before deciding whether to fire Billy, what additional information should JJ seek?

6. Is this a case in which keeping family harmony hurts the business?

7. Should family or business come first? Why? What other business stakeholders need to be taken into account?

8. Can JJ fire Billy if he has an outstanding performance record?

9. What should JJ do? Why?

APPALACHIAN COMMERCIAL CLEANERS: FAMILY DYNAMICS VERSUS THE BUSINESS

Johnny Jensen (JJ) attended high school in Charlestown, West Virginia. He enlisted in the army and served his country as an infantryman in the Vietnam War. He displayed valor and courage under fire, for which he received the Bronze Star, the Silver Star, the Distinguished Service Cross, and three Purple Hearts. Then he returned to his native West Virginia and got a job with a janitorial service company cleaning residential and commercial properties. He was promoted quickly because, owing to his military experience, he understood discipline, getting the job done, and how to lead by example.

After two years, JJ wanted to run his own business. Working for others had helped him "build" his business in his head. He decided that his business would be more professional. It would also be an "elite" business where people would be proud to work. He wanted to specialize in commercial cleaning services and have his employees wear nice uniforms and project cleanliness in their appearance. He figured the owners of commercial properties would pay for this quality cleaning service because it made their work environment more safe, healthy, and conducive to a professional atmosphere.

Case Study UVA-ENT-0126 © 2009 by the University of Virginia Darden School Foundation. This fictitious case was prepared by Edward D. Hess as a basis for class discussion rather than to illustrate effective or ineffective handling of an administrative situation.

In 1975, JJ started Appalachian Cleaning Services (Appalachian) and, over the next 25 years, built a successful family business. Appalachian became a family business because it ultimately employed five family members, including JJ, who was the CEO and chairman of the board. His brother Will was a crew chief; his brother-in-law Tom was in charge of supplies; his daughter Amy was chief accountant; and Amy's husband, Billy, rose to the rank of COO in charge of the 20 work crews, totaling 120 full-time employees. In effect, the business supported four families.

This structure worked well because it freed JJ from managing daily operations to focus on developing the business and expanding its customer segment into government contracting for city, county, and state office buildings. At the same time, he became quite active in state politics, making sure he knew politicians of both parties who had the power to influence the awarding of state contracts for cleaning the state's facilities. This proved to be a great growth initiative because government contracts were for a longer term than commercial contracts, and the government was a more stable client than businesses subject to the competition of the marketplace.

Another benefit of having Billy hire and manage the work crew was that it removed JJ from an area of responsibility that he found frustrating. As he grew older, he found it increasingly difficult to manage younger employees who, in his view, lacked the fundamental values of his youth that he thought had made this country great: working hard, respect for your elders, manners, discipline, and respect for authority.

The business ran smoothly for many years after its expansion into government contracting. One morning in April 2009, the smoothness was interrupted by two major events. First, JJ received a call from the chief operating officer of West Virginia's largest university asking JJ to come see him because he wanted to talk to him about outsourcing the cleaning of all university facilities to his company. This could triple the size of JJ's business.

The second event occurred when JJ's daughter Amy walked into his office and shut the door. "Daddy," she asked, "can we talk? I have some bad news." Then, his daughter informed him that she and Billy were getting a divorce. JJ understood that all marriages have rocky times, but he thought to himself that this would surely work out because he knew that Billy, besides being a good worker and COO, was a good man and father.

That night at dinner, JJ's wife insisted, "JJ, you have to fire Billy. He can no longer work in our family business." JJ's first reaction was one of disagreement because he knew Billy was a good worker and thought he would be able to work out the problems with his wife. He told his wife that it was not fair to fire Billy. But his wife continued, "JJ, our business is a family business and when you are no longer family, you do not belong in the business. That is why we always called it a family business."

Although surprised about his wife's strong views, JJ reminded her that no one in the company could do Billy's job. He also told his wife about the call he received that morning regarding the potential of Appalachian getting a new outsourcing contract with the state university that could triple its business. Then he told his wife that he wanted to think about it.

Two weeks later JJ's wife raised the issue again, and this time she demanded that JJ fire Billy that very week: "JJ, you know blood is thicker than water," she said. "How can you expect Amy to go to work every day and see Billy and deal with him? It is not fair to her, and it sends the wrong message to your employees—that you care more about money than values."

JJ faced a tough decision.

Better World Books

CASE DISCUSSION QUESTION
Having successfully scaled the business up to $30 million, Murphy now pondered his next move: He planned to scale the business further, to $75 million within the next three years. What were the critical management challenges or issues that he faced regarding people, strategy, capital, technology, operational, and business-model perspectives? How would you advise Murphy to meet those challenges while managing the risks of growth?

CASE
STUDY

BETTER WORLD BOOKS

Better World Books (BWB), headquartered in Mishawaka, Indiana, was a privately held Internet book retail business with a mission to fund literacy initiatives around the globe. It was the brainchild of Xavier Helgesen, Chris "Kreece" Fuchs, and Jeff Kurtzman, three 2001 graduates of the University of Notre Dame who came up with the idea of selling books online after graduation. What started as an effort to make some extra money while also helping out a local nonprofit evolved into a "self-sustaining, triple-bottom-line company," launched in 2003, that created social, economic, and environmental value for all stakeholders.[1]

The company acquired its growing inventory of used books from two primary sources: the Campus Collection program and the Library Discards and Donations program, working with more than 1,600 college campuses and about 1,000 libraries nationwide. BWB sold the books through a variety of established online marketplaces such as Amazon and eBay and its retail site, betterworldbooks.com. Every order was shipped carbon neutral with offsets from Carbonfund.org. The company donated 7% to 10% of its revenues to various global literacy initiatives, partnering with Books for Africa, National Center for Family Literacy, Room to Read, Worldfund, and Invisible Children.[2]

After developing the business for the first two years, the founders got a Small Business Administration–backed credit line in late 2004. In April 2008, the start-up raised $4.5 million in growth capital—$2 million from 18 private individuals and $2.05 million from its first institutional investor, Good Capital, a San Francisco–based

Case Study UVA-ENT-0146 © 2010 by the University of Virginia Darden School Foundation. This case was prepared by Senior Researcher Gosia Glinska and Edward D. Hess as a basis for class discussion rather than to illustrate effective or ineffective handling of an administrative situation.

1. Company Web site: http://www.betterworldbooks.com/info.aspx.
2. http://www.betterworldbooks.com/info.aspx.

investment manager of the Social Enterprise Expansion Fund.[3] After David Murphy came on board as president and CEO in August 2004, the company experienced triple-digit revenue growth that topped $30 million in fiscal year 2009.

More than 200 BWB employees collected 40,000 to 50,000 books every day and sold 10,000 or more books a day. Since its launch, the company had saved close to 31 million books from landfills and raised $7.5 million for literacy programs around the world.[4] It won the 2008 Fast Company Social Capitalist Award and was included on *BusinessWeek*'s 2009 list of the most promising social entrepreneurs. The admirable social and environmental mission that was drawing accolades was supported by a well-run, high-growth business that was expected to be profitable in 2010.[5] CEO David Murphy summarized his recipe for success:

Develop systems immediately that tell you the lifeblood of your company, even if it's not your financial system—and in many cases it's not. For us, it's all about inventory, and cash flow, what it truly costs us to acquire those books, how fast they sell, and at what price, and having arms around that lifeblood. Constantly evaluate and allocate your time and resources to cash-generating activities and to what people refer to as your "secret sauce." In our case, that secret sauce was technology. We had to keep building the technology, make it smarter, and make it better. We knew that there were things in there that were going to help generate our cash, especially in our pricing algorithms. I tell people, "If you actually look underneath the covers of Better World Books, once you move beyond our social mission, it's really a lot about technology and logistics."

Company History

In the summer of 2001, the best jobs Helgesen and Fuchs could get in an economy reeling from the dot-com bust were as calculus and computer-programming tutors for members of the Notre Dame football team. Strapped for cash, they decided to sell their used textbooks online. What the campus bookstore would not buy back, they sold on Half.com, an eBay company, for about $50 a copy. Even though it was the middle of the summer, Helgesen and Fuchs sold almost all of their used textbooks, as well as those of their roommates. "We realized we were on to something," Fuchs said.[6]

The First Book Drive

During the next few months, Helgesen and Fuchs often talked about collecting all the unwanted books piling up in Notre Dame students' rooms. In the spring of 2002,

3. Jim Meenan, "$4.5 Million Boosts Mishawaka's Better World Books," *South Bend Tribune*, April 8, 2008.
4. http://www.betterworldbooks.com/info.aspx.
5. Nick Leiber, "The Most Promising Social Entrepreneurs," *BusinessWeek*, May 1, 2009.
6. Ekjyot Saini, "Michigan: To One Charity, Old Books Mean a Better World," *Michigan Daily*, September 20, 2006.

they decided to make it happen. Having volunteered in the past at Notre Dame's Robinson Learning Center, they convinced its director to partner with them in running a book drive. Six months later, after collecting 2,000 books, the entrepreneurial duo sold them online for $20,000, earning $10,000 for the Robinson Center's after-school reading program.[7]

A Winning Business Plan

The success of the book drive encouraged Helgesen and Fuchs to draft a business plan with the help of their friend Jeff Kurtzman. The three former Notre Dame classmates envisioned a "different kind of company with a built-in social benefit."[8] They designed it as a for-profit business with a mission to capitalize on the value of used books to promote and fund nonprofit literacy programs. They called their company Better World Books and submitted the idea to their alma mater's business-plan competition.

In April 2003, Helgesen, Fuchs, and Kurtzman won for the Best Social Venture in the business plan competition at Notre Dame's Mendoza School of Business. In addition to $7,000 in prize money, the three founders impressed one of the judges, David Murphy, and gained a business mentor. A Notre Dame graduate as well, Murphy was a partner in a small equity firm, but after the business plan competition, he began working with BWB as a strategic advisor.

Murphy's Choice

Murphy watched BWB "as it went from almost nothing to the beginning of an actual business. He said he had first met Helgesen, Fuchs, and Kurtzman "when they had run just a handful of book drives and had a little bit of revenue. It was just the three of them." With Murphy on board using what he had learned studying for his MBA at Dartmouth's Tuck School, the fledgling business grew from three to about ten to fifteen employees by late 2004.

Over time, Murphy found himself increasingly drawn to the company's innovative business model and strong social mission. "I had my day job, and the book thing was starting to consume me in the evenings and on weekends," Murphy recalled. "And by the summer of 2004, I was saying, 'We need two things if we are really going to scale this business: a full-time CEO with experience and capital (preferably bank capital). The CEO must be instrumental in getting the company the capital it needed.'"

Having worked closely with the three founders for almost 18 months and understanding the core values and key business drivers embedded in the foundation of the growing business, Murphy took the plunge—and a big pay cut—and became

---

7. Stephanie Elam, "Building Better World a Book at a Time," *CNN*, July 2, 2009.

8. http://www.betterworldbooks.com/info.aspx?f=beginning.

president and CEO of BWB in August 2004. "I was willing to go periods of time without pay for the chance to build a great company, a different kind of company with a social mission at its center," Murphy said. "And certainly the risk also carried with it the chance to own a substantial piece of the company (equity)."

First Things First

Before Murphy joined the start-up full time, he conducted careful due diligence. "It was a proven model on a smaller scale. There were real revenues (less than $1 million annually), but very, very small," Murphy said. "To cast my lot with some young guys in a book business, I had to vet a lot and ask a lot of questions."

Shared Vision

Murphy first wanted to make sure that he shared the founders' vision for the company. "You've got to get the founders and the CEO, no matter what age they are, on the same page with regard to where they want take the company," he said. Because he was not interested in running a lifestyle business but wanted to scale the used-book venture, he made sure that the founders understood what high growth entailed. Murphy explained:

The first thing is alignment of the founders and all key people around the fact that that's exactly what you want, that this is no lifestyle business for some and a high-growth business for the others. So maybe stating the obvious, but really making sure that that's the vision that everybody shares, because that's also where you have common commitment and sacrifice. Those first three, four years, if you really want to scale, you're talking a lot of hard work. And if you're going to have everybody with their shoulder at the wheel, you have to make sure that they're all aligned around that vision and are willing to give extraordinary effort to get there.

Implementing a High-Growth Vision

In his conversations with the founders, Murphy honed his plans to implement the high-growth vision. He stressed the importance of putting the systems and processes in place, but "not to the point where it kills the company or saps innovation and creativity," he said. He and the founders also discussed the delicate subject of the founders' changing roles in a fast-growing enterprise. Aware that running a company required different talents, Murphy asked the founders, "Are you prepared to either step aside from senior-management roles, or shift gears, or possibly even leave, if that's in the best interests of the company?"

When Murphy joined BWB, its board of directors consisted of him and the three founders. By 2008, after raising outside equity, the company added two outside directors. Then Murphy raised the question of creating an advisory board, believing that having "outside eyes looking in is hugely important. Now that we've grown and our model has continued to evolve, we're talking about creating an advisory board in 2010."

Book Drives for Better Lives—Campus Collection Program

In late 2002 and early 2003, the entrepreneurs began contacting other Midwestern schools, including Purdue, Michigan, and Indiana, putting $7,000 in prize money won in the business plan competition into promoting Book Drives for Better Lives. In the summer of 2003, BWB had inventoried a total of 20,000 books. The company also had earned close to $10,000 for Minneapolis-based Books for Africa, its first international nonprofit partner.[9]

In 2003, Fuchs moved to Washington, D.C., Helgesen to San Francisco, and Kurtzman to Texas to begin coordinating book drives on a national level. About the same time, BWB hired regional directors in Boston and Atlanta to coordinate book drives.[10] In 2005, BWB had regional directors in offices in Los Angeles; Denver; Austin, Atlanta; Philadelphia; Seattle; San Francisco; Washington, D.C.; New York; Chicago; Boston; and Minneapolis.[11] By the spring of 2008, the number of regional directors in offices across the country had reached almost 20.

Recruiting Regional Directors

To fill the regional director positions, Murphy and the founders looked for young college graduates who found BWB's mission of social and environmental responsibility appealing. According to Murphy, "In those early days, we had a lot of liberal-arts grads. Smart people who had been in the work force for maybe a couple of years but were not happy and who wanted to work a couple of years before moving on to something else like grad school." He continued:

We got outstanding, hard-working, scrappy people who could work out of their apartment. We gave them health care and enough of a base salary—$26,000, $28,000—that they could have an apartment and maybe pay down some student loans. And some of them are still with us (although all of the book acquisition efforts are now centralized in Atlanta). They've been here four or five years. We looked real hard for the right blend of talented people who want to change the world, are naturally entrepreneurial, and good at sales.

Working with Volunteer Student Groups

Although the regional directors set up the relationships and offered help, BWB depended on volunteer student groups—such as an honors society, a service group

---

9. Gene Stowe, "Literacy the Bottom Line; ND Grads Begin 'Social Venture' to Put Old Books to Good Use," *South Bend Tribune*, January 24, 2005.

10. Stowe.

11. Stowe.

like Circle-K, a fraternity, or a sorority—to run campus book drives. Murphy said, "We make it extremely easy for the students to run a book drive on campus. Our regional directors are like our regional salespeople—they answer all the questions." He continued:

We told the students, "It will not cost you one dime. If you want to have a pizza party to kick it off and get your volunteers lined up, we'll pay for the pizza." So the message to student groups is threefold. First, it's easy because we've got all the materials you're going to need. Second, we align it with the notion of service—"You can make a difference." Third, we make it worth your while. Book drives are great fundraisers. If you run a book drive and get 20 volunteers out of a fraternity, and they get a check for $800, that's a lot of bake sales and car washes.

As soon as the collected books arrived at BWB's Mishawaka, Indiana, warehouse, their ISBN numbers were scanned into the database. Immediately, thanks to the smart intelligence built into the company's proprietary software, books were either accepted or rejected. "You don't want to throw books on your shelf that take forever to sell or will sell at a very low price," Murphy said. "Even if it's a reject, the book might actually look like a nice book, but we've set a threshold; we don't want more than 20 of these copies in inventory." Rejected books were either donated to various nonprofits (1.2 million thus far) or recycled to keep them out of landfills.

BWB paid $0.50 for what it considered a qualifying book. Most of the time, the company paid student groups for the books out of cash flow. For example, for the books collected during the spring book-drive season, which technically ended around June 30, BWB would cut the check in September of the same year. "We know that we're not going to sell those books until August or September," Murphy said. "We time the payment to the student groups to come out of cash flow, but if we needed to tap the credit line to honor our commitment to student organizations, we would."

Library Discards and Donations Program

In the fall of 2004, BWB launched the Library Discards and Donations program, targeting both the public and academic library communities. In September 2004, CEO Murphy brought in Dustin Holland, who had interned at the same private equity group where Murphy had worked. Murphy said, "Dustin, this is a big risk, and we don't know if there is a business there, but let's give it a shot." Murphy also recalled that "we went to trade shows, we started knocking on doors, and we began to talk to librarians about what they did with their books when they weeded them off the shelves. And we built it up." Holland rose to vice president of acquisitions and ended up overseeing not just the library but also the campus acquisition program.

By 2008, the library acquisition program contributed to the stability of the book-selling business. "It really helped us with the seasonal aspect of the [college] business. Before, we were in a feast-or-famine mode two times a year when college students bought their textbooks. We now get half of our revenues from libraries, and a much smoother distribution of revenue throughout the year," Murphy said.

The program also benefited libraries, most of which had no efficient way to dispose of their old or donated books. When Helgesen first went to a conference of the American Library Association, he heard stories of libraries "having to dump books down a well at midnight because they weren't allowed to even recycle them, but they didn't have any room on their shelves."[12]

By themselves, the best libraries could do was to sell the surplus books at cut-rate prices at sidewalk sales. This was where BWB and the power of the Internet came in. BWB's goal was to sell books at market value, thus improving returns for its library partners. Murphy stated, "We are a for-profit social enterprise; we believe in libraries, we want to create a revenue stream. Even if libraries could sell this book at a sale for $5, maybe somebody in London would pay $25 for it." BWB even covered all the shipping costs. "So it's no cash out of pocket for the library," Murphy added.

BWB's prescreen tools helped libraries determine which books to send to maximize their returns; children's books, cookbooks, coffee-table books, nonfiction, and biographies sold particularly well. "And here's where technology comes in," Murphy said. "We give librarians a portal, username, and password, so they could sign in. When the books were scanned into inventory, they could see that. It's updated in real time, and they can watch their sales."

BWB took the library books on consignment; the libraries got a quarterly commission on the proceeds. In addition, BWB donated a percentage of sales to a literacy nonprofit of a library's choosing. For example, one of BWB's biggest clients, the Brooklyn Public Library System (BPLS), had been supporting a literacy program known as Brooklyn Reads. "Every 90 days, one check goes to the BPLS, and one check goes to Brooklyn Reads," Murphy said, adding that since BPLS had partnered with BWB, library sales of di°scarded books had increased, as did funding for its affiliate literacy program. "Again, the power of the Internet, the power of selling books around the world at a higher price," Murphy said.

Expanding the Work Force

As the company grew, the founders realized that the friends and temp workers they hired for $8 an hour to help out during rush times were not enough. Among those first full-time employees was Aaron King, a South Bend native with a business degree from Purdue University. King took over management of the South Bend warehouse in the fall of 2003 and later became senior director of the central eastern division (overseeing some of the regional directors running book drives in the field).[13] The

---

12. Elam.

13. Gene Stowe, "BWB Revamping Its Process," *Tribune Business Weekly*, April 10, 2007.

company's social mission and charitable goals helped attract hard-working, motivated employees, such as Paul "Paco" Miller, who joined BWB as senior warehouse manager after a two-year stint in the Peace Corps.[14]

In late 2004, BWB had 10 to 15 full-time employees. In the seasonal textbook business, August and January were the busiest times, during which the warehouse staff increased to 50 employees. These employees sorted each incoming book by condition—acceptable, good, very good, like new—and attached stickers, including a code to identify its source. They scanned each book's bar code to enter information into a database, organizing the books as they came in. Thanks to the custom software, "With a team of eight people, we can get at least 5,000 books shipped in an eight- or ten-hour day," King said.[15]

As the number of collected books grew, BWB needed warehousing space, which, at first, was a 3,000-square-foot basement in Roseland. In December 2003, the founders moved their operation into the Sample Street Business Complex, a small-business incubator in South Bend, Indiana, which was the perfect environment for the fledgling company. "It allowed us to grow from 3,500 square feet to 75,000 square feet," said Fuchs.[16] In the summer of 2005, however, 75,000 square feet was no longer adequate. After several months of planning, BWB moved into part of the old Corrugated Paper Products factory on Currant Road in Mishawaka on April 1, 2006.[17]

Investing in Technology

The 2002 book drive at Notre Dame proved to be an invaluable learning experience and a lesson in the power of technology for the young entrepreneurs. Soon after they loaded the 2,000 collected books online, they were flooded with orders. At first, they filled orders manually: printing labels, packing, and shipping; however in August, the orders skyrocketed. "Those were the frenzied days of working 24/7 to get the orders out to the people who bought the books. And the founders said, 'Whoa, we can't do this again.'" They realized they needed to invest in technology to automate the process.

A driving force behind developing the custom software was Xavier Helgesen, an information-systems major and "naturally very, very tech-savvy entrepreneur," Murphy said. Helgesen and Kreece Fuchs felt they could develop the basic software architecture themselves. Having done everything manually, they knew what they needed to do it right. First, as soon as the books arrived, they wanted to be able to

14. Stowe, "Literacy the Bottom Line."
15. Stowe, "Literacy the Bottom Line."
16. Christina Hildreth, "Old Textbooks See New Use; BWB Donates to Literacy Charities," *South Bend Tribune*, June 6, 2006.
17. Hildreth.

scan their bar codes into a database. They also wanted to be able to post all the relevant information about the books online. Murphy explained:

They knew what was cumbersome—fulfilling the order and sending it out. Most customers would like a confirmation email that says, "Your order shipped." So they had to really think through all of it. How do you price the books? How do you perform customer service and inventory? How do you get that book and put it on the shelf? How in the heck are you going to know where it is? Because these are all random books placed haphazardly on the shelves.

Outsourcing Software Development

Designing the software architecture was one thing, but writing code was too time consuming. Cash-strapped, busy running day-to-day operations, and organizing campus book drives, the entrepreneurs found their solution on the Internet. Helgesen put the project up for bidding on eLance.com, the online exchange for private capital and professional business services. The job went to a firm in Russia "with all these PhD-level computer-science people, who did programming for $10 or $12 an hour," Murphy said. The outsourcing partnership worked out well for both sides. "To this day, we've got at least eight to ten full-time people in Russia with their heads down working on our software," Murphy said.

Developing Information Systems Where It Mattered Most

The founders understood early on that investing in technology—"and by technology I really mean software," Murphy said—was crucial to their company's survival, so they started developing information systems long before they managed to get outside funding. "They were really visionary in how to make sure the limited tech investment we could make was focused on the right things," Murphy said.

After Murphy took over and started implementing the high-growth vision, BWB's information systems needs grew more complex. As the founders hired regional directors to run book drives, they realized there was the need for a communication system that made it possible for directors to talk to each other and communicate with the warehouse. They needed to get supplies distributed to hundreds of college campuses without it becoming a nightmare of confusion. Murphy explained:

We were very focused on how you come up with systems that work. So we were early adopters of salesforce.com, for example, and we built it out. In fact, we're just about to hire a full-time sales force admin person because it's such a critical part to our business. It really is the technology that drives what I call the intake process. We are not selling as much as acquiring. So for us, it's not how many widgets we sell; it's how many books we collect.

Murphy emphasized that, when he came on board, "almost any available dollar we had, we put into technology." A key hire for the organization was Andy Warzon as CTO in January 2006. Murphy said that "Andy really took us to another level." Warzon ensured that the investment in technology was focused on what made the most business sense. Murphy continued:

We built some basic software that we needed to run our business. It was all about inventory flow control, pricing; it was the guts of our business. We built a system where we could get daily sales, daily pricing information; we could get a lot of things at our fingertips that told us how we were doing. So we got a very early grasp of cash flow, inventory, and what it was costing us to put books into inventory and how quickly that inventory was turning—not from a classic financial software package but homegrown.

The investment in technology continued even during "some dark, tough times," when the CEO and the founders had to forgo paychecks, stretch suppliers to 90 days, and "borrow money from friends and family." As the company grew, it needed more hardware (e.g., servers), but, according to Murphy, "The real dollars and the real payoff came from investing in systems and information that could best be described as 'high-powered analytics.'" Murphy explained:

We were building information into the system right from the get-go, but our critical resources were not put into the traditional "let's have a developed enterprise accounting system, and let's make sure our books are closed within five days." But if we knew inventory information and we knew cash flow and we knew pricing, the formal closing of the books would come later. Of course, as we grew, we were better able to capture even more traditional accounting metrics and information much more quickly.

While he invested in technology, Murphy wanted to make sure it was money well spent and spent in the areas that had the biggest impact on BWB's lifeblood. "We're forking over 20 grand a month to these Russians, and it's a lot like overhead to me," Murphy said, adding that he constantly monitored how investing in the software the company was using to acquire, process, inventory, and price incoming books was affecting cash flow. He continued:

Show me what this is getting us in terms of the impact on cash flow? What's its impact on our ability to really know the value of a used book, which, maybe it's not cash flow today, but it'll be cash flow in 12 months? We've invested automating this hard manual process or this pricing system, which has already improved us by giving us a 20% increase in our average sale price. We think we can get another 20%. It's investing in what is going to be one of our competitive advantages, and that's really strong technology, which takes data and turns it into really useful information to run our business.

Securing a Line of Credit

The information systems the founders developed proved to be a critical asset in running their business and also helped them secure the first line of credit to fuel the start-up's growth. Even though used books was not the most attractive asset to back a loan, and "our balance sheet looked like crap, and we were over-leveraged," Murphy said, the information they had at their fingertips "around those real key basics of cash flow" was enough for the banks to feel comfortable lending them money. Murphy recalled:

When we first started talking to the banks, they'd say, "Show us your most recent financial statement." What we sold the bank on was when we said, "Let's log on to our system and show you what we've got." When they could see that we really had inventory and cash flow and the predictability of our sales model, they said, "Okay, we're going to give you a $100,000 line of credit." After they put out $100,000 in June, and we told them, "We can pay this back by the end of August," and we paid it back once and then again, we built credibility. And then the line of credit went to $250,000 and then to $500,000.

Finding an HR Manager

When Murphy joined BWB, the company was so strapped for cash that hiring an HR manager was not an option, so he settled for creating a bare-bones employee handbook, which was reviewed by a labor attorney. Meanwhile, CFO Jeff Kurtzman handled the HR duties. Murphy recalled that, at the time, he told Kurtzman, "Just make sure everything's legal, safe, and bare basics." He continued:

Occasionally we would have to speak with outside experts to make sure we were doing things the way we should. And I was willing to take the risk, even if I had to have an occasional problem, or we dismissed somebody, and they wanted to come back and file some kind of complaint. That was a gamble I was willing to take. In the end, we had to be very flexible and fast-moving because I wanted to allow our unique and passionate culture to bloom rather than be stifled by too much HR bureaucracy.

Eight months into his tenure as the company's CEO, Murphy started to look for an HR manager. "We held the bar pretty high trying to find that right person," Murphy said. The challenge was to bring in someone who would not repress the young company's entrepreneurial spirit. As Murphy explained, "A true-blue traditional HR manager, who wants to come in and start putting in all kinds of policies and procedures, just wasn't going to work." He continued:

In the early days of building a company, you want to put in enough process, but not too much process. That's where you kill innovation, and you kill culture, and you kill that whole dynamic of, "Hey, we're young and it's exciting!" You want to be very careful—CFOs can do that as well. There are two groups of people where you probably have high turnover and some conflict. It's probably the accounting folks, and the HR folks because by nature, they're very process-oriented and legal minded, and they want to minimize risk at all levels in the company; gotta be right, gotta be perfect. And if you go too far that way early on, you just kill it.

Although the first manager hired lasted only a year, Murphy said, "He did a pretty nice job of getting us just the right level of structure given our size and growth." But Murphy wanted to stop relying on temp agencies and start recruiting more full-time employees. He embarked on another search for an HR manager, who joined the company in 2006. In 2008, Murphy stated, "As we've grown north of $20 million in revenue, we're up to 160 full-time people." He continued:

[Our HR manager] has helped bring us right up where we need to be. Today we have more structure. We need solid performance evaluations to take place systematically. We need pay systems that make sense. We're moving into more of what I call the enterprise culture of more systems, more accountability, and so forth.

Onward and Upward

Having successfully scaled the business up to $30 million, Murphy now pondered his next move: He planned to scale the business further, to $75 million within the next three years. What were the critical management challenges or issues that he faced regarding people, strategy, capital, technology, operational, and business-model perspectives?

C.R. Barger & Sons, Inc. (A)

CASE DISCUSSION QUESTIONS

1. How can Eric Barger take a small business with failing sales and a non-differentiated product with commodity pricing and create "growth boosters"?

2. If you were Eric, how would you grow this business?

3. Eric's father would like to see Eric's growth plan. Eric called you and asked you to prepare a PowerPoint presentation laying out how he can save the business. Please prepare the presentation.

C.R. BARGER & SONS, INC. (A)

Headquartered in Harriman, Tennessee, C.R. Barger & Sons, Inc., (Barger) operated two businesses: gas, water, and sewer-line installation and precast-concrete septic tank manufacture and sale. In 2002, after 35 years as a local supplier of septic tanks, that business had reached a plateau: Barger did not have a distinctive brand or product, and its sales were limited primarily to East Tennessee.

In early 2004, Eric Barger, the founders' grandson, assumed leadership of Precast Concrete Operations (PCO). Barger was on the verge of closing down that part of the business. Though still in his 20s, Eric had worked in the family business since he was a teenager and later after getting a civil engineering degree from Tennessee Technological University. Now the challenge Eric faced was how to take the precast septic tank, a nondistinctive commodity-priced product, and grow it into a viable growth business.

History

In 1967, Eric's grandparents, Charles (C. R.) and Mary Barger, started C.R. Barger & Sons, Inc. Straight out of high school, C. R. initially worked as a warehouse stock boy and then transitioned to plumbing work and building houses. In 1959, he purchased his grandfather's country store, Barger Groceries, but, as a side business, continued plumbing and building houses, and started installing septic tanks and field lines. C. R. ordered his septic tanks from third parties and often had problems receiving shipments on time, which frustrated his customers. One day, C. R. drove to a septic-tank-manufacturing plant in Georgia and observed how tanks were made and shipped. After the trip, he decided to make his own septic tanks to solve his supply-chain delivery problem.

Case Study UVA-ENT-0106 © 2008 by the University of Virginia Darden School Foundation. This case was prepared by C.R. Barger & Sons, Inc., and Research Assistant Shizuka Modica, under the supervision of Edward D. Hess, as a basis for class discussion rather than to illustrate effective or ineffective handling of an administrative situation.

C. R. and Mary made their first precast-concrete septic tanks in a small tin shed behind Barger Groceries. Together, they handcrafted the tanks with trowels, using a simple metal form. At that time, 750-gallon and 1,000-gallon tanks already were available on the market. The Bargers started by making only the 1,000-gallon tanks, and because the cement for each tank had to be individually mixed by hand with a shovel only one tank per day was cast.

After two months without making a sale, C. R. and Mary finally sold their first tank to a local resident. This single sale helped spread the word that there was a new family business in town, and soon the phone started ringing continually with customers asking for their handmade tanks. At a time when the concept of marketing was practically nonexistent in the industry, the Bargers' side business grew with every handshake into an eastern Tennessee precast-concrete-tank success story over the next three decades.[18] Mickey, one of C. R.'s sons, joined the company after obtaining a degree in business and helped to further grow the company.

Family Ties and Company Tradition

In January 2004, Mickey Barger passed the precast-division reins on to his 26-year-old son, Eric, although he retained management control of the utility division. The precast division was usually staffed with five employees, and the other divisions were made up of about forty employees. Eric took great pride in the family heritage and the traditions of his company; he considered his floor workers' and delivery drivers' positions to be as strategic as those of a winning Super Bowl football team: "The guys who make the tanks are critical—they're our offensive linemen. . . . And the drivers are similar to quarterbacks—everyone knows who they are; they're the first contact with clients. . . . A lot of the pressure is riding on them."[19]

The Business

When Eric took over PCO in early 2004, the division had two production employees, two delivery drivers, and a company secretary, who divided her time between the three divisions within the company. Eric had limited time to oversee his division because he was also heavily involved with the utility division.

Back in 2003, sales of precast-concrete products—primarily residential septic tanks and commercial grease interceptors—had reflected a 24% reduction over the previous business year and represented only $135,000 per full-time-equivalent employee. Word of mouth and an existing customer base drove precast sales. The entire cus-

---

18. Greg Snapper, "Lessons from the 'Little Guy': Smaller Precasting Outfits Like Barger & Sons Inc. Are Marketing Just Like the Big Guns," *MC Magazine* (July/August 2006): 42.

19. Snapper, 44.

tomer base of the company was located in Tennessee. About 30% of its business came from residential home builders and contractors and 70% came from the commercial and industrial segment; the 70% broke down further into 60% from utility districts and 10% from storm shelters and grease interceptors. The Barger market share of precast-concrete products, although believed to be small, was unknown. The Barger name was recognized by, at best, 20% of the licensed installers in the area, and the company's presence in the residential market segment was negligible.

Industry Character

The septic-tank manufacturing industry was mostly made up of small mom-and-pop businesses. As in any other industry, differentiating the products from those of other manufacturers was perceived to be essential to growing business. Because septic tanks were buried in the ground, however, they did not capture much attention. Usually, homeowners made decisions based on their contractors' advice without knowing much about the septic tanks they purchased; contractors relied on price alone when recommending specific tanks to their individual customers. And because little information on precast-concrete products was available to contractors, many of them thought that all septic tanks functioned equally. Therefore, it was hard to make the case that one manufacturer's tanks were better than another's.

The Goals

Although Eric knew his family was thinking about shutting down the septic-tank end of the business, he was determined to try and make it a success. So he set some audacious goals: (1) increase sales by a factor of three within four years to reestablish PCO as a viable, sustainable business entity; (2) build the highest-quality precast-concrete products in the area; and (3) establish a reputation as the premier source for precast-concrete-tank information and products. But because the future would be very different from the current reality of the business, the question was how to accomplish those goals. Eric contemplated his first moves.

C.R. Barger & Sons, Inc. (B)

CASE DISCUSSION QUESTIONS

1. Outline all the different ways utilized by Eric to reignite growth.

2. How did he get premium pricing?

3. How did he use technology to create differentiators?

4. How did his professional background help him achieve his objectives?

5. What are the geographical constraints on growing his business model?

6. How can he now scale production? Distribution?

7. Is he pursuing good growth or bad growth by considering the building of a concrete plant? How can that idea make strategic or financial sense?

8. Is Eric assuming that the recent past is a predictor of the future?

C.R. BARGER & SONS, INC. (B)

It had been almost four years since Eric Barger became president of the Precast Concrete Operations (PCO) division of C.R. Barger & Sons, Inc., (Barger). At the time he took over the position, the company was considering shutting down this division because of its persistently stagnant, flat revenues. But Eric had decided to give the PCO division his best shot.

By the end of 2007, Eric had turned the PCO division around and had grown it into a leader in the precast-concrete industry by implementing a multifaceted strategy. Eric accomplished this by differentiating the product and incorporating technology into the manufacturing process for higher quality and efficiency. He also expanded Barger's customer base geographically and added new customer segments after launching an aggressive Internet branding program and educational effort.

As a result, Eric's former challenges had changed dramatically—from how to save the PCO division to figuring out how to duplicate and improve on the results of his growth initiatives. In particular, Eric now was considering whether to build a new PCO plant at a cost of $3.8 million in order to accommodate future growth.

2004 Growth Strategy

When Eric took over the PCO division in 2004, Barger could not differentiate its precast-concrete tanks from those of other manufacturers in the area, in spite of

Case Study UVA-ENT-0107 © 2008 by the University of Virginia Darden School Foundation. This case was prepared by C.R. Barger & Sons, Inc., and Research Assistant Shizuka Modica, under the supervision of Edward D. Hess, as a basis for class discussion rather than to illustrate effective or ineffective handling of an administrative situation.

having been in the business since 1967. Basically, Barger sold a commodity product primarily to utility districts and had little market or brand recognition.

Eric's revitalization strategy had included seven goals: (1) create product differentiators; (2) increase manufacturing efficiency; (3) create brand awareness; (4) create new customers by expanding geographically; (5) create new customer segments; (6) be a first-mover incorporating new national standards; and (7) make service a differentiator.

In September 2004, the company got its grease interceptors H20-highway-traffic-rated to accommodate the Knoxville Utility Board's request. The H20-highway-traffic rating standards were applied in high-traffic areas as defined by the American Association of State Highway and Transportation Officials. Owing to rigorous standards, the new line of H20-rated products had price tags much higher than those of existing product lines. For instance, a 1,000-gallon non-traffic-rated grease interceptor cost about $400, but if it were H20-traffic-rated, it cost $2,500.

Barger became the only East Tennessee precast-concrete tank manufacturer offering watertight, traffic-rated grease interceptors, grit traps, and septic tanks. The company manufactured watertight 40- to 6,800-gallon tanks, including ones traffic-rated for H20 loadings and deep-burial applications.

The use of watertight, traffic-rated grease interceptors maximized tank performance and useful life, thereby enabling utility districts to effectively combat the problem of grease clogging municipal wastewater systems. Another critical design feature that further differentiated Barger products was its use of monolithic baffle walls that enhanced structural integrity, thereby eliminating premature failures.

Manufacturing Efficiency

Eric introduced the most rigorous industry standards into the company's manufacturing processes, which also enhanced product quality and further differentiated its products. In October 2005, the company was certified by the industry's leading trade association, the National Precast Concrete Association (NPCA) and became the only NPCA-certified plant in East Tennessee specializing in tank manufacturing.

The NPCA Plant Certification Program was a challenging test of a plant's ability to produce quality precast-concrete products. The program was administered by a world-renowned engineering and materials-science firm. Assigned inspectors comprehensively assessed all aspects of precast-concrete production at a plant. To be certified, plants had to meet high standards in all areas of production, safety, delivery of products, and information management.

Achieving this certification meant that Eric had to make the company's manufacturing process more disciplined; he maintained comprehensive manufacturing records and obtained required ACI certification for those employees performing the concrete testing.[20] According to Ty Gable, president of NPCA, Barger had proven its commitment to manufacturing the highest quality of precast products by joining this elite group of precasters.

As part of the NPCA certification process, Eric introduced innovative technology solutions in many ways and extended the company's computer network to include the manufacturing plant. The production side of technology solutions included the use of more precise concrete forms and the application of technically superior concrete, adhesives, and ASTM-compliant, chemical-resistant sealants.[21]

Concurrently, Eric developed and implemented two software systems that streamlined operations management. The first system, called PreCast-IT!, was an inventory-management software system designed specifically for manufacturing, delivering, and maintaining records for precast-concrete products. PreCast-IT! used bar codes and portable data terminals to maintain a complete history of each product manufactured and delivered to a customer, eliminating the time-consuming and error-prone manual data-entry method.

A second software system, Produce-IT!, provided detailed requirements for the materials for any selected time period based on the schedules, product structure, and bill-of-materials maintained in the system. Produce-IT! allowed manufacturing planners to easily schedule product pours and automatically generated a complete list of production-material requirements. The system allowed the user a five-day window into production schedules. The schedule for a specific concrete form could easily be shifted forward or backward in time to accommodate unforeseen demand or outages. Because Produce-IT! maintained complete product structure and bill-of-material records, it could generate a summary report on material requirements across any desired time period and facilitate efficient ordering of production materials.

Customer-Service Enhancement

Eric communicated Barger's commitment to providing excellent service both to his employees and to all customers. He wanted all employees to embrace the notion that excellence in service was not just an idea, but a way of life at Barger. He wanted all employees who came into contact with customers to be effective representatives of the quality of the company's product and guaranteed maintenance service. So, as part of customer-service enhancement, Eric demanded well-trained personnel for everything the company did and encouraged all employees to be certified in their relevant domains.

20. ACI stood for American Concrete Institute. Founded in 1904, ACI managed 14 certification programs to develop, share, and disseminate the knowledge and information needed to utilize concrete to its fullest potential.

21. ASTM stood for the American Society for Testing and Materials. This association set international standards for a wide range of materials, products, systems, and services.

Eric also led by example. For instance, he was dedicated to answering questions from customers and judiciously followed up on these inquiries by contacting them and/or sending AutoCad tank drawings and other relevant product information (Exhibit C.1) on the same day he received their inquiries.

On-time deliveries, which were rare in the industry, became the company's signature service, saving contractors the cost of having crews on standby for several hours waiting for a delivery. Not satisfied with this significant improvement, Eric pushed on-site delivery service to a different level, as proclaimed on the Barger Web site:

Delivery drivers are first-class people, willing to go the extra step it takes to ensure you are happy with your order. That includes handling the tank in a fashion that is safe and courteous, being on time for deliveries, and maintaining a good relationship with each customer. The drivers are just an extension of the business and the biggest representative that contacts the customer. Being able to make decisions on the job site, scheduling future deliveries and making sure that the customer has not ordered too much or forgotten a small item they may need.[22]

Additionally, both Barger's and Eric's personal expertise in utility operations helped enhance customer service in a way that other precast-concrete manufacturers could not. For example, Eric and several other employees held Water Treatment Plant and Licensed Distributionist certifications and could assemble water-meter vaults. To simplify the on-site tank-installation process, Barger started selling preassembled vaults to utility districts that were ready to be set in the holes and hooked up to the tanks.

Branding

Eric wanted to establish Barger as *the* underground-tank authority and to promote it as representing values that brought "old-school thought and 21st century marketing together."[23] Barger's marketing strategy encompassed various forms of awareness campaigns and education on product-design features unique to its products. This strategy was targeted toward all potential customers (i.e., individual homeowners, building contractors, engineers, architects, utility districts, and state and municipal regulators) who influenced the market.

Awareness Campaign

To raise awareness among prospective customers, Barger adopted the theme, We're Number One in the Number Two Business, which was carried throughout all PCO advertising. Because he did not have an expert marketing team on board at the time, Eric himself developed brochures, T-shirts, hats, and even pocket knives sporting the company logo. He filled a billboard with a display of the major Barger products and corporate theme and then had it placed strategically on Interstate 40.

22. http://www.bargerandsons.com/company/info.html (accessed 2 July 2008).
23. Greg Snapper, "Lessons from the 'Little Guy,'" *MC Magazine* (June/July 2006): 42.

The company advertised on the two Knoxville talk radio stations at a cost of $50,000 per year per station. Radio advertising by commercial voice-overs by well-known personalities helped inform Barger's target market about important product features and company attributes. It also hosted a four-hour radio show that ran five days a week on one of the stations whose radio waves reached five different states. This radio show's host unexpectedly became an advocate for Barger.

Some of Barger's employees, including Eric and his father Mickey, belonged to relevant industry associations and actively participated in trade associations and industry-standards groups. Eric served and networked with others in the industry as a member of the NPCA Quality Assurance Committee, as the director of the NPCA Educational Foundation, and as a member of ASTM committee, C27, Precast Concrete Products. While widely networking in the industry, Eric simultaneously pursued various opportunities for the company to be featured in articles in industry publications.

Community outreach was also expanded to sponsor direct delivery of industry trade-magazine subscriptions free-of-charge to decision makers, engineers, and utility owners. Barger also sponsored free technical classes where engineers and architects earned continuing education credits.

Internet Marketing

To promote education among prospective customers, a new Web site was designed without an emphasis on sales. The new site accommodated prospective customers' varying needs and interests. Anyone who visited the Web site was given unlimited access to detailed plans, design specifications and drawings, white papers, and published articles to use when designing and developing project specifications.

For nontechnical homeowners, the Web site also offered a list of frequently asked questions and provided information on how to best use and maintain a septic tank. This was different from the traditional way septic systems had been sold in the past when homeowners were seldom involved until the bill was presented to them. Eric's hope was that educating homeowners about residential septic systems would enable them to play a significant role in their purchase, a decision usually made by their contractors.

In designing the new Web site, Eric carefully chose metatags (keywords) embedded in each of the company's Web pages, so even with a quick search using a Web browser, Barger popped up on a computer screen for anyone looking for watertight concrete septic tanks, grease interceptors, and storm shelters.

The Results

Shortly after launching the new marketing strategy, Eric started getting phone and Web site orders from Georgia, Virginia, and Kentucky. When the company received sales inquiries from a new state, it quickly familiarized itself with that state's regulations governing its business to become compliant with relevant regulations. At the end of 2007, Barger had expanded its customer base from its home state of Tennessee to 12 more states, including Arkansas, North Carolina, South Carolina, Illinois, Mississippi, West Virginia, Ohio, and New York.

Thanks to its open-source Web site and customer-centered philosophy, Barger's quality products generated some unusual requests. For example, Eric received a call from a wildlife conservationist in San Juan, Puerto Rico, asking about a 5,000-gallon grease interceptor. This government official, who was responsible for the preservation of one of the most endangered birds in the world, had found Barger on the Internet. Situated in a remote location of the Caribbean National Forest, Luquillo Aviary was a captive breeding sanctuary for the Puerto Rican parrot. The sanctuary needed a cistern as part of the government's 19-year-old formal recovery plan for the parrot. The sanctuary bought Barger's grease interceptor as a rainwater storage tank to provide chemical-free drinking and bathing water for the birds. To ensure proper installation on-site, Eric filmed and narrated an instructional DVD that was shipped with the interceptor.

Now because of the order from Puerto Rico, Barger was advertised as a "parrot's best friend" in NPCA's industry magazine, *Precast Solutions Magazine*, in spring 2006.[24] Other media exposure included a feature article about the company, one about the lessons learned from the company's Web experience, and a technical feature presenting the results of a study on inflow and infiltration from unsealed septic-tank access ports. Eric's Web-savvy marketing also led to negotiations with American contractors in the Middle East.

By providing various technical white papers and personalized services to his customers, Eric built buy-in for high-priced, H20-highway-traffic-rated product lines. In 2006, Barger sold 60% more H20-rated products than products without the rating to both its commercial and industrial customers. H20-rated products buffered liability concerns customers had and helped them promote safe, ecologically friendly tanks.

Almost daily, new customers called or e-mailed. But attracting new customers was secondary to keeping existing business relationships thriving. At the end of 2007, Barger's customer base was 40% homebuilders (a 10% increase from the previous four years) and 60% commercial/industrial customers. This 60% broke down further to 40% utility districts and 20% grease interceptors.

The two software systems Barger developed to improve its production and management processes turned out to be great investments. Produce-IT! reduced the time required to develop pour schedules by 90%. In addition to saving several hours of effort per week developing pour schedules, Produce-IT! reduced the company's material supply stock by 50%.

Barger received the NPCA's Award of Excellence in 2007; it was one of only three plants in the United States to receive it. The award was based on scores from an inde-

24. Bridget McCrea, "Parrot's Best Friend," *Precast Solutions Magazine*, Spring 2006.

pendent, unannounced audit of the manufacturing plant, its processes, procedures, and employee qualifications. In 2007, Barger also received the Pinnacle Award, presented after a competition for the leading innovations, inventions, and ideas throughout the precast-cement industry. The award specifically recognized the PreCast-IT! inventory-management software as the most innovative industry development for 2007.

By charting and implementing a pathway to excellence, Barger's PCO reached a position of market dominance and preeminence in its field in four years. Gross sales for the 2007 fiscal business year exceeded 2003 sales by 400% and topped the goal established in 2004—these results reflected an average annual sales growth of 42% over the four-year period. The sales per full-time-equivalent (FTE) employee in 2007 were $202,000, reflecting an increase of 50% over 2003 figures. The number of FTE employees in the division alone grew from 4.5 in 2004 to 15 at the end of 2007.

When compared with the modest growth in construction in the area, Barger's 400% increase in sales suggested that some amount of business was taken away from competitors. According to the U.S. Census Bureau, new residential construction in 2007 decreased by almost 25% nationwide compared with new residential construction in 2006.[25] In early 2008, economists debated whether the United States was heading into a recession, and no one was quite sure about the magnitude of the impact of the subprime-mortgage crisis on the U.S. economy.

Growth Capacity: Build a New Plant?

Barger's success led it to wonder whether or not it should construct a new plant in an industrial park closer to the center of its market area. The new plant would increase Barger's production capacity, giving it the capability to expand its product lines. For about $3.8 million, the company could build a plant that would increase its concrete-production capacity by a factor of five from 40 to 200 cubic yards per day.

Barger had three primary reasons for wanting to build a new plant. First, by March 2006, the existing plant occasionally ran over capacity; in 2007, it ran over capacity more than 50% of the time and sometimes at 150% over capacity. But the bottom line was that the plant ran at over 100% capacity more than half the time. Second, Barger had no space for expansion on its existing one-acre property. Third, Eric wanted to improve the quality of the concrete the company used. Because the existing plant did not have the capacity to mix concrete, the company relied on purchased, premixed concrete. The new plant would give the company total quality control over the concrete.

Was it reasonable for Eric to expect that Barger could sustain the same growth rate in the future? Should Eric be satisfied with the company's 2007 revenue levels and focus on maintaining its product lines, market areas, and customer base? Or should Eric build the new plant and seek more growth?

---

25. U.S. Census Bureau, New Privately Owned Housing Units Started: Annual Data, http://www.census.gov/const/www/newresconstindex.html (accessed 21 July 2008).

Exhibit C.1 Why a Barger & Sons Septic Tank Is the Best Value for the Homeowner

Tank Feature	Barger's Approach	Other Manufacturers' Approach	Benefits to Homeowner
Zero Inflow and Infiltration			
Watertight tank	• Use ASTM C990 sealant and proven application methods • Joint design enhances seal	• Cheap sealant does not meet ASTM specifications and fails • Joint design and sealant size inadequate to assure water tightness	• Prevents expensive premature replacement of field line • Prevents raw sewage seepage to lawn surface
Tank Design and Construction			
Superior tank strength	• Engineered tank design • Superior 5,000 psi concrete strength • Prefabricated and precisely positioned rebar structure	• Do not have engineered design • May collapse after installation • Lack of or improperly positioned rebar can accelerate tank failure	• Prevents catastrophic failure due to ground pressure or riding lawn mowers • Septic tanks maintain structural integrity for at least 30 years
Zero baffle wall failures	• Thicker, monolithic wall baffle poured as part of tank walls, reinforced by rebar, remains perfectly positioned for life of tank, and functions perfectly to separate and retain solids from liquid waste	• Prone to failure due to thin design and being held in place by brick, baffle wall wobbles in place • Have no rebar reinforcing and are not tied directly into the tank walls • Exposed metal lifting wire leads to solids gathering around baffle wall passage	• Solids do not enter, increasing the life of the field line and decreasing system failure • Avoids replacement of septic tank due to baffle wall failure • Septic tanks perform like new 30 years after installation
Quality of Manufacturing			
Consistent manufacturing methods	• Zero defects quality philosophy • Methods validated by random audits by independent professional engineering firm • ACI-certified technicians and NPCA Production Quality School certified workers	• Do not employ ACI-certified technicians to ensure quality concrete • Production drawings are not available to manufacturing employees	• Ensures that each tank is built to the highest standards • Highest possible chance to receive a tank that has no defects
Recognized tank expertise	• Only septic tank manufacturing plant in East Tennessee that is NPCA-certified • Featured manufacturer in industry trade publications • Selected to provide products to solve international environmental issue on behalf of government agency • Manager serves on international tank quality assurance steering committee • Tanks used exclusively in more than 50 utility district projects	• Do not participate in recognized trade association	• Application of latest and best technologies • Continuous improvement through access to world-class experts
Life Cycle Cost			
Lowest cost to install and maintain	• High quality of tank design and construction maximize useful life of tank and field line • Provide lowest overall cost to install and maintain	• Faulty tank design and construction can lead to premature failure of tank and field line resulting in significantly increased operational costs	• Minimizes total cost to homeowner

SOURCE: Recreated with permission from C.R. Barger & Sons, Inc., from http://www.bargerandsons.com/site/demandbargerandsons.pdf (accessed 1 July 2008).

Defender Direct, Inc.: A Business of Growing Leaders

This case is embedded in Chapter 5 and can be found on page 108.

DEFENDER DIRECT, INC.: A BUSINESS OF GROWING LEADERS

Defender Direct is a good example of how an entrepreneur grew as his company grew. As you read the "Defender Direct, Inc.: A Business of Growing Leaders" case, focus on how Dave Lindsey's role changed as the company grew and how he evolved as a leader.

CASE DISCUSSION QUESTIONS

1. What do you think Dave means when he states, "Businesses don't grow—people do"?
2. What do you think Dave means when he states "Build a culture on purpose, not by accident"?
3. Why did Dave want to build a business that could be "McDonaldized"?
4. Explain how Defender's business model of simplicity was scalable.
5. What is the "Circle of Life"? Why is it important?
6. How did Dave evolve his business model?
7. "Businesses don't grow—people do." How did Dave grow? How did Dave's growth enable the business to grow?
8. What do you think Dave meant when he said, "Focus Equals Growth"?

Edens & Avant

This case is embedded in Chapter 9 and can be found on page 207.

This case is embedded in Chapter 9 and can be found on page 207.

<table>
<tr><td>CASE
STUDY</td><td></td></tr>
</table>

EDENS & AVANT

Now let's look at the issue of succession planning and how one successful entrepreneur using the philosophy and principles expressed in this chapter made the hard decision between three very different potential CEO successors. How did he balance the various needs of his family, his employees, his shareholders, and his personal desires for the company to be institutionalized beyond his tenure?

CASE DISCUSSION QUESTIONS

1. Put yourself in Joe Edens's shoes. What are your key concerns about succession? Your goals? Whose (stakeholders) interests do you need to consider?

2. How did Edens's family history impact his views about succession?

3. Joe Edens hires you as his advisor. He asks you to outline the pros and cons of each of the three candidates. What would you tell him?

4. Whom would you choose? Why?

5. What process should he use to get buy-in from the stakeholders?

6. What process should Joe use to pass on the CEO mantle to the successor?

7. Which succession choice has the least risk? Which has the most risk? Why?

8. Joe can pick only one successor. He has three good candidates, all of whom he wants to stay with the company as employees or, in the case of the outside candidate, as a consultant. As Joe's advisor, he asks you how he can accomplish that goal. What would you tell him?

15. Role play being the outsider who, if chosen, has discussions with the son and loyal employee trying to convince them to work for him.

Enchanting Travels

This case is embedded in Chapter 8 and can be found on page 183.

ENCHANTING TRAVELS

Enchanting Travels has grown using a joint venture model in Africa and an organic model in Argentina. Its challenge now is how to grow more quickly by expanding into new geographies. It has a scaling challenge, and the case raises the issue as to whether it should franchise to scale more quickly.

CASE DISCUSSION QUESTIONS

1. What was Enchanting Travels' differentiating customer value proposition?
2. Should Enchanting Travels franchise its business model? Why?
3. Explain the following statement: "What made Enchanting Travels successful limited its growth."
4. What are Enchanting Travels' major growth risks?
5. The founders had an usual philosophy of hiring. How does it contribute to their success and limit their success?
6. How can Enchanting Travels expand its business without opening new locations in new countries?
7. Do you think Enchanting Travels' business model is scalable? Why?
8. Would you buy this business? Why?

Eyebobs Eyewear, Inc.
This case is embedded in Chapter 1 and can be found on page 19.

EYEBOBS EYEWEAR, INC.

This story presents one entrepreneur's views about the risks of growth and why she turned away growth opportunities and certain large potential customers because of those risks.

CASE DISCUSSION QUESTIONS

1. Put yourself in Julie's shoes; why was she so risk averse?

2. What was consistent about Julie's attitude about financing her business and her product?

3. What were Julie's big concerns that drove many of her decisions?

4. Julie's life experiences prepared her to be a business builder—what were they and what did she learn?

5. Chart how Julie built the production and distribution parts of her business and explain her risk management thinking.

6. You are a writer for your school newspaper. Write a 250-word story that summarizes the Eyebobs case.

Freedom Technology Services

CASE DISCUSSION QUESTIONS

1. Build an argument that Jim Patterson should settle this matter quietly. What are the pros of that approach? What are the cons?

2. What values does a quiet settlement reinforce? What values conflict with a quiet settlement?

3. Build an argument that Patterson should seek a criminal prosecution. What are the pros of that course of action? What are the cons?

4. What values do a criminal action reinforce? What values conflict with that approach?

5. What impact do you think Patterson's failure to discover the fraud earlier should have on his decision? Is he exonerated by relying on the prior CPA audits?

6. How will Patterson's decision impact his employees?

7. What impact could his decision have on his government clients?

8. What would you do? Why?

CASE
STUDY

FREEDOM TECHNOLOGY SERVICES

Jim Patterson graduated from Virginia Tech in 1985 with a degree in computer science and spent the next 15 years as a technology consultant for IBM in the metropolitan Washington, D.C., area. His clients were usually large corporate or government entities. Patterson did a lot of classified cyber-security consulting for various top-secret U.S. military and intelligence units. He developed quite an expertise in this space.

By 2000, Patterson was ready to escape the big-company environment. He was encouraged to do so by many of his colleagues, who were convinced that his expertise and reputation would quickly generate lucrative business. Patterson took their advice and started Freedom Technology Services (Freedom) in Alexandria, Virginia. He immediately applied for contracts as a small business contractor to many of the intel agencies he had worked with during his time at IBM. Not surprisingly, he was awarded several contracts, which forced him to immediately hire 15 experienced consultants with whom he had worked on prior jobs. These consultants had the requisite security clearances and necessary experience with the specific contracting agencies.

Freedom prospered, earning Patterson more than $7 million in revenue by 2008. Approximately $4 million of this revenue was generated by Patterson's sole nongovernmental client—a major financial services company that had substantial cyber risks in its financial services business. Patterson attributed his success to the professionalism

Case Study UVA-ENT-0127 © 2009 by the University of Virginia Darden School Foundation. This fictitious case was prepared by Edward D. Hess as a basis for class discussion rather than to illustrate effective or ineffective handling of an administrative situation.

of his team and the family culture he built into the company, which contributed to Freedom's low employee turnover and high employee loyalty and productivity. Patterson rewarded this productivity and loyalty by paying above-market compensation and providing a Google-like nonbureaucratic no-rules-based environment. Freedom was consistently voted as a Great Place to Work by the local business newspapers.

Patterson believed in a lean management team because so many of his employees worked at client sites, including over one-half of them who worked on the financial services sites. His management team consisted of himself as CEO, three vice presidents of client service, a CTO, and a vice president of finance/human resources/administration, who was the only member of the management team that Patterson, in 2004, had hired de novo. She was a CPA and, coincidentally, the wife of the executive vice president of a large financial services client.

In early March 2009, the senior partner of Patterson's outside auditing firm called him at home on a Saturday morning. This auditing firm was the third to perform the required annual government audits since 2005; two other auditing firms had not met the CFO's standards for work quality. The senior partner asked if he could come over to Patterson's house to talk. When Patterson wanted to know why, the senior partner responded, "We have a major problem."

The senior partner arrived within the hour and told Patterson that he thought there was a high likelihood that fraud had been going on in the company since 2005 with respect to one of its large commercial clients. "I think your CFO has been embezzling money," he said.

Patterson was floored. How could this be? Patterson asked how much they we were talking about, hoping that this was not a big problem. But the senior partner responded, "Nearly a million dollars."

The senior partner recommended that Patterson get legal advice. They agreed to talk again Monday morning. Patterson immediately called his attorney, Charles Cuk, the senior partner at Cook, Cooke, and Cuk, who, after hearing the allegations, told Patterson that he would come over on Monday morning, and together they would confront the CFO. He also told Patterson he could sue in civil court to recover the money, or he could file a criminal complaint and have the CFO prosecuted and sent to jail. Cuk also said that in either case, Patterson could recover some of the money if he had insurance coverage for fraud.

But because he had all his books audited every year and only he and the CFO could sign checks, Patterson had not bought fraud insurance. It turned out that the fraud at Freedom was partially hidden by the bank line of credit that provided working capital for the business until checks came in for services rendered. Upon reflection, Patterson remembered wondering why the bank line of credit never was materially reduced.

On Monday morning, the senior partners of both the accounting firm and law firm arrived and met with the CFO. They asked for an explanation about the money that apparently was missing—more than $1 million for a four-year period. The CFO stated she had no idea, and she was sure there was an explanation the auditors had overlooked. She asked that Patterson leave the room. Then she then broke down and admitted to the senior partners that she had incurred debt by betting on horses and sports teams. She had borrowed money in 2005 to pay off these gambling debts without the knowledge of her family. She said she intended to repay the loan from her bonuses over the next two years so her husband would not know about her addiction. Unfortunately, her addiction had grown into a $1 million problem.

Crying, the CFO asked for forgiveness and stated that she would find a way to pay the money back but pleaded with them to keep this problem a secret. She did not want what she did to hurt her husband's standing in the community or impact negatively on his job. She reminded the senior partners in that room that her husband's employer was responsible for approximately 50% of Freedom's revenue.

Later, the senior partners briefed Patterson about the conversation. Cuk repeated the two legal options available to Patterson: a civil lawsuit if a quiet settlement could not be reached or criminal prosecution.

Patterson went home that night and discussed the situation with his wife. He wanted to do what was right in a moral sense and what was right for the business and its employees. Of course, the matter was made more complicated because the CFO was the wife of a key client contact; however, Patterson's reputation for integrity was the backbone of his government relationships. His wife pointed out that as CEO he could be held responsible for not discovering the fraud situation earlier and that it was obvious that the CFO had a mental addiction.

What should Patterson do? Why?

Global Medical Imaging, LLC

This case is embedded in Chapter 6 and can be found on page 136.

This case is embedded in Chapter 6 and can be found on page 136.

CASE
STUDY

GLOBAL MEDICAL IMAGING, LLC

Global Medical Imaging is a good illustration of how both the entrepreneur and the business evolve and change as the business grows. Ryan Dienst, the CEO, explains how he had to change, how he installed process, the challenges of building a management team, the tension of investing in infrastructure ahead of growth, and how the business model expanded to include service offerings.

CASE DISCUSSION QUESTIONS

1. What role did prior industry experience play in helping these founders avoid start-up failure?

2. Why did Scott and Ryan make good partners?

3. What are your 10 key take-aways about growing a business that you learned from this case?

4. How is managing a business with seven employees so different from managing one with thirty-five employees?

5. Why did GMI's experience so many people issues? What did they learn in the process?

6. What commonalities do you find in the Defender Direct and Global Medical Imaging cases?

Green Copier Recycling: Entrepreneur Meets Private Equity

CASE DISCUSSION QUESTIONS

1. Why did Patterson start his own company?

2. What were the keys to Patterson's success?

3. How would selling 70% of his company impact those keys to success?

4. Why should Patterson sell?

5. Why should Patterson not sell?

6. What issues are raised by the earn-out?

7. What concerns you about the proposed deal? Why?

8. Is Patterson receiving fair market value for his company? Why? How do you know?

9. What realistic alternatives does Patterson have?

10. What would you do? Why?

CASE
STUDY

GREEN COPIER RECYCLING: ENTREPRENEUR MEETS PRIVATE EQUITY

In 2000, Pat Patterson, at the age of 35, founded Green Copier Recycling (Green) after he had worked for 10 years in the equipment-recycling industry. Patterson's goal in starting Green was to have more control over his work destiny.

Green's business involved refitting and then reselling the used copiers turned in by leasing companies. The refitted-copier industry was highly fragmented and had no major national player when Patterson started his company. By 2008, however, Green had earned $80 million in revenues with a 15% EBITDA margin and had experienced double-digit compounded growth for some time.

Green had become *the* preferred recycling partner for many of the regional leasing companies who financed midsized and small businesses. Green's success was derived from its commitment to speed and quality and its money-back guarantees. After refitting the used copiers that came from the leasing companies, Green resold them through its Internet store to new buyers.

In early 2009, due to the economic recession, consolidation was taking place in the fragmented industry, and a private equity firm, looking for a platform company upon which it could consolidate, approached Green. Because of Green's stellar operating results and its reputation, it was the private equity firm's first choice for a

Case Study UVA-ENT-0125 © 2009 by the University of Virginia Darden School Foundation. This fictitious case was prepared by Edward D. Hess as a basis for class discussion rather than to illustrate effective or ineffective handling of an administrative situation.

platform company and a controlling investment. The firm made an unsolicited offer and gave Patterson a week to make a decision.

Patterson had not considered selling or relinquishing control of Green, nor had he considered acquiring other companies. If Patterson were to sell the company, the private equity investors would control the board and bring in a new COO of their choice; he would stay on as CEO under a contract for three years. Unfortunately, Patterson had no experience in financing or selling companies and neither did his CPA or attorney.

The Start-Up

In 1990, Patterson had received his BA from the University of Colorado, where he made the honors list and was elected head cheerleader for the football team and president of his fraternity. For 10 years after graduation, Patterson worked in the used-equipment recycling business, which included learning origination sources and the refitting process. While working in this business, he yearned to form his own company because he wanted the opportunity to do it his way, which he thought would lead to success. He decided to take the plunge in 2000. With his life savings of $5,000, he began his own equipment-recycling business in the garage of his home.

The Business

In 2005, 90% of Green's business was derived from service and sales commissions from regional banks and equipment-leasing companies; the rest was obtained from purchasing used copiers directly from businesses, refitting them, and selling them. Green's refitting process brought used copiers back to their original condition; the process covered nine areas: fusing assembly, imaging section, charge assembly, paper-feed assembly, document feeder, optics, testing, cosmetics, and prepackaging. Green specialized in copiers manufactured by Canon, Ricoh, HP, Konica, Sharp, Toshiba, and Minolta.

U.S. Equipment Leasing Association figures from 2005 showed that "U.S. leasing organizations financed $248 billion of a total of $800 billion in business equipment investments,"[26] which equaled 1.99% of the GDP. The equipment-leasing environment in the United States was very competitive and fragmented. For most categories of leased goods, the concentration of the largest eight equipment-leasing companies was less than 50%, and the copier-leasing industry was no exception. Green's product-origination sources were mostly regional banks and leasing companies, based on personal relationships that Patterson had developed while working at the previous company and through his own business. Approximately four companies accounted for 80% of Green's volume.

---

26. Equipment Leasing Sector, 2007" http://trade.gov/investamerica/leasing.asp (accessed March 6, 2008).

Green's customized refitting process tracked each asset and audited its activity from receipt to resale, providing a complete asset trail. Green operated out of its headquarters and its adjacent state-of-the art 45,000-square-foot facilities near the Denver International Airport.

Green guaranteed 100% customer satisfaction to the buyers of refitted copiers. Its business model was based on the following:

1. *Prices significantly lower than new copiers.* Although Green refitted only slightly used copiers, its resale prices were set significantly lower than the manufacturer's suggested retail price (MSRP) for a new copier. For example, Green's price for Toshiba's 310C color copier was $7,495 while the MSRP of a new model was $27,500.

2. *The best warranty and after-sale service in the industry.* All Green refitted copiers came with an 18-month warranty on all major parts, the best warranty possible for refitted copiers. Each refitted copier was certified, so the customer could put it on a manufacturer-designated maintenance-service contract as well as a 30-day complete warranty that covered the entire machine. If the customer was not 100% satisfied for any reason within 30 days, Green replaced the shipped copier with another model, free of charge.

Green promised its customers that it would refit copiers within seven business days and list those copiers on its Internet store within one hour of completing the refitting.

Revenue Model

Green's revenue model was based primarily on service and resale commission income from leasing companies. Because Green did not purchase used copiers from leasing companies, it utilized its working capital to stock parts. Once used copiers were on-site, they were refitted within a week and then placed on Green's online Internet showroom. Green's goal was to sell its products within 10 days of receipt.

The Unsolicited Offer

The copier refitting and resale industry was made up of many small players. The industry was ripe for consolidation and best-of-class business processes. This was the environment when Green was approached in early 2009 by a private equity firm looking for a platform company. The firm wanted to quickly acquire other players, build mass and scale, and then exit in the public markets or by selling to a strategic or financial buyer. The senior partner leading this initiative at the private equity firm was a former executive at one of Green's main leasing company origination sources—a regional bank equipment-leasing company.

At the time of the offer, Patterson had not considered selling: he wanted to grow his company. He knew the industry and the players. He was proud of Green's industry-leading margins, refitting processes, and its operations' reliability and speed. He also knew that most of the other players servicing his type of customers could not match Green's efficiency and profitability.

Patterson was aware that other investors were buying his competitors and had been told that the private equity firm interested in Green would buy another competitor if he did not take it up on its offer of $50 million in cash for 70% ownership. Green would be paid $30 million at closing and receive the rest over three years as an earn-out. Patterson would stay on as CEO for those three years, but at closing the private equity firm would bring on someone as COO who had big public company operating experience: another former executive at one of Green's primary origination sources. Of course, as majority owner, the private equity firm would control the board. Also, as part of the offer, Patterson would have to sign a three-year noncompete agreement that would come into effect after his employment ended.

Patterson had one week to decide.

Hass Shoes

CASE DISCUSSION QUESTIONS

1. The case raises a lot of theoretical ways in which Hass can increase its revenues. How would you evaluate those alternatives? What kind of decision process should Hass use?

2. Do you think Hass can "increase the reasons to buy shoes"? Why? How?

3. How can Hass make shoe buying "fun"?

4. What would you do if you were running Hass shoes? Why?

5. How can Hass try new things without running big financial risks?

**CASE
STUDY**

HASS SHOES

Hass Shoes (Hass), an independent shoe retailer located in Charlottesville, Virginia, had been in business for more than 15 years. In its freestanding store, Hass primarily carried quality shoes for men and women and accessories such as socks and hosiery. The store provided parking for its customers and, to better serve its working customers, was open from 12 P.M. until 8 P.M. on Monday through Friday; 9 A.M. until 6 P.M. on Saturday, and 12 P.M. until 6 P.M. on Sunday. Conscious of its membership in the community, Hass contributed to local charities and belonged to several civic and business clubs. In 2008, Hass joined the National Shoe Retailers Association (NSRA) and had been using the association's benchmarking process to track products, services, expenses, and inventory turns of its current performance against past performance and other best practices. Hass now operated above NSRA averages.

From its approximately 10,000 transactions per year, Hass grossed $800,000, averaging $80 per sale. The business turned its inventory 2.7 times a year and, after paying its owner's salary, netted a 7% before-tax profit. Hass did not try to compete on price but focused instead on service, selection of shoes, and maintaining a stock of hard-to-find sizes; however, Hass did not collect the usual data on individual customers such as number of visits, number of purchases, or the total average cost of purchases per year.

Hass had weathered the 2007 recession well, but its business had basically been flat since 2001. Now the shoe retailer wanted to grow its revenue by at least 10% per year and increase its net margin.

Business Advice

To get started on a plan to grow the business, Hass sought advice from professors at the Darden School of Business in Charlottesville. From them, the retailer learned about the two basic business models: the niche-value-added and the high-volume, low-cost. Hass also received the following suggestions for retail business growth:

- Increase the number of buying customers by either generating new buyers or by converting more existing shoppers into buyers;
- Increase the number of buys per year per customer;
- Increase the average purchase amount per customer;
- Add high-margin complementary products to inventory;
- Add high-margin-related services to its offerings;
- Add a new customer segment;
- Bundle offerings; and
- Increase reasons for customers to buy.

Role Models

Hass wanted to learn from other best-of-class retailers not part of the shoe or clothing sector and, to this end, studied the growth of Best Buy and Tiffany & Co. Back in 2005, Best Buy had changed its business model from a product-centric focus to a customer-centric one and to do so had conducted an in-depth study to identify its best customers, why they shopped, and when they shopped. Best Buy found that 80% of its profits came from 20% of its customers.

Hass also found that Best Buy grew its business by expanding its product offerings, selling more complementary products (e.g., accessories), adding services, selling warranties, and stocking such frequently sought products as CDs and DVDs in order to bring shoppers into the store more often. Last, to attract more shoppers and drive volume, Best Buy started to carry certain brands (e.g., Apple) that had broad appeal and captured more profit from the value chain.

Although Tiffany & Co. was mostly known as a top-of-the-line jewelry retailer, the store still sold sterling silver to many customer segments. At first, Tiffany customers typically bought for special occasions such as weddings, birthdays, anniversaries, graduations, and especially for the special holidays: Valentine's Day, Mother's Day, and Christmas. Then Tiffany increased its sales, by suggesting other reasons for celebration to shoppers beyond the special holidays, such as a good report card, a new home, or a business accomplishment.

Weighing Alternatives

Hass first considered offering women's handbags and scarves to match its shoes and adding men's belts to its inventory until other NSRA members described the high probability of risk involved in trying to match accessories with shoe purchases. Hass next thought about offering men's EEE- and EEEE-width shoes as a wholesaler to other shoe retailers in Virginia.

In the end, Hass decided it needed to learn more by finding the answers to some questions: How could it make shopping more fun and entertaining the way Sam Walton did in his early days of retailing at Wal-Mart? What could it do to attract customers without a specific need and then generate spontaneous buys? How could Hass make shopping more of a Starbucks experience, so the emotion of shopping at Hass would add 5% more margin? Could Hass produce an increase in purchases with a customer loyalty program such as airlines used? Could teaming with local Avon saleswomen increase sales? Should Hass buy a van and set up a booth at flea or farmers' markets? Should Hass sponsor community education on foot health? Should Hass go into the shoe-repair business?

Hass seeks your advice. What process should it use to weigh alternatives? How should it prioritize growth alternatives? What growth initiatives would you recommend?

James Abrams @ Clockwork Home Services, Inc.: Lessons from a Serial Entrepreneur

CASE DISCUSSION QUESTIONS

1. James Abrams founded three companies before Clockwork. What lessons did he learn from each that influenced Clockwork?

2. How did Abrams scale his consulting business?

3. What business model was Service Experts based on?

4. What drove its growth?

5. What did Abrams franchise? Why does the research show that buying a good franchise is less risky than starting a business?

6. Abrams built his business on four fundamental tenets. What are they? Why are they important to his business model? Are they transferable to other businesses? What kind of businesses? Why?

7. Were you surprised that franchisees pay him even though a sister company owned by Abrams may compete against the franchisee?

8. By growing his own companies, is Abrams cannibalizing his franchise model? Is that good or bad? Why?

CASE
STUDY

JAMES ABRAMS @ CLOCKWORK HOME SERVICES, INC.: LESSONS FROM A SERIAL ENTREPRENEUR

Clockwork Home Services, Inc. (Clockwork), a privately held company with headquarters in Sarasota, Florida, specialized in building national brands in the home-services contractor market. James Abrams, Clockwork's president and chief executive officer (CEO), launched the company in October 1998 with his business partner, John Young, and grew it from $2 million to $200 million in revenues in just 10 years.

Since its inception, Clockwork experienced strong organic growth, as well as growth from the acquisition of profitable home-services businesses. With 577 franchises for the plumbing, electrical and heating, ventilation and air-conditioning (HVAC) industries in the United States and Canada, Clockwork had 1,000 employees, including 220 in the parent company. In 2008, the company earned the 933rd spot on *Inc.* magazine's list of 5,000 of the fastest-growing private companies in the United States.

Case Study UVA-ENT-0117 © 2009 by the University of Virginia Darden School Foundation. This case was prepared by Senior Researcher Gosia Glinska and Edward D. Hess as a basis for class discussion rather than to illustrate effective or ineffective handling of an administrative situation.

Despite Clockwork's success, its 61-year-old CEO had no plans to rest on his laurels. During his 27 years as an entrepreneur in the home-services industry, Abrams had experienced his share of hits and misses, but he learned invaluable lessons along the way and applied them to each new enterprise he founded. He set up and then presided over several successful companies, including Service Experts, Inc., which was floated on NASDAQ in 1996 as the first publicly traded residential HVAC company in the United States.

Soon after taking Service Experts public, Abrams, faced with the pressure of Wall Street to deliver short-term results, decided to retire to Florida. But it turned out that beach living was not his style, and two years later he cofounded Clockwork—his fourth company. This time was different because the personal wealth, experience, and market know-how he had accumulated gave him the freedom to call his own shots. With a long-term view of building a strong, well-run company and in no rush to take Clockwork public, Abrams said:

What I wanted to do the first time around was build a business, and that's what I want to do this time. I feel that I've helped to lay the foundation for the company that can become the Home Depot of the home-services industry. To see it unfolding in reality is definitely a rewarding experience.[27]

The Founder—Plan or Be Planned For

James Abrams was born in 1947 and graduated from Western Michigan University with a BA in Business Administration. One day, while working as a schoolteacher in Detroit, Michigan, he accompanied a student, who was having problems at home, to a local social-services facility, where he encountered the sign Plan or Be Planned For. Abrams recalled:

Right behind that building was another very large building in Detroit, which was commonly referred to as the "projects," where they effectively housed people that had not planned very well for their life. So, it [had an impact] on me as a young man. I don't think I'll ever forget it—walking in there and seeing that sign and saying, "Oh my goodness, if one doesn't plan one's life, other people will have a plan for you that you may not like."[28]

The experience proved life-changing for the 21-year-old schoolteacher. First, Abrams, who weighed 247 pounds, enrolled in a Weight Watchers' program. After dropping 77 pounds, he became such a believer in the franchised weight-control concept that he went to work for the owners. Not only did he manage to keep his

---

27. Tom Bayles, "Franchisor Teaches Secrets to Success," *Sarasota Herald-Tribune*, May 14, 2007.

28. Brian Horn, "Timely Intervention: How James Abrams Uses His Strategic Plan to Predict Problems and Drive Clockwork Home Services to New Heights," *Smart Business* http://www.sbnonline.com/Local/ Article/14544/81/0/Timely_intervention.aspx?Category=104 (accessed 10 August 2010).

weight down, but he helped expand the Detroit Weight Watchers' franchise into the largest in the world, attracting some 8,700 customers a week.[29]

Earning His Spurs at Trane

In 1975, Abrams got a job with Trane Company, a La Crosse, Wisconsin–based manufacturer of air-conditioning and heating equipment, as an entry-level salesman. Within five years, he had risen through company ranks to the position of national residential-sales manager.

In the 1970s, when air conditioning (AC) was making inroads into the residential market,[30] Trane, which was ahead of its time, started recruiting business-school graduates, who developed a concept of direct marketing to consumers. Abrams said, "You'd send a salesperson out, explain why AC was becoming a way of life and, hopefully, sell it in the home that night." Trane's goal was to build a brand and transition the company from a manufacturing to a retail-oriented enterprise.

At Trane, Abrams met John Young, and together the future business partners realized the importance of consolidation and building strong brands in the fragmented home-services industry, which was chock-full of small businesses. Abrams explained:

Each owner was doing business in what I call egocentric methodology—everything circled around him. If his strengths were in sales, then you saw fairly strong sales but not necessarily good operational techniques. If he was an operator, you probably wouldn't see much growth, but he'd have excellent customer following and word-of-mouth type of advertising. But none of those guys had any accounting or administrative backgrounds, so their financial statements were all different. At the time, I read a book about an individual in the 1940s who convinced auto dealers to switch to similar financial statements. Before, dealers had failed at high percentage, but by going into standardized accounting methodology, they could understand, by comparing themselves to the best in class, here's how much rent should be as a percentage of sales, here's what I should pay in sales commissions, etc.

Air Experts, Inc.

As Trane was gearing up to acquire General Electric's central air-conditioning business, Abrams and Young both left the company and went their separate ways. Abrams moved to St. Louis, Missouri, where, in 1981, he founded Air Experts, Inc., an HVAC service and replacement company. As he said, "I was an accidental entrepreneur. I went into business because I couldn't support my family in any other fashion—I couldn't find a management job for myself out of La Crosse, Wisconsin. I had great success selling heat pumps in St. Louis."

---

29. Bayles.

30. In 1970, only 10% of U.S. homes had central air.

In just a few years, the "accidental entrepreneur" was ringing up $6 million in annual sales. In the early 1990s, Abrams sold Air Experts to a couple of employees, only to take it back two years later, after the company's profits started to plummet. After getting the business back on track, he sold it again. As word of his success spread, residential contractors started seeking Abrams's consulting services, and before long, he was advising 15 electrical utility companies on how to generate greater revenues in the most efficient way.

Contractors Success Group, Inc.

In 1988, Abrams and Young crossed paths again, and they started doing consulting work together for residential HVAC contractors. As their growing client list began making heavy demands on their time, however, they realized they had to change the way they worked. "We both failed at developing a staff that could relay our thoughts and methodologies to others," Abrams said. "And the contractors wanted either John or myself to come to their place of business. We said, 'Okay, let's have our clients come to us four times a year. And let's see if we can't license a territory where they can utilize our copyrighted materials and business methods within their marketplace.'"

In 1990, in St. Louis, Missouri, Abrams and Young founded Contractors Success Group, Inc. (CSG), a consultancy that offered marketing and management services to independent contractor-members. CSG clients attended an intensive four-day "boot camp" workshop on all facets of the business. Abrams described the situation:

Training was a key component. We'd give them copyrighted marketing materials on which they could put their names and use in their marketplaces. We developed new support materials for their field personnel. Each quarter we had a presentation, showing them what could be done. We'd bring them something a little bit different on what they could present to the consumer—a sales manual for the replacement salesperson, or a pricing book for the technician. Early on, we agreed on an accounting format. Here's what we want your income statements and balance sheets to look like.

In addition to having access to advisory services and proprietary products incorporating methodologies on how to run a successful contracting business, contractors benefited from their relationship with CSG in many other ways. For example, CSG discovered major price discrepancies among different geographical regions where manufacturers sold equipment to contractors. "Oklahoma and Arkansas were paying almost twice as much for the same equipment as Houston or Las Vegas," Abrams said. "So early on, our contractors acquired a huge competitive edge because they knew what equipment could be purchased for."

CSG charged its clients an initial $25,000 fee for an exclusive license to use CSG's services and products in their markets and $10,000 annually for continued support. "It was a lot of money for small independent contractors," Abrams said. "Our rationale behind charging a higher fare was that we would attract people who were sincerely interested in utilizing what we provided. They paid, and we had a very low turnover."

In 1995, participating contractors paid CSG more than $3.2 million in fees.[31] But it was money well spent; their businesses experienced significant improvement in their bottom line, moving from 3% to 5% net profit up to a range from 10% to 11%, with a few contractors making as much as 25% net profit.[32] Between 1990 and 1995, the CSG client list grew, largely by word of mouth, from 30 contractors to 292 contractors in the United States and Canada.

Service Experts, Inc.

Wanting to grow his company, Abrams embarked on a quest for financing. "I knocked on the investment bankers' doors for almost four years," he said, "before I finally convinced them, in late 1995, that if I had capital, I could expand the business rapidly."

In 1996, Abrams and Young started Service Experts, Inc., with the goal of buying out clients of CSG and becoming a nationwide residential HVAC-service company. In August 1996, Service Experts announced its initial public offering, raising $27.2 million.[33] At the same time, the company acquired 12 HVAC service and replacement businesses, with combined annual revenues of $60 million.

Abrams's goal was to create a consolidated, highly profitable company by streamlining the operations of the acquired businesses. Therefore, as he explained, "my plan at Service Experts did not call for keeping the former owner, who would always be saying, 'Here's the way I always did this.'"

The Pressures of Wall Street

Following a divorce in 1966, Abrams did not think the time was right for him to assume the CEO role at Service Experts. Instead, he and Young tapped Alan Sielbeck, who was CSG's Contractor of the Year in 1994. "That proved to be a huge error in terms of Service Experts' fate," Abrams said. "In fairness to the guy we picked, we went public during the go-go consolidation era, where Wall Street was rewarding anybody who could compile earnings."

Abrams, who became Service Experts' president and Chief Operating Officer (COO) and served on its board of directors, found it hard to submit to the pressure

31. Robert P. Mader, "Contractor Wants National Market," *Contractor*, September 1, 1996.

32. Robert P. Mader, "Investors Create HVAC Service Giant," *Contractor*, October 1, 1992.

33. Mader, "Contractor Wants National Market."

of Wall Street. In his opinion, "The public markets were simply capital to build a business." He elaborated:

At each board meeting I was lamenting that we were building a stock price rather than a business. But once shareholder value is increasing threefold over two years, people lose track of what it was that they began to build. Wall Street was there, seemingly throwing money at us, and I thought, "Okay, maybe this is the way big business works, and I just don't get it." So I got out of the way and retired.

In the meantime, Service Experts faced a serious threat from competitors, who started taking their companies public with a goal of consolidating the fragmented industry. "I didn't anticipate that two or three other companies would follow us and try to execute a similar plan," Abrams said. "And they targeted our clients, who were the best in the country."

Abrams's Second Act—Clockwork Home Services

In 1997, Abrams settled into retirement at his home on Siesta Key, off the coast of Florida. Each day, he walked up Crescent Beach and then swam back home. But he was bored. "I wasn't good at it," he said. "It was the wrong time to be retired."

So Abrams "went back to work" by studying the companies whose highly successful customer-service ideas he admired, such as Domino's Pizza and its "delivery in 30 minutes or it's free" policy or Federal Express and its "when it has to be there by 10 A.M." slogan. As Abrams said, "It seems to me that what they all have is a name that they drive into the public's mind, and it was something that mattered to the consumer. And they had a methodology of delivering the message to the consumer."

Abrams could not stop thinking about his former businesses and imagining ways to improve their systems and processes. As he said, "I thought: Last time around, this was just so burdensome. Is there a simpler way to do it?" It was not long before he was ready to launch a new business.

VenVest, Inc.

In 1999, Abrams and Young started a venture capital company, VenVest, Inc., in Clayton, Missouri, with the idea of consolidating and revolutionizing the home-services industry. Abrams said, "I thought, this time around I will not limit it to HVAC only. I'll do home services, which will give me a much bigger pool." Although the home-services industry was an $800 billion market, it was fragmented, with few recognized brands. Abrams said that he and Young

were absolutely convinced that he who gets there first with a brand name that means something in [the home-services business] wins. By wins, I mean that contractors can attract a large amount of customers in a different fashion than has been done in the past. A classic example is

Domino's Pizza in Detroit, where Tom Monaghan kept getting the message out to the public about who to call if they wanted pizza delivered in 30 minutes or less. Dominos built a multi-billion dollar business through franchising and a single concept—30 minutes or less delivery.[34]

VenVest managed to raise $6 million.[35] In addition to Abrams and Young, among the original 12 investors in VenVest were the founders' friends and associates, members of the Contractors Success Group, as well as the people whose skills and expertise the company needed. Abrams explained:

We are both relatively wealthy guys, so we didn't need their money. It was all about building this business, and we're managers more than entrepreneurs, so we thought, we're better working for other people—if we had others to report to, we'd probably be more productive. We tried to get guys who would be helpful to us, but that didn't work out as well as we thought. But we did get one guy, Tom Hopkins. He's the world's most prolific author of sales books. He invested with us, and he helped us get going with some understanding of the sales process that we'd be teaching.

Refining the Business Model

First, Abrams commissioned a study on what consumers valued most about home services. "Nobody had ever asked them," he said. "And they wanted service right now. And, if the service person couldn't get there right now, then get there when you said that you would." Armed with the findings of the study, Abrams collaborated with a software company. Said Abrams, "How many independent contractors could spend $2 million to develop a software package for dispatching? National consolidators can do exactly that. We can go to the software vendors and say, 'This is what I want.'"[36]

The technology that made it possible to have a technician appear at a customer's home within a one-hour window gave Abrams's new venture a clear advantage over the competition, which consisted of 80,000 mostly small mom-and-pop operations in the plumbing, electrical, and HVAC residential markets. Clockwork's sales pitch, which became a registered trademark—Always on Time . . . Or You Don't Pay a Dime!—was honored each time a technician was late for a scheduled appointment. "And that's what we began to build this business on," Abrams said. As he put it, Clockwork's goal was "to drive this concept into the mind of every consumer so that when they want service on time, they will think of us."

Abrams also introduced technological innovations for the various systems and software applications designed especially for business processes that enabled contractors

34. John R. Hall, "The Clock Is Ticking," *Air Conditioning, Heating & Refrigeration News*, June 16, 2003.

35. John Brinsley, "Plumber," *Los Angeles Business Journal*, May 3, 1999, http://www.labusinessjournal.com/news/1999/may/02/plumber (accessed 10 August 2010).

36. Thomas A. Mahoney, "'We'll Come as Competitors,' Consolidator Warns Contractors," *Air Conditioning, Heating & Refrigeration News*, June 1997.

to anticipate and sidestep the type of business "surprises" that plagued most small business owners. "We developed a number of different simpler systems in the business," he said, "and I got a couple of patents."

In 2005, VenVest changed its name to Clockwork Home Services, Inc., and moved its headquarters from Missouri to Sarasota, Florida. In 2008, Clockwork had franchises for the plumbing, electrical, and HVAC industries—Benjamin Franklin the Punctual Plumber, One Hour Heating & Air Conditioning, and Mister Sparky: America's On–Time Electrician, respectively. In addition, the parent company operated several subsidiaries, including Success Group International; BuyMax, an online discounted purchasing services; the U.S. retail business (company-owned franchises); and AirTime Canada, which offered group memberships to contractors in the HVAC industry and operated a handful of Canadian-based locations.

Success Group International

Success Group International oversaw several contractor affinity groups and educational training programs. Affinity groups provided consulting services to those contractors who wanted Clockwork's help in growing their companies but preferred to remain independent and keep their business identity. Group members had access to the same business-process tools and technical training as franchisees. Like CSG, Success Group charged contractors $25,000 for the initial equipment and training, plus $10,000 yearly for continued support, regional training, Internet assistance, and weekly teleconferences with an assigned advisor.

Based on his experience with CSG, Abrams knew that affinity groups in the home-services industry worked. "We have 1,200 clients in our affinity groups," Abrams said. "So that's evidence that this is something a contractor wants and will pay for." This time around, though, he did not limit himself to just one sector. "We run an affinity group for every trade that we target, and our core groups are plumbing and HVAC."

CSG's success had also proven that the affinity group was a great business model. Using a similar strategy with Clockwork, Abrams created communities of contractors who got together to share best practices and paid Clockwork for the privilege. "And then you take what you've learned, and you go out and recruit, and that's what you franchise," Abrams said.

Although Clockwork taught independent contractors how to boost their profitability, the company did not hide its intention to enter their markets. Using Federal Express, United Parcel Service, and DHL as examples, Clockwork showed its clients that ultimately three brands could be the top players in the marketplace at the same time. "We are honest with them, and we say, 'We're coming as competitors, but if you want to stay, we'll teach you how to stay,'" Abrams said. "We teach them how to build a strong brand. We know that there's no way in the service business that we will ever capture more than 40% to 50% market share anyway."

Success Group held semiannual meetings, attended by all affinity group members, during which Abrams and Young gave presentations. Abrams explained:

The meetings have to be entertaining, informative, and have to provide a struggling guy with hope. Part of the meeting is bringing up the success stories and then showing them that it can be done. The other part of the meeting is to deploy whatever we have improved upon in the business. We constantly look at the contractors, at where they put their time, and we measure that on three things, "Can we do it for them for less money?"

The Franchise Business

Where some independent contractors found membership in Clockwork's affinity groups appealing enough, others took note of a slew of support services Clockwork provided for its franchisees, including the same kind of benefits and retirement programs available at large corporations. For example, the company paid all of the medical and dental insurance premiums for its employees and, after they had been on the job for three years, their dependents as well.

In addition to teaching its franchisees how to generate greater revenue in the most efficient way and supplying them with proprietary software, Clockwork offered them access to equipment at discount prices through the company's online wholesale distributor BuyMax, whose more than 1,000 vendors guaranteed the lowest prices offered anywhere in the nation. In addition, at the end of the year, each franchisee received a rebate check for a percentage of everything it had spent through BuyMax.

But, most important, the franchise offered a strong, nationally recognized brand. As Abrams said, "In a fragmented world of HVAC and plumbing—the consumer doesn't know who to call. The franchise offers a brand. This identity package includes our name, logo, and message. This helps our franchisees become the dominant player in their respective markets."

Clockwork's marketing and communications efforts ensured strong brand affinity and high visibility wherever a franchise was located. "So some independent contractors draw the conclusion that if they latch onto a franchise they won't have to pay for their own advertising anymore," Abrams said. "They think, 'I don't have to worry about what my unique selling proposition is. I get a great deal of support, so I'm going to share their name and pay them more money.'"

Clockwork franchises were among the fastest-growing in the world (Exhibit C.2). As of December 2008, there were 250 Benjamin Franklin franchisees, 246 One Hour Air franchisees, and 81 Mister Sparky franchisees; however, becoming a Clockwork franchisee was not easy, and most of the companies that made the cut came out of

Clockwork's affinity group training. Abrams elaborated, "We're very selective. They have to be in the business already, and have a solid business plan, a solid balance sheet. They have to illustrate they have good business knowledge. Our model is that no franchisee will fail."[37]

Franchisee Support and Training

True to his word that "if we take their money, the franchisee won't fail on our part," Abrams continuously added new services and programs to help Clockwork franchises succeed. "We've made it easy for them," Abrams explained.

We provide all franchisees a full, comprehensive portfolio of programs, blueprints, software, and support systems that ensure their success. These include turn-key marketing programs, operating systems and procedures, recruiting tools for technicians, management systems, group buying power, patented pricing methods, online and classroom-setting training, model center support, and financial review procedures.

In 2009, Benjamin Franklin Plumbing and Mister Sparky: America's On–Time Electrician were ranked among the nation's top-115 franchise opportunities for franchisee satisfaction, according to independent research conducted by *Franchise Business Review*.[38]

Over the years, Clockwork's franchise support team had grown from two members in 2001 to more than forty in 2008, with one advisor assigned to support 20 franchises. Each advisor, a college graduate with either bachelor's or master's degree, underwent rigorous, industry-specific training in one of the industry schools owned by Clockwork.

"We have what we call four legs of that training," Abrams said. First, all new hires were required to read a book written by Abrams, which covered "all the challenges that a general manager could face in our industry," as he put it. The book had 30 chapters, and the trainees were assigned a chapter per week.

Second, the new hires had seven months to absorb the contents of a two-week-long general manager's course provided in DVD format. The course, which was an overview of general management, consisted of videotaped lectures given by various Clockwork instructors, who were specialists in the areas of marketing, finance, accounting, operations, etc.

The third leg of new-hire training involved employees mastering a 1,000-page-long, trade-specific manual called *Operational Excellence* or *Op-Ex*. After studying the

37. *Franchise Times* interview with One Hour Air Conditioning President and CEO James Abrams, March 3, 2006.

38. "Independent Research by *Franchise Business Review* Places Clockwork Home Services Brands Among Nation's Elite Franchise Opportunities," press release, Sarasota, Florida, March 10, 2009.

manual for approximately three months, the new hires were tested on their knowledge. According to Abrams, the manual covered:

How to hire people, what the right HR policies are to apply at the local level. Accounting systems. Software. It's got just about any answer that you can find. It's a living document. Anytime we come up with something in the field that requires a change, we're able to change it. It's got all the compensations in there, pricing, etc.

And finally, the fourth leg of new-hire training consisted of a series of classes taught at Clockwork's Success Academy. The new hires were required to take the classes available in the area of the trade they would be supporting.

Clockwork's Retail Business

Franchisees ran a vast majority of the plumbing, HVAC, and electrical businesses under the Clockwork umbrella, but the parent company owned and operated approximately two dozen of them. The company grew its retail business through acquisition of home-services contractors. Abrams said:

We only buy what we call market centers for us. We will not enter a market unless we acquire franchisees. Today, when I acquire a franchisee, I don't change the name. I don't change the software. I don't change the uniform. All I got to do is change the bank account.

Clockwork had company-owned One Hour Heating & Air Conditioning operations in nine states and throughout Canada; Benjamin Franklin Plumbing operations in six states; and Mister Sparky operations in three states.

Values, Culture, People

Abrams built his business on five basic tenets: superior business ethics; guaranteed service excellence; the place to be; equity opportunity; and home-services company. He elaborated:

From inception we said, "We're going to have superior business ethics and integrity here. We've got superior guarantees to our consumer." And then the third one is the way we define the place to be. We've put a lot of money into our facility, so it looks very nice. It's a comfortable place to come to work each day. Our fourth tenet is that we believe in sharing equity. So, all of my senior management team are multimillionaires. They understand that if we get to the public markets, they're going to become a lot wealthier—if we can succeed at getting that. And our fifth tenet—we intend to become the world's largest and most profitable home-services company.

Clockwork strived to be the most desirable place to work, offering the best pay, benefits, and work environment to all employees. "I have a dictum throughout the company that at every level we pay higher than anybody else for that job," Abrams said. "So every one of our people is the highest paid at what they do in the world." In addition, Abrams made it clear he was committed to promoting from within: "The finance department is the only exception that's got a lead from the outside in our company. Everybody else has come from the ground up."

Not surprisingly, Clockwork had no shortage of job applicants, and attrition was low; however, employees who did not live up to the high-performance standards were asked to leave the company. As Abrams admitted, "We require a lot of our people. I'm pretty demanding, and I expect my management team down the line to be very demanding. Since we're offering a lot, we're looking for the very best."

To ensure that Clockwork's 100% service guarantee was not an empty promise to the consumer, Abrams rigorously screened potential employees through reference checks and employment verification. In addition, all job candidates had to pass both a criminal record check and a drug test. In fact, because Clockwork was a drug-free company, all employees were subject to monthly drug testing. "We test 12.5% of our employee base," Abrams said, "and my name, just like everybody else's, comes out of the hat. Regardless of where we're at, we've got 24 hours to go and get drug tested." He continued:

There are certain marketplaces here in southern Florida where 85% of all the guys that come in either won't or can't pass the drug test or are ex-cons. And very few companies are setting up these types of standards. We have the on-time proposition to the customer, but behind the scenes, operationally, I've dictated that we have a "can't lose" proposition to the consumer, too. That's why we're constantly monitoring our personnel.

The Search for the Right CFO

One of the recruiting challenges Abrams faced was finding the right chief financial officer (CFO). First, a CFO brought in in 2005 did not work out. Then Abrams tapped Clockwork's vice president of mergers and acquisitions for the CFO position. Said Abrams:

In early 2005, I brought on a very sophisticated board, so I had the former worldwide chair of J&J Pharmaceutical, the former CFO of UPS, and the former CFO of Sprint on my board. The two CFOs made up my audit committee. So we chose an internal person who had a finance degree that was very operationally astute and moved her over to that role. That was a mistake.

Finally, in 2007, Clockwork found the perfect fit in Robert Clanin, a former CFO for United Parcel Service. Already a member of the company's board of directors, Clanin came out of retirement to assume the CFO position at Clockwork, taking over big-picture responsibilities for financial operations and assisting Abrams with planning strategies for growth. "He was so enamored with our business that he stepped in to help us," Abrams said.

Succession Planning

In 2008, Abrams had plans to stay at Clockwork's helm for at least four more years, but succession planning was something he took seriously. One of the contenders for Abram's position was Clockwork's group president of consumer services. "She's been with us for eight years," Abrams said. "This year her goal is to make sure that the retail division consistently delivers performance. If she does, she'll be promoted to COO at the end of this year. Either she or my CFO would become the heir apparent to my chair."

Funding Growth

From the onset, Abrams demonstrated his commitment and that of his management team to pursuing growth, which was part of the company's mission statement: "We intend to become the world's largest and most profitable home-service company." In 1999, a year into its operation, Clockwork pulled in revenues of approximately $2 million. After a steady climb, revenue jumped to $59.8 million in 2005, $111.9 million in 2006, and in 2007, the company posted revenue of $182.3 million.[39] Abrams commented on funding the company's growth:

We grew from zero to about $70 million in sales with no debt. We funded everything out of cash flow and were able to return substantial amounts to our shareholders. We are in a very high cash-flow business. The niche I'm in is residential service and replacement only. So when I see a customer, they pay me today. I make my payroll a week or two weeks from now, and I pay for the equipment or parts that I sold that customer today in 30 to 60 days from now. So I have a lot of float.

Growing a Business—Lessons Learned

Abrams credited Clockwork's speedy growth to his focus on planning. "It's our plan, really, that sets us apart from everybody else," he said. "The plan is allowing us to have this type of growth and generate profits each step along the way."[40] According to Abrams, the most important step in planning was to understand one's strategy and stick with it. Customer feedback helped him shape his strategy, which gave him clear insight into what customers really wanted. Abrams reflected on Clockwork's key success factors:

Know what it is that you're setting out to do with the end in mind. We have a very detailed plan, which gets updated each year. The next thing is the organization at different stages of the plan, so you know your organization on day one is not weighted with what your organization will look like 10 years later. And you have to understand the organization before you try to get the right people to fit those squares on the org chart.

An important aspect of Abrams's approach to managing people was staying within the boundaries of his company's organizational chart by filling each position with an employee whose specific skills were applied only to that position, instead of trying to

39. Horn.
40. Bayles.

get too much out of the employee by adding responsibilities that might dilute his or her strengths. He explained:

I might have somebody who is very talented so that perhaps I could exploit their talents and carry them over into a broader range of responsibility. But, ultimately, my experience has been that that will hurt the organization. For example, it's tempting to have someone who thrives in one area assigned another area of responsibility. I don't think that serves a company well in the long run. In the short run, it could work. In the long run, you end up with "Joe's job," rather than the defined operational position within the company.[41]

Building a Business, not a Stock Price

Taking Service Experts public proved to be an invaluable learning experience for Abrams. Staying private allowed Clockwork the flexibility to invest in long-term projects that did not give immediate payback, as opposed to being forced to focus on quarterly results to satisfy impatient Wall Street investors. Abrams explained:

We had inconsistency in terms of performance of our company-owned retail operations. And having been to the public markets before, I'm not going to take this company public until I know that not only does it perform on IPO, but it has sustainable performance for a decade. The good news is I'm already a wealthy guy, so I don't have to take this thing to the public markets to make me wealthier. The bad news for the company is that I'm not going to take it to the public markets until I'm 100% convinced in my bones that this thing will pay for a long time.

Exhibit C.2   Clockwork's Rankings

Clockwork Home Services'® HVAC, Plumbing and Electrical Units ranked in *Entrepreneur* Magazine's Franchise 500®

Mister Sparky Also Ranks on "Top New Franchises" List

Sarasota, FL January 6, 2009—Clockwork Home Services, Inc., (Clockwork) today announced that its One Hour Air Conditioning & Heating®, Benjamin Franklin Plumbing®, and Mister Sparky: America's On–Time Electrician® units are ranked among the nation's top 500 franchises for 2009, according to *Entrepreneur's* 30th annual "Franchise 500®." One Hour ranked #163, Benjamin Franklin ranked #140, and Mister Sparky ranked #387. The rankings are published in the January 2009 issue of *Entrepreneur.*

Entrepreneur compiles its list based on companies' financial strength and stability, growth rate and size of the franchise system. Other considerations include the number of years in business and length of time franchising, startup costs, low employee turnover, and whether the company provided financing.

In addition to its listing on the Franchise 500, Mister Sparky was listed #27 among "Top New Franchises," which are the top-50 brands that have been franchising since 2004.

SOURCE: Clockwork Web site; used with permission.

---

41. Horn.

Jeff Bowling at the Delta Companies: From Baseball Coach to CEO

CASE DISCUSSION QUESTIONS

1. Jeff described himself as an "accidental entrepreneur." Was he correct? Why?

2. What process did Jeff use in deciding to grow when he decided to "put this thing on steroids"?

3. What process should he have used?

4. Jeff called you today and, based on your knowledge of this case, asked you to prepare a talk entitled "Do As I Say, Not As I Did" for him to give to an entrepreneurship class on building a business. What should be the key points in his talk?

5. How did Jeff infuse his culture into new hires? Did you like his "cultural deposits"? Why?

6. How did Jeff manage his direct reports? Would you like to be managed his way? Why?

7. Is Jeff a CEO or a Coach? Why? What is the difference?

CASE
STUDY

JEFF BOWLING AT THE DELTA COMPANIES: FROM BASEBALL COACH TO CEO

The Delta Companies (Delta), headquartered in Dallas, Texas, was a privately held healthcare staffing and recruiting firm, specializing in permanent and temporary placement of physicians and mid-level healthcare professionals across the U.S. Delta's President and Chief Executive Officer (CEO) Jeff M. Bowling was a 20-something former baseball coach with no business background when he started the company in 1997 as Delta Medical Consulting. The start-up was funded by Dave Wood, a successful Texas businessman.

In 2003, when Wood decided to sell the company, Bowling sold everything he owned and bought it. Under Bowling's leadership Delta expanded from about 20 to 240 employees without any outside investments, and within five years, the company was the third-fastest-growing private healthcare staffing firm in the United States, with annual revenues of $60 million.[42]

Delta's stellar growth was fueled by a doctor shortage, especially in underserved communities, which found it difficult to attract the healthcare professionals they needed. As baby boomers were starting to retire, the need for healthcare professionals was growing, with an anticipated shortage of as many as 200,000 physicians by 2020.

Case Study UVA-ENT-0114 © 2009 by the University of Virginia Darden School Foundation. This case was prepared by Senior Researcher Gosia Glinska and Edward D. Hess as a basis for class discussion rather than to illustrate effective or ineffective handling of an administrative situation.
42. Staffing Industry Analysts, Inc., 2008 report.

Jeff Bowling, Accidental Entrepreneur

Baseball had always been Jeff Bowling's passion; he played at the University of North Texas in Denton, where he earned a B.S. degree in psychology, and after graduation he took a job as an assistant coach at a community college in the Dallas area. To supplement his income in the summer, Bowling coached select groups of high school kids. One of the teams he worked with, a group of 13- and 14-year-olds, was considered the best in Collin County, Texas.

One day, Bowling expressed a growing disenchantment with his life as a baseball coach to some of his players' parents, one of whom countered, "You're an excellent recruiter. You've recruited our son. Have you thought about just recruiting?" Bowling replied, "I haven't thought about anything but baseball for my entire existence on this planet."

The conversation inspired Bowling to research other career options. After identifying the leading healthcare recruitment firm in the country, the Dallas-based Merritt Hawkins & Associates (MHA)—the physician-staffing arm of AMN Services, Inc.—Bowling sent the firm his resume. Two weeks later, with a job offer on the table, he quit coaching baseball.

Although recruiting physicians came naturally to Bowling, and he enjoyed his newfound vocation, he still missed coaching. Fortunately, one year into his job at MHA, Bowling received a phone call from one of the parents whose son had been on Bowling's baseball team. The caller was local businessman, Dave Wood, owner of AMS Staff Leasing, which specialized in staff leasing services. Wood told Bowling, "The team you were coaching has gone to hell, and I need you to come back and coach." When Bowling explained that his heavy travel schedule had placed more demands on his time than ever, Wood made him an offer: "Why don't you start your own shop in my office? The deal is, you make yourself available to coach baseball."

Bowling left his job at MHA and, with Wood's help, started Delta Medical Consulting. Now he managed to have the best of both worlds—his own company and a talented baseball team to coach. As Bowling said:

Dave funded the business. And the interesting thing, talking about start-ups: had we sat down and had benchmarks or some level of expectation early on, or had he watched very closely what we were doing those first years, we wouldn't be here today. Dave allowed me to make some management mistakes, and I was able to further concentrate on the management as he took care of the back office details.

For several years, Bowling ran the recruiting business and coached the baseball team in his spare time, until 2001, when his team members started going off to college. Between 2001 and 2003, Delta generated annual revenues of $7 to $8 million.

"We ebbed and flowed between 20 to 30 people. In our industry, 50% turnover is a good thing," Bowling said. As he reflected on the start-up days:

I've told people, I'm not an entrepreneur. I was good at persuasion, getting people to sign deals, but that was it. I never had a great plan. I never expected to be doing what I'm doing today. It was all kind of accidental. We had grown the firm to about 20 people, just by accident, no strategic plans.

A Businessman Is Born

On August 14, 2003, Bowling was at a Six Flags amusement park with his daughter when he received an urgent call from Dave Wood, who announced he no longer wanted to fund and support Delta. But Bowling was not ready to give up a business he had built. As he said, "We had a good business and, essentially, that phone call started a two-week negotiation."

First, Bowling called a meeting with the 10 most senior people at Delta and explained what was happening. He offered them the option of leaving or staying to fight to save the company, which meant having to temporarily go without pay. Except for one person, who had no stomach for that kind of risk, no one jumped ship. Bowling recalled:

At the end of August, I purchased the company from Dave. Sold my house, sold my car, had to sell all the receivables to a factoring company to be able to do it. We had about $1.4 million in receivables, and I got the business from Dave for about $1.1 million. So we gave away our operating cash to get the business. A lot of the guys went without pay. Not only did they live off their credit cards, but they threw their credit cards down so Delta could exist. You find out real quick who is truly loyal.

The following six months of hard work paid off. In February 2004, "we were in a traditional bank with a traditional line of credit," said Bowling; furthermore, that year Delta generated $9 million in revenues.

But with the ownership of Delta came new challenges. Previously, the back-office function of the business—accounting, billing, and collections—had been handled by Wood's organization. Now, Bowling's company, which was essentially a sales organization, was forced to morph quickly into a full-fledged business—no small feat, considering that the newly minted business owner had no financial background. "I never knew what a cash flow statement was," said Bowling. "I never saw a profit or loss, not any more than what we thought it might have been, just through gathering the bills and knowing what receipts went out the door."

Growing the Business

Delta did so well in 2004 and 2005 that Bowling was able to pay off its creditors. On September 2005, he held a two-day off-site meeting with his senior management team to plan an aggressive growth strategy. "We kind of looked at each other and said, 'Hey, we're pretty good at this. We know what's going on.' We said, 'Let's put this thing on steroids.'"

In 2005, Bowling hired an accountant and a chief financial officer (CFO). "We took our money out of the traditional bank and put it with an asset-based lender, which was going to free up some dollars from a line of credit perspective," said Bowling. "We started a couple of sub-niches in healthcare staffing. And that was when we got really strategic about the growth of our business."

In 2008, Delta had five business units: Delta Physician Placement, which matched physicians in all medical specialties with permanent employment opportunities nationwide; Delta Locum Tenens, which specialized in temporary physician placement; Delta Healthcare Placement, which worked on behalf of healthcare facilities to locate therapists, technologists, pharmacists, practitioners, and executives; Liquid Medical Recruiting, a contingency healthcare recruiting firm specializing in personalized and efficient recruitment services that met the provider's professional and personal goals; and Delta Flex Travelers, which employed temporary allied healthcare professionals for the Delta Companies.

Delta partnered with its clients—clinics, hospitals, group practices, solo physicians, universities, and government and rehabilitation facilities—to continually place interested candidates. Through targeted ad campaigns, the company developed and maintained a database of tens of thousands of healthcare providers, who actively sought new job opportunities.

Bowling's Challenges

Bootstrapping the Business

One of the many challenges Bowling faced had been having the cash to fund growth. With no outside equity investors and only bank lines of credit on hand, Bowling had to finance current cash needs and fund his new business units until they generated enough cash flow to be self-funding. Bowling elaborated:

The biggest challenge that we've had—it's been bootstrapping this thing, cash-flow-wise. We have five business units, and each of those units has a vice-president. They each have an equity stake in their respective partnership. I mean, that's the way you retain people and show them that you care. In 2005, we understood that not being properly capitalized was going to be risky. If I could go back to 2003–2004 and change one thing, it would have been finding the right partner to be a CFO and provide them equity, because there have been a few close cash-flow calls. And had I had the right CFO, those mistakes wouldn't have been made.

Financial Management

Two critical aspects of cash flow management were managing accounts receivable and maintaining low general and administrative costs. An additional challenge for

Bowling was managing the cash needs of a rapidly growing business. Bowling knew that when revenues increased, so did risk. As he said, "The mistake you made at $20 or $30 million—you could sell your way out of. The mistake you make at $60 million—you can't sell your way out of it anymore."

Delta's business units kept their accounts receivable in check. The collection time was between 40 and 45 days. "Consolidated, we maintain 42, 43 days, which is world-class," Bowling said, "when you talk about collecting from healthcare facilities, which tend to get paid very slowly from insurance companies and the government."

In 2005, when Bowling and his executives planned aggressive growth, they expected their general and administrative expenses to skyrocket. One area with cost-cutting potential was payroll. "Our focus has been to get that fixed payroll down, as a percentage of total payroll," said Bowling. He explained:

Our recruiters and salespeople are on a small base, $24,000, $36,000 a year. Two-thirds to three-quarters of everybody's income is in commissions. And we don't pay until the money is in the house.

Although Bowling took advantage of a few cost-cutting opportunities, he admitted to some mistakes. One of them was leasing 96,000 square feet of office space that could accommodate 550 employees at a time when Delta had only 240. "It's going to take us a couple more years to get full. So the burden from a G & A standpoint is high," Bowling said.

Streamlining Financial Processes

Bowling invested heavily in technology to help make sound financial and managerial decisions. "When we decided to grow, we built up our infrastructure, hardware-wise," he said. "Virtual private networks and wireless, we're fine." What was more challenging, however, was the software side. Having used Intuit's QuickBooks Pro software for small-business accounting for awhile, Delta eventually implemented Microsoft's Great Plains, which tracked sales information, produced data for financial statements, calculated payroll, and issued invoices. "We were running $40 million a year in QuickBooks, and that was challenging," said Bowling. "And we still don't have good information flow."

Bowling understood that allowing business data to move easily across departments and achieving integrated, real-time visibility across key metrics was essential to managing growth. Therefore, he was continuously looking for ways to improve financial information flow. "We've been challenged with getting everybody to synch up," he said, "so we have begun implementing Microsoft's SharePoint program for our database, and we hired a full-time administrator, who was a senior vice president at a big company, to build and maintain the integrity of our data."

Learning to Lead

As Delta's CEO, Bowling was constantly learning and growing. He challenged himself to become the best he could be, and he expected the same from his executives. "So here's the dilemma that you go through as you try to grow this organization," said Bowling. "You discover that everybody has to grow their individual capacity to lead or to do their particular thing." Delta's chief marketing officer, for example, became an expert in his field by taking advantage of all kinds of educational opportunities available, such as executive seminars, trade shows, and subscriptions to trade journals.

Although he had no mentor himself, Bowling took his mentoring role seriously. For those who refused to grow and learn, there was no place in the organization. Far from being trigger-happy, Bowling made sure he gave his employees every chance to improve before he let them go. As he said:

My challenge as a leader was to transform away from performance management and metrics management to this more intangible thing of *leadership*, trying to increase people's capacities, or else they've got to "get off the bus," to quote Jim Collins. The difficult thing is being objective enough to look through the correct lenses and suggest to these people, "You can't stay here in the role that you're at." At the end of the day, I can still look myself in the mirror and know I gave it every stinking shot I could at transforming that person so that they grow in their capacity.

The Delta Culture

The company attributed part of its success to its culture, which was driven by its employees. As Bowling put it, "Our motto is We Hire Cool People Who Get S★★t Done." In 2007, the *Dallas Business Journal* voted Delta as one of the 25 Best Places to Work in the Dallas/Fort Worth market (Exhibit C.3).

In 2006, Bowling created the position of chief talent officer, who was responsible for the functions of the Human Resources department: the hiring and the education and leadership development programs for all personnel. He also managed the employee relations budget, which consisted of 1% of Delta's gross margin and covered companywide events such as pizza parties and outings to a ball game. Quarterly off-site meetings and awards ceremonies for every employee were also funded from the employee relations budget. For example, top sales reps and recruiters were rewarded with Rolex watches, and Platinum Club members won trips to the Caribbean.

Delta's new hires were immediately exposed to the eight core values: Focus, Speed, Passion, Expect It, Don't Play Scared, No Excuses, Clarity, and Finish, shared by all Delta business units. From the moment a candidate verbally accepted a Delta job offer, he or she started undergoing a disciplined and systematic on-boarding process, which began with email correspondence. During their first week on the job, they went to a new-hire class at which immersion in the Delta culture continued. Bowling also continued a Delta tradition of holding two 90-minute meetings with each new hire, during which he personally went over the company's core values. "I give them both empirical and anecdotal stories about the core values," he said.

All employees were encouraged to make "cultural deposits" by going above and beyond job description and common courtesy: planning social events, championing causes, and making Delta a fun place to work. Employees regularly initiated fundraising programs for community organizations. According to Bowling, "Everything we do for the new hires for the first 30 days is built around cultural deposits. Manners and respect are just the price of admission. And we expect these cultural deposits to be almost immediate."

To continuously engage and motivate its employees, Delta held quarterly off-site meetings, during which employee awards ceremonies were held. "We recognize people and throw their names up on 30-foot screens," said Bowling. "We have skits, and we allow people from the audience to get involved." While Bowling put a lot of emphasis on retaining and rewarding high-performing employees, he did not waste time keeping lame ducks. As he put it:

We hire cool people, but we make mistakes. You hire a resume, and a person shows up. Well, get rid of them real quick. In fact, I don't count retention in these scorecard meetings for the first 90 days. So if a director or a VP gets rid of somebody in 90 days, it doesn't go against their retention statistics.

Back to Coaching

Bowling considered management development his top priority, and he devoted 50% of his time to consistent coaching and to the professional growth of his eight direct reports, including the three Cs (chief talent officer, chief marketing officer, chief operating officer) and the heads of five business units. As Bowling explained:

My true desire is for them to be successful. That means financially and professionally. So that drives me first and foremost, because I'm not done there. They are not the best they can be. I'm not the best I can be. So it's a real drive and passion of mine to improve the lives of all my employees and to provide them with the best jobs they have ever had.

Bowling was a proponent of the "balanced scorecard"[43] approach, which was a method for selecting and measuring nonfinancial performance indicators, such as employee satisfaction, with work and customer loyalty. He held weekly team meetings during which, in addition to financial metrics, the less "tangible" metrics by which progress toward previously set goals was reviewed and discussed. Said Bowling:

Every Monday we meet at 4 P.M. after they're done getting the numbers calculated from the previous week. We pull up an overhead on the projector, and we look and see what they did

---

43. Robert Kaplan and David Norton, *The Balanced Scorecard: Translating Strategy into Action* (Harvard Business School Press, 1996).

from a KPI perspective, where their receivables are. We have a scorecard, where we measure things like retention, percentage of your team on goal, your KPIs, gross margin collection. And we sit down for two to three hours as a company, 20 to 25 directors, and the VPs, and all the Cs, and they have to present their numbers to their peer group and their superior. Well, I'll review that one-on-one with the VPs after the meeting.

In addition to the weekly team meetings, Bowling also held monthly one-on-one meetings with all of his direct reports. The meeting started at 10:30 A.M. An hour-long review of his reports' balanced scorecards was followed by lunch. "That's where we get into the intangible stuff," said Bowling, "and I help manage them from a personal perspective to some degree. I require all eight of my reports to give me their annual goals, and I talk to them about their spouses and how things are going at home."

In fact, Bowling did more than just talk to his executive team about their spouses; he took the time to get to know those spouses with whom he had face-to-face meetings at least twice a year. "One of the keys to our success is our close-knit, very collaborative relationship that the top eight to ten executives have," said Bowling. "Before I promote anybody, I'm going to get to know their spouse. The people who have passion and energy have a very supportive spouse. I am a direct example of that."

To get a well-rounded look at how his senior executives were performing, Bowling implemented 360-degree feedback, which was linked to the performance review process. A 360-degree review asked everyone who surrounded the executive (e.g., peers, reports, supervisors) to measure their competency. The process was part of Delta's strategy for creating a high-performance culture. It helped Bowling and his leadership to focus on what competencies were essential and make sure the leaders got the training they needed to improve their performance. As Bowling said, "They have accountability partners who work with them on that. And if it's calculated and you've objectified it enough, it becomes very easy."

Beyond Growth

In 2008, Delta moved up 589 spots on the *Inc.* 5000 list of America's Fastest-Growing Companies. In January 2009, despite the dire economic conditions, Delta forecast it would grow revenue by 27% in the coming year, which was 18 times the rate of the 1.5% at which the healthcare staffing industry was predicted to grow. To accomplish its revenue forecast, Delta planned to hire 61 new employees in 2009, growing its total headcount by more than 29%.[44]

Despite his company's continuing growth, the former baseball-coach-turned-CEO did not rest on his laurels. Delta was a great sales organization, but Bowling's

---

44. Delta press release, January 16, 2009.

ambition was to create a well-operating, profitable company; however, funding growth was expensive, and between 2006 and 2008 Delta incurred some calculated losses. Delta's top management worked on "ratcheting down that G&A percentage," among other things. As Bowling elaborated:

To call this business a success at this point would be dubious and premature. Because we haven't proven that we can be an effective business yet. And what drives me is, I don't want to be known as the cowboy who could drum up the revenue and then flip the business and retire.

Exhibit C.3   The Delta Companies' Awards and Recognition

- No. 2 Fastest-Growing Private Healthcare Staffing Company, Staffing Industry Analysts, 2007
- Dallas's 100 Fastest-Growing Companies, *Dallas Business Journal*, 2003–2004, 2006–2007
- Best Places to Work in Dallas/Fort Worth, *Dallas Business Journal*, 2006–2008
- Best Companies to Work for in Texas, Texas Monthly, 2007–2008
- Inc.'s 5,000 Fastest-Growing Private Companies, Inc. magazine, 2007
- CEO Jeff Bowling "Entrepreneur of the Year" Finalist, Ernst & Young, 2007
- "Awards of Excellence" for Advertising American Staffing Association Voice Awards, 2008

SOURCE: The Delta Companies; used with permission.

Leaders Bank: Creating a Great Place to Work

This case is embedded in Chapter 7 and can be found on page 158.

This case is embedded in Chapter 7 and can be found on page 158.

This case is embedded in Chapter 7 and can be found on page 158.

CASE STUDY

LEADERS BANK: CREATING A GREAT PLACE TO WORK

Leaders Bank set out to build a differentiating business model based on empowering employees to serve its customers. In order to achieve that result the management had to create a great place to work. As you read "Leaders Bank: Creating a Great Place to Work," please focus on the following questions.

CASE DISCUSSION QUESTIONS

1. What did Leaders Bank (Leaders) sell? Is it a commodity?

2. How did Leaders' "culture of respect" make money for its shareholders?

3. What is Leaders' customer value proposition? What are the necessary conditions for the Leaders business model to be successful?

4. How did Leaders achieve high employee engagement?

5. How did Leaders manage the risk of culture dilution as it grew?

6. What message was sent to employees by the "open book" policy?

7. How did Leaders structure its hiring processes to protect its culture?

8. What employee benefits programs did Leaders implement? Why? How did Leaders justify the added costs to the shareholders?

9. How did Leaders review performance and improve leadership skills?

10. Is Leaders' "people model" transferable to a non-banking business? What kind of business? Why? Are there businesses in which the Leaders "people model" will not work? Please explain why.

LG Investments, LLC: A Family Business in Generational Transition (A)

CASE DISCUSSION QUESTIONS

1. What were Tom and Carol's values?

2. What were their goals for their children?

3. What were their goals for the business?

4. What were their concerns or fears about wealth's impact on their children?

5. Did Tom and Carol create serious problems by making gifts of stock?

6. Why did they make those gifts?

7. How should Tom and Carol respond to the three questions asked at the shareholder meeting?

8. Each of the three questions raises serious family and business issues. For each question, what are those unstated issues?

CASE
STUDY

LG INVESTMENTS, LLC: A FAMILY BUSINESS IN GENERATIONAL TRANSITION (A)

LG Investments, LLC, was a Colorado family business created in 1947 by Tom Borne, a World War II veteran and hero. After the war, Tom spent one year in Walter Reed Hospital in Bethesda, Maryland, recovering from multiple wounds he had suffered in combat, for which he was awarded the Silver Star, the Distinguished Service Cross, and three Purple Hearts.

After his release, he returned to his native state to pursue a college degree at the University of Colorado in Boulder. While in college he started buying small duplexes and renting them out to fellow students. After graduating from college, he decided to stay in Boulder and make a living in real estate.

Tom first focused on buying residential rental properties, and then he slowly started buying commercial rentals downtown. For the next 25 years, Tom and his wife, Carol, worked hard, always with the goal of providing quality service and ethical behavior. They amassed the largest rental-property portfolio in the city along with dozens of commercial properties. Tom financed his real estate conservatively—all with no more than 50% debt loan to value, and all at a fixed interest rate in long-term life-insurance company loans.

Case Study UVA-ENT-0123 © 2009 by the University of Virginia Darden School Foundation. This case was prepared by Edward D. Hess as a basis for class discussion rather than to illustrate effective or ineffective handling of an administrative situation.

By 1975, Tom had decided that the town of Boulder could be a magnet for people who wanted to live and work in a beautiful environment, so he started buying farmland along the main highways connecting Boulder to Denver and Fort Collins.

By this time, Tom and Carol had four children, two sons and two daughters. Even though the family was wealthy, Tom and Carol raised their children with middle-class values and lived in a modest home in downtown Boulder. In 1975, the oldest son was 25, the oldest daughter was 23, and the other children were 21 and 19 years old.

In the 1990s, major changes occurred both in Boulder and in the family. Boulder was fast becoming the magnet that Tom had predicted, attracting wealthy Californians from Silicon Valley. Boulder's reputation in the field of technology was enhanced when IBM chose Boulder for the site of a major IBM facility. Boulder's entrepreneurial reputation was enhanced by its involvement with technology, running and Olympic training facilities, herbal teas, and books by Jim Collins.

Now, the farmland that Tom and Carol had bought increased in value from $100 an acre to more than $10,000 an acre along the corridor to Denver. Tom decided to contribute the land to several important commercial joint ventures, which included a major office park/hotel/golf complex and a large regional mall. By 2008, Tom and Carol's real-estate net worth totaled more than $500 million.

Years ago, Tom had created a family company called LG Investments. Tom, having never lost his sense of humor or his humility, viewed the family business as a way of passing on his wealth as well as his values to his children and grandchildren in such a way that kept them from becoming ne'er-do-wells. Thus, the initials "LG" in the family company name stood for Lucky Gene to emphasize and remind his children of the good fortune they had been born into, rather than having worked to build, and the responsibilities that went with it.

By 2008, LG Investments was earning $40 million in revenue a year and had expenses, including debt service, of $25 million, leaving a before-tax net profit of $15 million. The real-estate company used part of the net profit for capital reserves and funding new acquisitions.

Also by 2008, the family had grown, and its members were older. Tom at 82 and Carol at 78 were the first-generation shareholders (G1). The four children, aged 48 to 42, were the second-generation shareholders (G2), and the 16 grandchildren, who ranged from age 8 to 26, were the third-generation shareholders (G3). Heeding the advice of their estate-planning lawyer, Tom and Carol had started making annual gifts of LG stock years ago to the children and then to the grandchildren as they were born. In 2008, 40% of the stock was owned by the G1s, 40% by the G2s, and 20% by the G3s.

All the stockholders were family members, and all were bound by the stockholder restrictions that stipulated that no family business stock could be sold, transferred, or owned by any family member not a lineal descendant. For tax purposes, the stock was valued annually using a minority discounted-book-value methodology, a commonly accepted gift-tax practice. The stock had paid minimal dividends until 2005, when Tom and Carol had decided to pay a dividend of approximately $500,000 annually in total to all shareholders.

Of the four G2s, only one actually worked in the business—the youngest daughter. After getting her MBA degree at the University of Colorado, she became a CPA and spent five years as an accountant at PricewaterhouseCoopers in the Denver office. Then she joined the family business as vice president and CFO, earning a market salary of $125,000 a year plus all employee benefits, including life insurance, health insurance, car allowance, and club dues.

The other three G2s lived in the Boulder area and, over the years, had tried working in such different professions and entrepreneurial ventures as farming, childcare, and franchise restaurants. Although they all supported themselves, none of them had achieved the success that Tom and Carol had envisioned.

LG Investments' annual shareholder meeting was held, as customary, on December 23, 2008, at the Flagstaff House Restaurant, which overlooked Boulder and was known for its cuisine and impressive wine list. At that meeting, for the first time, several of the shareholders raised questions and concerns, catching Tom and Carol by surprise.

For instance, the oldest G2, a son, asked to be appointed vice chairman because "he needed to start preparing to take over for Dad upon Dad's stepping down as family patriarch."

The G2 sister not working in the family business asked that the other three G2s who did not work in the company have their dividend increased to an amount equal to the salary and benefits paid to the sister who was the vice president and CFO.

And one of the younger G-3s asked if he could have a job in the company upon graduation from college.

Tom and Carol responded that they would take these three questions under advisement, and after the holidays in February, 2009, Tom went to his lawyer Bob Hutson for advice. Tom and Carol realized that times had changed and that many of their children's friends were millionaires. Tom also knew that his family business was worth more than $500 million. Still, his goal had always been to create an enduring family business without making his children and grandchildren wealthy before they knew the meaning of hard work and competing in the marketplace.

How should Tom and Carol respond to the three questions?

LG Investments, LLC: A Family Business in Generational Transition (B)

CASE DISCUSSION QUESTIONS

Before responding to the three questions received at the Shareholder's meeting, Tom and Carol received four more questions from other family members. "When it rains, it pours."

1. How would you feel if you were Tom or Carol after receiving those seven questions?

2. What would you do ? Would you respond to each? Would you ignore them? What rights do the children and grandchildren shareholders have? Do Tom and Carol have to respond?

3. How should a family business determine whether and how much of a dividend it should pay?

4. Can a family business pay different dividend amounts to different family members if there is only one class of stock?

5. Should family members be restricted from selling their stock? Why?

6. Should family members be forced to remain as shareholders? Why?

7. Should Tom and Carol buy the granddaughter's stock? At what value? Why?

8. Should the family business hire the youngest grandson as an intern? What issues would that create?

9. What would you advise Tom and Carol to do?

CASE
STUDY

LG INVESTMENTS, LLC: A FAMILY BUSINESS IN GENERATIONAL TRANSITION (B)

Tom and Carol Borne pondered their responses to the shareholders' questions raised at the December 23, 2008, annual shareholder meeting. Then they were surprised to get the following letters from other shareholders:

1. G2—other son: "Dear Mom and Dad, As you know, the cost of living continues to rise, and we are now middle-aged. But we really have not been allowed to enjoy any of the wealth you created for us. None of us have ski homes in the mountains, and all of us have had to borrow money for our children's educational expenses, which are loans we would like to pay off. We request that you consider increasing the annual dividend payments from a total of $500,000 to an annual dividend of $3 million. We think this could be done without hurting the business. We also think that this dividend should only be paid to the G2 shareholders. You have enough money at this point in your lives, and your grandchildren are too young to receive money."

Case Study UVA-ENT-0124 © 2009 by the University of Virginia Darden School Foundation. This case was prepared by Edward D. Hess as a basis for class discussion rather than to illustrate effective or ineffective handling of an administrative situation.

2. G3—granddaughter: "Dear PaPa and Nana, I am sorry I could not attend the annual shareholder meeting because I was traveling in China on a college trip learning how to outsource manufacturing to that country. I am eagerly looking forward to getting my MBA in June and have decided to follow your footsteps and become an entrepreneur. I have created a plan to design a line of women's athletic clothes. I have asked Mommy and Daddy to help fund my start-up, but they have refused. The only asset I own is my LG stock. I would like to sell my stock. I understand that the Stock Restriction Agreement restricts the sale of my stock to only family members in my lineal line of descent. I have asked my siblings, but no one wants to buy it. I talked with a fellow MBA student, who is a finance major. He said my stock was worth much more than the annual book value we are given and thinks that I could easily sell my stock and have enough funds to start my company and pay my living expenses for five years. Would you buy my stock?"

3. G3—youngest grandson: "Dear PaPa and Nana, I love you so much. PaPa, you are my hero. Could I please have a paid internship this summer working for you?"

4. G2—daughter-in-law: "Dear PaPa and Nana, I am writing this letter on behalf of all of your daughters-in-law and sons-in law as well as the in-laws of the G3s. We feel excluded as family members because we cannot own stock in the family business nor attend the annual shareholder meetings. We do not understand why we are excluded. We are family too and the mothers and fathers of your grandchildren. Please consider changing this old-world concept. In addition, why are there no women on the board of directors other than Nana?"

After receiving these letters, Tom and Carol have sought your advice to find out what have they had done wrong.

LG Investments, LLC: A Family Business in Generational Transition (C)

CASE DISCUSSION QUESTIONS

1. How should Tom and Carol choose a successor to run the company?

2. How would you determine if the eldest son or the CFO were qualified to be the successor?

3. What would be the pros and cons of hiring a non-family member to be the CEO?

4. How do Tom's concerns and Carol's concerns differ?

5. What do you think of Jim Sharp's succession idea?

6. What do you think of Carol's idea of letting the children decide?

7. How can Tom control the process and get the right answer?

CASE
STUDY

LG INVESTMENTS, LLC: A FAMILY BUSINESS IN GENERATIONAL TRANSITION (C)

At first surprised by the shareholder demands of their children regarding the family business LG Investments, Tom and Carol Borne recovered enough to seek the advice of Dr. Family, a noted family-business advisor and psychologist with a practice in Denver, Colorado.

The goals and objectives for the business and the family were the first issues discussed. Tom stated that he would like LG Investments to stay a family business and as such to grow and be a source of financial security and enjoyment for his grandchildren and their children. But he wanted them to experience the hard work that leads to the joy of accomplishment. He was concerned that his children, grandchildren, and future generations of Bornes not end up as trust-fund babies.

In other words, Tom did not want any of his heirs to have too much money too soon. Carol agreed but added that she would like to see the children get involved in giving back to the community. She suggested that the family create a private charitable foundation that would provide financial support for the Boulder community. She thought that the foundation could be an avenue of employment for some of the Borne heirs and relieve her worries about too many family members working at LG Investments.

Dr. Family advised them to first deal directly with the issue of succession and to decide who was going to be the next leader of the business. Tom immediately responded that because his health was good, it was too early to make that decision. But

Case Study UVA-ENT-0133 © 2009 by the University of Virginia Darden School Foundation. This case was prepared by Edward D. Hess as a basis for class discussion rather than to illustrate effective or ineffective handling of an administrative situation.

Carol reminded him that their oldest son already had asked to be made vice chairman in order to be prepared for his succession.

When Dr. Family asked whether any of the children were working in the business, Tom told him about their daughter, the CFO. Then Dr. Family wanted to know whether their eldest son had real-estate experience or was competent enough to run a big business. Although Tom replied that his son had no experience and was not ready to run the business, Carol insisted that it was because he had never been given the chance to learn.

Dr. Family told them that every family succession involved someone taking over the job of running the business and ultimately becoming the family leader. And he added that successions generally did not work unless the retiring founder or head of the business had some meaningful activity to move on to such as charity work, politics, or multiple hobbies.

Tom and Carol had never discussed his retirement. His business was his full-time occupation; however, Tom realized now that this issue needed to be resolved while he could still control the outcome. He did not want his family to have come from humble beginnings to wealth and back to having no wealth within the space of two generations.

Tom thought about the best process to follow in making this decision. He wondered how to best balance family issues with the needs of the business. It was at that point that Dr. Family recommended that Tom and Carol go home and spend some time thinking about and discussing this issue of succession. He said there appeared to be three candidates for the job of the next CEO: their eldest son, their CFO daughter, or an outsider.

Tom was distressed. He told Carol he was going to stop by the Boulder Country Club on his way home to unwind with some of his pals. In the club's Grill Room, he saw his friend Jim Sharp, who had built a great tea company and then sold it for a tidy sum of money. Tom confided in Sharp about his meeting with Dr. Family, and Sharp said, "Tom, just sell the company and leave your kids what you want and move on." But Tom was still reluctant to take Sharp's advice about selling the company because he wanted the company "to live on and be a vehicle for the family to be engaged in the community."

Sharp answered, "Because your son is not qualified to run anything, make your daughter CEO and appoint him chairman of the board. Then everyone will be happy."

Was Sharp right, Tom wondered? Would this solve the succession issue?

He went home and told Carol about Sharp's advice. Carol responded, "Why don't we just ask the children what they think?"

LG Investments, LLC: A Family Business in Generational Transition (D)

CASE DISCUSSION QUESTIONS

1. You are the CFO. Create a dividend plan that meets Tom and Carol's objectives and can be defended in court if necessary.

2. How does a business balance shareholder dividend needs and company capital needs?

3. Should family shareholders be able to vote to increase dividends to such a large amount that the business stops growing, contrary to the founders wishes?

4. Should Tom and Carol follow Jim's advice in Case (C) and just sell the business and set up their estate in trusts in order to achieve their intended results?

<table>
<tr><td>CASE
STUDY</td></tr>
</table>

LG INVESTMENTS, LLC: A FAMILY BUSINESS IN GENERATIONAL TRANSITION (D)

Tom and Carol Borne each owned 20% of LG Investments. Each of their four children owned 10%, and the 16 grandchildren, in individual trusts, together owned the remaining 20%.

Tom and Carol's daughter had requested that LG Investments increase its dividend so that each shareholder who, like herself, did not work in the business received a dividend equal to the salary earned by the sibling who was the CFO. This amounted to approximately $200,000 per year plus benefits. Tom took this request to his daughter the CFO.

The CFO told her father that dividends were paid according to the percentage of stock ownership and that a 10% stockholder did not receive the same amount as a 20% stockholder. This meant, she told him, a 20% stockholder received twice the amount of money paid to a 10% stockholder, so her sister's idea made no business sense. She explained that if everyone received $200,000 plus benefits, the company would have to pay out $4.4 million, reducing its ability to make new deals and continue to grow. The CFO emphatically stated, "Dad, we need all the company money to invest in the next cycle of real-estate growth."

Tom then informed the CFO that her brother had requested that the company increase its annual total dividend from $500,000 to $3 million and that this dividend be paid only to the G2 shareholders, who were Tom and Carol's four children.

The CFO's initial response was that this plan was illegal and discriminatory—every shareholder was equal and had the same legal rights because there was only one class

Case Study UVA-ENT-0134 © 2009 by the University of Virginia Darden School Foundation. This case was prepared by Edward D. Hess as a basis for class discussion rather than to illustrate effective or ineffective handling of an administrative situation.

of stock. Tom wondered whether it was not discriminatory because each generation had different needs at different ages.

Then Tom went back to his daughter the CFO and asked her to come back with a plan that met both her siblings' needs for more money and the company's needs for preserving existing assets and growing the business. He stressed that her plan needed to recognize the different needs of the different generations of family members at different stages of their lives; it was a tough assignment. He also asked her to think about the request from one of the granddaughters who wanted the company to buy back her stock. It certainly begged the question: Should grandchildren be able to sell their company stock?

Mellace Family Brands, Inc.: Building a Socially Responsible Enterprise

CASE DISCUSSION QUESTIONS

1. What role did serendipity play in this company's start and success?

2. Describe the values and culture of Mellace Family Brands, Inc. (MFB).

3. Describe Mellace's supplier relationships and how those relationships helped create the business.

4. What were two critical inflection points in the growth of this business?

5. Does the business maximize shareholder value? Should it?

6. What does the Mama Cares Foundation do? How is it funded?

7. What were Mellace's key growth challenges?

8. How did Mellace's leadership manage the pace of growth?

9. Should they have outsourced manufacturing? Why?

10. How did Mike Mellace grow as a leader?

11. With its social policies, can Mellace be a public company?

12. Put yourself in the shoes of Mellace's leadership. You truly care about your unique business model of making money and doing good, yet you have investors. What would happen to your company and model if you receive a purchase offer from a big public food company at a high price of 20 times EBITDA? Because you have outside shareholders and employee shareholders, do you have to sell? Do you think the public company will continue the work of your Foundation?

CASE STUDY

MELLACE FAMILY BRANDS, INC.: BUILDING A SOCIALLY RESPONSIBLE ENTERPRISE

Mellace Family Brands, Inc., (MFB) was a privately held snack-food manufacturer with headquarters in Carlsbad, California. Two friends, Mike Mellace and Mike Runion, started the company in a garage in 2001. While holding down full-time jobs, they launched the Nut Hut, a small kiosk where they sold sugar-and-cinnamon-roasted almonds at fairs and festivals in Southern California. Soon after, they changed the name to Mama Mellace's Old World Treats as a tribute to Mellace's mother, Raffaelina, who came to the United States in 1962 from Calabria, Italy. In 2007, the founders settled on the name Mellace Family Brands to reflect more accurately the nature of their evolving enterprise.

Case Study UVA-ENT-0118 © 2009 by the University of Virginia Darden School Foundation. This case was prepared by Senior Researcher Gosia Glinska and Edward D. Hess as a basis for class discussion rather than to illustrate effective or ineffective handling of an administrative situation.

By the end of its first full year of operation, "the little nut business" pulled in $1 million in revenues. In 2007, Mike Mellace, the company's chief executive officer (CEO) and chief financial officer (CFO), earned entrepreneur-of-the-year awards from both the Carlsbad Chamber of Commerce and Ernst & Young. That same year MFB ranked number 1,678 on *Inc.* magazine's list of the 5,000 fastest-growing private companies in the United States.

Having grown from a small San Diego–based manufacturing operation into a coast-to-coast wholesale distributor, MFB counted Costco, BJ's, Target, and Staples among its clients. By 2008, the company had 105 employees and three product lines—Mama Mellace's Old World Treats, Snacktrition, and Mama Mellace's Nut Hut, which together generated more than $18 million in revenues. But making money was not what drove the MFB founders; these young entrepreneurs made social responsibility their top priority.

Of every MFB product sale, 2% went to support the Mama Cares Foundation, a nonprofit organization set up by Mellace and Runion to assist poverty-stricken families around the world and address the global problem of the hunger and malnutrition of children. "It's not just about a spot on the shelf," Runion said. "We can change our own little world, but if every small business did that, it would change the world. What really fills the human soul is giving."[45]

The Founders

Mike Mellace was born in 1974 and grew up in upstate New York with his parents and six siblings. His father owned the family market, which Mellace helped run before obtaining an accounting degree in 1996 from the State University of New York at Brockport. He worked first as a certified public accountant and later as a financial analyst for Ziff Davis Media, the publisher of technology-oriented publications.

Mike Runion was born in 1970 and grew up in Mira Mesa, a suburb of San Diego, California. After graduating from high school, Runion served as a staff sergeant in the United States Air Force and Air National Guard. In 1994, he received a communications degree from National University. Runion met his future business partner while working as a salesman at Total Gym. Later, after their nut-roasting business took off, Runion served as co-owner and sales manager for MFB.

The Genesis of the Entrepreneurial Venture

By 2001, Mike Mellace was a recent transplant to Southern California, where he ran a customer-service software business. One day, he and his associate Runion were making the rounds at a trade show in Chicago. Captivated by the aroma of roasted

---

45. Emily Vizzo, "Altruism in a Nutshell: Company Making Healthy Snacks Is Committed to Helping Feed the Needy," *San Diego Union Tribune*, February 15, 2009.

nuts, the future business partners followed it to a street vendor's cart, where they bought two bags of cinnamon-roasted almonds. Runion remembered, "According to Mellace, you see them at festivals a lot. I had never seen them before, and they're a real big hit on the East Coast. So we start eating them, and I go, 'These things are great!'"

The two men went back and bought several more bags of nuts. "And we started talking about how cool it would be to have something on the side for fairs and festivals," said Mellace.[46] The next day, Runion recalled that all he could think about was "those darn nuts." By the time they returned to San Diego, the two Mikes had decided to give the nut-roasting business a try.

The Nut Hut

Mellace and Runion bought a nut-roasting kettle and began experimenting by making small batches of flavored nuts in their homes. By August 2001, their Nut Hut business was doing so well at regional fairs and festivals that in September, they set up a stall at Street Scenes, the downtown San Diego music festival, and sold roasted nuts as fast as they could scoop them into paper cones. At one fair, they were assigned a spot next to an ice-cream vendor. "It was 110 degrees, and they put us next to Baskin-Robbins!" Mellace remembered. "Could it get any worse? But we had about as long a line as they did, selling our hot nuts. That's when we really knew we were onto something."[47]

Encouraged by their success, Mellace and Runion erected a pop-up tent at the University Towne Centre Mall in the La Jolla neighborhood of San Diego. "People would walk around the mall going, 'Man, what's that smell?' and then they'd come over. They'd try the nuts, and it was great," Mellace said.[48]

While their wives worked at the tent by day, the two entrepreneurs, who were not quite ready to give up the security of a paycheck, went to their regular jobs. After work, they spent their evenings cooking nuts in their garages. Before long, they were pulling all-nighters to fill holiday orders. "Real-estate agents would come by and say, 'I need 300 bags by tomorrow,' and we would say, "No problem," and then stay all night cooking them," said Mellace.[49]

The Costco "Road Show"

After six months of scooping nuts into paper cones, the entrepreneurs had their first big break. They caught the attention of a Costco Wholesale buyer, who invited them

---

46. Tracy Sellers, "Creativity Helps California Nut Thrive," *California County*, California Farm Bureau Federation, 2009.

47. Becky Ebenkamp, "Mama's Boy Goes from Software to Salted Nuts," *Brandweek*, June 9, 2008.

48. "Carlsbad Company Caters to Nuts," March 2, 2009, CBS 8, San Diego, California.

49. Rachel Laing, "Going Nuts: Proprietors of Mama Mellace's Old World Treats Expect $10M Profit," *San Diego Union-Tribune*, June 5, 2005.

to sell a packaged version of their product at a road show the big-box retailer held at its San Diego area stores to test the potential traction of new brands. Mellace and Runion could not believe their good luck. "We were like 'you guys are Costco; we are in a tent!'" Mellace said.[50] At their first Costco road show, they gave away samples but soon were selling their product on consignment.

By now, Mellace and Runion figured that the name "Nut Hut" was not going to cut it in the long run. "We wanted this brand to be more about comfort food, and that really didn't embody that," Mellace said. "We tried all kinds of names, and then someone suggested, 'How about your mother? She's famous for her cooking and [she represents] family.'"[51] The founders settled on Mama Mellace's Old World Treats because it evoked nostalgia for family recipes and home cooking.

Managing the Supply Chain

From the beginning, Mellace and Runion were committed to producing natural, healthy snacks made from high-quality ingredients. They did not have to look far to find top almonds: California, the only state in the United States that grew almonds commercially, was the home to more than 6,000 almond farmers.

Mellace and Runion turned to one of the largest and most respected farms in the business—the Stewart and Jasper Farm in the San Joaquin Valley, whose owners decided to take a chance on the small company because, as Mellace put it, "They loved our growth story. They loved how we operated with integrity."

At first, Mellace and Runion would order only a few cases of almonds from Stewart and Jasper. "We felt their quality was fantastic," said Mellace. "Today, we're buying millions of pounds from them every year." During the next seven years, the two companies formed a unique strategic partnership. Mellace elaborated:

We've really built a relationship of trust and integrity. We know each other's families. We've gone through hard times with them in terms of their short supply. They'd call us up and say, "Look, you have this contract for this, but we can only supply you with this other grade. Can you work with us?" And, of course, we can work with them. And then we'd call them up and say, "Look, we're having cash-flow problems, and we've got to get this big order out, can you increase our limit or can you give us some reprieve?" And they would come back and say, "Yeah, we'll work with you." So we've been through that sort of give-and-take relationship.

For cashew nuts, the entrepreneurs turned to Indonesian cashew farmers in Southeast Asia. "I have a direct relationship with a Christian grower in Indonesia with whom we do ministry work," Mellace said. "Our employees have supported some of their employees to go to school and provided scholarships for their kids to go to school. We've supported some of the orphanages there too." Mellace emphasized that

---

50. Vizzo.

51. Ebenkamp.

having suppliers who were more than just suppliers has helped his company weather many storms. "They are partners," Mellace said. "They are brothers in Christ."

Beyond the Garage

To keep up with the growing demand after the successful Costco road show, Mellace and Runion bought a few more roasting kettles but still had neither automation nor manufacturing facilities; it was the entrepreneurs and their wives who did all the filling, labeling, and safety-sealing of the bags and jars by hand, often with fingers raw from twisting ties on the bags and, after switching to jars, with "scooper shoulder"— muscle soreness from repetitive scooping.

In 2002, the partners rented a warehouse for $500 a month in Oceanside, where they packed nuts all night and still worked at their jobs during the day; however, by August 2002, they realized they could not continue running their nut-roasting operation on the side. To Mellace, a certified public accountant, the numbers looked good. So both men gave up their jobs to focus completely on growing their start-up. Also, Runion, in a leap of faith, sold his house and put the equity into the business.

With their nut business booming, they outgrew the Oceanside warehouse as well and moved to a 6,000-square-foot facility in San Marcos. Then they had to buy more equipment to support the expanding business and ended up storing their packaging material in the parking lot during the day to provide employees with enough working space.

In 2004, Mellace and Runion moved their company to a new location in Carlsbad, and two years later acquired an adjacent property, bringing their facility's size to approximately 41,000 square feet. Now there was room for the large bed roaster, several industrial kettle roasters, and the baking ovens that made it possible for MFB to turn out thousands of pounds of nuts, snack mixes, and treats each day. In an adjacent room, chocolate and caramel bubbled in huge vats, ready to coat the nuts and other snack foods. Automated bagging, labeling, and jar-filling machines got products quickly off the line and into boxes destined for distributors and retailers around the country.

The Competitive Landscape

The snack-food-manufacturing industry in the United States included about 400 companies with combined annual revenue of $23 billion. Most snack companies were divisions of highly diversified corporations such as PepsiCo's Frito-Lay, Kraft's Nabisco subsidiary, and Kellogg's retail snacks business. The industry was concentrated—the top 50 companies accounted for 75% of industry revenue.[52] Mellace commented on the competition:

We certainly run up against the big guys from a competitive standpoint in the marketplace, but they are not coming after us yet. What I've heard is when you get between $50 and $100 million

---

52. 2008 Hoover's industry report.

in revenues—as seen with Vitamin Water—big companies come in because you've proved the concept. They feel they can take your product through their distribution channels and their connections and get it into the market and get the revenue up to a billion very quickly.

Social Responsibility as Highest Priority

Since their company's inception, Mellace and Runion made sure that reaching out to the community was part of its corporate culture. Through the Mama Cares Foundation, which they described as the "eBay of peoples' needs," they sent money and supplies to an Indonesian orphanage, helped feed needy families in San Diego, and continued to support the men and women of the armed forces with snack donations. Working with various organizations in the United States, such as Grower's First, Big Brothers Big Sisters, and Hope for the Children Foundation, MFB actively lived its social responsibility policy. Mellace explained:

Our company vision is "inspiring the world through simple products, solving complex problems." We may be in the business of making simple snack foods, but our goals are set much higher than product innovation and revenue growth. We want to use our success and resources to take on some of the biggest problems we face on this earth—poverty, hunger, hopelessness—and solve them.[53]

Mellace became involved in alleviating child hunger after visiting Indonesia and Ethiopia. World Health Organization statistics indicating that 20 million children suffered from severe malnutrition got him thinking about the nut parts left over from his processing line—those thousands of pounds of nut scraps deemed too small for packaging that were wasted. "These are the crumbs that Americans don't want in their bags," Mellace said. "Imagine tons and tons and tons of this."[54] Those nuts scraps became an ingredient in a fortified nut butter his company developed for distribution to hungry children around the world.

The Founders' Challenges

As MFB evolved from a two-man tent in the shopping mall to a 105-employee operation, so did the challenges facing the founders. "The first thing is to not get overwhelmed by the fires," said Mellace, who had to tackle many increasingly complex challenges simultaneously. "You have to focus," he emphasized. "You have to look at what's the biggest impact on the company. And you go from there."

Funding Growth

Every dime the company earned the founders reinvested in the business, and they took on bank debt to further its expansion. They also worked with leasing companies

53. *San Diego Examiner* and *Uptown Daily Business Report*, January 17, 2008.
54. Vizzo.

and private investors to obtain much-needed cash. Mellace admitted that managing cash flow and getting funding proved to be among the biggest challenges he and Runion faced:

You have to focus on infrastructure. You have to hire people before you actually get the revenue to offset them. And so your P&L suffers as a result. When you start putting the infrastructure in place, you're going to lose money because you stop the growth. But banks look at that and say, "Well, gosh, you're not growing, anymore, you're dying." And so they start cutting your funding, because they feel like there's too much risk there. So that becomes a sort of a vicious circle.

Raising capital was challenging in itself, but applying the principles of their Christian faith to all aspects of running their organization created an additional layer of obstacles. As Mellace explained:

We have a corporate chaplain. We have a director of social responsibility. We do a lot of giving back to the community. And that delayed us getting financed. We'd have investors and bankers come in and say, "You're not maximizing shareholder value. You're losing money and you're giving to all these different programs. You've got to stop." Those weren't the investors we were looking for. So I went back to the board, and I said, "If we stop giving and being socially responsible, then I don't need to be CEO, because I believe that's our core value. That's why our people are here. And we have to stick to it." So we had to wait until we could find the right investors, and, eventually, we did. It took us longer, but, in the long run, it was a blessing.

The founders stuck to their guns, and their company more than doubled its revenues each year.

Growing Beyond a Mom-and-Pop Business

By 2005, MFB had grown to approximately $10 million in annual sales and 55 employees. But making a leap from $10 million to $20 million in revenues proved to be another tough challenge for the founders. Mellace elaborated:

When you get to $10 million in revenues, everything about the company changes. It goes from being a mom-and-pop family business to more of a real enterprise. You have to have controls, processes, and systems. You are sort of under the radar, especially in the food business, when your company is under $10 million. Then once you get on everyone's radar you start catching QA attention and some of these bigger accounts want to see your audited reports and things like that. That is when you realize you don't have what you really need to go to the next level.

Mellace continued, "The other side we experienced was the automation side." Mellace said that at first "we did a lot of stuff by hand, a lot of our personal involvement—myself, my partner, our wives, friends, and family"; however, at some point, it became impossible to fill the orders without investing in the required equipment and putting processes and systems in place. Although Mellace focused on the operations side of the business, he said he did not "grow out the sales side at the same time, and that slowed us down a little bit."

Now, with experience and a better understanding of what was required, Mellace reflected on what he and Runion could have done differently, in terms of scalability:

There were certainly a number of things that we could have put in place from the very beginning that would have been scalable. And I would have definitely tried to do that ahead of time, because it would have helped us tremendously. . . . But it's harder to do at $25 million than it is at $100 million, but it's easier to do it when you're at zero than it is at $25 million. It's like building a house and just saying, look, we're going to put a plumbing outlet here just because it's there. It's cheaper to put it there now when you're building the house than it is to try to rip up the walls later and put it in.

Supplier to a Fortune 500 Company

Mellace and Runion's commitment to social responsibility made it harder to attract bankers and investors but easier to form a partnership with a Fortune 500 coffee company, which had a long history of integrating social conscience into all aspects of the business and required its suppliers, most of who were coffee farmers, to comply with certain standards. These suppliers were graded on such criteria as product quality, economic accountability, social responsibility, and environmental leadership by independent verifiers. Businesses qualified as preferred suppliers if their scores were above 60% in those areas and could demand premium prices if they scored higher than 80%.

As a result of passing the social responsibility audit with flying colors, MFB became the coffee company's nut supplier. Mellace described the audit process:

They send two people to audit your company. They spend several days on-site, confidentially interviewing your staff, reviewing all of your records, such as payroll, your worker's comp, insurance, reviewing what you're doing in terms of giving back to the community, your relationships with suppliers, etc. And of all the companies that they've ever audited on a global basis, we were the only company to have passed that audit 100%. And that just blew the bars away. So all those dollars that everybody kept telling me that we shouldn't be putting back into the company, that it was a waste of money—it ended up being the best dollars we could have spent.

Managing People, Becoming a Leader

Mellace was convinced that because he and Runion ran the company according to Christian principles, they were able to attract quality employees with "tremendous talent" they would not have been able to afford otherwise. "We have been extremely blessed," Mellace said. "Some of my employees have taken a pay cut to come here to work, solely for the chance of making a difference in the world." While Mellace did not deny having "employee issues," he emphasized the integrity of his senior staff. "I would trust them with my son," he said.

Trusting his employees enough to let go of control, however, was not easy for Mellace, and he admitted it took a lot of commitment on his part. When he first started the company, he "led a lot by fear and intimidation," he said, "because that's how I learned from my father growing up in the business, that you sort of demand respect." As soon as he realized how counterproductive this attitude was, he was determined to change it. "I said, 'Okay, my employees need to be empowered, and they have to have the freedom to make decisions and fail, in order for them to grow.'" Mellace remained committed to working on his communication and management skills:

Today, I have more of a servant-leader leadership style. A servant leader determines vision and values. Once you determine that, you flip the pyramid upside down and empower your people to actually implement it and to make it happen on a daily basis. Things happen where they can't depend on me to make a gut call. I've got to trust that they're going to make the right decisions, and they know that I stand behind them.

Keeping in mind that his best employees were motivated by doing good more than by financial gain, Mellace nevertheless believed in rewarding them for good performance through equity sharing. "We're going to do a management carve-out and add additional options for the new staff," he said. "There are many people who do have these options and others who do not, but the plan is that within the next 12 months everybody—that is, mainly professional staff—will be on the same page."

The Gevity Partnership—Outsourcing the HR Function

As the company grew, acquiring more and more employees, MFB partnered with Gevity, a professional employer organization based in Bradenton, Florida. Under the co-employment arrangement, Gevity took over responsibility for health benefits, workers' compensation claims, payroll and tax processing, unemployment insurance, 401(k) retirement options, and human resource services. "We've outsourced the whole thing, but we control our hiring, culture, and quality," Mellace said. While Gevity focused on the administrative solutions and helped MFB reduce administrative costs, Mellace focused on growing the company's core business. He explained the rationale behind partnering with Gevity:

When we started to grow and put the processes in place, as I looked around at every different aspect of the company, I said, "Is it scalable?" In everything we do, my question right now is, "Is it scalable beyond what our need is today?" So I wanted to be able to grow incrementally as we grow now. A mistake that I made initially is I invested in the short term, not in the long term. On the HR side, I felt we needed to do something that was scalable there as well.

Foundation for Success

Putting social responsibility above mere profits reflected Mellace and Runion's Christian faith, which, in turn, served as a guiding light on their entrepreneurial journey.

Both partners viewed the business as a ministry and themselves as servant leaders, dedicated to improving the lives of others. Not surprisingly, when Mellace shared his business insights, he stressed the importance of defining success as something achieved by more than making money. "If [making money] is the reason for your business, you're going to fail right from the get-go," Mellace said and explained:

You need to have a purpose that's bigger than profit; bigger than the company itself, and you have to get people to believe in it. And so that's why I come to work every day, believing that I can make a difference in the world in some small way. I often tell people, define success before you get started, or it will get defined for you. You have to decide why you're doing this, because that's going to be called into question every day. Every difficult situation you're going to come to, you're going to ask yourself, "Why the heck am I doing this?" And the answer better not be because I want to make lots of money.

Mellace believed that all entrepreneurs should define their personal values before building a business. "If you don't have a solid footing—you're dead," he said. "I've read an article recently that said 25% of the bones in your body are in your feet. So, it's about your foundation. If the foundation of your body isn't right, you're not going anywhere." And for Mellace that "solid footing"—the unshakable foundation underlying every business decision and every relationship—was integrity. In fact, he considered *Integrity* by Henry Cloud one of the best business books he had ever read:

[*Integrity*] talks about how every decision you make, everybody you talk to—you should look at it though the lens of integrity. Before something comes out of your mouth, make sure it's with integrity. Are you telling somebody something that you cannot honor? Are you knocking people down, or are you building them up? So it's all about integrity.

Last but not least, Mellace emphasized the importance of building mutually beneficial and lasting relationships with stakeholders—"relationships with bankers, with your employees, with your customers," he said. "When you don't have a relationship, you have nothing."

Motor City: A Disruptive Business Model (A)

CASE DISCUSSION QUESTIONS

1. Describe Dr. Jones's business model.

2. What was its differentiating customer value proposition? Was this CVP defensible or hard to copy?

3. What were the limitations in scaling the business model?

4. In order to scale the business, what does Dr Jones need?

5. Should Dr. Jones accept GM's requirement of actual equity ownership? What are the pros and cons of accepting? What are the pros and cons of not accepting?

6. How could he structure equity ownership to mitigate risks of such ownership?

7. Is Dr. Jones's goal of being another Kroc or Walton a risky ego trip?

CASE
STUDY

MOTOR CITY: A DISRUPTIVE BUSINESS MODEL (A)

In 1986, Steve Jones (Jones) was the leading cardiologist in Kansas City, Missouri. He had built a cardiology practice with ten doctors, four physical fitness trainers, two nutritionists, and two social workers plus twelve cardiac nurses that served the Midwest region of the United States. His state-of-the-art facility included a fully equipped physical-fitness facility and an all-suites hotel for visiting patients and families. His practice was affiliated with several major hospitals to which it sent patients in need of surgery.

Jones grew his practice by attracting patients from other parts of the United States, Mexico, and South America. He invested his wealth in several entrepreneurial ventures in the Kansas City area alongside members of the elite families of the region. He was a passive investor in land-development deals, a regional shopping mall, and several major apartment projects; however, his cardiology practice left him little time for active management of his business investments.

Besides work and his family, Jones's other passion was cars, especially foreign high-performance cars. He was a regular at Kansas City luxury car dealerships, where he bought two new cars every six months, drove them until he wanted to try something different, and then traded them in on new cars. Over the years, he became friends with both the owner and the general manager of the biggest BMW dealership in Missouri and learned the financial side of the car business. In doing so, Jones became interested in how car dealers financed their car inventory through manufacturer floor

Case Study UVA-ENT-0130 © 2009 by the University of Virginia Darden School Foundation. This fictitious case was prepared by Edward D. Hess as a basis for class discussion rather than to illustrate effective or ineffective handling of an administrative situation.

plans and their used cars through bank lines of credit. Dealers generally held used cars for short periods of time and then sold the cars at one of the two big national used-car auction houses. Dealers did not want to carry a large inventory of used cars because their focus was on the sales and service of new cars.

At the same time, Jones began visiting used-car lots and found that, unlike the large car lots of the new-car dealers, most used-car lots were small and owned by a former car salesman or car finance officer. He also discovered that the used-car market was fragmented and, in general, its reputation was regarded as questionable by most people.

Jones sensed an opportunity. Why not build a new modern car facility that was as nice as a luxury-car facility, hire professional staff, and sell late-model used cars to the public with a no-hassle policy, good financing, and guarantees on all the cars? In other words, why not professionalize the used-car business?

Jones's plan was to not only attract used-car buyers but also compete for new-car buyers by only selling used cars that were no more than three years old. His facility's sales pitch would remind customers that the used cars they bought would not depreciate 25% in value when they were driven off the lot. He also planned to offer a 120-day guarantee on all cars. Thus, the idea of Motor City was born.

Jones tested his idea out on his friends at the BMW dealership, and the owner told him that he was crazy. But the general manager thought it was a great idea. Jones hired a leading car-dealership architectural firm and had it design a facility that BMW would have approved of for a new-car dealership. He purchased land on Interstate 435's beltway around Kansas City with good access to the area and hired a finance manager from the BMW dealership to manage this dealership. Motor City opened in the fall of 1987 with the following advertisement: "Motor City is the premium used-car dealership in the Midwest offering no-hassle sales, professional sales and finance service, plus 120-day money-back guarantees." Its logo was the picture of a large X on top of a yellow lemon to suggest Not a Lemon on Our Lot. Motor City was an instant success, netting $1 million its first year. The cost of building the dealership plus funding the opening operating deficits was $1.5 million.

Jones was thrilled. He had always dreamed of being an innovator like Ray Kroc or Sam Walton. He had wanted to build a national high-quality used-car dealership company. By now, he had learned enough about business to know that anyone could copy his idea, so he thought he needed to quickly open more dealerships. He planned to extend his footprint within three years to St. Louis, Missouri; Des Moines, Iowa; Tulsa, Oklahoma; and Dallas, Texas.

Jones understood that quality was his underlying competitive advantage. He bought his used cars only from reputable dealers and auction houses; he performed a 50-step quality inspection before putting a car on his lot; and he reduced the bonuses of the service managers and senior mechanics if any cars were returned because of problems. He ran a spit-and-polish type of operation requiring all cars on the lot to be cleaned every day, the showroom to shine and sparkle, and all personnel inspected each day for cleanliness and professional appearance. In keeping with this, all personnel were trained in customer service with luxury-hotel-training techniques. The dealership's culture was the golden rule.

Jones trademarked the Motor City name and logo and registered the business in all 50 states. His financial plan was to take the profits from the first Motor City dealership to open another dealership. Then, with the net profits from the two existing dealerships, he would open two more dealerships. He was ready to embark. All he needed was someone to drive and lead the expansion.

Jones was much more comfortable hiring someone he knew rather than hiring an unknown, so he approached the general manager at the BMW dealership and began exploratory talks. That person had 20 years of experience in the car business, no record of criminal or civil litigation, was well-regarded in the community, and a leader in his church. Also in his favor, he had taken all of BMW's online management training programs and had been awarded BMW's General Manager of the Year award for the Midwest region several times.

Jones offered the general manager the position of CEO at a $200,000 base salary plus 5% of the net profits from any dealerships he opened. Such net profits would be computed on a combined basis for new dealerships; therefore, if a new dealership operated at a loss, the loss would reduce the net-profit number. This package was a much better deal for the general manager than the one offered in his current compensation. In addition, he would have generous employee benefits that included full use of two demonstrator vehicles.

The general manager knew that in the car business it was unusual for a general manager to have equity ownership and thought that, if he was going to take this risk and create all this wealth for Jones, he wanted to share in the money pie: He wanted the 5% equity ownership to be vested at 1% a year based on performance.

Jones sought the advice of his brother, who happened to be a leading corporate and tax lawyer in Washington, D.C. His brother had extensive experience in these matters, including minority shareholder lawsuits. His brother explained to Jones that, as the majority shareholder, he would have a fiduciary duty to a minority shareholder and have to use corporate money and assets only for arm's length purposes. The brother also told him he could accomplish the same thing just as economically through a phantom stock plan. Under a phantom stock plan, the general manager would receive all the economic benefits of owning stock, including equity participation, but would not be a legal stockowner.

Jones took this counter proposal back to the general manager and explained it to him. The general manager rejected the proposal and stuck to his position that he wanted real stock ownership and not some legal phantom ownership.

Jones had a tough decision to make.

Motor City: A Disruptive Business Model (B)

CASE DISCUSSION QUESTIONS

1. Why should Dr. Jones continue to grow his business?

2. Using the Growth Decision Template found in Chapter 1 on page 15, what issues should he think about?

3. Using the Growth Risks Audit on page 16, what are the risks of growth he should manage?

4. How does Dr. Jones deal with his CEO's lack of enthusiasm for growth?

5. How does Dr. Jones deal with his CFO's ambition?

6. How does he create a unified team?

7. What are the pros and cons of each of the three financing alternatives?

8. What would make the private equity firm offer more enticing?

9. How can Dr. Jones assess whether he is getting a fair offer from the private equity firm?

10. What lessons about scaling a fixed-asset-based business can you learn from this case?

11. Should Dr. Jones accept the private equity firm offer? Why?

CASE
STUDY

MOTOR CITY: A DISRUPTIVE BUSINESS MODEL (B)

Steve Jones (Jones) reluctantly agreed to the new CEO's stock-ownership demand, and they embarked on their expansion plan. To manage his risks, Jones hired a senior audit partner from a national accounting firm, with extensive multiunit car-dealership experience, to be the CFO and chief administrative officer of the holding company, giving him stock ownership in the company as well.

The first Motor City expansion was to St. Louis, Missouri, where it took a year to find the right piece of land to buy and then to build and staff the dealership. Much like the Kansas City dealership, this dealership was well received and started turning a positive cash flow after four months. Once this occurred, the CEO turned his attention to the next dealership opening planned for Des Moines, Iowa.

The operating profits from the Kansas City and St. Louis dealerships financed the Des Moines dealership, which opened one year after the one in St. Louis had opened. The CFO told Jones that this method of financing dealerships meant that pace of openings would be slow, and therefore it would be hard to open multiple new dealerships in one year. The CFO advised Jones that if his goal was speed—first-mover

Case Study UVA-ENT-0131 © 2009 by the University of Virginia Darden School Foundation. This fictitious case was prepared by Edward D. Hess as a basis for class discussion rather than to illustrate effective or ineffective handling of an administrative situation.

advantage—then he needed to finance some of the dealership openings with debt financing.

The CFO explained further that debt financing would most likely be local bank debt for each dealership, at least until the holding company had enough income to get entity-level debt financing from a major bank. He told Jones that this local bank financing could fund the costs of the land and construction, but it would require Jones's personal guarantee. A personal guarantee meant that Jones's entire net worth would stand behind each dealership loan. As the CFO pointed out, if Jones wanted speedy openings, then this was what it would cost.

Jones decided to open a Motor City dealership in Tulsa, Oklahoma, the conventional way, on the basis of the cash flow from other dealerships, and by the end of 1993, he had four dealerships producing earnings of $6 million before taxes and depreciation. His concept was a success. It had been proven in four different markets, and he had been able to attract quality management.

At this time, Jones's holding company had a CEO, CFO/CAO, chief legal officer, vice president of human resources, marketing-advertising manager, and chief technology officer. In December of 1993, Jones held a shareholder meeting with the two other shareholders—the CEO and the CFO. They talked about the strategic plan for the next five years.

The CEO asked that the expansion plan be speeded up because his wife was starting to complain about his frequent travel. He was concerned that their lucky streak was going to end. He was earning more than $500,000 a year and that was more money than he needed or ever dreamed of earning. The CFO was enthusiastic about using bank debt to add three new dealerships a year and believed the next openings should be in Texas; southern California; Atlanta, Georgia; and northern Virginia to stake out a national map. He also thought that, if there could be dealerships at 15 geographically dispersed locations within three years, Motor City could go public, and then they all would be very rich.

After the shareholder meeting, the CFO told Jones in private that he would like to become CEO and lead the expansion because he thought the current CEO did not have the drive or passion to grow the business. According to the CFO, "the business has outgrown him," and the CFO said he wanted to work at a growth company.

Jones was not sure what he wanted. Clearly his two "partners" had different viewpoints. The three shareholders agreed to table the discussion until after the holidays and to meet again on January 15, 1994. For the holidays, Jones was taking his family to their home in Beaver Creek, Colorado, where they had a 10,000-square-foot mountainside home in an exclusive section and were members of two clubs. During the holidays, when he was at one of these clubs, Jones sought the input of his friend Steve Sams, who happened to be the senior partner of a large private equity firm.

Sams was interested to learn about the business and thought Jones had a good concept. He talked about the challenge of the divergent management team views that Jones faced and questioned him about his endgame. For Jones, all of this conversation was helpful.

Three days after that meeting, Sams called Jones and asked to meet for dinner on January 4th. He said that a couple of his partners were flying into Beaver Creek on the firm's Gulfstream jet, and he wanted Jones to hear their views about Motor City. At dinner, the visitors were enthusiastic about Motor City's potential and advised Jones to take advantage of his opportunity before someone else preempted him. After getting over his surprise that the men were so young, Jones had listened but wondered how these young guys who had never built a business themselves knew so much.

After dinner, Sams asked his friend Jones to stay and have an after-dinner drink with him. Then he told Jones that his firm would be willing to put up all the money for a fast national rollout of Motor City for majority ownership. Sams's firm would fund the expansion with enough equity to allow entity-level nonrecourse debt financing with Jones having no personal liability. Jones would not be selling any stock but would have his ownership percentage reduced to a negotiated level. As majority owners, the private equity firm would control the board of directors and therefore the management team. Sams stated that this was the way for Jones to accomplish his dream without risk.

On January 12th, Jones and his family were flown home on the private equity firm's jet to Kansas City, where Jones continued to ponder his choices.

Octane Fitness, Inc: The Power of Focus
This case is embedded in Chapter 2 and can be found on page 46.

This case is embedded in Chapter 2 and can be found on page 46.

CASE
STUDY

OCTANE FITNESS, INC.: THE POWER OF FOCUS

A good example of an entrepreneur who, with others, built a successful growth business is Dennis Lee of Octane Fitness. As you read the case focus on strategic focus, critical growth processes, and the people aspect of growth.

CASE DISCUSSION QUESTIONS

1. Why was Octane Fitness able to achieve $6 million in revenue in its first year of operations?

2. Octane Fitness has hired you to prepare a speech titled "The Keys to Success: The Octane Fitness Way" to be given at your school by the founders. Please create a PowerPoint presentation.

3. Do you think the founders made a good or bad decision in selling part of their company?

4. What was their biggest challenge in building the business?

5. Why are their current challenges harder than even their start-up challenges?

Room & Board

This case is embedded in Chapter 3 and can be found on page 65.

ROOM & BOARD

CASE DISCUSSION QUESTIONS

1. Put yourself in John Gabbert's shoes. What were your goals in starting your own business, and how does Room & Board's business model reflect those goals?

2. Explain how John elegantly designed Room & Board's culture, structure, leadership model, and human resource policies to consistently create the right environment to attract the right people (customers and employees) to Room & Board.

3. If John wants to institutionalize his business beyond his life, why doesn't he take Room & Board public?

4. What are the biggest risks of John's business model?

5. Why did John disclose the company's financials to his employees?

6. Would you want to go to work at Room & Board? Why?

Sammy Snacks (A)

CASE DISCUSSION QUESTIONS

1. What motivated Peterson to start a pet-food business?

2. Peterson followed entrepreneurial best practices prior to opening her store. Please explain.

3. What was her first major mistake? Why?

4. It could be asserted that Mr. Big's investment condition fundamentally changed the game for Peterson. Do you agree or disagree? Why?

5. Were you surprised that Mr. Big was willing to invest in Sammy Snacks? Why?

6. What alternatives did Peterson have if she just wanted to operate a lifestyle business?

7. What process should Peterson have used in weighing Mr. Big's offer?

SAMMY SNACKS (A)

Pamela Peterson slumped into her comfy chair, exhausted from the work of the day. Sam Peterson made a few circles before settling on a spot on the floor next to Peterson's chair. Sam, Peterson's Labrador retriever, had provided the inspiration for Sammy Snacks, a retailer of super-premium-branded holistic dog and cat food. With the success of the Charlottesville, Virginia, store, Peterson now turned her attention to the expansion of her vision. By late April 2005, the second retail location in Richmond, Virginia, had opened after much anticipation. Peterson reflected on the tasks of the last month that had been required in getting the Richmond store opened. Although mentally drained, she could not help but think about the next store opening. Her management team planned to open 10 stores by the end of 2007, and 20 stores by mid-2010. Opening a second retail location had required an evaluation of the existing operations of the company, but Peterson knew the proposed changes would not be sufficient for the entire expansion strategy. She wondered how much the operations would dictate the expansion strategy for Sammy Snacks.

The Pet-Food Industry[55]

The U.S. pet-food segment was part of a relatively mature $19 billion pet-products industry. Dog and cat food represented almost 70% of the market and had grown at the industry-compounded annual growth rate of almost 4% (Exhibit C.4). Nestle Purina continued to dominate the dog and cat food sector since Nestle purchased

Case Study UVA-OM-1177 © 2005 by the University of Virginia Darden School Foundation. This case was written by David Eakes (MBA '05) and revised by Assistant Professors of Business Administration Timothy M. Laseter and Gregory B. Fairchild as a basis for class discussion rather than to illustrate effective or ineffective handling of an administrative situation.

55. Euromonitor report.

Ralston Purina in 2001. Industry forecasts predicted that pet products would close in on $20 billion by 2007, with dog and cat food accounting for almost $12 billion.

The pet-food industry had benefited from the recent phenomenon where Americans tended to humanize their pets and, accordingly, applied higher standards to pet-care products and services. Thus, despite the mature nature of the industry, new product development had been fairly elevated. These developments included dietary supplements, pet toiletries, and kennels with Webcam. In the services segment, virtually any medical procedure available to a human could be performed on a pet, from knee surgery to face-lifts. Not surprisingly, veterinary insurance and emergency care facilities had also emerged and grown in response to this phenomenon. By comparison, premium pet food represented a rather simple response to the humanization movement.

Premium-pet-food growth had been stimulated primarily from new products and enhanced distribution. The current health movement had transcended humans and spawned innovative brands of cat and dog food. Not only were the new foods made with better ingredients, but they were also specifically formulated to address pet-health needs. Two significant events had influenced the transformation of pet-food distribution. First, Procter & Gamble ensured the presence of premium pet food in grocery stores with its acquisition of Iams brand. Previously, premium pet foods had been distributed to pet stores and veterinary hospitals but not to grocery stores. Second, the explosion of pet superstores dramatically increased the number of distribution channels. Premium pet food, specifically dog and cat food, had steadily increased as a percentage of the total pet food offered. At over 40% of the total, premium dog and cat food was estimated to grow to over $5.5 billion by 2007, increasing share of the segment to more than 46% of the total.

Specialty Retailing

Specialty retailing represented approximately 75% of the almost $3.5 trillion U.S. retail business.[56] The classification specialty suggested a retailer that focused solely on a specific product or category. Given the narrow focus, specialty retailers extended across a wide spectrum of industries. The top-ten retailers included companies such as Home Depot (home improvement), Best Buy (consumer electronics), Gap (apparel), and Staples (office supplies). Traditional department stores had consistently lost market share to specialty retailers, as malls lost favor to superstores. While these large retailers garnered the spotlight, the entire industry continued to be extremely fragmented and dominated in number by small firms.

Specialty retailing exhibited some unique characteristics. While subject to the macroeconomic factors that influenced the overall retail environment, these retailers also faced events inherent to their specific segment of industries. A focused product

---

56. Standard & Poor's 2004 Industry Survey.

offering implied a narrow target market and reinforced the importance of customer loyalty and retention. Customer loyalty had been achieved through various methods, including private label credit cards and private label merchandise, which created a retailer-specific awareness with consumers. In the mid-1980s, "category killers" described specialty retailers that leveraged high volume in a discrete retail category to take market share from smaller players. The 1990s introduced "gnategory killers," microspecialty stores offering usually one item or a narrow range of items to compete with category killers. Currently, specialty retailing seemed to be shifting from a focus on price competition to "lifestyle" positioning, as Wal-Mart has dominated the low-price position across a range of product categories, while companies such as REI or Starbucks try to connect with the consumer as an embodiment of their personal lifestyle.

Sammy Snacks

The Sammy Snacks business operated at the intersection of the premium-pet-food and specialty-retailing industries. Providing high-quality dog and cat food, the company also operated an experiential retail business based on customer education and high-touch customer service.

From the Home Oven to the Farmer's Market

Although Pamela Peterson incorporated Sammy Snacks in April 2003, the business truly began in 2000. At the time, Peterson was working in marketing and public relations for an online gaming company. When she was not spending time writing press releases and organizing media events, she was attempting to create nutritious and tasty treats for Sam with recipes that were based on the cookies and pastries she loved. Because Peterson loved chocolate chip cookies and knew that ingredients in chocolate could be toxic to dogs, she created a carob chip treat for Sam. The smells emanating from her kitchen were divine, and she began to share her creations with coworkers. After a number of delicious turns as taste testers, Peterson's coworkers suggested she take her treats to the local farmer's market.

In the days leading up to the farmer's market, Peterson decided that she would brand her treats after their inspiration, Sam. She also decided that a fair price for the treats would be $0.25 each. Her first market test proved conclusive: She sold out of her entire stock. She decided to continue selling in the market through the remainder of the summer, but the demand she was creating in the community meant that she baked almost every night after returning home from work. Over time, she developed a following within her town's pet-owning community. As treats were being sold, a community was being created: between Peterson, Sam, customers, and their pets, and between the pet-owning families that bought Sammy Snacks. The knowledge that she was providing a nutritious *and* delicious product to pets and facilitating a social community gave her great satisfaction.

Less Excitement in the Day Job

As the summer ended and her weekends at the market came to a close, Peterson found that she was getting less satisfaction from her day job. First, she had begun to question the market strategy and a few of the ethical decisions made by the management of the firm. Fundamentally, Peterson valued building brands and loyal customers through quality products, but she increasingly questioned whether the choices being made by management would achieve that end.

Second, her mentor had recently left the company, and her new boss had more education than insight. Peterson's own approach was to value the education that comes from interaction with real-world problems. During her childhood, she learned at the knee of her father. From him, she gained a passion for creation by putting things that seemed unrelated together. The contrast between the passion she was getting from providing the treats her customers loved and the anxiety of working with people she did not respect was stark. To keep her internal fires burning, she decided that she would begin making treats for the wholesale-pet-food market, while continuing her full-time job. When she was not baking, Peterson was reading everything she could find on dog nutrition. She created a logo for her company, and soon thereafter her loyal customers began finding her treats at a local independent grocery store.

Counting the Costs

Peterson's father passed away unexpectedly that fall, and in the aftermath, she reflected seriously on the things that she valued. That process led to her resignation from the company (many of her co-workers would eventually follow). One morning, she picked up Sam's bag of dog food, which now was well known and had a reputation among consumers of being nutritious. Armed with her recent research on dog nutrition, however, Peterson knew better. What she recognized that many dog owners did not was how much poor nutrition affected the demeanor and health of dogs. She decided that she could make Sam (and dogs everywhere) a better food and that better nutrition would mean healthier, happier dogs and families. During that time, Peterson generated a number of ideas to achieve that end. One vision was a juice bar for dogs and their owners. Another idea was for a dehydrated dog food. Later, she teamed with a nutritionist who had developed a formula that met her uncompromising expectations; the formula provided the recipe for Sam's best dog food.

Peterson began talking with everyone she knew about these ideas, including a retail store that would combine food with gifts, clothing, information, and interaction. The retail store concept appealed to her desire to create a community for pets and their owners. During this time, she sought advice from a national business-mentoring organization that paired potential entrepreneurs with retired local executives, but the response she received about her ideas was not positive.

Undaunted, Peterson continued to work on developing her formulas and her business ideas. She felt pet foods were recession-proof. Even if there were market upturns and downturns, owners always would feed their pets. She went to a local bank and was able to secure a business loan that was guaranteed by the Small Business Administration. The loan officer had a number of impressive educational credentials but was inexperienced in lending. In fact, Peterson's loan was the officer's very first. In June 2003, the first retail location opened in downtown Charlottesville. Then Peterson was able to move her operation out of her kitchen and into its own space. She was on her way to achieving her dream. She convinced one of her former co-workers, a graphic artist and advertising expert, to join her in the business as an employee and limited investor.

The community she envisioned was becoming a reality, and market support was building. One customer gave her a loan purely because of the friendship they had built. Another mentioned that he knew a very successful entrepreneur who might be a source of capital and advice. Peterson felt these were strong votes of confidence in her concept. Another indicator was her growing sales, for by early 2005, she was averaging $20,000 in revenue per month.

Still, not everything was perfect. One decision Peterson later regretted was bringing her friend and former co-worker into the business. As she had with her father, Peterson learned how to do much of the advertising and graphics through interaction and observation. She eventually could match her friend's expertise. Her friend had little to no interest in the other necessary elements of a manufacturing and retail operation. She did not have the same passion, and it began to show in the quality of work. Peterson wondered how she could motivate her.

Product Offerings

Premium dog and cat food provided the majority of the business volume at Sammy Snacks, with approximately 70% of total revenue. Dog food was offered in Puppy, Adult, and Senior formulas in a variety of flavors and sizes (Exhibit C.5). Of the total pet-food volume for the company, dog food represented about 95%. Demand in size varied, with the 33-pound bag totaling 60%, the 16.5-pound bag 30%, and the 5.5-pound bag comprising the last 10%. Cat food accounted for the other 5% of the pet-food business, with one flavor available in each size. The breakdown in sizes generally mirrored that of the dog food. Customers could purchase food at the retail location or through wholesale channels. The company offered to deliver for both retail and wholesale customers.

The remaining business volume was split evenly between treats and specialty accessories. The scent of fresh-baked treats flowed throughout the store. FDA approved for people and pets, these treats allowed Sammy Snacks to reinforce the natural, healthy ingredient recipe used for the bulk dog food. Pet accessories added local flair as the feeding bowls and beds were products provided by community artisans and businesses. Despite a relatively minor contribution to company revenues, these two product categories defined the specialty retail nature of Sammy Snacks.

Pet-Food-Ordering Process

With a two-week lead time for delivery, pet-food orders were placed with the mill in Hamlin, Texas, on a monthly basis. Current order quantities were set to cover approximately four weeks of demand for all stock-keeping units. The manufacturer shipped products on mixed pallets and did not charge a premium for this service. Peterson knew that the mixed pallets and relatively small order sizes clearly added cost for the manufacturer, and thought that it might be possible to negotiate a discount of 5% once the shipment volumes grew enough to justify ordering full-pallet quantities.

Pet-Food Transportation

All products traveled directly from Texas to the Charlottesville store. The food was received and inventoried in a storage space in the backroom of the retail location. Rates for a full truckload (not exceeding 39,600 pounds) cost $1,985 per shipment. Over the past year, Peterson had ordered monthly to keep inventory fresh and at a reasonable level even though most orders did not completely fill up the truck. Storage space in the Charlottesville store provided just enough space for a typical shipment with some room to spare for safety stock. With the opening of the second store in Richmond, additional product was ordered to fill the pipeline, but the Richmond retail store would not be able to hold much more than a week's worth of inventory. Accordingly, Peterson planned to supply the Richmond store from the Charlottesville store. The Charlottesville store supplied the new store during the ramp-up period due to the proximity. The pet-food bags were delivered via a local carrier on a weekly basis.

Enter Mr. Big

As Peterson was growing the top line of her firm, she began to face an unanticipated challenge: cash flow demands. She realized she needed assistance to know what she did not know, but the demands of the business provided little time for study. She needed money, and fast. Then she remembered the customer who had offered the assistance of a local businessman and former entrepreneur. Peterson, her customer, and the former entrepreneur met for lunch, and she was impressed with his interest in her business. He asked her a number of questions such as "Why not a wholesale business?" and "What makes your product special?" He wondered if she was selling at the right price. Peterson liked debate, especially on a topic about which she was passionate and knowledgeable. Only later did Peterson learn about his reputation within the local business community as a success in his past ventures. She decided her ignorance about him was a beneficial happenstance. She was less deferential to him than she might have been otherwise (and less deferential than many in the local community were to him).

Months later, the entrepreneur decided to make a small investment in the business. Peterson learned that in the intervening period, he had sent in secret shoppers to test the quality of her product and service and that he also quietly had made inquiries in the community about her. What he found encouraged him to make the first of a number of investments in Sammy Snacks. In one of their early conversations, he let her know that his investments came with a cost: He would only invest if Peterson wanted to grow a professionally managed firm and not a "lifestyle" business. Peterson knew that this would mean the business would be a developmental opportunity for her in which her skills as a well-rounded manager would grow as the firm grew. It would mean she would need to be more than a business owner. She would need a strong team, and she would eventually need to be the CEO.

Mr. Big turned out to be more than just a source of capital. He provided perspective and advice. He even helped out in the business itself, moving furniture and helping with stock. Even after learning about his great past successes, she maintained the tone of friendly debate they had established in their first meeting. While it was not always flattering, Peterson strove to be as quick to admit her mistakes as she was to voice her opinions. As she said, "You need backbone. Backbone to eat crow when you need to, and backbone to stick to your values and ethics because you will be challenged."

During his visits, Mr. Big would discuss, little by little, key issues of concern. One of those was her friend's commitment and value to the business as it grew. With his gentle nudging, Peterson began to realize that her friend would need to change, or the firm would need to change. These conversations led Peterson to make the tough decision to help her friend find a new career.

Expansion Strategy

Peterson intended to expand the Sammy Snacks business model outside of the local area. The geographic footprint would cover a driving radius of roughly two to three hours from the flagship store. Probable targets included cities within Virginia and North Carolina. Expansion would occur over a number of years, generally defined by two phases. The first phase involved the development of the first 10 stores by the end of 2007 and the second set of 10 stores by mid-2010.

By the end of the first phase, average store sales were expected to be 50% higher than the current Charlottesville store, as the new store locations (including a planned relocation in Charlottesville) would place Sammy Snacks in high-traffic strip-mall locations rather than the current sub-prime retail spot. With a full 20 stores with a stable sales base by the end of 2010, the average sales volume per store would double from the 2007 averages—representing a tripling over the current sales rate. Extrapolating from current weekly sales figures, Peterson estimated the sales by SKU at the end of the Phase I expansion (Exhibit C.6).

While expansion efforts were underway in Richmond, Peterson understood the current operation changes represented short-term solutions. Before opening a third store, she wanted to specifically evaluate the impact the store footprint would have on the logistics costs for the bagged pet food because it represented a significant line item for the business. To simplify the analysis, Peterson developed two expansion scenarios. The first would try to build a broad footprint and minimize cannibalization by opening a single store in as many different cities as possible. The second would focus on maintaining operational efficiency by concentrating the store openings in as few cities as possible (Exhibit C.7).

In each case, it would be necessary to engage a third-party logistics company (3PL) to serve the stores in a "hub and spoke" structure. Shipments from the manufacturer would arrive at the warehouse for eventual distribution to the respective retail locations. The 3PL would handle the inbound transportation from the manufacturer as well as outbound transportation to the stores. Each shipment would be priced based upon various combinations of the starting and ending points, independent of how full the truck was loaded vis-à-vis its 39,600-pound capacity limit (Exhibit C.8).

Peterson anticipated serving the stores on a weekly basis to minimize the use of expensive retail space for storage with the added benefit of making "milk run" shipments in the more concentrated markets where appropriate. For milk runs, the trucking company charged an additional fee of $100 per incremental stop, so a milk run from Richmond to three stores in Washington, D.C., would cost $750 (the $550 basic rate plus another $100 each for stopping at the second and third stores). The 3PL would charge a handling fee of $1.50 for each pallet inbound and outbound and a $3.00 storage fee for the average number of pallets held in stock each month. The 3PL also offered to create mixed pallets from full pallets for a fee of $30 per finished mixed pallet.

Final Thoughts

Lost in thought, Peterson had not realized that Sam was now propping his head in her lap. She rubbed behind his ears, and he wagged his tail in approval. Still reflecting on the early success of Sammy Snacks, she knew considerable changes were ahead. The short-term operations solutions for the Richmond expansion would work for now, but how would she effectively serve a larger region? Peterson wondered if decisions would differ for opening only 10 stores instead of 20. While assessment of the transportation and warehousing costs seemed obvious, she contemplated the less tangible costs and thought about what other costs would arise based on the expansion selection.

One critical issue was how she would staff the expansion. Where would she find someone who would complement her own skills? She knew that she needed a key

partner within the firm, most likely someone with accounting and financial skills.
She had not written a job description, but she felt that the person would be someone
older. There also needed to be a basic understanding of the value of pets. The person
need not be a dog owner but did need to have an appreciation for the importance
of the relationship between dogs and their owners. Peterson believed that something
was fundamentally missing in people who did not like dogs.

It seemed fitting that Sam was sharing the moment with her because Sam, after
all, had triggered the whirlwind of events of the past few years. She glanced up at the
whiteboard in her office at one of her favorite quotes:

1. Know where you are.
2. Know where you are going.

      —Paul Myhre

Exhibit C.4 Pet Food Industry Statistics

Market Sectors	2003 Sales (MM)	% Total	CAGR
Cat food	4,533.50	23.7%	3.20%
Dog food	8,794.60	46.0%	3.94%
Other pet food	438.80	2.3%	3.07%
Pet care products	5,343.30	28.0%	4.14%
Total	19,110.20	100.0%	3.80%
Dog and Cat Food	13,328.10	69.7%	3.68%

Premium Pet Food Trends

US$ MM	2000	2001	2002
Premium dog food	2,401	2,722	2,994
Total dog food	6,249	6,581	6,882
Percent premium	38%	41%	44%
Premium cat food	1,473	1,613	1,729
Total cat food	3,834	4,042	4,218
Percent premium	38%	40%	41%
Dog and cat percent premium	38%	41%	43%

2003 Share of Market

Nestle Purina PetCare Co.	30.0%
The Iams Company	14.2%
Hill's Pet Nutrition, Inc.	9.5%
Kal Kan Foods, Inc.	9.0%
Del Monte Foods Company	7.6%
Private Label	3.2%
Other	26.5%

SOURCE: Euromonitor.

Exhibit C.5   Product Offerings and Specifications

Formula	Flavor
Puppy	Lamb meal and pearled millet
	Chicken meal and pearled millet
Adult dog	Lamb meal and pearled millet
	Chicken meal and pearled millet
Senior dog	Rice and chicken
Cat	Chicken meal and rice
Treats	CranOat
	Garlic
	Cheese
	Carob chip

Product Specifications

		Retail
Puppy food	33 lbs	40.99
	16½ lbs	24.99
	5½ lbs	12.99
Dog food	33 lbs	38.99
	16½ lbs	22.99
	5½ lbs	10.49
Senior dog food	33 lbs	38.99
	16½ lbs	22.99
	5½ lbs	10.49
Cat food	33 lbs	44.99
	16½ lbs	24.99
	5½ lbs	12.99

SOURCE: Company Website.

Exhibit C.6   Weekly Unit Sales Forecast by SKU for 2007

Formula	Flavor	33 lbs	16.5 lbs	5.5 lbs
Puppy	Lamb meal and pearled millet	9	10	7
	Chicken meal and pearled millet	12	14	8
Adult dog	Lamb meal and pearled millet	15	12	7
	Chicken meal and pearled millet	18	14	8
Senior dog	Rice and chicken	22	14	16
Cat	Chicken meal and rice	6	5	3
	Units per pallet	60	120	180

SOURCE: Company interviews and casewriter estimates.

Exhibit C.7   Potential Store Locations

| City | State | Distance from Charlottesville (mi) | 2007 Footprint Options | | Planned Footprint | Warehouse Location |
			Minimize Overlap	Maximize Density	Footprint 2010	
Charlottesville	VA	N/A	1	1	1	Richmond, VA
Richmond	VA	65	2	3	3	Richmond, VA
Virginia Beach	VA	175	1	3	3	Richmond, VA
Washington	DC	100	1	3	4	Richmond, VA
Winston-Salem	NC	200	1		1	Winston-Salem, NC
Greensboro	NC	175	1		1	Winston-Salem, NC
Roanoke	VA	120	1		1	Winston-Salem, NC
Charlotte	NC	300	1		3	Winston-Salem, NC
Raleigh/Durham	NC	145	1		3	Winston-Salem, NC
Total			10	10	20	

SOURCE: Company interviews and casewriter estimates.

Exhibit C.8   Freight Rates

Origin	Destination	Truckload Rate
Hamlin, TX	Charlottesville, VA	1,985
Hamlin, TX	Richmond, VA	1,985
Hamlin, TX	Virginia Beach, VA	2,200
Hamlin, TX	Washington, DC	2,125
Hamlin, TX	Winston-Salem, NC	1,815
Hamlin, TX	Greensboro, NC	1,815
Hamlin, TX	Roanoke, VA	1,815
Hamlin, TX	Charlotte, NC	1,715
Hamlin, TX	Raleigh/Durham, NC	1,950
Richmond, VA	Charlottesville, VA	420
Richmond, VA	Richmond, VA	200
Richmond, VA	Virginia Beach, VA	435
Richmond, VA	Washington, DC	550
Winston-Salem, NC	Greensboro, NC	250
Winston-Salem, NC	Winston-Salem, NC	200
Winston-Salem, NC	Roanoke, VA	400
Winston-Salem, NC	Charlotte, NC	430
Winston-Salem, NC	Raleigh/Durham, NC	525

SOURCE: Casewriter estimates.

Sammy Snacks (B)

CASE DISCUSSION QUESTIONS

1. Evaluate the outside consultant's recommendations. In what ways were they unique or unusual?

2. Should Mr. Big have given Pamela a chance to implement the consultant's recommendations? Why?

3. Operating at capacity, how could the Charlottesville store earn enough income after tax to pay back the investors' capital plus return?

4. What are the major constraints on growth faced by this business?

5. How could you grow this business without more capital?

CASE
STUDY

SAMMY SNACKS (B)

The Situation

In April 2005, a time when the retail market was hot, Pamela Peterson, CEO and founder of Sammy Snacks in Charlottesville, Virginia, expanded the geographic scope of her business by opening a second store in Richmond. Peterson's strengths were her vision, passion, and marketing skills. When she made her first planned expansion by opening the new store in Richmond, she took on the responsibility of operating it on a daily basis, commuting to and from Richmond every day.

The Richmond store never achieved profitability, in spite of investments in excess of $200,000. The store's fixed occupancy (rent) cost was $8,000 a month, but the business was never able to sell more than $9,000 worth of products a month, at a gross margin of nearly 50%, before closing in 2006. Opening the second store had diverted Peterson's time and focus, as well as the resources from the Charlottesville store, which was operating at a loss by the end of 2006. Operating losses for 2006 were funded by the investors and a bank line of credit, but Sammy Snacks still had some long-term bank debt.

The Charlottesville store was located in Barracks Road Shopping Center, an area with a high traffic count. Sammy Snacks Treats for dogs and cats were created and baked right in the store. These small treats were not only nutritious and wholesome for animals but also for humans—giving Sammy Snacks product differentiation. In 2006, in addition to Pamela Peterson, the Charlottesville store employed a full-time manager and accountant, a part-time retail salesperson and warehouse worker, and a

Case Study UVA-OM-1350 © 2008 by the University of Virginia Darden School Foundation. This case was prepared by Edward D. Hess as a basis for class discussion rather than to illustrate effective or ineffective handling of an administrative situation.

baker who worked two-thirds of the time. The store's primary product was dry dog food, which included chicken and lamb flavors for variety.

Peterson's love for her product did not diminish in spite of the store's dismal financial situation in 2006. She still wanted to reach more pet owners and to deliver the highest-quality nutritional dry dog food possible. She continued to outsource manufacturing to a Texas company, and she continued to build a Charlottesville client list of over 2,000 customers. In January 2007, faced with these disappointing results, the increasingly impatient investors brought in a consultant, Matthew Frey, to analyze Sammy Snacks' costs and operations in an attempt to discover why the business was losing money.

Frey's Plan for 2007

Frey spent the months of January and February 2007 reviewing the accounting records of Sammy Snacks, interviewing the employees, studying the premium-natural-dog-food market, and then submitting a plan to turn the business around by reducing warehousing costs, shipping costs from the manufacturer, and personnel, and increasing revenue through the wholesaling of Sammy Snacks–branded products. Frey prepared three PowerPoint presentations: "Costs Analysis," "Inventory Analysis," and "Going Forward," and he made the following recommendations:

1. Reduce head count in the Charlottesville store by curtailing the hours of the full-time CPA and reduce retail staff.
2. Store dry-dog-food inventory at the store rather than off-site.
3. Reduce shipping costs per bag by ordering in larger quantities.
4. Reduce out-of-stock incidents and lost sales by better inventory management.
5. Grow the wholesale business, as its net margins were significantly higher than retail net margins.
6. Do not open more stores.

It was understandable that the current management did not take kindly to this outside critique. Frey's report also brought to light inventory-management issues and cash flow problems. In March, in a move to help Frey execute his plan, the investors hired him as president and CEO. Based on the 2006 results and Frey's report, the investors requested that Peterson resign as CEO. The new president invested cash in the company, received a stock-incentive grant, and bought the company. Peterson resigned her officer position but remained a major stockholder and board member.

One of the first things the new CEO did was to meet with the baker. Frey knew he needed her to stay, as she was a hard worker and the mainstay of the branded product. He also thought the dog-treat business could be increased by 50% very quickly. He was frank with her about the distressing state of the business and asked her to give him a chance. To show his respect for her abilities, he increased her responsibilities, hours, and hourly pay by more than 30%. Frey could afford these costs, as he had terminated the full-time CFO, eliminated third-party warehouse costs, and reduced the number of retail employees to one.

Results

By the summer of 2007, Sammy Snacks had regained a positive monthly cash flow. Major factors that contributed to this result were a reduced annual employee cost of approximately $30,000, a reduced annual off-site warehousing cost of $14,000, a reduced shipping cost of $8,000, an increase in the sales of dog treats, and the wholesaling of Sammy Snacks–branded dry dog food to six stores in Richmond. At the time, sales were also helped significantly by the recall of dog-food products made or manufactured in China, resulting in the heightened sensitivity and demand for quality U.S.-manufactured dog food. This increased demand strained the Sammy Snacks supply chain and cash reserves, but sales were never lost because of stockouts.

In the three months of the last quarter of 2007, the business sold $45,000, $48,000, and $60,000 of retail and wholesale products. Approximate retail net margin was 52%, and the wholesale net margin was 33%. Cash flow reduced payables and lowered the line of credit needed to buy inventory. The highest fixed cost was the approximately $4,700 a month in rent that Sammy Snacks paid for its store space in the Barracks Road Shopping Center.

The business finished 2007 with strong last-quarter results, including a net profit of $21,000, after a first-quarter loss of $38,000. If the business continued to operate at this financial level, it would show a net profit in 2008 of $100,000. For 2007, approximately 20% of Sammy's revenue had been from the wholesaling of product.

During 2007, the CEO had been working from 70 to 80 hours a week. The CEO believed the Charlottesville store was operating at its gross-income capacity, with little room to cut costs further. The company could redo its Web site to make it a channel of distribution, but the fact remained that the market for high-end premium dog food was limited, and there were many competitors, including the two big natural brands with significant marketing clout: California Natural and Wellness.

Another Decision

The CEO knew that the retail pet-store business, in general, was dominated by three large national chains, but he also knew that the market did accommodate a large number of mom-and-pop retail outlets, run primarily by animal lovers who were not business lovers. With the president and shareholders—who had invested more than $500,000—looking at him to grow Sammy Snacks in order for them to realize a return on their investment, the CEO knew he had to consider his growth options.

Sammy Snacks (C)

CASE DISCUSSION QUESTION

1. Should the CEO follow the board's advice to hire a full-time wholesale salesperson at a cost in excess of the next two years' projected net profits? Why?

CASE STUDY

SAMMY SNACKS (C)

In 2007, Sammy Snacks implemented the recommendations of its consultant, Matt Frey, and made him CEO of the company. These recommendations resulted in a small net profit for that year.

In 2008, Frey focused on expanding the wholesale business by personally calling on other privately owned boutique dog stores in Virginia. This strategy of wholesaling the firm's dog foods and snacks experienced a sixfold increase in net profits and increased its wholesale sales from 10% to 17% of the revenues.

In December of 2008, the Sammy Snacks board met and proposed that Frey hire a salesperson to focus full-time on wholesale sales to individual retail stores.

Frey estimated the cost of a salesperson for a year would be $120,000 dollars, which included salary, bonus, car allowance, employee benefits, and travel expenses; however, that estimated cost exceeded not only the net profit for 2008 but also the projected net profit for 2009. Frey responded that he had planned on using the projected net profit from 2007 and 2008 to build a new Sammy Web site to increase online sales, to increase Sammy's advertising, and to purchase a delivery truck.

The board told Frey that it wanted to grow the business faster and if he did not want to hire a full-time salesperson to call on the boutique retail stores, then he should come back in January with a strategic plan on how to grow the business quickly.

Case Study UVA-OM-1398 © 2009 by the University of Virginia Darden School Foundation. This case was prepared by Edward D. Hess as a basis for class discussion rather than to illustrate effective or ineffective handling of an administrative situation.

Sammy Snacks (D)

CASE DISCUSSION QUESTIONS

1. What strategy did Frey pursue? Why?

2. What event created a new opportunity for the company?

3. What were the benefits of selling to a regional wholesale distributor? What were the challenges?

4. List each management challenge created by the new growth opportunity and outline different ways to meet each challenge.

5. Assume that Frey is able to successfully bring the new distributor on board. What is the resulting business model? Should he retain his Charlottesville store? Why? What does he own that is unique or differentiating? How does he scale all his products without losing his differentiator?

**CASE
STUDY**

SAMMY SNACKS (D)

Frey rejected the board's suggestion that he hire a full-time salesperson because he was concerned about spending more than two years of projected net profit ahead of earning it. He began 2009 by continuing to personally call on more retail stores and sign them up to buy his products wholesale. By midyear, he had signed up twelve new stores in northern Virginia and seven grocery and convenience stores in Charlottesville.

Frey also signed up Sammy Snacks with an online virtual wholesaler, Wholesale Pet.com, which sold pet supplies for 120 vendors. Then, in early 2009, one of Sammy's competitors experienced a recall. This created an opportunity: A large distributor that sold to dog stores in five states approached Sammy about becoming its exclusive distributor in those states. The distributor would buy two to four truckloads of Sammy's products a month. This would increase Sammy's annual revenue by 90%. But with this opportunity to sign on with a five-state regional distributor came several challenges.

Wholesaling to big regional distributors would be a big step for Sammy. Yes, it would increase sales, but selling through distributors instead of directly to stores would reduce Sammy's profit per bag of dog food by more than 30%. Furthermore, each regional distributor would require Sammy to hire a regional salesperson at a cost of approximately $90,000 to work with that distributor educating its retail store customers about the products, design marketing programs, and setting up store displays.

Case Study UVA-OM-1399 © 2009 by the University of Virginia Darden School Foundation. This case was prepared by Edward D. Hess as a basis for class discussion rather than to illustrate effective or ineffective handling of an administrative situation.

Wholesaling would also require Sammy to invest $90,000 in preprinting the labels on the dog-treat bags at the manufacturing plant for these big distributors rather than its usual practice of affixing the labels manually in the store after it received shipments from its manufacturer in Texas. This cost would have to be paid before the dog food was manufactured. Although distributors generally paid for purchases 30 days after delivery, Sammy paid its manufacturer COD.

Wholesaling created another challenge for the business. Sammy now baked its dog treats in its Charlottesville store, where its manufacturing capacity was 400 pounds a day. A regional distributor would buy 5,000 pounds of dog treats per week. Outsourcing the production of the dog treats created quality control issues and, more important, required Sammy to disclose for the first time its proprietary dog-treat recipe. The dog treats could only be manufactured in a facility that met human standards because the market differentiator for Sammy's Treats was that they were so good that they were edible by humans.

As expected, Sammy's board was gung-ho to sign on with the five-state regional distributor because its members thought this was a good way to grow the business. But Frey had several management challenges to overcome to make this opportunity work.

SecureWorks

This case is embedded in Chapter 4 and can be found on page 86.

SECUREWORKS

Michael Cote took over as CEO of SecureWorks, a company with a proven product but not enough sales. Cote put in place processes, people, and focus to grow the business.

CASE DISCUSSION QUESTIONS

1. In his second year as CEO , Michael Cote was able to grow sales 8X. Why was he able to achieve that result?

2. Put yourself in Michael's shoes. You are a "911" CEO. Where do you start? People? Process? Strategic focus? Please explain.

3. How did Michael align SecureWorks' culture with the processes he put in place?

4. SecureWorks' private equity investors want to use this story as a teaching story for other companies in their investment portfolio. They ask you to prepare a PowerPoint presentation of no more than five slides titled " Lessons from Michael." Please do so.

5. Why was Michael's redefinition of the business so important? By redefining the business what was he trying to accomplish?

6. Would you want to be Michael's co-pilot? Is he a good leader? Why? Is he an inspiring leader? Why?

7. What does he mean when he says, "It's all about people"?

Students Helping Honduras

CASE DISCUSSION QUESTIONS

1. List all of Students Helping Honduras's (SHH's) growth initiatives.

2. Using the Growth Decision Template on page 15, what initiatives should SHH undertake?

3. Using the Growth Risks Audit on page 16, what are SHH's major growth risks? How should SHH manage those risks?

4. What are SHH's real problems? Has SHH outgrown its management team?

5. Do you think SHH can do more harm by doing more good? How? How does SHH prevent this from happening?

CASE
STUDY

STUDENTS HELPING HONDURAS

Students Helping Honduras (SHH) was a student-founded, student-led nonprofit organization dedicated to helping Hondurans escape from the cycle of poverty. SHH was founded in 2006 at the University of Mary Washington (UMW) by Shin Fujiyama and his sister, Cosmo. Its mission was twofold: to empower communities in Honduras by providing educational and economic opportunities and to cultivate a spirit of volunteerism and global responsibility. SHH accomplished this by engaging college students in its projects from beginning to end. Its aim was to co-create sustainable ways out of poverty with Hondurans, while simultaneously developing a new generation of leaders and social entrepreneurs through the transformational volunteer experience.

By spring of 2008, SHH had begun three major projects in Honduras. SHH supported 10 student chapters at colleges and universities in Virginia, and had more than 250 students involved in its projects. It operated with a $65,000 yearly budget, augmented by student fundraisers, which had raised more than $678,000. Operating costs had been funded by a grant from the Sunshine Lady Foundation—the private foundation of Doris Buffett. Exhibit C.9 provides the 2007–08 operating budget that enabled SHH to use 100% of the proceeds from fundraisers for its projects.

By the summer of 2008, SHH increased the number of its full-time employees living in Honduras to three and had an ambitious business plan. SHH wanted to expand the number of college chapters, substantially increase its student-volunteer visits and summer service-learning internships, continue its three existing projects, and begin

Case Study UVA-ENT-0105 © 2008 by the University of Virginia Darden School Foundation. This case was prepared by Edward D. Hess and Research Assistant Shizuka Modica as a basis for class discussion rather than to illustrate effective or ineffective handling of an administrative situation.

three new ones. This plan was expanded further by requests from SHH chapter leaders. They wanted more tools and a manual to run the chapters and fundraisers, to update project videos, to increase communication between chapters, to send monthly newsletters, to form an SHH alumni group, and to have better preparation for site visits.

SHH, however, had limited resources—people and money. Having given $54,000 to SHH already to partially fund its operating costs for 2008–09, the Sunshine Lady Foundation felt it had served its purpose and would not fund more operating expenses. SHH was also challenged to build stronger relationships with its two major constituencies—the Honduran people and its student-volunteer graduates.

Facing this difficult financial reality, the SHH leadership team now questioned SHH's future. Should it expand the number of student chapters at colleges? Should it undertake new projects? How would it fund ongoing operations? How could it increase the effectiveness of its programs with a substantive number of people? How could it institutionalize its cause beyond its founders' daily involvement? How should it prioritize its many opportunities?

History

During his first year at UMW, Shin frequently traveled overseas to play soccer. Taking advantage of his fluency in Portuguese, Shin lived for nearly a year in Brazil before starting at UMW, where he majored in international affairs and premed. His sister, Cosmo, a student at the College of William & Mary (William & Mary), also was multilingual and spent many of her vacations as a volunteer in Latin America. She took on a variety of activities—teaching English in Peru, working at a women's center in Nicaragua, and leading trips for Habitat for Humanity International. As a women's studies major, Cosmo gravitated toward activities promoting women's rights. The origin of SHH was explained by Shin:

The two of us went on short-term volunteer trips throughout Latin America during college and felt unsatisfied with them. We felt as if we were spreading ourselves too thin by going to [different] locations every time, providing bandages to problems that needed comprehensive and long-term work, and [we did] not have a way to stay involved back at home in an organized manner. In the summer of 2005, we both found ourselves in Honduras.

In the city of El Progreso, we witnessed hundreds of children without adequate housing, health care, or access to education. Both of us came to the conclusion that we needed to do more than just help out one or two weeks out of the year and focus our time and resources in a specific location. Upon returning to our campuses, we began to advocate for change in El Progreso—in particular, to benefit the children of the overcrowded Copprome Orphanage and the families of the area's largest squatter community, Siete de Abril.[57]

---

57. From founder Shin Fujiyama's statement in one of the SHH grant applications.

Returning from Honduras at the end of the 2005 summer, Shin and Cosmo started collecting pens and pencils on their respective campuses to send to schools in Honduras. Their grassroots efforts to help Honduran children soon grew into a larger Christmas-card fundraiser to raise money for school uniforms and tuition. By now, many students and young professionals had joined Shin and Cosmo in their efforts to help improve the lives of Honduran children, who lived in one of the poorest countries in the Western Hemisphere; almost 50% of Hondurans lived in poverty. Honduras had the highest HIV/AIDS infection rate (1.8%), highest unemployment rate (27.9%) in Latin America, and nearly 40% of the Honduran population comprised children under the age of 14.[58]

In February 2006, Shin and Cosmo founded SHH as a spin-off of the UMW Human Rights Club. SHH successfully secured a two-year grant from the Sunshine Lady Foundation, which partially covered SHH operating expenses. In July 2007, SHH became a 501(c)(3) nonprofit organization; Shin was elected CEO, and Cosmo became president.

Three months after the official launch of SHH as a nonprofit organization, students from UMW and William & Mary organized the first Walkathon for Hope, raising $148,000 to build an education center and begin some projects at Copprome. The second walkathon in 2007 was organized by students from five universities with a goal of raising $100,000. More than 3,500 people turned out for the event, and SHH raised $288,000, including a Sunshine Lady Foundation matching grant. This total also included $20,000 from the Dodge Motor Company to acknowledge that SHH was the first nonprofit organization to collect 20,000 votes in an online voting campaign called "GrabLife GiveLife."

Their dedication to helping Honduran people in desperate need earned Shin and Cosmo recognition and accolades while they were still in college. When both Shin and Cosmo graduated in May 2007, they committed themselves fully to SHH. This meant that Shin postponed his plan to attend medical school, and Cosmo deferred a job with Teach for America.

The siblings' approach to working with impoverished people was getting to know them first before committing to a big project. This allowed time for frequent interaction, so friendships, understanding, and trust could develop. In fact, some girls that Cosmo worked with even asked her to be their godmother. Soccer played a critical role in connecting SHH staff and volunteers with Hondurans of all ages. Relationships that developed around the sport resulted in constructive partnerships being formed with members of a community and fostered a sense of ownership in a project among all parties. SHH believed that the impoverished Hondurans were strong,

---

58. Information from public Web site: *USAID/Honduras*, http://www.studentshelpinghonduras.org/honduras.

capable, and intelligent people. The organization emphasized full participation and independence from its constituents and selected only those projects that promised sustainability.

Reflecting SHH's success in recruiting student volunteers, more than 150 students and adults traveled to Honduras on various service trips in 2007. Because it was apparent that SHH was making a relatively immediate and significant difference in the lives of Hondurans, 90% of the student volunteers who returned from service trips there continued to raise funds for the organization. As of June 2008, SHH had grown from four volunteers to nearly 500 committed young people, and it had established 10 chapters at colleges and universities, including Virginia Tech, University of Virginia, Penn State, and Georgetown University; new chapters were starting up at Barnard College, Boston College, and Western Illinois.

To manage growth, SHH expanded its full-time paid personnel from two to three in the summer of 2008. Alex Escobar, a Honduran citizen, joined Shin and Cosmo in Honduras as the chief operating officer after completing his studies for an MBA at the Darden School of Business. He had been a dedicated SHH volunteer and board member, alongside Shin, since his undergraduate days at UMW. Escobar's primary responsibility was to strengthen SHH's vision and fundraising capability as well as ensure the long-term sustainability of the organization. His plan was to turn the popular and low-cost SHH volunteer-service trips into income-generating ventures by adding a small fee to help with operational expenses.

Existing Projects

The municipality of El Progreso was the fourth-largest city in Honduras and represented one of the most marginalized communities that included squatter villages, orphanages, and a displaced-persons camp. SHH chose to partner with El Progreso to directly carry out sustainable community-specific initiatives (i.e., education, health, housing, women's empowerment, family planning, infrastructure, environmental management, and business development).

Copprome Orphanage

SHH became one of Copprome's top-tier donors in 2006. Still, Copprome had been financially struggling since its inception. In 1982, Sister Teresita Gonzalez had founded the small orphanage with support from El Progreso community members. Copprome provided housing, nourishment, and schooling to approximately 60 children, who had been orphaned, abused, and/or abandoned. The children ranged in age from 4 to 21, and most of them were girls; boys transferred to another facility when they turned 13. A large number of girls left Copprome when they graduated from high school.

With limited funds, Copprome had to prioritize its spending on the children's basic needs—housing, food, and clothing. Copprome children did not get Christmas gifts, so in 2005, SHH had started bringing donated gifts, which were partially funded by the sale of Christmas cards that the children created. Copprome children did not attend school every day because they could not afford bus fare; many children performed poorly at school and dropped out. Even those who persisted did not have adequate space, tools, or support. They worked on their homework on their beds or in the bathroom stalls. Out of 20 students enrolled in high school, 11 were failing at least one class for such reasons as lack of motivation, low self-esteem, and lack of a remedial curriculum for those children who had a late start.

In many ways, Copprome was fighting a losing battle because most of the girls left the orphanage with minimal skills and became housemaids, earning $3 per day. A poor education, a limited network, limited life skills, and the sheltered life at Copprome all worked against these young women. Some became single mothers, some fell into prostitution, and others went missing. In fact, no Copprome graduate had ever earned a college degree. SHH saw that education could break the cycle of poverty and identified three fundamental issues to address: (1) financial support for students, (2) emotional stability, and (3) higher education.

The SHH staff and Copprome children together developed a plan to build the Sunshine Education Center, which was completed in May 2007. It had a large classroom, a small library of donated books, a kindergarten, a computer lab with wireless Internet, a study room, and an arts-and-crafts center. SHH funded a full-time certified Honduran teacher to oversee the center for approximately $6,000 a year.

The Sunshine Education Center offered various after-school programs for the children. In the Leadership Program, high-school girls interned with SHH volunteers to learn various administrative and project-management skills. The arts and crafts the children made brought in additional funds to the center—approximately $500 in the first year. SHH believed that the center's offerings would enhance the children's confidence, discipline, focus, and, eventually, emotional stability, which, in turn, would serve to improve academic performance.

In addition, SHH began providing scholarships to the teenage girls, so they could attend the best private high schools in the city, as opposed to the dilapidated public schools. The total cost to maintain the scholarship program was about $6,000 per year. By August 2008, SHH had nearly $66,000 left from the $148,000 it had raised for Copprome in 2006. The SHH staff had numerous meetings to decide how best to invest this fund to finance annual costs.

The Neighborhood of Siete de Abril

In 2005, Siete de Abril was the largest and poorest squatter community in El Progreso and housed approximately 75 families, including 200 children. Families lived in shacks made of cardboard, plastic, and rusted tin without electricity or plumbing and did not have access to clean water or health care. The residents were susceptible to preventable diseases such as malaria and water-borne illnesses. And most homes used inefficient wood stoves that produced intense indoor air pollution—the fifth leading cause of death in developing countries and a contributor to chronic illnesses such as asthma.

Of the residents in Siete de Abril, 30% made less than $20 per month. Without adequate education, most of the men were destined for a lifetime of temporary manual labor for minimal pay. Because men were the only wage-earners for most families, the income base fluctuated considerably in this community. Much like other squatter communities, Siete de Abril had its share of social problems involving violence, robbery, and drugs. A sense of community and trust was lacking among the residents.

Very few of the children in Siete de Abril regularly attended primary school, and even fewer went to secondary school. Many of the children were either too sick to attend school, could not afford bus fare, or had to work to help support their families. At the secondary-school level, transportation was an even bigger challenge because secondary schools were located farther away than primary schools. Concerned parents started a makeshift open-air school with plastic chairs and a few desks. The parents tried to teach math and reading to their children literally on a patch of dirt, so whenever it rained, the school had to close. To remedy the situation, in August 2006, SHH and the residents together planned and completed a temporary structure that became the School of Hope, with assistance from the Campus Christian Community, Immanuel Presbyterian Church, Rotary International, and James Monroe High School. Although the school still needed reinforcing with cinderblocks and steel, nearly 100 children attended it in the spring of 2008.

As for housing, most residents could not afford to make major improvements on their homes. And there were other obstacles. The village was built on a floodplain and flooded regularly. Minor improvements could not survive floods. Moreover, families did not own the land on which they lived. SHH and the residents decided to build new homes in Siete de Abril.

Once the locals learned that SHH was interested in building homes in Siete de Abril, however, several individuals claimed ownership of the land and went to court to settle the dispute, which could have taken three to five years to resolve. Faced with the real possibility that the legal landowner could take away any homes they would build, SHH and Siete de Abril residents collectively decided, in October 2007, to purchase a piece of land and build the new village of Villa Soleada. In November, SHH purchased a large plot of land for $66,741 in Las Brisas, four miles from Siete de Abril. The future residents of the new village, SHH staff, and over 150 volunteers from the United States began construction on Villa Soleada. The groundbreaking attracted some dignitaries, including Roberto Micheletti, the president of the Honduran National Congress, and Alexander Lopez, the mayor of El Progreso.

Still, some residents chose to stay in Siete de Abril because of their ties to the nearby churches and for transportation and work-related reasons. For those who decided to move, SHH began constructing steel-reinforced cinderblock homes in December 2007. Each unit cost from $4,000 to $5,000 and was designed to withstand earthquakes and hurricanes.

The housing project was expected to take from 12 to 18 months to complete. The families were responsible for almost all the labor and for raising funds to pay for skilled labor. Villa Soleada would consist of more than 50 small, three-bedroom homes, each with a toilet and a shower. Over the next three years, SHH intended to raise $200,000 to help the families achieve their ambitious plan to install a water well and a low-maintenance purification system, purchase malaria bed-nets and fuel-efficient cooking stoves to fight chronic health problems, and establish a free clinic run by local and international doctors.

SHH and Villa Soleada residents had many long-term goals that would require more financial resources. They wanted to install electricity, roads, and wireless Internet. They wanted to make loan services for the least privileged (microcredit) available and build a center for small businesses to increase employment opportunities. They wanted to build a library and additional classrooms in neighboring schools to increase the level of education. They wanted to build a communal center for church gatherings and town meetings, a school, a library, a soccer field, vegetable gardens to promote a sense of community, and some land for sustainable businesses. They also wanted to hold seminars on sex education and women's rights to promote family planning and gender equality.

Por Venir School

In the fall of 2007, the 500-person community of Por Venir approached SHH asking for help in building a school for their children. Although Por Venir was a poor community, it was closely knit and not trapped in as dire a situation as Siete de Abril. Por Venir's school building had a severely leaking roof that disrupted classes. Moreover, the building was only one large single room for the first five grades and overcrowded to the extent that middle-school classes were held at night.

In spite of the two projects that it had already undertaken, SHH agreed to help Por Venir parents, but because of its limited resources, SHH had one stipulation: Por Venir would cover half the cost of the necessary construction or all of the labor. The community wasted no time springing into action. Parents organized soccer tournaments and raffles and raised enough money in just a few weeks to contract five masons. SHH did its part by winning a $10,000 online-voting-campaign award sponsored by Razoo, a social networking Web site. SHH received the award in October 2007 and construction started in January 2008. Ten volunteer parents worked every day at the construction site. The Por Venir community already planned to add a kindergarten building in due time.

New Projects

Indoor Air Pollution Initiative for Siete de Abril

In the spring of 2008, a team of seven UMW students and an economics professor conducted extensive interviews and assessed the respiratory health of more than 50 families suffering from indoor air pollution (IAP) caused by wood-burning stoves. SHH planned to raise enough money to provide every family in Siete de Abril with improved cook stoves and institute a mechanism to monitor air quality in homes. The stoves cost $83 each, and SHH's plan was to match a donor with each family. The Honduran Association for Development would train the villagers on how to use the new stoves properly.

Women's Academy for Copprome Graduates

As in any other country, higher education in Honduras raised the standard of living. Although only 5% of Hondurans had college degrees, SHH saw a college degree as a more permanent solution than others in breaking the cycle of poverty. It planned to establish a comprehensive support mechanism to help its female graduates. SHH raised $200,000 in 2008 to help Copprome open the Women's Academy to transition these women into the outside world. It would offer transitional group housing, college scholarships, life-skills training, and connections to local businesses for part-time job opportunities.

Monte de Olivos

SHH began forming partnerships with 300 residents of the displaced-persons camp in Monte de Olivos, a community of landless farmers who lived on the outskirts of El Progreso. In 2007, the Honduran government demolished their homes with bulldozers so that the United States Agency for International Development (USAID) could build a water oxidation plant on the land. Neither the Honduran government nor USAID offered alternative housing to these displaced residents: They were forced to live near sewage runoff.

Growth Strategy

The SHH leadership team was confronted with some difficult issues. It had lost its major funding source (the Sunshine Lady Foundation), and it had only three full-time employees. SHH's growth strategy was to have a lasting impact through its three existing projects, add three more projects, triple the number of its campus chapters each year, and double the number of student visits.

Yet the leadership team felt ill-equipped to face the overwhelming rate of growth they had seen in the past 27 months and needed to make changes. During the summer of 2008, it carried out a comprehensive evaluation of the organization by analyzing data and interviewing dozens of student members. Many questions arose during these interviews: Why not specialize in one specific cause or project instead of pursuing multiple projects that were vastly different from each other? How could the ever-increasing number of chapters be managed? Did the name Students Helping Honduras alienate nonstudents from joining the cause?

SHH's full-time leadership was limited to three people: Shin, Cosmo, and Alex Escobar, and they had some important questions to answer: What should each do? How should they proceed? Should they expand the number of college-student chapters? Should they undertake the three new projects? How would they fund ongoing operations? How could they increase the effectiveness of their programs to involve a substantive number of people? How would they institutionalize their cause beyond their daily involvement? How should they prioritize their many opportunities?

Exhibit C.9   Annual Operating Budget for Students Helping Honduras

Expenditure	2007–2008 (in dollars)
Salaries	
Chief executive officer	14,400
President	14,400
Staff accountant	2,160
Health insurance	1,783
Professional services	
Rent (house times two)	2,743
Rent (office)	1,685
Utilities (water, electricity, and gas)	500
Internet and telephone	1,392
Equipment and supplies	
Furniture and supplies	3,426
Furniture and supplies maintenance	100
Office supplies	469
Equipment (laptop and software)	6,064
House security (fencing)	400
Staff polo shirts	201
Transportation	
Truck	10,000
Car maintenance	606
Travel	
International travel	2,550
Business trips in Honduras	342
Grants and conferences	
Grant-writing conference	1,700
Project Honduras conference	300
Total expenditure	65,221

SOURCE: This table was prepared by the case writer based on information provided by SHH.

Trilogy Health Services, LLC: Building a Great Service Company

CASE DISCUSSION QUESTIONS

1. What is Trilogy's differentiating customer value proposition?

2. What is necessary in order for Trilogy to execute and defend this customer value proposition?

3. Why does Trilogy support the proposition that "growth is much more than just a strategy"?

4. How did Trilogy achieve high employee engagement and low turnover?

5. How did Trilogy manage the risk of growth diluting its culture?

6. What hiring and on-boarding processes did Trilogy use to promote high employee engagement?

7. How did Trilogy's leadership combat elitism and arrogance?

8. What do you think are the critical factors in this business model that limit growth?

TRILOGY HEALTH SERVICES, LLC: BUILDING A GREAT SERVICE COMPANY

Trilogy Health Services, LLC, (Trilogy) was a privately held senior-living-services company with headquarters in Louisville, Kentucky. It was launched in December 1997 by Randall J. Bufford, Trilogy's president and chief executive officer (CEO), whose vision was to create "health campuses" that provided a continuum of personalized care—from independent and assisted living to skilled nursing and rehabilitative services—for older adults.

Under Bufford's leadership, Trilogy grew to 17 facilities in seven years. In 2004, Frontenac, a Chicago-based private equity firm, bought the company with the intention of further expanding its network of facilities. Three years later, when Trilogy had 44 health campuses, another private equity firm, Swiss-based Lydian Capital, bought it for $350 million.

With Bufford still at the helm, Trilogy continued to grow, maintaining its focus on under-served, nonurban communities in the Midwest. Rising demand for Trilogy's services, fueled by an increasingly large senior population, allowed its facilities to operate at nearly full capacity—just above 90%.[59] Trilogy's revenues hit $257.8 million in 2007, having shot up 200.4% from its revenues in 2004, just enough for the company

Case Study UVA-ENT-0122 © 2009 by the University of Virginia Darden School Foundation. This case was prepared by Senior Researcher Gosia Glinska and Edward D. Hess as a basis for class discussion rather than to illustrate effective or ineffective handling of an administrative situation.

59. The U.S. Census Bureau has projected that the population of senior citizens will double between 2010 and 2030, from 35 million to 72 million; if these projections hold, one in five Americans will be 65 or older in 2030.

to be ranked 1,871 on *Inc.*'s list of the 5,000 fastest–growing private companies in the United States in 2008. In addition to earning top ratings in customer-satisfaction surveys, Trilogy was voted the Best Place to Work in Kentucky by its employees two years in a row, not a small feat in an industry where turnover rates were as high as 150%.

By 2009, Trilogy operated 56 health campuses in Kentucky, Indiana, Ohio, Michigan, and Illinois, all based on a culture of compassionate service. Bufford firmly believed that it was Trilogy's culture—with its emphasis on people and service before earnings—that formed the company's competitive edge. "We have a simple philosophy," Bufford said. "If we take great care of our employees, they take great care of our customers, and we have a bottom line. Our challenge as we grow is to make sure that we keep the culture high and don't lose sight of our mission."

The Founder

Bufford was born in the Midwest. His father was a career military man in the U.S. Air Force, and Bufford grew up on bases across the country. After graduating from the University of Louisville with a bachelor's degree in accounting in 1981, he started his career as auditor with the accounting firm of Arthur Young & Company. Then he held various positions at the Cardinal Group, a Louisville, Kentucky–based nursing-home company, where he rose to the position of chief financial officer.

In 1993, Bufford started Transitional Health Services, a senior-care company in Louisville, and, in a management-led buyout, acquired selected assets of the Cardinal Group. He served as the company's general manager and CEO until it merged with Centennial HealthCare Corporation.

During his tenure at Centennial, Bufford was the executive vice president of business development. He oversaw the operations of Centennial's ancillary service companies, participated in the 1997 IPO, and played a role in the company's acquisition efforts.

Trilogy Health Services: A Cash-Starved Start-Up

As Bufford rolled out Trilogy's first 10 health campuses in 1997, the business community was in the midst of the Internet bubble, and one of the biggest challenges his company faced was access to capital. "We're a very capital-intensive sector," Bufford said and added that, at a time when his business was in need of funding, "there was no capital—zero—being given to any organizations."

Bufford and his management had been aware that the Balanced Budget Act of 1997 was going to affect nursing homes, and they planned accordingly when making their financial projections. What Bufford and his executives did not realize, however, was the effect the Balanced Budget Act would have on Trilogy's peers, and "how that would ripple down into lack of investor confidence in the sector as far as making investments," Bufford said. He continued, "Seven out of the top nine public companies in the senior-living-services sector went bankrupt. We could not convince people that we were a viable model."

To fund the start-up, Bufford said:

We primarily relied on management's capital and then some of the real estate investment trusts; we partnered with them for bridge loans. I had one debt piece. Our new CFO looked at it and said, "Is that right? Is that 22% interest?" I'm, like, "Yes sir, it is, but it kept us out of bankruptcy."

To make matters worse, "While we were starting our business, we went through a very difficult time in our sector as far as reimbursement," Bufford said. To ward off failure and avoid sharing the fate of many of Trilogy's peers, "We had to do a good bit of juggling and emptying our own piggybank to make sure we had sufficient resources to run the company on a day-to-day basis." And, Bufford continued:

We stretched our vendors pretty thin. But we did that with good communications; we had one-on-one meetings with all of our major vendors, our top 20 that get 80% of our vendor dollars. We never stretched the little guys, who are probably not as well capitalized, and they're in our local community. So we pushed our top 20 vendors hard.

The Trilogy Health Campus

Before Bufford launched Trilogy, he canvassed potential customers and used their feedback to put together a business plan for a group of nursing facilities in Kentucky. He learned that the elderly preferred to stay at home and receive any needed health-care services in the least-restrictive setting and were willing to pay for such services. Based on his research on the evolving needs of older adults, Bufford developed an innovative senior-care model, which offered a continuum of services on one health campus: adult day care, assisted living, and skilled nursing. According to Bufford, the services were affordable to middle-income seniors.

Trilogy's prototypical campus covered approximately 48,000 square feet, and was built on a "town-square" model. Residents usually lived in private rooms configured in "neighborhoods" that surrounded a town square. Each neighborhood had a small, one-person nursing station instead of the more common large central one. To encourage consistent and personalized care, caregivers were assigned to only six or seven residents in a neighborhood. Bufford thought that "the neighborhood concept lends itself to person-centered care."[60]

A 60-bed skilled-nursing facility and an assisted-living facility with 35 apartments were separate buildings located on opposite sides of the campus. Each had its own

---

60. Jane Adler, "Trilogy Boosts Nursing and Assisted Care Holdings with $34.5 Million Purchase," *Penton Insight*, April 27, 2009.

parking, entrances, dining room, and common-space areas but shared infrastructure, which contributed to operating efficiency. On most campuses, the assisted-living operation consisted of 23 traditional units and a separate, secure wing with 12 apartments for elderly residents who suffered from dementia.

Trilogy management took great care to ensure that senior-living centers they operated had state-of-the-art facilities. In some markets, Trilogy established independent living villas and patio homes surrounding its health campuses. Overall, Trilogy buildings had a less institutional feel than older facilities found in many senior-living communities.

A Culture of Service

Having attractive facilities certainly enhanced the environment in which Trilogy residents lived, but it was Trilogy's culture of compassionate service that convinced many visiting seniors to stay. "We've tried very hard to ensure that we have high standards at each of our communities," Bufford said, adding that one of the vital elements of Trilogy's culture was an understanding that growth in earnings was an outcome of great customer service, not the other way around, and that focusing on financial returns ahead of service almost always guaranteed failure (Exhibit C.10). Bufford emphasized that Trilogy's commitment to providing exceptional customer service was what differentiated his company from its peers:

I can assure you that our financial results are not what we think about first thing in the morning. It's important that we keep track of those and make capital investments in our information systems, but those don't ensure success. In fact, if you're not doing well, all those will do for you is tell you how bad you're doing. We're in a business that's all about service and all about taking great care of people. And that's one key ingredient that's often missing.

Creating the Best Place to Work

Bufford asserted that the best way to ensure customer satisfaction was to create a nurturing environment for Trilogy's front-line employees—the caregivers, nursing assistants, nurses, and others. "I want them to say that this is the best place they've ever worked," Bufford admitted, emphasizing that "if we take great care of our employees, then they'll take great care of our customers." He and his management team worked hard to promote "the kind of culture where our employees feel supported by a culture that says, 'No person is any more important than others.'" Bufford thought that the right attitude at the top was essential to unlocking the potential of front-line employees:

It starts with a culture of management where we are leading our employees, not directing them. We have executive directors, and I've even pondered whether that is the right title because we don't direct anybody to do anything. As soon as you start ordering people around, you get the bare minimum performance.

Bufford and his executives devoted a lot of time to coaching Trilogy's midlevel managers, encouraging them to read and educate themselves to become better leaders. "We read books as a company," Bufford said, citing Ken Blanchard's *Know Can Do!* as one of the reading assignments. "We took some thoughts from it to help [our managers] understand how to lead our people into wanting to have the right performance and creating an environment where they'll do the right thing without thinking about it," Bufford said.

In his coaching efforts, Bufford stressed that leadership was not an innate gift that some had and others lacked. "We tell our managers that leadership is a learned business skill," Bufford said. "It starts with somebody who's willing to humble themselves for the benefit of others. We work hard on humility."

Even Trilogy's mission statement (Exhibit C.11), which was printed on the back of everyone's name badge, addressed the issue of humility. One of the bullet points stated, "Take what the company is doing very seriously but not yourself," which was followed by a tagline, "Our company has zero tolerance for egos or politics." Promoting humility companywide went hand-in-hand with fighting arrogance. "Overall, we've got a good culture of not having arrogance," Bufford said. "And when I see it, I really emphasize that it can tear you down pretty quickly."

Walking the Talk

In addition to offering a competitive benefits package for its employees, Trilogy put in place a number of policies and programs to help retain and motivate them. "We walk our talk, and we back it up with tangible things. We have employee retention programs into which we pour literally seven figures every year," Bufford said and added that in 2008 when gasoline prices were rising, every full-time employee who had been with Trilogy six months or longer was eligible for a $30-a-month subsidy to cover increasing commuting costs. "Whether they're line staff or managers, everybody in the company gets it, except for ownership," Bufford said. He continued:

Once a month we do a recognition party; we call it the ER3 party. If it's your six-month anniversary—you get recognized. If you have perfect attendance—you get recognized. If you had a baby or your daughter-in-law had a baby, we give you a Trilogy baby onesie. All those things create an environment where it's going to be a little easier not to get burned out.

Employee Training and Education

At Bufford's direction, Trilogy emphasized employee education and training early on. "We've always understood that we're a service business, and we've invested heavily in training our staff," Bufford said. "There's no better way to show employees that you care about them than investing in them."

For Trilogy's new hires, learning started on their first day of work with a 30-minute customer-service training program, followed by two hours of in-service training.

Adhering to the principle of always putting residents and their needs first was at the core of Trilogy's training program and an important part of what differentiated the facility.

In an effort to make the training program engaging, Trilogy tried to mix in elements that were fun. For example, one year's theme was "A Race to Customer Service," and the winner received tickets to the Indy 500 and an overnight hotel stay. The program also covered such customer-service basics as speaking to anyone within close proximity (10 feet), regardless of whether that person was a patient, family member, co-worker, or vendor; making eye contact; speaking clearly; displaying good body language, hygiene, and overall demeanor; and speaking positively about the facility when out in the community.[61]

Trilogy's customer-service principles were reinforced monthly through posters and payroll stuffers, "something that will reintroduce and remind people of that principle," said Rhonda Sanders, a registered nurse and one of Trilogy's trainers. "Randy Bufford can have the vision, but it takes each person to make the difference," said Sanders, adding that at Trilogy, they talked constantly about the importance of each and every staff member.[62]

Employee Communications

In addition to training and education, Bufford invested in employee communications, which, he believed, was essential for gaining buy-in for company and facility goals. "The more investments we make in two things—training and communications—the better we get with our employees," he said. Employees received company and campus newsletters containing messages from Bufford. A bulletin board at each facility displayed messages about Trilogy goals and progress. Facility leaders routinely pulled aside five or six employees for "coffee breaks" at which they received coffee and donuts while learning about a new initiative or goal. Bufford believed that reaching employees in a small-group setting helped maintain a consistent message.

Recruiting

Bufford's efforts to create a culture focused on people—residents and employees—paid off: In 2008, Trilogy applied for the "Best Places to Work in Kentucky" program and was the number one company in the small/medium category; it repeated the feat the following year. Snatching the top spot two years in a row was a great morale boost; it also helped Trilogy compete for the best healthcare workers.

Bufford took recruiting seriously. "First and foremost, you have to get the right employees," he said and revealed that Trilogy had a simple question on its job applica-

61. Marla Fern Gold, "New-Venture Profits Help Balance SNF Shortfalls," *Provider*, February 2003.
62. Gold.

tion: "Do you love the elderly?" Bufford described the ideal candidate Trilogy was trying to attract:

We want to find somebody who's looking for a compassionate return, who is not there just to pick up a check, because that person is not going to find satisfaction in the difficulties we face. And we don't beat around the bush about the difficulties. We tell our potential employees, how many businesses are open 24/7, 365 days a year with customers who really don't want to be with us?

Lowering Employee Turnover

Trilogy's turnover was significantly lower than the industry norm, and a distinct advantage for Trilogy, which competed in an industry rife with transience. According to Bufford, employee turnover rates in the healthcare industry averaged between 90% and 150% a year. Trilogy's turnover rate in 2009 was only 36%, a figure Bufford planned to shrink to 25% by 2011.

Training and Retaining New Hires

The comparatively high employee retention rate at Trilogy was partly due to the time, care, and expense the company invested in the on-boarding and training processes. In 2004, Trilogy launched a Caregiver Preceptor Program to help new hires acclimate. "We've got a buddy who's been specially trained in on-boarding leadership, making sure new employees feel like they're part of the family," Bufford said. Trilogy preceptors also conducted culture and leadership training for new employees at off-site retreats.

Because approximately 80% of Trilogy's turnover took place in the first six months of employment, during that time the new hires wore blue name badges. "The idea behind it is that we all know you're new, we're giving you extra love, we're telling you that we want to celebrate that badge turning white with you," Bufford explained. Employees who satisfactorily completed six months on the job took part in a special celebration and became eligible for a base-wage increase and additional benefits.

More Effective Hiring Practices

Trilogy's management worked hard to address the issue of employee turnover by reviewing its hiring practices and trying to improve them. Bufford admitted that the reason front-line employees left the company—or were asked to leave—was twofold:

We hire the wrong people, or the people we hire say the right things in the interview process, but they really don't mean it when it comes to how hard we work and not playing politics. So, some of that turnover is a result of us saying, after the 90-day trial period, "Hey, you're probably not the right person for us." And the other part is—we don't do a good job screening. We've never gotten great results out of the reference process, but we're trying to intensify that from a networking standpoint, trying to find people who have known this person in employment in our communities, versus what this person puts on their reference sheet.

To get a better shot at improving employee retention, Trilogy put in place an internal referral program and awarded its employees bonuses for referring candidates that the company brought on board, provided that they stayed for at least a year.

Trilogy's Growth Strategy

Trilogy grew its portfolio of senior-living communities by building brand-new health campuses in attractive markets and through acquisitions of well-run nursing homes, whose management and culture were in line with Trilogy's. After buying land adjacent to the newly acquired properties, Trilogy would then build state-of-the art facilities to replace the old ones.

Bufford's preference was to own Trilogy real estate rather than lease it. But when Trilogy was a start-up, it was so cash-starved that leasing was the only viable option. In 2008, however, the company was in a position to negotiate a purchase of 14 of its leased facilities. "It's a good time for us to buy since we have capital," Bufford said. "It's tough for them to raise capital so they're selling assets. We probably won't ever get to owning 100%, but, I'd say, within two years we'll be pretty close to about 90%."

Bufford's expansion efforts centered on underserved, nonurban markets, where Trilogy was growing in clusters, "branching out from outposts, and filling in and backfilling," as Bufford explained it. In reviewing Trilogy's disciplined expansion strategy, Bufford attributed the company's success to "staying focused on how we grow the tight markets we are in, where they're located in proximity to other markets." He continued:

We've had a chance to go to a small town in Tennessee that on paper looks great, but it's a long way from Louisville, and we don't have any sister facilities there. We first determined the depth of the market around that location in Tennessee and whether we could get five facilities in that area. We studied Michigan that way, and we took our lone outpost to southern Michigan, near our Indiana properties, and we're now up to three properties with a fourth coming. That's our opportunities—to remain focused on our geographic area and do the filling in. We like clustering because it's easier to grow that way and transfer the culture.

Transferring the Culture

For Bufford, successful culture transfer started with getting the right people on a new facility's management team, which often meant pulling some of Trilogy's seasoned veterans from other locations. For example, when Trilogy opened a new health campus in Bellevue, Ohio, in 2008, four members of its ten-person team of department heads came from two other nearby Trilogy facilities.

But conquering new markets also required tapping the outside talent pool. "We look for what I call the 'providers of choice' to recruit from, primarily through cold calling, to see if we can find leaders who match up with our culture." The select candidates for top management positions were routinely invited to spend time on Trilogy's health campuses about 120 to 180 days before the hiring process started. Bufford explained:

They live in a hotel for a week or two at a time, visiting our four or five campuses. Just meet our people, understand what we do, and start capturing the culture and the leadership components by seeing it in action versus us sitting at a new location, telling them. We do peer reviews, which are twice a year inspections, so, for example, they would go and spend time on peer reviews.

Building the Talent Bench

When Bufford started hiring more senior people, the COO position was the toughest to fill. "We're an operations-oriented company, and the depth of talent in our sector is not that strong," Bufford said. The first COO, who came on board when Trilogy had only 10 health campuses, could not keep up with the growing company, and his job soon outgrew him. "I knew that he didn't have the capacity," Bufford said. "I pretty much had to set his agendas and follow up, and we need to be self-starters to grow."

In 2002, after an intensive search, Bufford hired Philip Caldwell, who proved to be the right man for the job. "He's been with us six years. I brought him in as co-COO while we worked the other gentleman into the idea that maybe he couldn't be the COO forever."

Bufford worked with Caldwell to ensure that Trilogy had a deep talent bench, "assembling that next layer of operational management," as he said and added, "We have four out of five, we're very solid. We have one gentleman who's willing to learn, so Phil and I are investing a lot of time with him, because we think it's probably easier to grow him into the position then to find somebody else."

Leadership of Continuous Improvement

Despite Trilogy's success, Bufford remained acutely aware that failure was always close at hand. He kept his finger on the company's pulse, making an effort to visit Trilogy campuses at least twice a year. "A big part of our business is that we don't run it out of a corporate office," Bufford said. He explained:

Even though we have a central office, our business really happens in the field. Our employees see a lot of me, and also the COO and the area managers. Occasionally, I'll sub in if we have an area manager's position open. I might grab two or three facilities and just take those under my wing, because it keeps me close to the business and sharp on management and things on the field level.

Bufford understood the dangers of success; he knew it could breed complacency and arrogance, which he worked hard to fight. For Trilogy to continue to thrive, he argued, its management had to lead by example, focusing on how to do things better. "We call it LOCI—Leadership of Continuous Improvement," Bufford said and then elaborated:

If I don't put my feet on the floor every day, thinking about how this organization's going to get better, and if our employees and our executives aren't doing the same exact thing, we got a good shot at going backwards. It's almost like you're on a treadmill and you better keep working it, because as soon as your employees think that it's not important to you, it becomes unimportant to them. As long as we continue to get better at each and every campus, we're going to continue to grow at eight or ten units a year. And I manage that way, I tell people we have lots of metrics and numbers, and the number really is not important to me; it's really the delta in the number. Everything we do is pretty much keyed around, "Are we getting better, and can we do that better?"

Exhibit C.10   Our Culture—"E"'s to Successful Customer Service

---

Expectations

- We have high expectations of Excellence in customer service for our residents.
  - Zero tolerance for failure to execute our Trilogy Service Standards
  - Zero tolerance for failure to have prompt response and resolution of customer needs and concerns
- We have high expectations for employee conduct.
  - Zero tolerance for patient abuse
  - Zero tolerance for harassment of any type
  - Zero tolerance for ethical misconduct
- Set high expectations for yourself . . . you'll be surprised at what you achieve.
- Campus leaders have the responsibility to communicate our company's expectations to their staff! We take very seriously our leadership of high expectations! You cannot ask someone to do something you will not do yourself!

Excellence

- We should strive to exceed our Customer's Expectations at all times. Our focus is CUSTOMER SERVICE EXCELLENCE!
- Excellence is achieved by having COMPASSION for our residents. You have to love the elderly to work for this company!
- Small things are what create excellence:°
  - Everyone does the basics.
  - Pay attention to details as they are the ingredients to Excellence.
  - Excellence is created by the execution of our Trilogy Service Standards.
  - Go out of your way to help our customers or another employee . . . your efforts will return dividends to you.

Exhibit C.10   Our Culture—"E"s to Successful Customer Service, Cont'd.

Employees

- The Right Employees make the difference!
  - Great Physical Plant + Average Employees = Average Facility
  - Average Physical Plant + Great Employees = *Great Facility*
- The Right Employees have the following attributes:
  - Compassion for service to others.
  - Willingness to support the team ahead of themselves.
  - Understanding of the importance of details in achieving service EXCELLENCE.
  - Readily embrace hard work as a key to success.
  - Willingness to be an example and leader for others.
- Employees must work as a team.
  - Everyone pulls on same rope . . . customer service.
  - To get everyone on the same rope—communicate!
    - ⋆ Communication must be effective and often.
    - ⋆ Communication goes both ways . . . input and feedback are EXPECTED!
- When employees are treated like royalty, they will treat our customers like royalty.

Empowerment

- Every employee is empowered to improve our services for our customers.
  - Empowerment means saying yes first and then figuring out how to meet the objectives.
  - We have to be solution oriented to have Empowerment in Customer Service.
- Leadership and Education unlock the empowerment door.
- Employees need training on Customer Service . . . it is an absolute must to create Empowerment!
- Entrepreneurial spirit means the most important people in the organization are the people closest to our customers . . . our caregivers!

Education

- Education and Training are Customer Service Separators.
  - Employee orientation, in-service and seminars, is an essential part of employee retention and customer service success.
  - The most effective education is done by Example. We teach and train best by being role models of our culture, customer service, operating procedures, etc.
  - Training is a personal responsibility that runs on a two-way street.
- There is no better way to show your commitment and caring to an Employee than through Education and Training.
- Education is the best investment our company makes!

Exhibit C.10 Our Culture—"E"'s to Successful Customer Service, Cont'd.

Earnings

- We have a responsibility to our shareholders to achieve a return on their investment.
  - Positive financial returns will allow for re-investment in improving our services and campus environment.
  - Earnings generated in the local market can be returned to the community through taxes and charitable contributions or services.
  - We should seek out ways to be a partner to our community, both on a financial and service approach.
- Improvements in service lead to growth in earnings, which allows the company to invest in more ways to improve service. This is known as the Flywheel to Success!
- Focusing on Earnings ahead of Service is a start to the "Doom Loop." We understand that financial returns follow great customer service and not vice versa!

Execution

- Now all we have to do is execute.
- Execution does not happen by accident. LEADERSHIP is required to spur along the right combination of execution ingredients.
  - Hard work
  - Teamwork
  - Compassionate commitment
  - Communication
  - Trilogy Service Standards
- Execution success requires connecting the values of the company to what the task at hand involves!

SOURCE: Adapted by the case writers from data on Trilogy's Web site.

Exhibit C.11 Trilogy's Mission Statement

- We are committed to exceeding our customer's expectations.
  - Excellence is achieved by execution of our Trilogy Service Standards.
- The right employees make the difference.
  - Communication and training are the keys to success.
- The team approach works best.
  - Let everyone contribute to his or her fullest potential.
- Pay attention to the details.
  - The details separate the winners from the losers.
- Take what the company is doing very seriously but not yourself.
  - Our company has zero tolerance for egos or politics.

SOURCE: Adapted by the case writers from data on Trilogy's Web site.

Valley-Wide Health Systems, Inc.

CASE DISCUSSION QUESTIONS

1. Why was it so important that Valley-Wide use business best practices?

2. What lessons should Valley-Wide learn from its Durango experience?

3. How does Valley-Wide resolve the conflict between its social justice mission and the need to strategically focus?

4. What lessons can every not-for-profit learn from Valley-Wide?

CASE
STUDY

VALLEY-WIDE HEALTH SYSTEMS, INC.

Valley-Wide Health Systems, Inc. (Valley-Wide), was a private not-for-profit corporation that delivered primary health care, dental care, and ancillary health services to underserved populations in 20 rural counties in southern Colorado. It was also one of the most successful and one of the largest rural community health centers in the United States.

Valley-Wide operated 19 primary care and dental clinics that served 40,000 patients. It had more than 350 full-time employees and an annual budget of $32 million. Since 1989, Marguerite Salazar had served as CEO and, with a passion for healthcare justice, she had built Valley-Wide into a national model for rural health care by utilizing business-management best practices.

Valley-Wide's continued success and innovation was an example of how business-management best practices could be used to foster social good. In its role as a high-performance business, Valley-Wide consistently focused on the operational excellence and financial accountability enabled by both technology and its highly engaged, loyal, and productive work force.

For more than 30 years, Valley-Wide had grown and expanded geographically. It increased the number of customer segments it served, added more services, expanded its professional staff, built a management team, and enlarged its revenue model, while adding the processes, controls, and state-of-the-art technology to manage a growing business and oversee patient data, records, and quality. Besides its goal of delivering world-class health care, Valley-Wide also wanted to be a good steward of the money received from patients and funding sources by utilizing best-of-class business operating processes and controls. "Using federal and state taxes to provide health care is a huge responsibility. We wanted to show that we are a good investment by putting this funding to prudent use," said Salazar.

Case Study UVA-ENT-0145 © 2009 by the University of Virginia Darden School Foundation. This case was prepared by Edward D. Hess as a basis for class discussion rather than to illustrate effective or ineffective handling of an administrative situation.

History

In 1976, the only available health care in the San Luis Valley for people without health insurance or money was in the emergency room at the local hospital. In the United States, emergency rooms were required to treat everyone who presented with an emergency regardless of their ability to pay. The situation changed in 1976, when a group of citizens established two health clinics in the San Luis Valley and hired Valley-Wide's first doctor. Valley-Wide's budget for that first year was $135,000, which included a $65,000 Federal Rural Health Initiative grant.

During the early 1980s, Valley-Wide, with its five doctors, was a major health-care provider to migrant workers and their families, serving approximately 8,000 patients. By 1985, Valley-Wide had expanded to four counties and had an operating budget of approximately $2.4 million: $700,000 from patient fees, $1.5 million from federal grants, and $100,000 from Colorado's Office of Economic Development grants. During that time, a medical social worker, who provided mental health and social services through local hospitals and clinics, was asked to join Valley-Wide as the director of community health: That person was Salazar.

Salazar

Born in the San Luis Valley, Salazar had attended Colorado State University and Adams State College in Alamosa, Colorado, earning a bachelor's degree in psychology/sociology and a master's degree in counseling psychology. After graduating, she worked as a mental health therapist for the Community Mental Health Center in Alamosa and left in 1982 to set up her own medical social-work service company, which she ran until 1989. As an entrepreneur, Salazar quickly learned that cash flow was the lifeblood of every business regardless of its market focus. As a result, she became proficient at healthcare finance and insurance reimbursement, managing more than 10 separate provider contracts.

The competitive advantage Salazar brought to the hospitals, nursing homes, clinics, and veteran's center she served was cost-efficient measurable quality service. Her entrepreneurial spirit and common-sense approach was to run nonprofits just like businesses; doing so accomplished the most good for the most people. Efficiency, productivity, return on investment, controls, constant improvement, and challenging the status quo were all lessons she had learned in private practice.

By 1985, Valley-Wide administered the Federal Migrant Health Program for the valley and served approximately 25% of valley residents through five clinics and 40 personnel. In 1989, as president and CEO, Salazar began the task of applying sound business practices in health-care delivery. To accomplish this, Valley-Wide installed new electronic information systems and established a formal finance department staffed with CPAs. It continued to open new clinics for underserved populations, and, by 1995, it had an operating budget of $11 million and a staff of 150 who treated more than 18,000 people. By now, Valley-Wide's medical staff included seven family-practice and four internal-medicine physicians and ten physician assistants and nurse practitioners. COO Konnie Martin described the situation:

During this period of time, we became large enough to convert several business practices into our internal process, including billing, payroll, and reporting requirements for the federal government funding. We have continually evolved to utilize technology to keep us in the forefront of key operations.

Valley-Wide upgraded to state-of-the-art scalable software packages to prepare it for future growth, placing it ahead of other nonprofits and positioning it at the leading edge of utilizing best business practices. In 1995, it expanded its services to include a full-service dental clinic and began focusing on children and high school students.

Throughout its history, Valley-Wide had served insured and uninsured men, women, and children, offering a wide range of services, clinics, and education programs on topics such as allergies, arthritis, asthma, cancer, dental, diabetes, geriatrics, heart disease, intestinal disorders, nutrition, obstetrics, pediatrics, pharmacy, physical therapy, prenatal care, preventive medicine, social services, and surgery. Patients were covered under federal and state grants, Medicaid, Medicare, commercial insurance, self-pay, CHP+ (program for low-income children), and migrant worker and state indigent-care programs.

Business Philosophy

Salazar modeled Valley-Wide as a successful for-profit business with a budget, frequent financial reports, and plans to build revenue streams independent of private charitable or federal grants. She was concerned that the financial viability of the organization and the thousands of clients dependent on it for their and their families' health care was supported by only one primary funding source or federally funded program. Therefore, Salazar expanded contracts with insurance companies to provide services so she had a base of nongovernmental income to cover costs.

In 2009, Valley-Wide generated approximately 40% of its revenue from commercial insurance companies, 40% from Medicare and Medicaid, and 20% from federal and state grants.

Management Team

Valley-Wide's management team in 2009 was made up of six individuals who served as COO, medical director, director of programs, CFO, dental director, and head of compliance/HR. The COO had been with the organization since 1985; the CFO since 1987; the director of programs since 1989; the compliance/HR head since 1990; the medical director since 1999; and the dental director since 2000.

Interestingly, most of the management team had grown professionally along with Valley-Wide by acquiring more skills and knowledge through training and education. For example, the COO participated in the UCLA/Johnson & Johnson Health Care Executive Program, and both she and the compliance officer were fellows in the Regional Institute for Health and Environmental Leadership through the state of Colorado. The director of programs, who provided leadership in quality management, was trained at the Quorum Health Resources, Inc., quality school, and all members of the management team regularly attended Joint Commission Accreditation and Medical Group Management Association (MGMA) training. This was outside the realm of nonprofit management, but because Valley-Wide competed with private physician groups, it was imperative that the management team understood best business practices while implementing them.

With the management team in place, Salazar changed the organization's structure. She worked hard to build a collaborative team environment and an organization-wide family atmosphere. She always looked first and foremost at cultural and mission-fit as she hired and promoted employees.

Building this team allowed Salazar to spend 50% of her time on local, state, and national policy issues, strategic issues, and funding issues. She pushed herself to learn from business best practices in industries other than community health. She explained:

We are trying to be a best-of-class organization as compared to world-class for-profit organizations. We have to keep raising our performance and the operational bar. We cannot become complacent. We deal daily with issues of justice around a culture of poverty. Our work is not done.

Valley-Wide clearly had perfected delivering broad-based community health services in rural Colorado. Then, in 1998, the company was approached about the possibility of offering primary family health-care services in a different demographic setting in the wealthier area of Durango, Colorado, a town with a ski resort that attracted skiers and vacationers. Valley-Wide's management team saw it as an opportunity to help more people. Of course, Valley-Wide would expand: That was its mission.

The Durango Experiment

In 1998, Valley-Wide was invited to begin discussions with Mercy Hospital, which wanted to close three primary-care sites (one of which served indigent patients) that were losing substantial amounts of money. Mercy Hospital wanted to outsource that patient segment and was willing to subsidize Valley-Wide for taking on that responsibility to the tune of $500,000 per year for three years. It was hoped that any remaining costs could be covered through state and federal grants.

Valley-Wide hired outside financial experts and lawyers to do due diligence and build a five-year financial plan based on Mercy Hospital's financial history for the prior five years. The financial advisors decided that Valley-Wide needed to be subsidized for at least three years during which it would seek additional funding, including federal funding. The financial analysis was completed by late 2000, and, in March 2001, Valley-Wide took on the Durango project, relying heavily on the three-year subsidy package.

Unfortunately, the three-year funding that was so carefully researched and planned for began to unravel in early 2002, as Colorado reduced its statewide funding due to the economic downturn after 9/11. Also, significant federal funding did not materialize because, on a national competitive basis, the Durango community as a whole was considered too comparatively affluent. A perfect financial storm ensued in May 2003, forcing Valley-Wide to reduce the Durango work force to cut costs. But funding was not the only issue.

The culture and work ethic of the Durango work force turned out to be different from Valley-Wide's culture and expectations of service. Durango's staff, including doctors, wanted not only multiple days off during the week, but they also wanted to close the clinics during spring break. In addition, the Durango professional staff did not accept Valley-Wide's high accountability business processes. Valley-Wide management met with Durango staff individually and held retreats with the entire staff in an effort to influence the corporate culture and integrate this new community into its well-established, stable organization. The company logo was also changed to reflect the addition of the new area, so Durango staff would not feel like stepchildren.

At the same time, Valley-Wide reached out to the community with a plan to set up and attend multiple meetings to talk about the need for community health care and its philosophy of helping the underserved. A local advisory board was established, and two members of that board were elected to Valley-Wide's board of directors. The local board met monthly, and Salazar and key management-team members attended in person.

By March 2004, Valley-Wide faced substantial financial exposure and a difficult community and work force environment, which it had not faced before, even when it had expanded in rural southwest Colorado. It underwent a multidisciplinary analysis to answer the question: "Can we have the success we desire in Durango?" By then, it was clear that neither Mercy Hospital nor the Durango community were willing financial partners. Still, Valley-Wide was so mission-driven to serve underserved populations that it continued to try and make the Durango setup work. Because of the 9,000 Valley-Wide patients dependent on it in Durango, getting out would be difficult from a cultural as well as a mission standpoint.

In fall 2004 and throughout 2005, Valley-Wide doubled its efforts to get funding from federal programs, Catholic health programs, and local sources; however, there was no new funding, including a local tax that was defeated in a public referendum in May 2006. That public vote was the clincher for Valley-Wide: It could no longer subsidize Durango if the community did not want to help. Valley-Wide had done everything it could do but could not continue to allocate resources to Durango. It was time to cut its losses and endure its first failure at expanding health care in Colorado. In December 2006, the Valley-Wide board voted to close Durango operations by March 31, 2007.

Valley-Wide's leadership team mourned the Durango loss and after some time began an analysis of it to learn where it went wrong. There were questions that needed to be answered. Should Valley-Wide not have expanded outside its primary market in rural southwest Colorado? How could it have balanced strategic focus against having a well-proven business-operations model and a nationally recognized health-care-delivery model that served underserved populations—a big national need?

Bibliography

Astrachan, J. H., and M. C. Shanker. "Family Businesses Contributing to the U.S. Economy: A Closer Look." *Family Business Review* (September 2003).

Blanchard, Ken. *Know Can Do! Put Your Know-How Into Action.* San Francisco: Berrett-Koehler Publishers, 2007.

Buckingham, Marcus, and Curt Coffman. *First, Break All the Rules: What the World's Greatest Managers Do Differently.* New York: Simon & Schuster, 1999.

Cameron, Kim S., Jane E. Dutton, and Robert E. Quinn, eds. *Positive Organizational Scholarship.* San Francisco: Berrett- Koehler, 2003.

Collins, James C., and Jerry I. Porras. *Built to Last: Successful Habits of Visionary Companies.* New York: HarperBusiness Essentials, 2002.

Dutton, Jane E. *Energize Your Workplace: How to Create and Sustain High-Quality Connections at Work.* San Francisco: Jossey-Bass, 2003.

Heskett, James L., W. Earl Sasser Jr., and Leonard A. Schlesinger. *The Value Profit Chain: Treat Employees Like Customers and Customers Like Employees.* New York: Free Press, 2003.

Heskett, James L., W. Earl Sasser Jr., and Leonard A. Schlesinger. *The Service Profit Chain: How Leading Companies Link Profit and Growth to Loyalty, Satisfaction, and Value.* New York: Free Press, 1997.

Hess, Edward D. "3 Fellers Bakery" Case Study UVA-ENT-0137. University of Virginia Darden School Foundation, Charlottesville, 2009.

Hess, Edward D. "10 Keys to Raising Growth Capital." *The Catalyst*, April 2004.

Hess, Edward D. "Appalachian Commercial Cleaners: Family Dynamics Versus the Business" Case Study UVA-ENT-0126. University of Virginia Darden School Foundation, Charlottesville, 2009.

Hess, Edward D. "Are Your Employees a Means to your End?" *The Catalyst*, May 2004.

Hess, Edward D. "Darden Private Growth Research Project." 2008.

Hess, Edward D. "Defender Direct, Inc.: A Business of Growing Leaders" Case Study UVA-ENT-0115. University of Virginia Darden School Foundation, Charlottesville, 2009.

Hess, Edward D. "Edens & Avant" Case Study UVA-S-0146. University of Virginia Darden School Foundation, Charlottesville, 2007.

Hess, Edward D. "Family Business Succession: The Duality Principle." *The Catalyst*, February 2004.

Hess, Edward D. "Freedom Technology Services" Case Study UVA-ENT-0127. University of Virginia Darden School Foundation, Charlottesville, 2009.

Hess, Edward D. "Green Copier Recycling" Case Study UVA-ENT-0125. University of Virginia Darden School Foundation, Charlottesville, 2009.

Hess, Edward D. "Hass Shoes" Case Study UVA-ENT-0142. University of Virginia Darden School Foundation, Charlottesville, 2009.

Hess, Edward D. "LG Investments, LLC: A Family Business in Generational Transition (A)" Case Study UVA-ENT-0123. University of Virginia Darden School Foundation, Charlottesville, 2009.

Hess, Edward D. "LG Investments, LLC: A Family Business in Generational Transition (B)" Case Study UVA-ENT-0124. University of Virginia Darden School Foundation, Charlottesville, 2009.

Hess, Edward D. "LG Investments, LLC: A Family Business in Generational Transition (C)" Case Study UVA-ENT-0133. University of Virginia Darden School Foundation, Charlottesville, 2009.

Hess, Edward D. "LG Investments, LLC: A Family Business in Generational Transition (D)" Case Study UVA-ENT-0134. University of Virginia Darden School Foundation, Charlottesville, 2009.

Hess, Edward D. "Managing the Family Business: Golden Goose." *The Catalyst*, May 2003.

Hess, Edward D. "Motor City: A Disruptive Business Model (A)" Case Study UVA-ENT-0130. University of Virginia Darden School Foundation, Charlottesville, 2009.

Hess, Edward D. "Motor City: A Disruptive Business Model (B)" Case Study UVA-ENT-0131. University of Virginia Darden School Foundation, Charlottesville, 2009.

Hess, Edward D. "Organic Growth—Lessons from Market Leaders." Working paper, 2007.

Hess, Edward D. "Rapid Growth: Be Careful What You Ask For." *The Catalyst*, July 2003.

Hess, Edward D. *The Road to Organic Growth*. New York: McGraw-Hill, 2007.

Hess, Edward D. "Room & Board" Case Study UVA-S-0150. University of Virginia Darden School Foundation, Charlottesville, 2008.

Hess, Edward D. "Sammy Snacks (B)" Case Study UVA-OM-1350. University of Virginia Darden School Foundation, Charlottesville, 2008.

Hess, Edward D. "Sammy Snacks (C)" Case Study UVA-OM-1398. University of Virginia Darden School Foundation, Charlottesville, 2009.

Hess, Edward D. "Sammy Snacks (D)" Case Study UVA-OM-1399. University of Virginia Darden School Foundation, Charlottesville, 2009.

Hess, Edward D. "Silver Bullet of Leadership." *The Catalyst*, November 2004.

Hess, Edward D. *Smart Growth: Building an Enduring Business by Managing the Risks of Growth*. New York: Columbia Business School Publishing, 2010.

Hess, Edward D. *The Successful Family Business: A Proactive Plan for Managing Both the Family & the Business*. Westport, CT: Praeger, 2006.

Hess, Edward D. "Students Helping Honduras" Case Study UVA-ENT-0105. University of Virginia Darden School Foundation, Charlottesville, 2008.

Hess, Edward D. "Valley-Wide Health Systems, Inc." Case Study UVA-ENT-0145. University of Virginia Darden School Foundation, Charlottesville, 2009.

Hess, Edward D. "What Do Good Leaders Actually Do? (Part I)." *The Catalyst*, September 2003.

Hess, Edward D. "What Do Good Leaders Actually Do? (Part II)." *The Catalyst*, November 2003.

Hess, Edward D. "When Should Your Business Stop Growing?" *The Catalyst*, March 2004.

Hess, Edward D., and Kim S. Cameron, eds., *Leading with Values: Positivity, Virtue and High Performance*. Cambridge: Cambridge University Press, 2006.

Hess, Edward D., and Gosia Glinska. "Better World Books" Case Study UVA-ENT-0146. University of Virginia Darden School Foundation, Charlottesville, 2010.

Hess, Edward D., and Gosia Glinska. "Eyebobs Eyewear, Inc." Case Study UVA-ENT-0139. University of Virginia Darden School Foundation, Charlottesville, 2009.

Hess, Edward D., and Gosia Glinska, "Global Medical Imaging, LLC" Case Study UVA-ENT-0143. University of Virginia Darden School Foundation, Charlottesville, 2009.

Hess, Edward D., and Gosia Glinska. "James Abrams @ Clockwork Home Services, Inc.: Lessons from a Serial Entrepreneur" Case Study UVA-ENT-0117. University of Virginia Darden School Foundation, Charlottesville, 2009.

Hess, Edward D., and Gosia Glinska. "Jeff Bowling at the Delta Companies: From Baseball Coach to CEO" Case Study UVA-ENT-0114. University of Virginia Darden School Foundation, Charlottesville, 2009.

Hess, Edward D., and Gosia Glinska. "Leaders Bank: Creating a Great Place to Work" Case Study UVA-ENT-0128. University of Virginia Darden School Foundation, Charlottesville, 2009.

Hess, Edward D., and Gosia Glinska. "Mellace Family Brands, Inc.: Building a Socially Responsible Enterprise" Case Study UVA-ENT-0118. University of Virginia Darden School Foundation, Charlottesville, 2009.

Hess, Edward D., and Gosia Glinska. "Octane Fitness, Inc: The Power of Focus" Case Study UVA-ENT-0141. University of Virginia Darden School Foundation, Charlottesville, 2009.

Hess, Edward D., and Gosia Glinska, "SecureWorks" Case Study UVA-ENT-0140. University of Virginia Darden School Foundation, Charlottesville, 2009.

Hess, Edward D., and Gosia Glinska, "Trilogy Health Services, LLC: Building a Great Service Company" Case Study UVA-ENT-0122. University of Virginia Darden School Foundation, Charlottesville, 2009.

Hess, Edward D., and Robert K. Kazanjian, eds. *The Search for Organic Growth*. Cambridge: Cambridge University Press, 2006.

Hess, Edward D., and Shizuka Modica. "C.R. Barger & Sons, Inc. (A)" Case Study UVA-ENT-0106. University of Virginia Darden School Foundation, Charlottesville, 2008.

Hess, Edward D., and Shizuka Modica. "C.R. Barger & Sons, Inc. (B)" Case Study UVA-ENT-0107. University of Virginia Darden School Foundation, Charlottesville, 2008.

Hess, Edward D., Monidipa Mukherjee, and Sanju Jacob. "Enchanting Travels" Case Study UVA-ENT-0144. University of Virginia Darden School Foundation, Charlottesville, 2009.

Hess, Edward D. "Entrepreneurial Leadership: Why Should Anyone Follow You?" *The Catalyst*, June 2003.

Laseter, Timothy M., Gregory B. Fairchild, and David Eakes. "Sammy Snacks (A)" Case Study UVA-OM-1177. University of Virginia Darden School Foundation, Charlottesville, 2005.

McGregor, Jena. "Room & Board Plays Impossible to Get: Private Equity Sees Growth for the Retailer but Founder John Gabbert Prefers His Own Pace." *BusinessWeek*, October 1, 2007.

O'Reilly, Charles A. III, and Jeffrey Pfeffer. *Hidden Value: How Great Companies Achieve Extraordinary Results with Ordinary People*. Boston: Harvard Business School Press, 2000.

Michel Robert, *Strategy Pure and Simple: How Winning Companies Dominate Their Competitors*. New York: McGraw-Hill, 1993.

Smart, Bradford D. *Topgrading: How Leading Companies Win by Hiring, Coaching, and Keeping the Best People*. New York: HarperCollins, 2005.

Recommended Reading

Books

BUILDING A COMPANY

Bethune, Gordon. *From Worst to First*. New York: Wiley, 1998.

Chouinard, Yvon. *Let My People Go Surfing*. New York: The Penguin Group, 2005.

Collins, James C. *Good to Great: Why Some Companies Make the Leap . . . and Others Don't*. New York: HarperBusiness, 2001.

Collins, James C., and William C. Lazier. *Beyond Entrepreneurship: Turning Your Business into an Enduring Great Company*. Paramus, NJ: Prentice Hall, 1992.

Collins, James C., and Jerry I. Porras. *Built to Last: Successful Habits of Visionary Companies*. New York: HarperCollins, 1994.

Dell, Michael, and Catherine Fredman. *Direct from Dell*. New York: HarperBusiness, 1999.

Hess, Edward D. *Smart Growth: Building an Enduring Business by Managing the Risks of Growth*. New York: Columbia Business School Publishing, 2010.

Hess, Edward D. *The Road to Organic Growth*. New York: McGraw-Hill, 2007.

Hess, Edward D., and Charles F. Goetz. *So! You Want to Start a Business*. Upper Saddle River, NJ: FT Press, 2009.

Marcus, Bernie, and Arthur Blank, with Bob Andelman. *Built From Scratch: How a Couple of Regular Guys Grew the Home Depot from Nothing to $30 Billion*. New York: Times Books, 1999.

Meyer, Danny. *Setting the Table*. New York: HarperCollins, 2006.

O'Reilly, Charles A. III, and Jeffrey Pfeffer, *Hidden Value: How Great Companies Achieve Extraordinary Results with Ordinary People*. Boston: Harvard Business School Press, 2000.

Roddick, Anita. *Body and Soul*. New York: Crown Publishing Group, 1991.

Schultz, Howard, and Dori Jones Yang. *Pour Your Heart Into It*. New York: Hyperion, 1997.

Truett, Cathy S. *Eat Mor Chiken: Inspire More People*. Decatur, GA: Looking Glass Books, 2002.

Walton, Sam, with John Huey. *Sam Walton, Made in America: My Story*. New York: Doubleday, 1992.

BUSINESS STRATEGY BOOKS

D'Aveni, Richard A. *Hypercompetition*. New York: Free Press, 1994.

Joyce, William F., Nitin Nohria, and Bruce Roberson. *What Really Works: The 4+2 Formula for Sustained Business Success*. New York: HarperBusiness, 2003.

EMPLOYEE ENGAGEMENT

Buckingham, Marcus, and Curt Coffman. *First, Break All the Rules: What the World's Greatest Managers Do Differently*. New York: Simon & Schuster, 1999.

Cameron, Kim S., Jane E. Dutton, and Robert E. Quinn, eds. *Positive Organizational Scholarship*. San Francisco: Berrett- Koehler, 2003.

Dutton, Jane E. *Energize Your Workplace: How to Create and Sustain High-Quality Connections at Work*. San Francisco: Jossey-Bass, 2003.

Heskett, James L., W. Earl Sasser Jr., and Leonard A. Schlesinger. *The Service Profit Chain: How Leading Companies Link Profit and Growth to Loyalty, Satisfaction, and Value*. New York: Free Press, 1997.

ENTREPRENEURSHIP BOOKS

Drucker, Peter F. *Innovation and Entrepreneurship*. New York: HarperBusiness, 1993.

Gerber, Michael E. *The E-Myth Revisited: Why Most Small Businesses Don't Work and What to Do About It*. New York: HarperCollins, 2001.

FAMILY BUSINESS BOOKS

Hess, Edward D. *The Successful Family Business—A Proactive Plan for Managing the Family and the Business*. Westport, CT: Praeger, 2006.

Ward, John L. *Perpetuating the Family Business*. New York: Palgrave MacMillan, 2004.

LEADERSHIP BOOKS

Badaracco, Joseph L. *Leading Quietly: An Unorthodox Guide to Doing the Right Thing*. Boston: Harvard Business School Press 2002.

Behar, Howard, and Janet Goldstein. *It's Not About the Coffee: Leadership Principles from a Life at Starbucks*. New York: Penguin, 2007.

Cameron, Kim S. *Positive Leadership: Strategies for Extraordinary Performance*. San Francisco: Berrett-Koehler, 2008.

Collins, James C. *How the Mighty Fall: And Why Some Companies Never Give In*. New York: Jim Collins, 2009.

George, Bill. *Authentic Leadership: Rediscovering the Secrets to Creating Lasting Value*. San Francisco: Jossey-Bass, 2003.

Gergen, David. *Eyewitness to Power: The Essence of Leadership: Nixon to Clinton*. New York: Simon & Schuster, 2000.

Goldsmith, Marshall, with Mark Reiter. *What Got You Here Won't Get You There: How Successful People Become Even More Successful*. New York: Hyperion, 2007.

Goleman, Daniel, Richard E. Boyatzis, and Annie McKee. *Primal Leadership: Realizing the Power of Emotional Intelligence*. Boston: Harvard Business School Press, 2002.

Greenleaf, Robert K. *Servant Leadership: A Journey into the Nature of Legitimate Power and Greatness*, edited by Larry C. Spears. New York: Paulist Press, 2002.

Hess, Edward D., and Kim S. Cameron, eds. *Leading with Values: Positivity, Virtue, and High Performance.* Cambridge: Cambridge University Press, 2006.

MANAGEMENT BOOKS

Bossidy, Larry, and Ram Charan, with Charles Burck. *Execution: The Discipline of Getting Things Done*, New York: Crown Business, 2002.

Finkelstein, Sydney. *Why Smart Executives Fail and What You Can Learn from Their Mistakes.* New York: Portfolio, 2003.

Kaplan, Robert S., and David P. Norton. *The Balanced Scorecard: Translating Strategy into Action.* Boston: Harvard Business School Press, 1996.

Magretta, Joan, with Nan Stone. *What Management Is: How It Works and Why It's Everyone's Business.* New York: Free Press, 2002.

Sullivan, Gordon R., and Michael V. Harper. *Hope Is Not a Method: What Business Leaders Can Learn from America's Army.* New York: Broadway Books, 1997.

MARKETING AND SALES BOOKS

Kotler, Philip. *Kotler on Marketing: How to Create, Win, and Dominate Markets.* New York: Free Press, 1999.

Sheth, Jagdish, and Rajendra Sisodia. *The Rule of Three: Surviving and Thriving in Competitive Markets.* New York: Free Press, 2002.

Articles

Collins, James C. "Level 5 Leadership: The Triumph of Humility and Fierce Resolve." *Harvard Business Review* 79 1 (2001): 66–76.

Drucker, Peter F. "Managing Oneself." *Harvard Business Review* 77, 2 (1999): 64–74.

Magretta, Joan. "Governing the Family-Owned Enterprise: An Interview with Finland's Krister Ahlstrom." *Harvard Business Review* 76, 1 (1998): 112–123.

Porter, Michael E., Jay W. Lorsch, and Nitin Nohria. "Seven Surprises for New CEOs." *Harvard Business Review* 82, 10 (2004): 62–72.

Rogers, Paul, Tom Holland, and Dan Haas, "Value Acceleration: Lessons from Private Equity Masters." *Harvard Business Review* 80, 6 (2002): 94–101.

Slywotsky, Adrian J., and Richard Wise. "The Growth Crisis and How to Escape It." *Harvard Business Review* 80, 7 (2002): 72–83.

Index

Lightning Source UK Ltd.
Milton Keynes UK
UKHW031334091218
333620UK00015B/713/P